INTRODUCTION TO WEB TECHNOLOGY

INTRODUCTION
TO
WEB TECHNOLOGY

By

ANURANJAN MISRA
Associate Professor
ABES Engineering College,
Ghaziabad (U.P.)

ARJUN KUMAR SINGH
Associate Professor
ABES Engineering College,
Ghaziabad (U.P.)

UNIVERSITY SCIENCE PRESS
(An Imprint of Laxmi Publications Pvt. Ltd.)
An ISO 9001:2015 Company

BENGALURU • CHENNAI • GUWAHATI • HYDERABAD
KOCHI • KOLKATA • LUCKNOW • RANCHI
NEW DELHI

Printed and bound in India
First Edition : 2011, Reprint : 2013, 2017, 2022, *Edition* : 2026
ISBN : 978-93-8085-698-8
UWT-9600-729-INTRO TO WEB TECHNOLOGY-MIS

Price: ₹729.00

Branches

✆	Bengaluru	080-26 75 69 30
✆	Chennai	044-24 34 47 26
✆	Guwahati	0361-254 36 69
✆	Hyderabad	040-27 55 53 83
✆	Kochi	0484-405 13 03
✆	Kolkata	033-40 04 77 79
✆	Lucknow	0522-430 36 13
✆	Ranchi	0651-224 24 64

Published in India by

UNIVERSITY SCIENCE PRESS
(An Imprint of Laxmi Publications Pvt. Ltd.)

An ISO 9001:2015 Company
113, GOLDEN HOUSE, GURUDWARA ROAD, DARYAGANJ,
NEW DELHI - 110002, INDIA

Corporate Office : B-33, Sector-5, Noida,
Gautambuddha Nagar (U.P.) - 201 301, INDIA
Telephone : +91-120-44 46 900
www.laxmipublications.com
info@laxmipublications.com

CONTENTS

PREFACE

The growth, integration and sophistication of information technology and communications are changing our society and economy. Today, computers and other electronic devices increasingly communicate and interact directly with other devices over a variety of networks, such as the Internet. For developing good quality software the analysis of system is done and system must be properly designed. Since there were a lot of organizations, which were opting for automation, it was felt that some standard and structural procedure or methodology be introduced in the industry so that the transition from manual to automated system became easy. The concept of system life cycle came into existence then. Life cycle model emphasized on the need to follow some structured approach towards building new or improved system. There were many models suggested. System development begins with the recognition of user needs. Then there is a preliminary investigation stage. It includes evaluation of present system, information gathering, feasibility study and request approval. Feasibility study includes technical, economic, legal and operational feasibility. In economic feasibility cost-benefit analysis is done. After that, there are detailed design, implementation, testing and maintenance stages.

This book incorporates following 19 chapters as well as Examples, Interview Questions and Answers, Multiple Choice Questions, and Review Questions.

1. Introduction to Web Technology, 2. Introduction to Cyber Laws in India, 3. Introduction to International Cyber Laws, 4. Web Projects and Web Team, 5. Web Development Strategies, 6. Quality Assurance and Testing, 7. HTML, 8. DHTML, 9. Java Script, 10. VbScript, 11. XML, 12. Active Server Pages, 13. Introduction to Perl, 14. RMI and COM/DCOM, 15. Java Beans and EJB, 16. Servlets, 17. Java Server Pages, 18. Database Connectivity and 19. Introduction to Web Services Management.

The book also contains three appendixes: J2EE Interview Questions and Answers, Glossary on Web Technologies and Introduction to XHTML.

Since rapid changes can be witnessed in the area of Information Technology and Web Technology is not left untouched. I have taken my best efforts to incorporate the latest updates taking in the Web Technology. Furthermore your views, suggestions, comments and recommendations are invited and will be highly appreciable. Simultaneously please do not hesitate to write me at e-mail anuranjanmisra@gmail.com, and I promise you to revert at earliest.

We have tried to bring the book free from errors. However, it is not unusual that certain flaws might have crept into the body of the text. I take personal responsibility for the same and request to let know of those misprints or mistakes. I assure the readers to remove them in the next addition of this book.

—Authors

1

INTRODUCTION

1.0 HISTORY OF WEB

The World Wide Web largely realized the dreams of Vannevar Bush, J.C.R. Licklider, Marshall McLuhan, Ted Nelson, and others for the potential use of information technology. The web was also the key technology that popularized the Internet around the world.

There have always been things which people are good at, and things computers have been good at, and little overlap between the two. I was brought up to understand this distinction in the 50s and 60s and intuition and understanding were human characteristics, and that computers worked mechanically in tables and hierarchies. The word "hypertext" was first coined by Nelson in 1963, and is first found in print in a college newspaper article about a lecture he gave called "Computers, Creativity, and the Nature of the Written Word" in January, 1965:

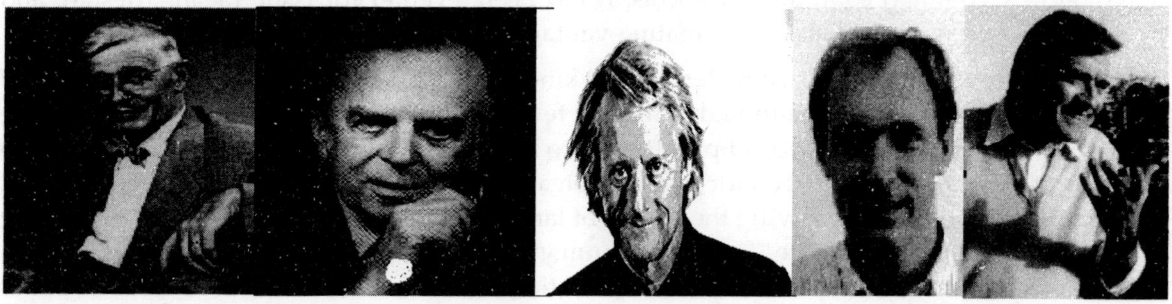

Vannevar Bush, J.C.R. Licklider Ted Nelson, Tim Berners-Leev & Robert Cailliau

One of the things computers have not done for an organization is to be able to store random associations between disparate things, although this is something the brain has always done relatively well. In 1980 I played with programs to store information with random links, and in 1989, while working at the European Particle Physics Laboratory, I proposed that a global hypertext space be created in which any network-accessible information could be refered to by a single "Universal Document Identifier". Given the go-ahead to experiment by my boss, Mike Sendall, I wrote in 1990 a program called "WorlDwidEweb", a point and click hypertext editor which ran on the "NeXT" machine. This, together with the first Web server, I released to the High Energy Physics community at first, and to the hypertext and NeXT communities in the summer of 1991. Also available was a "line mode" browser by student Nicola Pellow, which could be run on almost any computer. The specifications of UDIs (now URIs), HyperText Markup Language (HTML) and HyperText Transfer Protocol (HTTP) published on the first server in order to promote wide adoption and discussion.

The dream behind the Web is of a common information space in which we communicate by sharing information. Its universality is essential: the fact that a hypertext link can point to anything, be it personal, local or global, be it draft or highly polished. There was a second part of the dream, too, dependent on the Web being so generally used that it became a realistic mirror (or in fact the primary embodiment) of the ways in which we work and play and socialize. That was that once the state of our interactions was on line, we could then use computers to help us analyse it, make sense of what we are doing, where we individually fit in, and how we can better work together.

The first three years were a phase of persuasion, aided by my colleague and first convert Robert Cailliau, to get the Web adopted. We needed Web clients for other platforms (as the NeXT was not ubiquitous) and browsers Erwise, Viola, Cello and Mosaic eventually came on the scene. We needed seed servers to provide incentive and examples, and all over the world inspired people put up all kinds of things.

Between the summers of 1991 and 1994, the load on the first Web server ("info.cern.ch") rose steadily by a factor of 10 every year. In 1992 academia, and in 1993 industry, was taking notice. I was under pressure to define the future evolution. After much discussion I decided to form the World Wide Web Consortium in September 1994, with a base at MIT is the USA, INRIA in France, and now also at Keio University in Japan. The Consortium is a neutral open forum where companies and organizations to whom the future of the Web is important come to discuss and to agree on new common computer protocols. It has been a center for issue raising, design, and decision by consensus, and also a fascinating vantage point from which to view that evolution.

With the dramatic flood of rich material of all kinds onto the Web in the 1990s, the first part of the dream is largely realized, although still very few people in practice have access to intuitive hypertext creation tools. The second part has yet to happen, but there are signs and plans which make us confident. The great need for information about information, to help us categorize, sort, pay for, own information is driving the design of languages for the web designed for processing by machines, rather than people. The web of human-readable document is being merged with a web of machine-understandable data. The potential of the mixture of humans and machines working together and communicating through the web could be immense.

1.1 GROWTH OF THE WEB

The web has grown very fast. In fact, the web has grown substantially faster than the Internet at large, as measured by number of hosts.

The rate of the web's growth has been and continues to be exponential, but is slowing in it's rate of growth. For the second half of 1993, the Web had a doubling period of under 3 months, and even today the doubling period is still under 6 months.

Results Summary			
Month	# of Web sites	% .com sites	Hosts* per Web server
6/93	130	1.5	13,000 (3,846)
12/93	623	4.6	3,475 (963)
6/94	2,738	13.5	1,095 (255)
12/94	10,022	18.3	451 (99)
6/95	23,500	31.3	270 (46)
1/96	100,000	50.0	94 (17)
6/96	230,000 (est)	68.0	41
1/97	650,000 (est)	62.6	NA

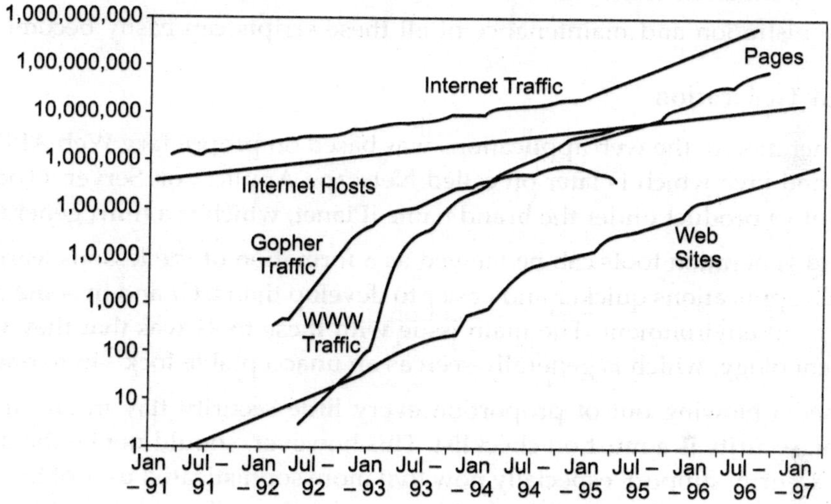

Growth curves for the Internet and the WWW on a logarithmic scale.

1.2 EVOLUTION OF WEB APPLICATIONS

Web applications are different from ordinary applications in the following ways:

1. Your Application can have millions rather than thousands of customers, and many more simultaneous clients than in normal client - server systems. Scaling your application is a big problem, and this is not going to go away, as the Internet expands and extends to mobile phones.
2. HTTP is a stateless protocol, which does not have the concept of a client session.
3. The key to web success is provision of dynamic data on rapidly developing sites. Managing this, as a developer and a system - admin, can be a headache.
4. Transactions and security are needed for the purpose online. The Internet is a public network, and that makes authorization and encryption critical.
5. Impersonal as the web interface appears to be, you can and must make your customers feel welcome, perhaps personalize their view of the site information, and otherwise help them find what they want otherwise the competition is just a click away.

Web applications can be seen as going through three generations during their evolution.

1.2.1 First Generation

The first generation is based on Common gateway Interface(CGI) technology. CGI applications are independent applications, originally implemented for Unix platforms , which are invoked by web servers - CGI providing the gateway between the Web and the existing applications. It is incredible to see how many perl, C shell, and Bourne shell scripts control the guts of e-commerce.

The main problems with this approach are:

1. Scalability is one of those things that people do not think about when they start a project but that becomes a major problem when it is successful. It's difficult to retrofit scalability, as architecture is everything.
2. Session handlingis the application's responsibility – and CGI only provides primitive runtime information from the web server.
3. The administration and maintenance of all these scripts can easily become a nightmare.

1.2.2 Second Generation

The second generation of the web applications was based on proprietary Web API's for example NetDynamics and kiva which is later on called Netscape Application Server. (Today both tools have merged into a product under the brand name iPlanet, which is a third generation product).

These second generation tools cab be viewed as a formation of the lessons learned with CGI. They made web applications quicker and easier to develop than CGI and in some cases included fancy development environment. The main issue with these tools was that they were based on proprietary technology, which is generally seen as an unacceptable lock - in to one vender.

With the media blowing out of proportion every little security flay in any Internet-related tools or system, security is a must on checklist. This however, should not be the only reason for having a solid security support, especially now that more sophisticated uses of the Internet really require it. Security is not only a matter of perception for the end users, but also something that should be included from the outset, in the design of the application.

Both generations often lacked built in support for most important functionality the main problems with this generation are:

1. Something that is absolutely required in today's e-commerce is transactional support. A transaction is a series of steps or processes that are treated as a single unit of work. A transaction is successful when all the steps are completed successfully, otherwise, if any step fails, the transaction as a whole fails.
2. There are a number of other issues we need to mention, which can be grouped under the operations, administration, and management umbrella. First and second generation web applications and tools generally did not consider anything related to these issues as they were mainly designed to cover the needs of developers.

1.2.3 Third Generation

The third generation of web applications forms a new market segment called application server. Application servers support a multi-tiered architecture rather different from a standalone, monolithic application-meaning that multiple components compose the application server. Applications that run in these servers typically have separate parts for clients/UI, business logic and database/persistence layer. In its most basic form, an application form, an application server can be viewed as **middleware**, that is, it act as glue that holds together web-based clients and existing applications or data stores.

1. The clients can be browsers, Java-based programs, or other web-enabled programming environment running on the first tier.
2. The second tier(The glue) is the middleware, an application server. This is not absolutely required, you can always use the middle tier just as funnel to existing applications or data stores. But normally the second tier will host a combination of presentation logic and business logic.
3. The third tier is generally a combination of existing applications and data stores.

As compared with the traditional two tier client-server systems, the multi-tier systems have the following benefits:

1. **Scalability and reliability** — decoupling two tiers and three tiers means that workload can be split between machines, and multiple machines in each tier, if necessary. Clustering is an option here.
2. **Easier management** — enabling division of jobs into presentation, business logic and data management.
3. **Security** — the application server is a client of the database, and so browser clients cannot access all the data, only selected parts.
4. **Simpler integration** — existing applications can be fitted into the architecture as just another data source, or become a web application server themselves, accessed through a URL.

1.3 PROTOCOLS GOVERNING THE WEB

The TCP/IP suite of protocols is the set of protocols used to communicate across the internet. It is also widely used on many organizational networks due to its flexibility and wide array of functionality provided. TCP/IP is a set of protocols which is used to govern the web. The division of TCP/IP protocols layer wise and function wise is as follows:

TCP/IP by Layer

Link Layer

- **SLIP** — Serial Line Internet Protocol. This protocol places data packets into data frames in preparation for transport across network hardware media. This protocol is used for sending data across serial lines. There is no error correction, addressing or packet identification. There is no authentication or negotiation capabilities with SLIP. SLIP will only support transport of IP packets.
- **CSLIP** — Compressed SLIP is essentially data compression of the SLIP protocol. It uses Van Jacobson compression to drastically reduce the overhead of packet overhead. This may also be used with PPP and called CPPP.
- **PPP** — Point to Point Protocol is a form of serial line data encapsulation that is an improvement over SLIP which provides serial bi-directional communication. It is much like SLIP but can support AppleTalk, IPX, TCP/IP, and NetBEUI along with TCP/IP which is supported

by SLIP. It can negociate connection parameters such as speed along with the ability to support PAP and CHAP user authentication.

- **Ethernet** — Ethernet is not really called a protocol. There are also many types of ethernet. The most common ethernet which is used to control the handling of data at the lowest layer of the network model is 802.3 ethernet. 802.3 ethernet privides a means of encapsulating data frames to be sent between computers. It specifies how network data collisions are handled along with hardware addressing of network cards.

Network Layer

- **ARP** — Address Resolution Protocol enables the packaging of IP data into ethernet packages. It is the system and messaging protocol that is used to find the ethernet (hardware) address from a specific IP number. Without this protocol, the ethernet package could not be generated from the IP package, because the ethernet address could not be determined.
- **IP** — Internet Protocol. Except for ARP and RARP all protocols' data packets will be packaged into an IP data packet. IP provides the mechanism to use software to address and manage data packets being sent to computers.
- **RARP** — Reverse address resolution protocol is used to allow a computer without a local permanent data storage media to determine its IP address from its ethernet address.

Transport Layer

- **TCP** — A reliable connection oriented protocol used to control the management of application level services between computers. It is used for transport by some applications.
- **UDP** — An unreliable connection less protocol used to control the management of application level services between computers. It is used for transport by some applications which must provide their own reliability.
- **ICMP** — Internet control message protocol (ICMP) provides management and error reporting to help manage the process of sending data between computers. (Management). This protocol is used to report connection status back to computers that are trying to connect other computers. For example, it may report that a destination host is not reachable.
- **IGMP** — Internet Group Management Protocol used to support multicasting. IGMP messages are used by multicast routers to track group memberships on each of its networks.

Application Layer

- **FTP** — File Transfer Protocol allows file transfer between two computers with login required.
- **TFTP** — Trivial File Transfer Protocol allows file transfer between two computers with no login required. It is limited, and is intended for diskless stations.
- **NFS** — Network File System is a protocol that allows UNIX and Linux systems remotely mount each other's file systems.
- **SNMP** — Simple Network Management Protocol is used to manage all types of network elements based on various data sent and received.
- **SMTP** — Simple Mail Transfer Protocol is used to transport mail. Simple Mail Transport Protocol is used on the internet, it is not a transport layer protocol but is an application layer protocol.

- **HTTP** — Hypertext Transfer Protocol is used to transport HTML pages from web servers to web browsers. The protocol used to communicate between web servers and web browser software clients.
- **BOOTP** — Bootstrap protocol is used to assign an IP address to diskless computers and tell it what server and file to load which will provide it with an operating system.
- **DHCP** — Dynamic host configuration protocol is a method of assigning and controlling the IP addresses of computers on a given network. It is a server based service that automatically assigns IP numbers when a computer boots. This way the IP address of a computer does not need to be assigned manually. This makes changing networks easier to manage. DHCP can perform all the functions of BOOTP.
- **BGP** — Border Gateway Protocol. When two systems are using BGP, they establish a TCP connection, then send each other their BGP routing tables. BGP uses distance vectoring. It detects failures by sending periodic keep alive messages to its neighbors every 30 seconds. It exchanges information about reachable networks with other BGP systems including the full path of systems that are between them. Described by RFC 1267, 1268, and 1497.
- **EGP** — Exterior Gateway Protocol is used between routers of different systems.
- **IGP** — Interior Gateway Protocol. The name used to describe the fact that each system on the internet can choose its own routing protocol. RIP and OSPF are interior gateway protocols.
- **RIP** — Routing Information Protocol is used to dynamically update router tables on WANs or the internet. A distance-vector algorithm is used to calculate the best route for a packet. RFC 1058, 1388 (RIP2).
- **OSPF** — Open Shortest Path First dynamic routing protocol. A link state protocol rather than a distance vector protocol. It tests the status of its link to each of its neighbors and sends the acquired information to them.
- **POP3** — Post Office Protocol version 3 is used by clients to access an internet mail server to get mail. It is not a transport layer protocol.
- **IMAP4** — Internet Mail Access Protocol version 4 is the replacement for POP3.
- **Telnet** is used to remotely open a session on another computer. It relies on TCP for transport and is defined by RFC854.

Bandwidth Control

- **BAP** — Bandwidth Allocation Protocol is a bandwidth control protocol for PPP connections. It works with BACP.
- **BACP** — Bandwidth Allocation Control Protocol.

TCP/IP by Function

Packaging and Low Level

- **IP** — Internet Protocol. Except for ARP and RARP all protocols' data packets will be packaged into an IP data packet. IP provides the mechanism to use software to address and manage data packets being sent to computers.
- **SLIP** — Serial Line Internet Protocol. This protocol places data packets into data frames in preparation for transport across network hardware media. This protocol is used for sending data across serial lines. There is no error correction, addressing or packet identification.

There is no authentication or negotiation capabilities with SLIP. SLIP will only support transport of IP packets.

- **CSLIP** — Compressed SLIP is essentially data compression of the SLIP protocol. It uses Van Jacobson compression to drastically reduce the overhead of packet overhead. This may also be used with PPP and called CPPP.
- **PPP** — Point to Point Protocol is a form of serial line data encapsulation that is an improvement over SLIP which provides serial bi-directional communication. It is much like SLIP but can support AppleTalk, IPX, TCP/IP, and NetBEUI along with TCP/IP which is supported by SLIP. It can negociate connection parameters such as speed along with the ability to support PAP and CHAP user authentication.
- **Ethernet** — Ethernet is not really called a protocol. There are also many types of ethernet. The most common ethernet which is used to control the handling of data at the lowest layer of the network model is 802.3 ethernet. 802.3 ethernet privides a means of encapsulating data frames to be sent between computers. It specifies how network data collisions are handled along with hardware addressing of network cards.

Transport and Basic Functions

- **TCP** — A reliable connection oriented protocol used to control the management of application level services between computers. It is used for transport by some applications.
- **UDP** — An unreliable connection less protocol used to control the management of application level services between computers. It is used for transport by some applications which must provide their own reliability.

Network Management

- **SNMP** — Simple Network Management Protocol is used to manage all types of network elements based on various data sent and received.
- **ICMP** — Internet control message protocol provides management and error reporting to help manage the process of sending data between computers. (Management). This protocol is used to report connection status back to computers that are trying to connect other computers. For example, it may report that a destination host is not reachable. This protocol is required for basic TCP/IP operations.
- **ARP** — Address Resolution Protocol enables the packaging of IP data into ethernet packages. It is the system and messaging protocol that is used to find the ethernet (hardware) address from a specific IP number. Without this protocol, the ethernet package could not be generated from the IP package, because the ethernet address could not be determined. protocol is used to report connection status back to computers that are trying to connect other computers. For example, it may report that a destination host is not reachable. This protocol is required for basic TCP/IP operations.

Host Management

- **BOOTP** — Bootstrap protocol is used to assign an IP address to diskless computers and tell it what server and file to load which will provide it with an operating system.
- **DHCP** — Dynamic host configuration protocol is a method of assigning and controlling the IP addresses of computers on a given network. It is a server based service that automatically assigns IP numbers when a computer boots. This way the IP address of

a computer does not need to be assigned manually. This makes changing networks easier to manage. DHCP can perform all the functions of BOOTP.

- **RARP** — Reverse address resolution protocol is used to allow a computer without a local permanent data storage media to determine its IP address from its ethernet address.

Mail Protocols

- **SMTP** — Simple Mail Transfer Protocol is used to transport mail. Simple Mail Transport Protocol is used on the internet, it is not a transport layer protocol but is an application layer protocol.
- **POP3** — Post Office Protocol version 3 is used by clients to access an internet mail server to get mail. It is not a transport layer protocol.
- **IMAP4** — Internet Mail Access Protocol version 4 is the replacement for POP3.

Multicasting Protocols

- **IGMP** — Internet Group Management Protocol used to support multicasting. IGMP messages are used by multicast routers to track group memberships on each of its networks.

Routing Protocols

- **BGP** — Border Gateway Protocol. When two systems are using BGP, they establish a TCP connection, then send each other their BGP routing tables. BGP uses distance vectoring. It detects failures by sending periodic keep alive messages to its neighbors every 30 seconds. It exchanges information about reachable networks with other BGP systems including the full path of systems that are between them. Described by RFC 1267, 1268, and 1497
- **EGP** — Exterior Gateway Protocol is used between routers of different systems.
- **IGP** — Interior Gateway Protocol. The name used to describe the fact that each system on the internet can choose its own routing protocol. RIP and OSPF are interior gateway protocols.
- **RIP** — Routing Information Protocol is used to dynamically update router tables on WANs or the internet.
- **OSPF** — Open Shortest Path First dynamic routing protocol. A link state protocol rather than a distance vector protocol. It tests the status of its link to each of its neighbors and sends the acquired information to them.

EXERCISE

1. Discuss history of web in detail.
2. Discuss growth of web in brief.
3. Describe different generations of web applications.
4. What are the drawbacks of first generation of web?
5. What are the drawbacks of second generation of web?
6. What are the advantages of Third generation of web?
7. Discuss protocol governing the web in detail.
8. Discuss the protocol used by transport layer.
9. List the protocols used by application layer.
10. Discuss routing protocols.

2

INTRODUCTION TO CYBER LAWS IN INDIA

2.0 INTRODUCTION

Cyber law is a much newer phenomenon having emerged much after the onset of Internet. Internet grew in a completely unplanned and unregulated manner. Even the inventors of Internet could not have really anticipated the scope and far reaching consequences of cyberspace. The growth rate of cyberspace has been enormous. Internet is growing rapidly and with the population of Internet doubling roughly every 100 days, Cyberspace is becoming the new preferred environment of the world. With the spontaneous and almost phenomenal growth of cyberspace, new and ticklish issues relating to various legal aspects of cyberspace began cropping up. In response to the absolutely complex and newly emerging legal issues relating to cyberspace, CYBERLAW or the law of Internet came into being. The growth of Cyberspace has resulted in the development of a new and highly specialised branch of law called CYBERLAWS- LAWS OF THE INTERNET AND THE WORLD WIDE WEB.

2.1 CYBER LAWS IN INDIA

The beginnings of Internet were extremely small and the growth of subscribers painfully slow. However as Internet has grown in our country, the need has been felt to enact the relevant Cyberlaws which are necessary to regulate Internet in India. This need for cyberlaws was propelled by numerous factors.

Firstly, India has an extremely detailed and well-defined legal system in place. Numerous laws have been enacted and implemented and the foremost amongst them is The Constitution of India. We have interalia, amongst others, the Indian Penal Code, the Indian Evidence Act 1872, the Banker's Book Evidence Act, 1891 and the Reserve Bank of India Act, 1934, the Companies Act, and so on. However the arrival of Internet signalled the beginning of the rise of new and complex legal issues. It may be pertinent to mention that all the existing laws in place in India were enacted way back keeping in mind the relevant political, social, economic, and cultural scenario of that relevant time. Nobody then could really visualize about the Internet. Despite the brilliant acumen of our master draftsmen, the requirements of cyberspace could hardly ever be anticipated. As such, the coming of the Internet led to the emergence of numerous ticklish legal issues and problems which necessitated the enactment of Cyberlaws.

Secondly, the existing laws of India, even with the most benevolent and liberal interpretation, could not be interpreted in the light of the emerging cyberspace, to include all aspects relating to different activities in cyberspace. In fact, the practical experience and the wisdom of judgment found that it shall not be without major perils and pitfalls, if the existing laws were to be interpreted in the scenario of emerging cyberspace, without enacting new cyberlaws. As such, the need for enactment of relevant cyberlaws.

Thirdly, none of the existing laws gave any legal validity or sanction to the activities in Cyberspace. For example, the Net is used by a large majority of users for email. Yet till today, email is not "legal" in our country. There is no law in the country, which gives legal validity, and sanction to email. Courts and judiciary in our country have been reluctant to grant judicial recognition to the legality of email in the absence of any specific law having been enacted by the Parliament. As such the need has arisen for Cyberlaw.

Fourthly, Internet requires an enabling and supportive legal infrastructure in tune with the times. This legal infrastructure can only be given by the enactment of the relevant Cyberlaws as the traditional laws have failed to grant the same. E-commerce, the biggest future of Internet, can only be possible if necessary legal infrastructure compliments the same to enable its vibrant growth.

All these and other varied considerations created the conducive atmosphere for the need for enacting relevant cyberlaws in India. The Government of India responded by coming up with the draft of the first Cyberlaw of India — The Information Technology Bill, 1999. One question that is often asked is why should we have Cyberlaw in India, when a large chunk of the Indian population is below the poverty line and is residing in rural areas ? More than anything else, India, by its sheer numbers, as also by virtue of its extremely talented and ever growing IT population, is likely to become a very important Internet market in the future and it is important that we legislate Cyberlaws in India to provide for a sound legal and technical frame work which, in turn, could be a catalyst for growth and success of the Internet Revolution in India.

India woke up to the Internet reality, albeit late in the day, and brought into force the IT (Information Technology) Act, 2000, which derives its flavor from UNCITRAL's (United Nations Commission on International Trade Laws) Model Law on e-commerce. A UN General Assembly resolution in 1997 advocated the adoption of UNCITRAL Model Law in the local laws of member countries to maintain uniformity in practice. The IT Act primarily seeks to recognize transactions carried out by electronic means and to provide a framework for the development of e-commerce and e-governance. Amongst other things, the IT Act provides for: Legal recognition of electronic records Facilitation of electronic filing of documents with government agencies Authentication and certification of electronic records by means of digital signatures Transaction of business through electronic data interchange and electronic communication Prevention of computer crimes, etc Amendment of Indian Penal Code, 1860, Indian Evidence Act, 1872, Bankers Book Evidence Act, 1891 and the Reserve Bank of India Act, 1934 to bring them in tune with the information-technology regime Where the IT Act fails The IT Act has many inherent limitations and shortcomings. The most significant one amongst them are: The Act makes no reference to the protection of intellectual property like copyrights, patents or trademarks on the Net. It is also silent on domain-name infringement and cyber squatting. This seriously inhibits corporate bodies to invest in the IT infrastructure It extends the application of its penal provisions to persons outside India, irrespective of their nationality if the offence under the Act relates to a computer located in India. Such extra-territorial jurisdiction is fraught with limitations as to its enforcement.

In May 2000, both the houses of the Indian Parliament passed the Information Technology Bill. The Bill received the assent of the President in August 2000 and came to be known as the Information Technology Act, 2000. Cyber laws are contained in the IT Act, 2000.

This Act aims to provide the legal infrastructure for e-commerce in India. And the cyber laws have a major impact for e-businesses and the new economy in India. So, it is important to understand what are the various perspectives of the IT Act, 2000 and what it offers.

The Information Technology Act, 2000 also aims to provide for the legal framework so that legal sanctity is accorded to all electronic records and other activities carried out by electronic means. The Act states that unless otherwise agreed, an acceptance of contract may be expressed by electronic means of communication and the same shall have legal validity and enforceability. Some highlights of the Act are listed below:

Chapter-II of the Act specifically stipulates that any subscriber may authenticate an electronic record by affixing his digital signature. It further states that any person can verify an electronic record by use of a public key of the subscriber.

Chapter-III of the Act details about Electronic Governance and provides inter alia amongst others that where any law provides that information or any other matter shall be in writing or in the typewritten or printed form, then, notwithstanding anything contained in such law, such requirement shall be deemed to have been satisfied if such information or matter is rendered or made available in an electronic form; and accessible so as to be usable for a subsequent reference.

The Said Chapter Also Details the Legal Recognition of Digital Signatures

Chapter-IV of the said Act gives a scheme for Regulation of Certifying Authorities. The Act envisages a Controller of Certifying Authorities who shall perform the function of exercising supervision over the activities of the Certifying Authorities as also laying down standards and conditions governing the Certifying Authorities as also specifying the various forms and content of Digital Signature Certificates. The Act recognizes the need for recognizing foreign Certifying Authorities and it further details the various provisions for the issue of license to issue Digital Signature Certificates.

Chapter-VII of the Act details about the scheme of things relating to Digital Signature Certificates. The duties of subscribers are also enshrined in the said Act.

Chapter-IX of the said Act talks about penalties and adjudication for various offences. The penalties for damage to computer, computer systems etc. has been fixed as damages by way of compensation not exceeding Rs. 1,00,00,000 to affected persons. The Act talks of appointment of any officers not below the rank of a Director to the Government of India or an equivalent officer of state government as an Adjudicating Officer who shall adjudicate whether any person has made a contravention of any of the provisions of the said Act or rules framed there under. The said Adjudicating Officer has been given the powers of a Civil Court.

Chapter-X of the Act talks of the establishment of the Cyber Regulations Appellate Tribunal, which shall be an appellate body where appeals against the orders passed by the Adjudicating Officers, shall be preferred.

Chapter-XI of the Act talks about various offences and the said offences shall be investigated only by a Police Officer not below the rank of the Deputy Superintendent of Police. These offences include tampering with computer source documents, publishing of information, which is obscene in electronic form, and hacking.

The Act also provides for the constitution of the Cyber Regulations Advisory Committee, which shall advice the government as regards any rules, or for any other purpose connected with the said act. The said Act also proposes to amend the Indian Penal Code, 1860, the Indian Evidence Act, 1872, The Bankers' Books Evidence Act, 1891, The Reserve Bank of India Act, 1934 to make them in tune with the provisions of the IT Act.

2.2 ADVANTAGES OF CYBER LAWS

The IT Act 2000 attempts to change outdated laws and provides ways to deal with cyber crimes. We need such laws so that people can perform purchase transactions over the Net through credit cards without fear of misuse. The Act offers the much-needed legal framework so that information is not denied legal effect, validity or enforceability, solely on the ground that it is in the form of electronic records.

In view of the growth in transactions and communications carried out through electronic records, the Act seeks to empower government departments to accept filing, creating and retention of official documents in the digital format. The Act has also proposed a legal framework for the authentication and origin of electronic records/communications through digital signature.

From the perspective of e-commerce in India, the IT Act 2000 and its provisions contain many positive aspects. Firstly, the implications of these provisions for the e-businesses would be that e-mail would now be a valid and legal form of communication in our country that can be duly produced and approved in a court of law.

Companies shall now be able to carry out electronic commerce using the legal infrastructure provided by the Act.

Digital signatures have been given legal validity and sanction in the Act.

The Act throws open the doors for the entry of corporate companies in the business of being Certifying Authorities for issuing Digital Signatures Certificates.

The Act now allows Government to issue notification on the web thus heralding e-governance.

The Act enables the companies to file any form, application or any other document with any office, authority, body or agency owned or controlled by the appropriate Government in electronic form by means of such electronic form as may be prescribed by the appropriate Government.

The IT Act also addresses the important issues of security, which are so critical to the success of electronic transactions. The Act has given a legal definition to the concept of secure digital signatures that would be required to have been passed through a system of a security procedure, as stipulated by the Government at a later date.

Under the IT Act, 2000, it shall now be possible for corporates to have a statutory remedy in case if anyone breaks into their computer systems or network and causes damages or copies data. The remedy provided by the Act is in the form of monetary damages, not exceeding Rs. 1 crore.

2.3 ISP GUIDELINES

The Government has issued guidelines for providing Internet Services on a license on a non-exclusive basis. Some of the salient points of the guidelines include the following:

A company registered in India under the Companies Act, 1956 will be eligible. Foreign equity, if any, shall be as per the Government Policy and guidelines from time to time. At present, the foreign equity is permitted to the extent of 49 percent.

A company registered in India under the Companies Act, 1956 will be eligible. Foreign equity, if any, shall be as per the Government Policy and guidelines from time to time. At present, the foreign equity is permitted to the extent of 49 percent.

Separate licenses will be granted to an applicant company for each service area classified as Category "A", "B" and "C" respectively.

Applicants will be required to submit separate applications for each service area. The ISP will be required to set up his nodes *i.e.* Routers/Servers within the geographical limits of the service area. An applicant may be granted any number of licenses. The leased line subscribers shall be from within the service area. However, the ISP can offer dial-up services from any part of the country.

Existing email and VSAT service licensees may also obtain separate ISP licenses for any number of the above mentioned service areas subject to the fulfillment of the eligibility criteria.

Direct interconnectivity between two separately licensed ISPs is permitted. Authorised public/government organisations are allowed to provide Internet Gateway access including international leased circuits directly without going through VSNL gateways. Private ISPs are allowed to provide such International Gateways after obtaining security clearance.

Flow of obscene, objectionable, unauthorised or any other content infringing copyrights, intellectual property right and international and domestic Cyber Laws in any form over ISP's network is not permitted.

ISPs are allowed to put their own Internet Gateways subject to security clearance.

Cyber Laws in India Fails to Protect Cyber Piracy and Address Patent and IP Issues

Although, this seeks to afford protection for Indian cyber space from intruders from other countries but the example of Dawood and Quattrochi clearly bare the ineffective enforcement machinery in India It excludes property transactions to be carried out on-line due to the necessity of payment of stamp duty and registration of documents The Act fails to address the issue of cross-border taxation that may arise in international contracts. The question of jurisdiction of a particular country over on-line transactions, which involves more than one jurisdiction, has also been left open It does not deal with Internet privacy issues like prohibition of unsolicited commercial mail (spamming) and unauthorized use of private data collected on-line It binds digital signatures to the asymmetric encryption system, limiting the scope of innovation in technology. This is a serious drawback especially since the technology is being replaced with a more secure system soon It fails to cover control of cyber laundering of money, which can easily be used for criminal or terrorist activities especially given the situation post September 11. E-commerce The IT Act provides that electronic records can substitute written paper-based records, digital signatures can substitute physical signatures wherever such records are required to be maintained by law. Thus, the days of bulky documentation for business transactions and requirement of main- taining voluminous records are over. But this good news for corporate India comes with a rider! Negotiable instruments like cheques, drafts, bills of exchange, etc., wills, powers of attorney, trusts and documents related to sale, lease, mortgage, etc., of immoveable property still remain inaccessible electronically. Digital signatures The Act provides for the authentication of electronic records by affixing digital signatures. This process requires the use of a pair of electronic keys. If you are signing an electronic document, then one of the keys (private key) is in within your control. You give the other key (public key) to the person to whom the electronic document is addressed. He can use that key to verify that the electronic document bears your signature and there has been no manipulation since the document was electronically signed. Since the process of digital signatures is unlike the normal process where your handwriting determines your signature, you must remember to preserve the private key. This can be done by storing the electronic private key in a smart card or password-protected environment on a computer. Public and private keys are made available by a digital signature-certifying authority. The Controller of Certifying Authorities licenses a certifying authority (may include private and foreign certifying authorities). Unfortunately, though it has been more than a year since the IT Act was enforced, certifying authorities and the digital signature infrastructure are still not in place. E-governance The IT Act enables the filing of any form, application or other document, issue or grant of license, permit or approval by the government and receipt and payment of money to be done by electronic means prescribed by government. It also enables rules, regulations, orders, by-laws or notifications to be issued by the government in electronic form. This is a very decisive step towards e-governing the country. Andhra Pradesh has already successfully adopted it Changes have been made in the criminal procedure laws of Andhra Pradesh such that an accused can be brought before a judge through video-conferencing. Government offices are inter-connected and regular feedback on development of various projects is obtained, bringing efficiency in the system. One only hopes that the other states would follow suit. Cyber crimes Hackers beware! Destruction, deletion or alteration of information contained in any computer, computer network, database or software, or fiddling with the information so as to cause serious harm can attract a punishment of up to three years imprisonment and a fine of up to Rs 2 lakh. Publication or transmission of pornographic material is a serious offence under the IT Act and attracts a punishment of five years imprisonment and a fine of Rs 1 lakh for the first instance; penalties double for subsequent instances. Strict penal provisions also exist for frauds in digital signatures, tampering with computer source codes, securing unauthorized access to protected systems, etc. Where the IT Act fails The IT Act has many inherent limitations and shortcomings. The most significant one amongst them are: The Act makes no reference to the protection of intellectual property like copyrights, patents or trademarks on the Net. It is also silent on domain-name infringement and cyber squatting. This seriously inhibits corporate bodies to invest in the IT infrastructure It extends the application of its penal provisions to persons outside India, irrespective of their nationality if the offence under the Act relates to a computer located in India. Such extra-territorial jurisdiction is fraught with limitations as to its enforcement. Although, this seeks to afford protection for Indian cyber space from intruders from other countries but the example of Dawood and Quattrochi clearly bare the ineffective enforcement machinery in India It excludes property transactions to be carried out on-line due to the necessity of payment of stamp duty and registration of documents The Act fails to address the issue of cross-border taxation that may arise in international contracts. The question of jurisdiction of a particular country over on-line transactions, which involves more than one jurisdiction, has also been left open It does not deal with Internet privacy issues like prohibition of unsolicited commercial mail (spamming) and unauthorized use of private data collected on-line It binds digital signatures to the asymmetric encryption system, limiting the scope of innovation in technology. This is a serious drawback especially since the technology is being replaced with a more secure system soon It fails to cover control of cyber laundering of money, which can easily be used for criminal or terrorist activities especially given the situation post September 11. n Civil offences You have to pay damages up to Rs 1 crore if without being authorized you secure access to a computer system or download or copy sensitive information or introduce a virus into a computer or in any other manner causes damage to a computer or computer system or network. The penalty imposed under the foregoing provision affords no immunity from prosecution under other laws. ISP immunity ISPs (Internet Service Providers) have been exempted from any liability that may arise for any third-party acts but only if he is able to prove that the offence was committed without his knowledge or he had taken reasonable steps to prevent such offence. ISPs must, thus, be careful with the data being transmitted over their networks. They should install appropriate software for preventing pornographic material from being transmitted over their networks and protection against known viruses. Surprisingly, our IT Act has turned into an exportable commodity! New Zealand expressed a desire recently to frame its IT laws on the lines of our IT Act, which speaks volumes about the cyber legislation. Maybe some criticism of the Act is unjustified especially considering the Utah example where the law was in place in 1995 but till 1997 no certification authority had been established. Some of the notable exclusions from the Act may be because its parent's (UNCITRAL) thrust is on trade and commerce only. A decisive step towards rationalization of cyber laws is the Convergence Bill-which seeks to bundle up information, communication and entertainment into a comprehensive legislation-pending in Parliament. Jasmeet Singh Wadehra.

2.4 LEGAL REQUIREMENT(S) OF ELECTRONIC COMMERCE

The legal requirement is to establish the authenticity of an electronic message or document. This includes integrity, confidentiality, and non - repudiation of origin and receipt of an electronic document in case of dispute. The UNCITRAL model EDI/EC laws defines an electronic data message as follows:

"2a Data message means information generated, stored or communicated by electronic, optical or analogous means including but not limited to, electronic data interchange (EDI), electronic mail, telegram, telex or telecopy".

This law proposes legal recognition of data message, and defines writing, signature and their admissibility and evidential value. Individual countries have been advised to enact this law with suitable modification that may be necessary in the national context.

In order to prevent fraudulent changes of electronic records, civil and criminal liabilities for misconduct are necessary to deter criminals, whether corporate insiders of hawkers, through appropriate promulgation of the computer misuse act of amendment of the existing criminal code. This would help protect against unauthorized use of, or access to computers, as well as unauthorized alteration or destruction of data. Likewise, the digital signature act has also to be enacted to give sanctity to digital signatures, which is central to authenticating electronic documents. Alongside the law/or rules for the establishment of certification authorities, electronic Notaries would also be essential to permit then states to have access to keys for deciphering and tapping messages over the network to keep criminals under check and surveillance. This is necessary for the national security, as also for preventing the use of this technology by smugglers, drugs peddlers and other criminals.

EC on the Internet will soon far surpass commerce conducted over private VANs. The use of the Internet for commerce opens up a pandora's box of problems that come with it. The legal issues revolve around protection of copyrights, trademarks, patents and electronic controls on the web. The privacy of individual stands threatened.

Since data could be downloaded from various sited and ugly heads, since it is difficult to define where the transaction has taken place and on what date/time, for purpose of attributing responsibility.

2.5 LEGAL ISSUES FOR ELECTRONIC COMMERCE

E-commerce raises legal issues through the provision of the following services:

- Online Marketing
- Online retailing ordering of products and services.
- Financial services such as banking and trading in securities.
- Exchange of electronic message and documents.
- EDI, electronic filling, remote employee access, electronic transactions.

EXERCISE

1. What do you mean by cyber laws?
2. Discuss cyber laws in India.
3. What are the advantages of cyber laws?
4. Discuss ISP guidelines for cyber laws.
5. What are the legal requirements of electronic commerce?
6. Discuss legal issues for electronic commerce.

3

INTRODUCTION TO INTERNATIONAL CYBER LAWS

3.0 INTRODUCTION

In the today's era of rapid growth, Information technology is encompassing all walks of life all over the world. These technological developments have made the transition from paper to paperless transactions possible. We are now creating new standards of speed, efficiency, and accuracy in communication, which has become key tools for boosting innovations, creativity and increasing overall productivity. Computers are extensively used to store confidential data of political, social, economic or personal nature bringing immense benefit to the society.

The rapid development of Internet and Computer technology globally has led to the growth of new forms of transnational crime especially Internet related. These crimes have virtually no boundaries and may affect any country across the globe. Thus, there is a need for awareness and enactment of necessary legislation in all countries for the prevention of computer related crime.

Globally Internet and Computer based commerce and communications cut across territorial boundaries, thereby creating a new realm of human activity and undermining the feasibility and legitimacy of applying laws based on geographic boundaries. This new boundary, which is made up of the screens and passwords, separate the "Cyber world" from the "real world" of atoms. Territorially based law-making and law-enforcing authorities find this new environment deeply threatening.

In the today's era of rapid growth, Information technology is encompassing all walks of life all over the world. These technological developments have made the transition from paper to paperless transactions possible. We are now creating new standards of speed, efficiency, and accuracy in communication, which has become key tools for boosting innovations, creativity and increasing overall productivity. Computers are extensively used to store confidential data of political, social, economic or personal nature bringing immense benefit to the society.

The rapid development of Internet and Computer technology globally has led to the growth of new forms of transnational crime especially Internet related. These crimes have virtually no boundaries and may affect any country across the globe. Thus, there is a need for awareness and enactment of necessary legislation in all countries for the prevention of computer related crime.

Globally Internet and Computer based commerce and communications cut across territorial boundaries, thereby creating a new realm of human activity and undermining the feasibility and legitimacy of applying laws based on geographic boundaries. This new boundary, which is made up of the screens and passwords, separate the "Cyber world" from the "real world" of atoms. Territorially based law-making and law-enforcing authorities find this new environment deeply threatening.

3.1 WHY CYBER LAWS AT ALL?

We may ask why is there a need for a separate law to govern the Cyber World?

This may also assume significance looking to the fact that the phenomenal spread of Internet has been enabled mainly due to the absence of a centralised regulating agency. Anyone who has access to a computer and a telephone network is free to get hooked to the Internet. This uncontrollable growth of the Internet makes the need for regulation even more badly felt.

Systems across the globe have many different rules governing the behavior of users. These users in most of the countries are completely free to join/ leave any system whose rules they find comfortable/ not comfortable to them. This extra flexibility may at times lead to improper user conduct. Also, in the absence of any suitable legal framework, it may be difficult for System Administrators to have a check on Frauds, Vandalism or Abuses, which may make the life of many online users miserable.

This situation is alarming as any element of distrust for Internet may lead to people avoiding doing transactions with online sites thereby directly affecting e-Commerce growth. The (Mis)Use of Internet as an excellent medium of communication may in some situations lead to direct damage to physical societies. Non-imposition of taxes on online transactions may have its destructive effect on the physical businesses and also government revenues. Terrorists may also make use of web to create conspiracies and make violence in the society.

Therefore, all of us whether we directly use Internet or not, will like to have some form of regulation or external control for monitoring online transactions and the cyber world for preventing any instability.

3.2 CYBER CRIMES

"Computer or Cyber crimes are considered as illegal, unethical or unauthorized behavior of people relating to the automatic processing and transmission of data, use of Computer Systems and Networks".

Common types of Cyber Crimes may be broadly classified in the following groups:-

1. Against Individuals:
   - (*a*) Against Person:
     - (*i*) Harassment through e-mails.
     - (*ii*) Cyber-stalking.
     - (*iii*) Dissemination of obscene material on the Internet.
     - (*iv*) Defamation.
     - (*v*) Hacking/cracking.
     - (*vi*) Indecent exposure.

(*b*) Against property of an individual:
   (*i*) Computer vandalism.
   (*ii*) Transmitting virus.
   (*iii*) Internet intrusion.
   (*iv*) Unauthorised control over computer system.
   (*v*) Hacking /cracking.

2. Against Organisations:
   (*a*) Against Government, Private Firm, Company, Group of Individuals: -
      (*i*) Hacking & Cracking.
      (*ii*) Possession of unauthorised information.
      (*iii*) Cyber terrorism against the government organisation.
      (*iv*) Distribution of pirated software etc.
3. Against Society at large:
   (*i*) Pornography (specially child pornography).
   (*ii*) Polluting the youth through indecent exposure.
   (*iii*) Trafficking.

3.3 BASIC APPROACHES FOR CREATION OF CYBER LAWS

Following are the basic approaches for creation of Cyber Laws, which will ensure the smooth governance of Internet globally:

(*a*) Formulation of new laws and amendment of existing laws by nations within their present territorial boundaries thereby attempting to regulate all actions on the Internet that have any impact on their own population.

(*b*) Nations may enter into multi-lateral international agreements to establish new and uniform rules specifically applicable to conduct on the Internet.

(*c*) Creation of an entirely new international organisation, which can establish new rules and new means of enforcing those rules.

(*d*) Guidelines and rules may naturally emerge from individual decisions like domain name and IP address registrations and by websites and users deciding about whom will they patronise.

3.4 DEFINING CYBER LAWS

Cyber law encompasses a wide variety of legal issues related to use of communications technology. It includes use of Internet as well as any other form of Computer or Digital Processing Devices. It includes intellectual property, privacy, freedom of expression, and jurisdiction.

As the law of **Cyber Space**, as envisioned by **William Gibson** in his novel **Neuromancer**, **Cyber Law** addresses the issues of **Virtual Property** and **Virtual Persons**. It covers rights of **Netizens** who are the citizens of Cyber Space and regulation of the Cyber Space for a peaceful and harmonious existence of Netizens.

The biggest challenge before **Cyber Law** is its integration with the legacy system of laws applicable to the physical world.

Since **Cyber Space** has no geographical boundaries, nor the **Netizens** have physical characteristics of **Sex, Age** etc., several conflicts surface when the rights of Netizens are viewed in the eyes of Citizens of a physical space. This is well reflected in the conflict between the Trade mark Laws and system of Domain Names.

There are several countries which have enacted special laws for regulating Cyber Space Transactions of Citizens within their Physical Jurisdiction and these are recognized as the Cyber Laws of the Physical Jurisdiction.

3.5 ESTABLISHING A SUITABLE FRAMEWORK

There is a dire need for the emergence of a well-defined framework of Cyber Laws, which should be able to do the following:

1. Create and implement a minimum set of guiding rules of conduct that would facilitate efficient Communications and reliable Commerce through the use of Electronic medium.
2. Define, punish and prevent wrongful actions that attack the electronic medium or harm others.

One of the greatest concerns of the field of Cyber Laws has been the absence (or rather delay) of a well-defined and comprehensive framework of law across the globe. Today's *Internet* was born in the early 1960's while the initial efforts for its regulation could only surface in the late 1990's. This problem has been further aggravated by the steep rise in usage of Internet in the recent years all over the world and that too in the absence of any appropriate legal framework.

Surely, the Cyber Law scenario is globally more complicated than traditional laws owing to the reason that the range of activities which are to be governed by these laws are largely technology driven, an area which is dynamically changing and is beyond anyone's control. However enactment of these laws pose opportunities for nations to carve model Cyber Societies for the future thereby taking a lead in becoming Global IT Powers.

Effective Implementation of any law is as critical an exercise as its enactment. A law-implementing agency has to focus on the following major areas to be effective:

1. Creating a suitable climate thereby Inducing Self Compliance by the Society.
2. Regular monitoring of the scenario for reliable feedback.
3. Offering Openness and Flexibility to accept and incorporate necessary modifications at appropriate times.
4. Distinctly establishing the Authority-Responsibility guidelines for the Implementing Agency.

In order to be effective, it has to be ensured that the Law is Simple, fair and full of clarity. Failing this, the law may be misused to harass individuals resulting in its defiance. The implementing agency will then be compelled to take corrective actions to ensure implementation. This whole process may result in spread of corruption and polluting of the overall sentiments in society making the job of law implementing agencies more difficult.

3.6 CYBER LEGISLATIONS WORLDWIDE

To meet the challenge posed by new kinds of crime made possible by computer technology including telecommunication, many countries have also reviewed their respective domestic criminal laws so as to prevent computer related crimes. Some of these countries are USA, Austria, Denmark,

France Germany, Greece, Finland, Italy, Turkey, Sweden, Switzerland, Australia, Canada, India, Japan, Spain, Portugal, UK, Malaysia and Singapore.

However, no country has fully resolved all the issues such as legal, enforcement and prevention of crime. The legislations enacted by different countries cover only few of the classified computer related offences. However, looking to the dynamic and fast changing technology, new types of offences may pop-up frequently.

Some of the major types of offences against which many countries across the globe have enacted various Acts (mostly at preliminary levels) are as follows:

1. Unlawful access to data in computers.
2. Damaging data in computer etc.
3. Possession of device to obtain unauthorised telephone facilities.
4. Unauthorised access to computer and computer material.
5. Committing mischief with data.
6. Data spying.
7. Computer fraud.
8. Forgery of prohibitive data.
9. Alteration of data.
10. Computer sabotage.
11. False entry in an authentic deed.
12. False entry in permit licence or passport.
13. Electronic record made wrongfully.
14. Electronic record made wrongfully by public servant.
15. Interferences with business by destruction or damage of computer.
16. Interferences with computer.
17. Destruction of public document.
18. Destruction of private document.
19. Unauthorised access with intention to commit offences/computer crimes.
20. Unauthorised use and interception of computer services.
21. Knowingly access of computer without authorisation related to national defence or foreign relation.
22. Intentional access of computer without authorisation to obtain financial information.
23. Unauthorised access of computer of a Govt. Deptt. Or agency.
24. Knowingly causing transmission of data/program to damage a computer network, data or program or withhold or deny use of computer, network etc.
25. Knowingly causing transmission of data/program with risk that transmission will damage a computer network, data or program or withhold or deny use of computer, network etc., an unauthorised access of computer with intent to defraud.

3.7 THE LEGAL ISSUES IN CYBER LAWS

In its recent Communication on Electronic Commerce, the European Commission stressed that "in order to allow for electronic commerce operators to reap the full benefits of the Single Market, it is essential to avoid regulatory inconsistencies and to ensure a coherent legal and regulatory framework for electronic commerce". The types of pitfalls that are facing any company or person wanting to set up a distance selling activity on the Internet, offering goods or services to consumers and businesses located world wide are numerous, they vary according to the type of relation you are considering entering (consumer, business), and according to the legal framework you are accustomed to operating in. To make things even more difficult, the answers are often unclear, non existent, contradictory and constitute real obstacles to conducting a commercial activity on the network. As governments continue to consider how best to enforce their interests in electronic transactions, technical standards and traditional contract principles will provide a private source of law to govern online transactions. Conceptual, operational and intellectual property issues are raised by electronic commerce, and organizations actively involved in intelligent transactions must conduct legal risk assessment in order to document their information policies.

When the World Wide Web Consortium (W3C) officially adopted the eXtensible Markup Language (XML) in mid-February 1998, the Internet finally came to what users of SGML have been enjoying for years, a meta-grammatical modeling language. The difference is, these newcomers brought millions and millions of dollars and users with them. At a time when Microsoft and Sun Microsystems fought each other in a courtroom over the future of Java, the two companies co-sponsored the 1998 XML Conference in Seattle, Washington. Wait a minute. What's going on here? and why?

Electronic commerce is what is going on, and there appears to be enough for everyone. [ELGIN1] Companies like Microsoft, Sun Microsystems and Adobe are finally working with SGML veterans like SoftQuad, ArborText and Inso because the information needs generated by electronic commerce are powerfully addressed with the modeling tools of SGML. The whole global information infrastructure could benefit from this fact, as first commercial transactions and then non-commercial transactions are transformed into a rich, rapid and accurate intelligent information stream, and structural innovation becomes a competitive market instead of a birthright of the next business cycle.

As the mechanism for mediating the exchange of value between intelligent information systems, meta-grammatical standards like XML and SGML play the same role that the law plays in mediating the exchange of value in the real world. As such, these technical standards act as a source of law for online transactions and therefore must be reliable, detailed and accurate enough for real jurisdictions to rely upon them in addressing the multitude of legal issues generated by electronic transactions.

With the passage of only one statute, digital signature laws, the way humans do business will never be the same. For as secure digital commerce evolves, the sheer number of transactions possible predicts that entities will be party to dramatically more contracts. Where there are contracts, there is litigation. Whether, when and how legal institutions will give legal effect to online transactions is the greatest challenge confronting both the legal and technological communities. Even though there are no clear answers, there are some important questions that need to be asked. This paper will attempt to spot the important legal issues generated by electronic commerce, detail the benefit of an international, content-neutral regulatory structure and suggest a semantic framework for understanding and distributing the risks of electronic transactions.

Most importantly, it is my desire to generate a dialogue among participants regarding these issues before the next generation of innovation for the global information infrastructure moots many of these questions. There is a tension between governmental bodies and the private sector over the development of a legally-sufficient electronic infrastructure, and so far, governments are waiting to see what the private sector does first. SGML/XML and the standards-based content interchange industry have an opportunity to provide that infrastructure in a vendor-neutral way, while at the same time creating a whole new and level market for semantic information tools. The Internet is a new economic environment with tremendous potential. But if the economic infrastructure of the Internet only mimics current markets, then much of that potential will be lost, and in the end, your PC will look more like the soda machine down the hall then the intelligent access point it can be.

The legal framework we are operating in is increasingly becoming complex and burdensome in one single jurisdiction alone, let alone when you are faced simultaneously with hundreds of potentially applicable legislations because you are entering agreements with customers located anywhere in the world. Besides, a number of companies and consumers are still unaware of the legal constraints they may encounter by entering electronic transactions. The objective of this present draft is to fill this gap by providing an overview of relevant legal issues raised by the development of electronic commerce.

Taxation Law

- What criteria may be used to associate on line transactions with the territory of a country?
- How can double taxation be prevented?
- How do the direct taxes rules apply in an electronic environment, both for businesses and for individuals?
- Do general taxation, VAT and custom duties regimes apply to electronic transactions?
- What is the nature of supplies on the Internet? Are the products delivered electronically goods or services?
- How can digital documents comply with existing administrative requirements to keep written evidence of commercial operation and registration in accountancy?
- How can the place and the time of the supply be determined?
- Are electronic transactions exports or imports pursuant the European VAT directives?

Electronic Payments

- What are the existing advantages and obstacles to introducing technical systems that enable electronic payments in an electronic transaction?
- Are banking regulations applicable to issuers of cybercash and cyber credit cards? Does such electronic cash constitute legal tender?
- How can credit cards and other electronic payments satisfy the legal requirements in electronic environments?
- How can privacy, consumer protection and bank secrecy be fulfilled in an electronic banking relationship?
- What is the situation concerning the use of electronic negotiable documents?

Contract Law and Evidence

- Which are the nature , parties and subject matter of the contracts?
- How to enter contracts electronically?

- What is the value of an electronic document and a digital signature?
- Where and when does the offer take place?
- What are the terms and conditions governing the contract?

Liability

- What type of liability could the various actors (service provider, access provider, TTP, seller, banking institution,) involved in the offering of goods or services face?
- What type of damages are covered?
- What are the causes of liability?

Intellectual Property Rights

- How to protect a web site, a domain name, a trade mark or any other type of intellectual property right against illegal misappropriation?
- How to control the use of protected material on the global infrastructure?
- Which rights are concerned when downloading, viewing or printing a protected work? Is there a exhaustion of rights?
- How can the rightholder expect to obtain remuneration?
- How can his moral rights be ensured?
- How should licence agreements be drafted?
- What is the legal protection of the integrity of ECMS?
- Is it possible to detect illegal use?
- Who can be considered as liable in case of copyright or trade mark infringement?

Consumer Protection

- What general or specific rules must be respected when entering a contract with a consumer or when advertising a product?
- What is the regulation of offers and marketing practices?
- What are the abusive terms of a contract?
- What type of information has to be included in a web site?
- How is the distance selling contracts regulated?
- What is the regulation of product and services liability and of products labelling and packaging?
- How can consumers have easy access to jurisdiction and which are the possibilities for consumer associations to defend consumer's interests?

Privacy Issues

- What are the applicable general and specific legislations?
- Can personal data be transferred?
- What are the technical developments currently undertaken to improve the protection of privacy on the Internet? How do they comply with privacy provisions?

International Private Law

- What are the competent jurisdictions and the applicable law in the following matters: Contracts, Liability, Intellectual property Rights, Marketing and competition law, electronic payments and banking issues
- What are the specific mandatory criteria in the context of consumer protection?
- How can a jurisdictional decision be enforced in another country?
- Is online litigation and arbitration in commercial cases relevant?

Legislative developments are facing a new challenge brought on by the rapid development of the on-line technology and by the newly created difficulty of applying existing regulations in a networked environment. Simultaneously, technology provides more and more solutions to the threats created by the emergence of this new technology. Lawyers and technicians can no longer consider each other as enemies but have to collaborate. Technology and law must develop along each other's progress and integrate mutual input. Such connections between both already exist in a number of fields. Many examples may be mentioned such as TTPs, Privacy Enhancing Technology, ECMS, etc. Systems as PICS can also be applied to a growing number of fields, such as protection of copyright, protection of minors, consumers, etc.

Forthcoming legislative initiatives will necessarily have to encounter these technical solutions in order to address regulatory responses to the growth of electronic commerce.

EXERCISE

1. Discuss the need of international laws.
2. Why Cyber Laws At All?
3. What do you mean by cyber crimes?
4. Discuss Common types of Cyber Crimes.
5. Discuss Basic approaches for creation of Cyber Laws.
6. Define Cyber laws.
7. Establish a suitable framework for cyber laws.
8. Discuss Cyber Legislations Worldwide.
9. Discuss The Legal Issues in Cyber laws.
10. Discuss International Private Law.

4

WEB PROJECTS AND WEB TEAM

4.0 WEB PROJECTS

Web Projects are Internet enabled project, by using the web project user can share data, browse data, apply some operations on the data etc., all over the world. Web project are differ from software and traditional projects.

Comparison of web projects with software projects, advertising projects and traditional projects is as follows:

S.No	Web Projects	Software Projects	Advertising Projects	Traditional Projects
1.	Project Managers are not always client managers.	Different	Similar	Different
2.	Development Schedules are dramatically short.	Can be Similar; called "death march" projects	Similar, though manageable since there is no technical component	Similar
3.	New, often beta, technologies are used, often without technical support.	Different	N/A	N/A
4.	Scope changes occur during the implementation phase.	Similar, though not without dramatic change in cost and time	Different	Similar
5.	A pricing model for web Project does not exist.	Similar	Different	Different
6.	Standards for web production do not exist.	Different	Different	Similar
7.	Team roles are less specialized.	Different	Different	Different
8.	Clients are often unwilling to bear the costs of Web development, especially during planning phase.	Different	Different	Different
9.	The project manager's responsibilities are very broad.	Different	Similar	Different

4.1 CHARACTERISTICS OF WEB PROJECTS

The basic characteristics of a web project are as follows:

1. Project managers are not always client managers.
2. Development Schedules are dramatically short.
3. New, often beta, technologies are used, often without technical support.
4. Scope changes occur during the implementation phase.
5. A pricing model for web projects does not exist.
6. Standards for web production do not exist.
7. Team roles are less specialized.
8. Clients are often unwilling to bear the costs of web development, especially during the planning phase.
9. The project manager's responsibilities are very broad.

4.2 SKILLS OF A PROJECT MANAGER

A project manager must have following skills:

- Software of film project management experience.
- Rigorous understanding of scheduling, budgeting and resource allocation.
- Superior written and verbal communication skills.
- Ability to lead effective meetings.
- Detail oriented.
- Pragmatic
- Good sense of humor
- Ability to stay clam during disasters
- Development or production experience in Web, multimedia, software or film.

4.3 PHASES OF A WEB PROJECT

A Web project has many phases. The main phases of a web project are as follows:

1. **Define a Project :** Defining a project means that to understand and communicate in written the mission of the project, objective of project, risk and requirements. A project can be defined quickly and easily by following steps:
   (*a*) **Write a Project Mission Statement :** Writing a project mission statement is the first step towards defining a project. By mission statement we describe the solution of the problem that our web project is going to solve. It answers three following basic questions:
   - What are we going to do?
   - For whom we are doing it?
   - How do we go about it?

   (*b*) **Identify Objectives :** Objectives helps our creative team to design the best graphics for the site, they help the programmers. Understood how the web site might grow, and they tell the writers what tone or information is critical to the site. Mr. James Lewis had defined five characteristics of the objectives; they are:

- Specific
- Measurable
- Attainable
- Realistic
- Time - limited.

(*c*) **Identification of Target Users :** Targeted user of a web project must be identified. Content of the web site will be determined by the users whom you want to visit the site. User can be identified by using four sources:

- Market Resource
- By previous History
- Focus Groups
- Understanding Internet Audiences.

(*d*) **Determine the Scope**

The scope of the web project must be determined in the beginning. In order to nail down the scope, we must understand the project completely.

(*i*) **Factors that contribute to scope are:**

- Time and cost
- Web site is perceived as being easily changeable.
- How to communicate with your client and your team.
- Amount of money that your client want to spend.

(*ii*) **Key elements can be determined as:**

- Site design
- Navigation architecture
- Copywriting
- Quality assurance testing

(*iii*) **Breaking down components:** Now that you have identified the key elements of your web site, you are ready to investigate the time, effort and cost associated with each element. You will be breaking down each element into tasks, analyzing the tasks and the time it will take to complete them and making some decisions about how to implement the features so that you stay within a budget and on schedule.

(*iv*) **Writing the scope document:** The scope document is the culmination of your effort to define the project. The work breakdown structure that you created is essentially the scope of your project. In your scope document, you reiterate the mission and objectives of your Web project along with the features that you will build to meet the project goal. Your scope document should be easy to follow and must include a sign-off page. The sign-off page is for you and your client to put in writing your agreement on the features on the site.

2. **The Budget :** Your budget is your fully defined project with a price tag. The better you become at defining your project's scope, the more accurate your budgets will be. Creating a perfect budget is the Web project manager's lifetime project. It's almost impossible to do it; but each time you create a budget, you will get better at it.

(*a*) **Budget Categories :** Your budget categories come directly from scope document and work breakdown structure (WBS). Every task that you outlined in your WBS becomes a line item in your budget as well as your project plan. Your budget may be short, long or medium.

(*b*) **Assumption for Budgeting :** Your budget is also a set of assumptions about things that are to be delivered not only by you to the client, but also from the client to you. Assumptions about the budget should be written up either as part of the scope document or in an appendix to the budget. The following are possible assumptions about the budget:

- All content provided by the client should be delivered in Microsoft World.
- The client has 72 hours to approve design.
- The Web team will present two design concepts.
- Media buying is not part of the strategic plan.

(*c*) **Hidden Costs :** Every time meet informally about your project or pick up the phone to discuss something with your client, you are incurring a cost. The costs may be small, but they add up. It's important that you include a cushion in your budget for these kinds of untraceable and unexpected costs. Some of the most widely forgotten cost ate the following:

- Meeting with the full team
- Phone calls
- Photo or art research
- The Scope document
- E-mail and administration
- Setting up the review site
- Setting up a development site

(*d*) **References :** To make a budget of a web project, project manager takes the help of several prepared budget of different projects as a references.

(*e*) **Tools :** Every project manager has his/her own set of preferred tools. Some of them are:

- Email with integrated task management
- Microsoft Excel
- Microsoft Project

3. **More Preliminary Planning Issues :** While you are scooping and budgeting for the project, you need to be thinking about two things: your team and your infrastructure. Your infrastructure is the supporting environment for your project. It consists of your communications system (e-mail), your tools (software and hardware) and any other tangibles or intangibles that are important for providing an environment in which to build your web site. Some issues are:
   - Set up an e-mail alias for your project
   - Develop an e-mail convention for your subject line, so that all team members can easily recognize e-mail pertaining to your project.
   - Make sure you have all the documents you need for client sign-off. These could be legal contracts, non-disclosure agreements or your own scope document.

4.4 WEB TEAM

Because of the rapid growth of Internet and web applications, web team is evolving. The need of separate web team have been arrived, because of the following reasons:

- Business leaders are beginning to understand that the web is transferring the way business id done.
- Leaders are realizing the need to bring this medium into the overall, long term business plan and treat it as they would any other significant component of their business

Different web projects require different web teams; it totally depends on the web project that who are the team members. Common compositions of web team can be categories into three types.

1. **Core Team Members :** There are some core role and responsibilities, which are carried out by core team members of a web project. Core team members are the basic bone. Example of core team members is Project manager, Technical Leader, Web production Specialist, Creative lead, Designers Production artist, and Quality assurance leader.
2. **Extended Team Members :** Extended team members are people whose skills might not always be necessary or who might have cross-functional roles and needed for a short period in the development of the web project. Examples of extended team members are Account manager, Programmer, Network engineer, Information architect, and tester.
3. **Special Team Members :** Special team members are people whose services are taken to solve special purposes. They are specialist of their field and needed in a web project for a short period. Examples of special team members are Security expert, Audio engineer, Video engineer, #-D modeler, Web Cast specialist, Media buyers, and strategic planner

4.5 ROLE AND RESPONSIBILITIES OF WEB TEAM MEMBERS

To do the proper work, role, responsibilities and the way of interaction of each team member must be properly defined. Team composition varies depending on the scope, audiences and levels of complexity of the web projects. As defined above web team contains three types of members: Core team members, Extended team members and Special team members. Role and responsibilities of web team members are as follows:

1. **Project Manager :** The project manager is responsible for planning and managing all the human and technological elements of a web development project, from concept to completion. These responsibilities include: liaising with the content expert or client; planning, budgeting and preparation; concept design and arranging user research; briefing and managing the rest of the web team; overseeing the content, creative and technical development; overseeing site testing, release and evaluation; bringing the project to completion, within the time-frame and budget; and trouble-shooting.
2. **Account Manager :** The account manager is generally present in agencies or companies who follow the agency model. The account manager is responsible for selling in different projects and providing the project team with necessary consumer insight and information. The account manager interacts with the client, the project manager and the creative leader.
3. **Technical Leader :** A technical leader oversees the project from a technical point of view. The technical leader assists the project manager in ensuring that the technical strategy is sound, manages the programmers and chooses specialized team members such as security experts, database programmers, and other system integrators. The technical leader prepares

technical brief and communicates with the project manager, technical team members, and members of the client's technical team.

4. **Network Engineer :** A network engineer is responsible for setting up and configuring a Web server. A network engineer is also a database administrator or security expert. A network engineer is also responsible for registering domain names and sometimes responsible for setting up e-mail servers as well.
5. **Information Architect :** The information architect is responsible for the process where we help our client determine the structure of their site. Information architecture includes deciding how to organise the content so that it makes most sense to the users; how to link the pages together; and how to navigate through the pages.
6. **Information Designer :** The information designer is responsible for the process through which information is configured for effective communication. Information design helps make information understandable and easy to use by incorporating good-practice issues of graphic design, typography, systems and usability.
7. **Instructional Designer :** Instructional design is a process whereby learning objectives are matched with the most appropriate instructional practices and strategies. An instructional designer is responsible for creating engaging learning activities.
8. **Interaction Designer :** The interaction designer is responsible for developing the user experience in a website or other digital medium, focusing on elements such as navigation, layout and user interactions.
9. **Visual Designer :** The visual designer is responsible for creating the overall look and feel of the web site and the visual style of the individual web pages. The visual designer solves problems relating to graphic layout of web pages, typography, colour selection, branding and overall consistency.

   Common tasks include: image processing and web optimisation, developing HTML templates and browser/platform testing of the HTML layouts. Where necessary the visual designer may create original animation, illustration and photography.

   During the concept design stages, the visual designer collaborates with the project manager, client and content developer to determine the information needs of the users, and to come up with a look and feel for the user interface that will work in an interactive form. During design production, the visual designer works with the content developer and programmer to build the web site.
10. **Content Developer/Web Writer:** The content developer/web writer creates the web site content — the information presented on the web site. The content developer/web writer's responsibilities depend on what kind of content is required, and may include: assessing and analysing content needs and designing content layout solutions; researching content; developing and writing new content or rewriting/editing existing content into a form that is appropriate for interactive media and adds value to the content materials; html coding and validating; inserting copy into templates or content management systems; processing images; and maintaining live web site content.

    During content production, the content developer works with the content expert, information architect, visual designer and programmer, and may provide advice relating to the presentation of site content.
11. **Programmer :** The programmer builds the web site's functionality — the things it can do. A web project may need just one or a number of different programmers, depending

on the size of the site, what you want it to do, and which programming languages are required to make it work. Programmers use authoring software tools to bring a web site to life and make it work. For example, they code web sites that can publish data dynamically to the web using combined html and database technologies, and they build roll-over and fly-out navigation, interactive elements like games and forms, and user interfaces like embedded content management systems.

The programmer may be involved during project planning, to provide technical advice on the proposed web site. During production, the programmer works with the information architect, content developer and visual designer.

12. **Security Expert :** A security expert is someone who provides security strategy for Web Sites. This person knows and has implemented sites using various types of encryption and can discuss the pros and cons of each with your team and your client.
13. **Web Production Specialist :** A Web production specialist is the person who integrates the site using HTML or javaScript, and is generally the hub of the site. This is usually the person who codes the HTML pages, integrates Java or Shockwave applications, integrates images and animations and hands the project off to the QA depertment.
14. **Copywriter :** Copywriter prepares all the text and Images and material which is to be put on the web site. Usually, the client supplies copy and the information architect or designer makes it Web — readable.
15. **Production Artist :** A production artist the artwork that the designer creates into Web ready art. The production artist obtains Photoshop files from the designers and cuts up the files into individual graphics, and then optimizes the graphics into Web file formats. The production artist must be skilled in color reduction and image compression techniques.
16. **Quality Assurance Leader :** A quality assurance leader makes sure that the product you delivers meets the critriea specified in the scope document and functional Specification. The QA person interacts with developers during bug - fixing time and with the producer to ensure that all bugs are addresses and resolved when project is delivered.
17. **Tester :** A tester test the Web project based on the test plan that the QA leader writes.
18. **Audio Engineer :** An audio engineer designs sounds for web sites. These sounds could range from music to sounds that happen when the user does something. The audio engineer usually interacts with the creative and technical leader.
19. **Video Engineer :** The video engineer creates video images and delivers them in digital formats to the creative leader or the Web production specialist.
20. **3-D Modeler :** A 3-D modeler creates artwork that is in 3-D and usually works with the creative leader.
21. **Web Cast Specialist :** A Web cast specialist is usually a third party vendor who specializes in Web casts.
22. **Media Buyer :** A media buyer is usually part of the client's advertisement agency. If your project is an advertising campaign, the producer will interact with the media planner to obtain specifications on the media buy so that the web team can create advertisements based on the sizes in the buy.
23. **Strategic Planner :** A strategic planner is the person who delivers the consumer insight to the team. This person generally conducts market research on the client's audience and delivers a brief to help the creative team understand the mind of the target auidence.

24. **Photographer :** To take original phtographs for the web site.
25. **Evaluationexpert :** To conduct user research and user testing.
26. **Compatability/Useability Tester :** To test the web site during the final stages of production, to make sure it works on a variety of platforms and that there are no bugs.

4.6 PUTTING TOGETHER RIGHT TEAM

To get a right team for work is a typical task. The right team is that will fulfill your Web site objectives most successfully. It is east to choose the wrong people for Web teams, especially because some of the tasks involved with putting up a Web site can be perceived as easy. To get a right team the following aspects must be needed.

(*a*) **Identify Necessary Skills :** To get a right team you must be sure about that the following skills are covered:

- **Project Management Skill :** The ability to see and communicate the big picture to the team and your client and make sure the site gets built according to specifications, on time and on budget.
- **Information design/Architectural skill :** The ability to design a usable and useful user interface that includes how the user will interact with the interface and navigate the site.
- **Graphic design skill :** The ability to transform the information design into a visual design.
- **Graphic production skill :** The ability to create Web graphics that are fast loading and that look great on all browsers.
- **Content development skill:** The ability to develop both written and interactive content for Web sites. This includes copy, video, audio, and anything that is not part of the user interface.
- **Programming skill:** The ability to create Web pages using HTML, JavaScript and other client/server scripting languages.
- **Technical/network infrastructure skills:** The ability to understand the requirements for servicing a Web site on the Internet and to recommend the best strategy based on the client's or stakeholders needs.

Assessing Skills: The site of different team members must be assessed. Whether they are competent in their work or not.

Building a Team: Finding the right people is a difficult task, but an even more challenging task is matching team members both to the task and to each other. If you are managing multiple Web Projects, then you have probably faced the dilemma of choosing the right combination of people for a particular project.

You might find yourself having to choose between similar people to do a certain task. To make a good choice, it's important to think about several things:

- Is there is a critical deadline for the task? If so, choose the person with the better track record for meeting deadlines. This will reduce the risk of missing the deadline.
- What risks do I take if I put this person on the task? If you know that one person is more prone to mistakes, then you can assign him or her tasks with lower risk.

- How does this person interact with the rest of the team? If either person has a history of not getting along with one of your team members, then you can decide whether to take risk of having to manage interpersonal problems as well as project-oriented issues.

(*b*) **Managing the Team :** To manage a team according to their work is a typical task. The web teams have to perform their work in a given time schedule. There are many, many more risks because there are more unknown factors and development times can be longer and more costly.

One of the more challenging aspects of web project management is managing human resources — from different departments or different teams on one project or over several projects.

(*c*) **Leverage the Central Web Team's Skills :** You are faced with parallel Web development efforts and limited resources, including your own time and expertise. Your obstacles are the following:

- You don't have people on staff that shoots video.
- You need to have the new site designed.
- You need to have the new site coded.
- You cannot interrupt the project in process.
- You have a small budget for the second project, but you can cover the cost of video shooting and production.

It is important to develop processes that each team member follows. When you have a method of doing things, people get more and more efficient and save time. Once you get past design and into production, it's essential that your team be able to work efficiently.

(*d*) **Cross-functional Teams :** A cross-functional team is made up of individuals who perform different functions within the team. For example, a producer might also be an information designer. A designer might also be an HTML coder.

4.7 TEAM DYNAMICS

(*a*) **Virtual Management :** There will ultimately be occasion where your Web teams will be in different locations, working simultaneously on a Web project. If you have to manage resources at different locations then you have to prepare for traveling. The following point must be kept in mind for managing a Web team:

- **Set clear Guidelines :** When members of a team are scattered in various locations, nothing becomes more important than a clear understanding of what everyone's roles are, including who does what, when and how. It's critical to provide team members with information about the other team members, what their roles and deliverables are, and how they will deliver their piece of the project.
- **Set up a review site :** A very important tools for the virtual team is the review Web site. This is a Web Site that lists everything about the project, from contact names and addresses to the scope document, schedule and schematics of the site. As well it has a link to the staging site, which is where your team will work collaboratively on the site.

(*b*) **Working With the Client's Resources :** The most important thing for you to do as a project manager is to be open to using these resources. Never refuse them. Doing so would only cast you in a negative light to your client. The right thing to do is to find a job for them. If they are IT people of employees who have learned web production, then pair them with people from your team and give them low risk tasks to do. Of they prove themselves to be competent, then you have just earned another resource, and you can use your own team resource on another project.

(*c*) **Outsourcing or Working With Vendors :** Every now and then you will need to work with an outside resource on a project. Either you will need to hire a specific resource, such as coder or designer, or you might need to form a partnership with a vendor to provide services to your Web team does not provide, such as networking infrastructure, production or strategic planning.

(*d*) **Sorting the Suitable Person According to Their Work :** You should sort the people according to their suitability of work. Your responsibility is to develop an environment of communication and production systems that help your team do the best job possible.

- **How programmers work :** Programmers are solitary beings. They are used to getting a requirements document, designing a specification, and then coding. They do not respond well to having to write documentation, but they know they have to. Some programmers will not speak up and will defer to the loudest voice.
- **How designers work :** A clear iteration of the marketing goals and key consumer insight can be invaluable in helping a designer get the concept right on the first try. Giving the designer a production assistant to do photo research is also a good idea—this way the designer does not spend too much time getting artwork and can focus on sketching and design.
- **How writers work :** Writers need to know who the audience is and what the project's objective is or they will be writing in a vacuum. Your creative or strategic brief should contain what the writer needs to develop copy that is appropriate for the audience.

EXERCISE

1. Define web projects.
2. Give a comparative study of web projects with software projects, advertising projects and traditional projects.
3. Describe Characteristics of a web project.
4. What are the skills of a project manager?
5. What are the phases of a web project?
6. How we define the budget of a web project?
7. What do you mean by web team?
8. What are the categories of a web team?
9. Discuss Role and Responsibilities of Web Team Members.
10. How we put a right team together?
11. Discuss team dynamics.
12. How we manage a team?
13. What do you mean by cross functional team?
14. What do you understand by team dynamics?
15. How you ensure that your team does the best job possible?

5

WEB DEVELOPMENT STRATEGIES

5.0 COMMUNICATION ISSUE

Good Communication is critical to every project, but how easy is it to identify "what is good communication?" Good communication comes from learning, occurs over time, and must be practiced between people. You could have the world's best communication process, in which people meet daily and follow up each meeting with good notes that are dispersed to the whole team and still have poor communication. There are many causes of poor communication; some of them are as follows:

5.0.1 Cause of Poor Communication

1. People come different environment
2. Personalities
3. Lack of mutual understand of terminology
4. Hidden agenda
5. Proximity
6. Assumption
7. Poor infrastructure and support
8. Ineffective meetings
9. Being and expert
10. Hesitation
11. Lack of good communication structure

1. **People come different environment :** People specialized in different stream such as some people are expert in design some people are expert in programming some are expert in sales etc. people who come from different stream all can understand each other but they could have to work on communicating with people outside of their stream.
2. **Personalities :** If two or three people have more difficult time communicating with each other then they do with other people for solving a problem.

3. **Lack of mutual understanding of terminology :** If people are different stream use their own terminology, which might cause confusion among other team members.
4. **Hidden agenda :** Hidden agenda is very big problem for understanding the people because they had their motivating factors. They will not ready to listen others suggestions, alternations and changes.
5. **Proximity :** People who are the members of your team may be from different cities, state and country. This means that the meetings you will be largely conference call or videoconference.
6. **Assumptions :** Often people make assumption and these assumptions can load their ability to communicate.
7. **Poor infrastructure and support :** This is the main cause for poor communication the following are the reasons for this.
   (*a*) Computer Troubles
   (*b*) Lack knowledge of computer
   (*c*) E-mail handling problem
   (*d*) File format incompatibility
   (*e*) Other system failures

   If any one of the above problem occurs, then communication effected.
8. **Ineffective meetings :** Meetings always waste of time if they are not led well. Due to following reasons ineffective meetings are occurred
   (*a*) Big personalities
   (*b*) Agenda not proper
   (*c*) Communication Gaping
9. **Being an expert :** It is very big problem that expert are not listen to others in the meetings. Unfortunately they do not know what is the impact of the piece of site on which they are working on other people work.
10. **Hesitation :** Hesitation is the biggest barrier to good communication. The following reasons are given below:
    (*a*) New place
    (*b*) New topic
    (*c*) New audience
11. **Lack of a good communication structure :** Often there is not a good communication structure. The reasons of bad communication structure are as follows:
    (*a*) Fit the way people work
    (*b*) Made up of emits
    (*c*) Usable
    (*d*) Easy to use
    (*e*) Does not have unnecessary information

    Some of these are the causes of miscommunication are critical.

5.0.2 Good Communication System

A system with good communication is perfect, healthy and work properly.

1. **Evaluate the way your team communicates :** Reasons for evaluating the current communication structure of web team are as follows:
   (*a*) What is your current communication structure? How can you leverage the existing system structure . which types of information effect your system
   (*b*) If you have a face problem for open and reading a file attachment for team members.
   (*c*) Do you frequently go over budget on your project?
   (*d*) Do you often find out things " through the grupevine"

   If you realize that your answer " Yes" to some or all of these questions then you have weakness in your communication structure that you need to address.
2. **Translator :** Due to different languages, team face problem then team should be include translator. Translator understand the language well and communicate to each other . If you have work in a very large project then your technical leader must be able to act as a translator.

5.0.3 Chain of Communication

Chain communication is a good way of passing the new information to each others suppose that project manager is responsible for alerting the project team and all members. Project manager should get the team input first and then communicate to the client.

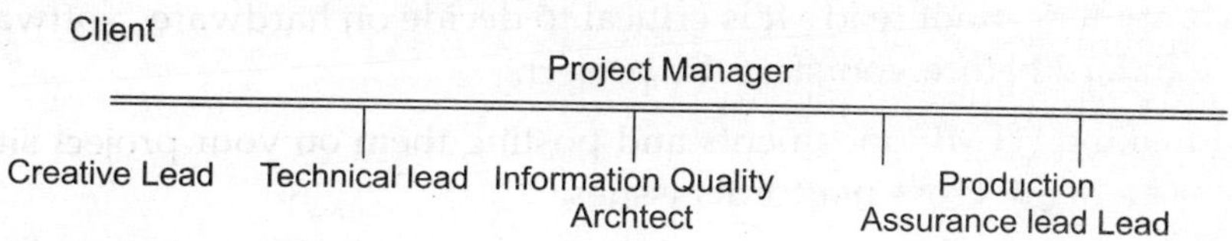

Creative lead communicate to :

(*a*) Copy write
(*b*) Designers
(*c*) Sound designers
(*d*) Video designers
(*e*) Animators

Technical lead communicate to :

(*a*) Script writers (client + server side)
(*b*) Database Archtect
(*c*) Security expert
(*d*) Programmers
(*e*) Network Administrator

Information architect communicate to :

(*a*) Focus groups

Quality assurance lead communicate to :

(*a*) Testers

Production lead communicate to :

(*a*) HTML Coders
(*b*) Art Production

Symbology : Symbols are very power full when accept the users their appearance can make many people act in a known and consistent manners

Example: when drivers see red light they know to stop the bus so symbol is also useful for web development team. Think about how often you have encountered a communication problem over how something is going to work on a web site. So symbol is very useful for web development team because he/she know the meaning the symbol.

Style guides : A style guide is important but a good web style guide is a hard commodity to find. A style guide offers a consistent guide to word and acronym usage.

Production guides : From a communication point of view the production guide is a valuable tool in case of the new to add or change production staff quickly. The guide gives new staff and overview of the production aspects of a project such as

- Server access information
- Directory Structure
- File naming Convention
- File formats
- Production art statistics

Infrastructure : Nothing is more frustrating for a team members then receive documents in a format his or her computer cannot read . It is critical to decide on hardware , software and other platforms related standard before you start the project.

I recommended making HTML documents and posting them on your project site as often as possible this eliminates many cross platforms issues.

If you use some other tools such as Excel or word, make sure your team has access to these tools.

Automating communication : Certain programs like team manager by Microsoft allows you to set up a system that alerts team members when people have achieved certain programming milestones, for example once a person has finished a task he sends an email to the project manager and the schedule is automatically updated with the new information.

Leading effective meetings : We have attended so many unfocused and unproductive meetings that waste time and frustrate team members. Some guidelines for effective meetings and some format of meetings must be followed.

Some guidelines for the effective meetings are:

- The meeting leader call the meetings
- The timekeeper keeps track of time
- The minute taker takes notes during the meetings

There are eight steps in the format of the meetings

(*a*) Establish who will be the minute taker and who will be the timekeeper

(*b*) First agend define and then discuss

  (*i*) Content : What is topic

  (*ii*) Process : How will the topic be discussed

  (*iii*) Resolution : It is a decision needed

  (*iv*) Action : Record the action decided

(c) Summarize the meetings and every one agree
(d) Review the previous week meetings
(e) Display the of notice board
(f) Evaluate the meetings
(g) Close the Meetings.

5.1 CLIENT

The client is the person who has contracted you to build a web site.

There are two types of Clients:

(a) Internal Clients
(b) External Clients

Difference between external clients and internal clients

Internal Clients	External Clients
In some organization so many departments if you can select in house development project in any department then internal politics will be excuse	No such internal politics is involved
It is very difficult to satisfy internal clients	External clients can be easily satisfied

5.1.1 Client Education Process

The client should be educated, it means not only educated in web site but also educated in project managing process. The client education process should be include following steps.

1. Build a structure within the budget
2. Explain each phase with importance so that he pays for each and every phase
3. Communicate your work or project process to your clients
4. Explain various technical issues to the client

5.1.2 Guideline of Clients Point of View

From client's point of view web site is very important aspect of his overall business. So it is very important for web site development that the site must according to the clients business.

Your relationship with your clients will benefits if you take the time to understand his overall business position not just when the web site is concerned. It is very important thing that you can work under the budget of the clients.

Client's positions can be got by using the following two methods:

(a) **Research :** Study about clients business marketing brand and competitors, find out what yours clients competitors are doing.
(b) **Ask questions :** What is risk for your client? How does the web site objective and fit into the overall business objective for the clients?

5.1.2.1 Communicate to Your Clients About Project Process

It is important to take the time to communicate your work process to your clients. Methodologies are very important to communicate to the clients. Having an explanation of your work process in your business proposal might give you a competitive edge over other web and new media companies, if you already informed to the client about changing anything then you will be paid.

(*a*) **Setting clear expectations:** You will provide clear instruction to the client and give them following in written.

(*i*) **Deliverables:** For delivery purpose the following questions must be cleared

- What will you be delivering to your client?
- What does your client need to deliver to you in order to move forward?
- Who is the person which provides content for the site

(*ii*) **Approvals:** The following questions must be cleared

- How will approvals be handled?
- What is the minimum time required for approvals

(*iii*) **Policies:** If You have policies for change order process then the client should know about them formally

(*b*) **Writing contact reports:** You should write a contact report each time so clients know each and every thing.

5.1.2.2 Getting "BYE — In"

If your client resists paying the costs of development and production then you need to educate your clients, with regard to the value of your process and its impact.

Two points are important to emphasize.

(*a*) **Overall cost savings:** check all technical points before the delivery to the clients so project solution become feasible.

(*b*) **Better results:** If you give time in strategic planning and concept development to solve a business problem then you will be closer to getting the results

In developments and production process involves

- Analysis and design phase
- Complete with black and white semantics of screen elements and functionality
- Significant documentation
- Prototype application
- Full testing cycle

5.1.2.3 Explaining Technical Issue to Clients

If clients are none technical person then you will never use jargon words. You must use day-to-day words.

If clients are technically sounds then:

- Don't try to over simplify
- Preface you discussions with good words
- Try to documents conversation with clients in a contact report

5.1.2.4 Building Communication Structure into the Budget

It is a hard thing to track but the cost of communicating with your client regularly. It is significant, if done on a regular basis like traveling frequently to a client's place of business. It is very compulsory to build communication cost into the budget.

5.2 COMMUNICATION THROUGH THE PROJECT

Without proper communication with the never do any thing.

Communication start from—

- Transfer the message to any one
- Getting the business
- Web site development
- Developing the concept

As the relationship develops with your clients leads to certain level of familiarity. It is important that you remain consistent in your approach to communication so that your client will trust you. There are two types of communication

- Legal Communication
- Project Communication

5.2.1 Legal Communication

In legal communication some major issue are:

- Letter of agreement
- Non—discloser agreement
- Contracts

(*i*) **Letter of agreement :** Without letter agreement never start project work because how to trust the clients so letter agreement is very essential work for starting the project.

(*ii*) **None—disclosure agreement :**

(*a*) any information shared between the two parties remains confidential

(*b*) Your clients trade secrets and other information must also remains confidential

(*iii*) **Contracts :** A contracts is critical for the contractual web developer. Your employer legal department handles contract. In contract is also defined in your payments mode.

5.3 PROJECT COMMUNICATION

Always communicate the client is better manner. Every conversation should be documented so that cost will not increase. Communication is cleared between you and clients. Projects communication includes are

(*a*) Assumptions

(*b*) Scope and cost

(*c*) Interactive approach for design phase

(*d*) Approvals documents

(*e*) Conducting effective reviews

(*f*) Giving the project back

(*a*) **Assumptions :** Every project has assumptions all the deliverables that you determine in your scope documents are made with certain assumptions. If some document is to be received from the client then you and client both are safe because both know date schedule about project delivery and payment mode.

(*b*) **Scope and cost :** The major issue of project management include scope cost and what can be done by the deadlines. In most web application the scope is defined after the discovery phase in which you and your client discuss the projects objective and requirements. Once requirements are determined you can enter into the design phase with a sense of the project scope.

(*c*) **Iterative approach for design phase :** Every feature screen and elements such as text image ,video etc should be fleshed out in the design phase black and white schematics for each page even every single element should be fail down most of design is iterative in terms of effects that are interactive.

(*d*) **Approvals documents :** The approvals documents is a document in which your client signs off on features that make up the web site live items in an approvals documents might be navigation visual design forms , data schema, network configuration, copy site architecture.

(*e*) **Conducting effective reviews :** You should conduct effective reviews with the client about the project. People for a client review by having an internal review first. Write down the important points to hit, and try to guess your clients reactions. A client might react to certain aspects.

(*f*) **Giving the project back :** After the completion of the last phase of project is given back to the client. At this point you consider two things

(*i*) Site maintenance

(*ii*) Provide either training and maintain the site

When to Hand the Project Back

It is important to hand the project back when it makes business sense to do so when you have delivered the project up to the standard of your test plan and when your client is prepared to receive the project though these may not occur at the same time.

Some time clients are interested in keeping the team involved in the project to perform site maintenance functions such as adding a page here and there or putting up a link. It is the best way to handle this kind of relationship is to negative a service agreement and change for time and material for site maintenance.

5.4 MULTIDEPARTMENTAL AND LARGE SCALE SITES

Multidepartmental means many departments exist in one system. A large scale or multidepartmental site holds challenges for even the most experienced project manager who must fully understand them in order to lead a successful web project.

5.4.1 Internet Department

If you have been chosen or have volunteered to create, revise or maintain a large corporate web site or Internet. At the end of 1998, few businesses had dedicated team to handle their own corporate web or Internet site.

Until recently web development efforts were driven by ad-hoc coalitions. Small group that were thrown together to get a web site together. The problem with these coalitions is that there is little executive support and strategy to address the critical questions " what is our on line objective" as well as to provide the funding necessary to meet the objective. If your company does not have a dedicated department for on line development being talking about it. A dedicated group will provide the authority strategic vision funding and cohesion that a large-scale development effort needs.

5.4.2 Company has on Line Strategy

It is critical on a large-scale development effort to make sure you have executive level support. This support comes in the from of the strategic vision for the site not a part on the back. What you want from executive management team is a statement of what the web role is within the company. Is the site to be used solely for marketing or will the web interface with the rest of the existing system such as library or customer services? This statement will help you develop measurable objective so that you can benchmark the success of the site.

5.4.2.1 Audience Know

A large scale web site or internet usually has a diverse audience. Different audience in different section and different place of the site, from resellers to international business customer to individual network engineers seeking support.

As a project manager your job is to plan a project that meets certain objectives, to do so you must figure out how to reach a large part of your target audience.

5.4.2.2 Balancing the Needs of Different Units

If you are hired to develop a large web site for any organization with many departments or business units, how do you represent each of those units? How can you be sure the site you build is the site that the end users need? Balancing the needs of different department and business units is difficult and sensitive especially if each unit is using its own budget to fund the overall the web site. There will be lot of politics. Before you start your project first of all decided single person should be senior executive in hole project and he will take decision. If you have do not have this person you might find yourself dealing with managers for each department. Without some one to give the final world you spend a lot of time making decisions you should not make. The best way to balance the needs of different departments and business units is to make sure you have an overall corporate objective or mission statements for the entire site.

5.4.2.3 Making the Needs of Different Audiences

What your clients believe their users need and what your team believes they need almost always will be different. In the case of the corporate Internet it is important to conduct interviews with each department so that you can identify the key pieces of information that reach the greatest audience.

Corporate Politics

It is important to know of any corporate politics that might affect the web project. Being aware of the political landscape in your internal organization and your client organization is very important, for obvious reasons. If your clients are facing internal political struggles the outcome could affect you either positively or negatively. Being aware and alert, yet objective and professional is the way to handle corporate politics especially when they are put directly in front of you. People you interview or meet with will most likely talk to you do not offer advice and maintain a professional distance.

Quality Issue

How do you ensure that your large scale web site or Internet is bug free, has no spelling errors or broken links and adheres to corporate standards with regard to logo usage font and other corporate identity elements? There are many quality issues for you to consider for both a development and maintenance point of view.

In a large scale web site where there are multiple content authors and servers and production system you will face big challenge in ensuring that all subsections of the site are up to an acceptable level of quality.

5.5 TECHNOLOGY ADVANCES AND THE IMPACT ON WEB TEAMS

No one really know the future but it is not too difficult to take an education guess about what the future might hold for web teams and people looking to provide web services to client.

5.5.1 Emerging Technology and Changing Needs

The web has many audiences, all of whom come looking for information goods and services on demand. It is an active medium, users for the most part, seek information at their own level of desire. This kind of information on demand has been the most prevent kind of web application. However people begin to use the web for more and more consumer purpose, such as comparison shopping or advertising the web will become more like television and radio where information is pushed toward the consumer through channels or other yet to be developed means.

5.5.1.1 The Web as Interactive Television

One of the biggest changes on the horizon is broadband internet access. With broadband Internet access the web can provide richer types of media such as audio, video and virtual reality. With cable companies getting into business and providing internet access, we can expect to see the web become more accessible from television sets and information kiosks in the home or stores and organization.

Web TV allow users to have both a TV interface and a web interface simultaneously appear on screen. People with experience in television production, scriptwriting, sound, design and videography will all become part of the web team that provides content for interactive television.

5.5.1.2 The Web as Information Store

What if the web became the central repository of information for national and international organizations like the postal service, libraries and universities? Certainly the ability to search effective for data is one of the key requirements for this kind of web project. A web team would necessarily have to include a librarian and perhaps a team of programmers to customize or create software that could search information accurately in both textual and binary formats. As well significant usability testing is critical because these sites base their effectiveness on how well people can find information. If there are millions of records in a database how does this data get displayed in a meaningful way to the user? So data maintain in web application is very difficult task.

5.5.2 The Web and Electronic Commerce

If every kitchen has a web kiosk where consumer can log on to order groceries find recipes, shop for merchandise and interact with other users and the brands themselves then what does that mean for consumer brands? Consumer risk being literally inundated with information and choices. Consumers will naturally choose brands they can interact with in a meaningful way.

It means that companies who want to sell their products and increase brand awareness on online will have to provide experiences for the consumer in order to do so. A sample banner advertisement will not be enough. The advertisement space in the web of the future is still undefined but the team of the future needs to embrace whatever technologies emerges and is able to build these interactive experience by understanding the users psychology and techno profile.

On the technical side web team that provides electronic commerce application needs to include security expert database programmers and network engineers. Engineers and architect are working towards integrating the electronic transactions into the entire organization, business system meaning that a web transaction will be the first in a series of transaction that are automatic ordering shipping, updating inventory, invoicing and replenishing inventory.

Many vendors offer e-commerce solutions and packages. Some tips to keep in mind when looking for an e-commerce partner.

Will the Vendor work with staff and provide specification so your team can build the user interface? It is important that a representative be available and that the relationship is not an " install and run relationship.

Understand what you are doing. There is a lot of information about e-commerce on line. Read and understand the issue and the electronic commerce cycle. Some web sites name is given below.

- www.google.com
- www.llec.com

5.5.3 Portable Web : Convenience and Access

The way in which people access the web has a huge impact on web site development and design. Monitor size, modem speed and browser already have dramatic impact on the web teams develop web sites and on the cost of web site development. If you have a very diverse users and audience you are naturally going to want to provide the best experience for each user. We all would like to see some standardization with regard to browsers and platforms so that our job as web developer is easier, but that is not going to be the case. If anything it will be harder and harder as people being to access the Internet with their palm pilots their televisions sets. So develop the site useful and usable and profitable.

5.5.4 Tools

Web developers use certain tools to create web content designers use Photoshop, animator's use after effect. So many tools are available in market for web development use Photoshop, Flash, html, xml etc.

5.5.5 Preparing for Change

Technological change has many effects on web teams. There is technological change in terms of how people create web application as well as how the team interacts.

As technology changes new tools will be created and new skill will be necessary. Web teams will be incorporating specialized members in addition to the central core of team members. It will be critical to be able to communicate to your team development process to these new team members succinctly. Specialized team members will not be always part of the web team but he will support.

5.5.6 Change in the Process

When I develop static web site the process is fairly straightforward. I can design a navigation system and individual pages that are finite and easy to test and troubleshoot. Programming these pages in html is very straightforward and even if you use a perl script or java script to process data or produce effects you still are working with elements that remain the same after you create them.

With web data driven sites Page is created in dynamically based on the users input. The process for creating these kinds of web site is different because here is user interaction is more. Web site changes according to customer feedback or user handling problem and main quality of web application.

5.6 SECURITY ON THE WEB

Security is and always will be important to consumers and to business that are selling products and services on line. However consumers will begin to accept certain levels of security on the web as increased good press and experiences spread by word of mouth or other channels. A web developer's ability to gain consumers trust is critical. Providing interface that walk users through the payment sequence and reinforce the security level is an important part of the design process.. Hackers also break big financial sites. The leading companies that provide firewall protection and other security products.

5.6.1 Privacy

Security issues surrounding your web site you also have to gain public confidence if you want people to give you information including their credit card numbers or other personal information.

EXERCISE

1. What do you mean by communication issues?
2. What are the causes of poor communication?
3. Discuss good communication system.
4. Discuss the Chain of communication.
5. Define client.
6. Discuss types of client.
7. How you communicate to your clients about project process?
8. Discuss Communication through the Project.
9. What do you mean by Legal Communication?
10. Discuss multidepartmental and large web sites.
11. Discuss Emerging technology and changing needs.
12. Discuss web and Electronic Commerce.
13. Discuss Security on the Web.
14. Discuss tools for web developer.
15. Discuss web as information store.

6

QUALITY ASSURANCE AND TESTING

6.0 INTRODUCTION

Information quality and quality of software, which is used for analyzing information, is major concerned in any computerized organization. In this unit we will discuss the meaning of quality assurance, Why software quality assurance is needed, the software quality, software quality assurance, Management Role in Software Quality Assurance, Formal Quality Assurance Measures/Structure and the ETHICAL AND SOCIAL DIMENSIONS in quality assurance.

6.1 QUALITY ASSURANCE

6.1.1 Introduction

Historically speaking, application of Information Technology was initially confined to scientific and research-related activities, where time was not considered to be a constraint. However, as the I.T., capabilities and their impact on organizational functioning became apparent, I.T., emerged as a new, powerful tool to out-perform business rivals and gain competitive advantage by improving product quality, adding value to quality, facilitating product delivery and changing the very processes in an organization.

I.T., applications and, of course, the I.T., software then became a 'HOT thing, the end-user, surprisingly, being at the 'receiving end' and the software developer in the 'driver's seat.' No wonder then that the development of software, application software in particular, used to put an over-emphasis on schedule and cost, to the detriment of quality.

It is now being realized that the development of Information Systems requires a constant trade-off of Schedule and Cost Vs. Quality. With operational snags emerging after the installation of the systems and with the soaring maintenance costs, it is also being realised that there is an urgent need that software products, like any other product in the market, should also be evaluated carefully before they are delivered and implemented.

There is yet another dimension to Software Quality Assurance.

Software is ubiquitous and people often behave as if they had complete confidence in it.

For example: The ATMs or Computerized Railway Bookings or the Telephone Network. People do not expect them to fail!

Software failures can now impact upon many areas of the people's lives and are much less likely to be tolerated than in the past when software was used only by a small number of people who understood that they were using an inherently unreliable system.

Software failures can now affect people who were unaware of the fact that they were using software.

It is, therefore, the responsibility of the software developers and providers to develop and provide a software of a "Fail-safe" quality which justifies this level of public confidence.

Hence, the expectation and demand for the most stringent Software Quality Assurance Programme to provide the required degree of confidence.

6.1.2 Why Software Quality Assurance?

Apart from the factors discussed earlier, Software Quality Assurance is also required for the following reasons:

(*a*) Avoiding legal liability if the software fails.

(*b*) Proving, with due documentation, that the software was developed using the best practices techniques embodied in various standards.

(*c*) Convincing the users or prospective clients that the developer has a satisfactory Software Quality Assurance Programme in place.

(*d*) Being able to develop/deliver a good quality product which, in turn, may enable the developer to offer guarantees with software as a part of marketing strategy.

(*e*) Making software development more cost-effective.

(*f*) Taking advantage of a rigorous Quality Assurance Programme as a marketing 'USP'.

(*g*) Taking the user/client from "Customer Satisfaction" to "Customer Delight" to "Customer LUV" and ensure "Customer Loyalty".

6.1.3 What is Software Quality?

Let us first discuss the two terms separately, before discussing Software Quality.

6.1.3.1 *Software*

Generally, software is defined as a set of instructions. In the context of Software Quality Assurance, let us now view the software as:

"All instructions and data which are input into a computer to cause it to function in any code".

Includes "operating systems, supervisory systems, compilers and test routines as well as application programmes. It also includes the documents used to define and describe the Programme, including flow charts, network diagrams and programme listings — as well as specifications, test plans, test data, test results and user instructions".

6.1.3.2 *Quality*

"Quality indicates the degree of excellence of a product or service".

According to DoD 1985, Quality means the degree to which the attributes of the software enable it to perform its specified end item use.

According to ISO 1986, Quality means the totality of features and characteristics of a product or service that bear on its ability to satisfy stated or implied needs.

As could be observed, the ISO definition clearly reflects the desire to define quality in a way which captures the current concept of quality as customer satisfaction in the broadest possible context.

Now that we have noted the definitions of 'Software' and 'Quality', let us now move over to Software Quality.

6.1.3.3 *What is Software Quality?*

- Software Quality is the inherent ability of a software to be used for a specified purpose as the software possesses certain features and characteristics and which enable it to be used for that purpose.
- Software Quality is the ability of a software to be fit for its purpose and capability to ensure that:
  - (*a*) It is reliable.
  - (*b*) It is doing what it is supposed to do.
  - (*c*) It is performing according to its specifications.
  - (*d*) It is doing efficiently.
  - (*e*) It is working efficiently for the time for which it is predicted to work.
- Software Quality would also simply
  - (*a*) Quality of Conformance, reflecting the extent to which the developer has succeeded in producing software which implemented the design, and
  - (*b*) Quality of Design, which reflects the extent to which a given software product meets a customer's expectations.

After having noted the definitions of software quality, let us now broadly summarise the attributes of quality known as **Quality Factors**.

- Aesthetics
- Conformance
- Correctness
- Durability
- Efficiency
- Extendability
- Integrity
- Inter-operability
- Maintainability
- Openness
- Perception/Perceived quality
- Portability
- Reliability
- Reusability

- Security
- Serviceability
- Survivability
- Testability
- Understandability(Comprehensibility)
- Usability
- User-friendliness

6.1.4 Software Quality Assurance

6.1.4.1 Quality Assurance

Quality Assurance is, "a planned and systematic pattern of all actions necessary to provide equate confidence that the item or project conforms to established technical requirements."

6.1.4.2 Software Quality Assurance

Software Quality Assurance, accordingly, lays considerable stress on getting the design it, prior to coding, although the increasing use of prototyping in systems development is producing the differences between the production stages of Hardware and Software.

Software Quality Assurance must also:

(*a*) Provide for exhaustive testing.

(*b*) Obtain a mathematical proof of correctness.

(*c*) Convince oneself that the output from each phase of the development process, which will be a different representation of the software, is functionally equivalent to its predecessor.

6.1.5 Management Role in Software Quality Assurance

The failure of the Management to properly plan and control the software development process is now felt to have been responsible for much of the poor quality software developed/produced in the past. In fact, one of the major roadblock in software quality was the belief/attitude that problems can be sorted out at the end of the development process.

It is now generally recognised that—Management has a key role to play in the production/development of Quality Software, as the Software Quality Assurance, like any other form of quality assurance, is highly dependent upon management attitudes. While the organisational structures could be created and put in place any time, the real change required is the change in managerial attitudes.

The management must manifest and transmit a greater desire to produce high quality product. The Management must also commit 'commensurate resources' to ensure this. In turn, the software developers must plan and implement software development projects with the objective of "building in" quality.

Towards this end, they must

(*a*) Establish and maintain the requirement specifications.

(*b*) Establish and implement a process for developing the software.

(*c*) Establish and maintain an evaluation process.

Further, the "Discipline Triangle" must be applied to produce quality software successfully. "The Discipline Triangle" would contain Management, Software Development and Product Assurance Discipline.

The 'Management Discipline' would include both Project Management and General Management.

The 'Software Development Discipline' would involve such activities like analysis, design, testing etc.

The 'Product Assurance Discipline' would include quality assurance, test and evaluation and configuration management.

6.1.6 The Formal Quality Assurance Measures/Structure

The formal Quality Assurance structure would need to be woven around the ISO-9000 Standard. ISO-9001 defines a minimum set of requirements for Quality Management. It includes Quality Assurance, Quality Control, Process Control, Change Management and Formal Review.

ISO-9001 is acknowledged as requiring additional features for software development.

ISO-9001 Standard with the IEEE-1298 Standards and the ISO-9000.

3 Guidelines would be required to be considered for Software Quality Assurance.

6.1.7 Additional Considerations

In addition to the standards mentioned earlier, due attention should also be given to the following:

(*i*) Quality Profile Model

(*ii*) Constructive Quality Model

(*iii*) "TickIT" Initiative

6.1.7.1 Quality Profile Model

To ensure quality assurance, it is imperative to keep in view the quality profile of software. A Quality Profile Model, proposed by Kaposi and Kitchenham as a way of structuring the analysis of the quality of a piece of software is presented below:

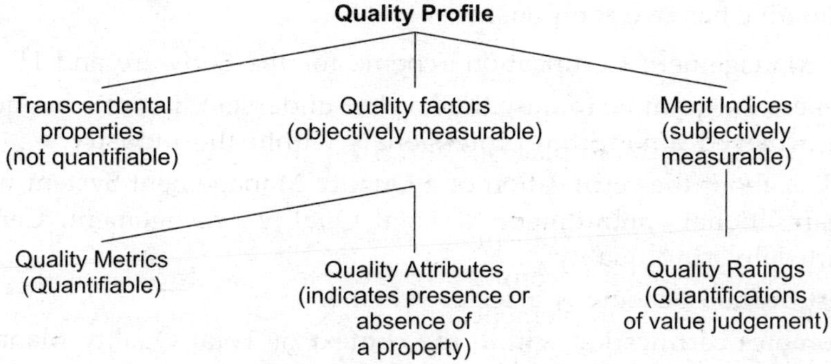

Fig. 6.1 *Quality Profile Model*

6.1.7.2 Constructive Quality Model

Kitchenham has also discussed the development of a Constructive Quality Model, known as COQUAMO'.

The Model attempts to make explicit the dependence of the achievement of a quality factor upon activities undertaken throughout the life cycle. In each stage of the life cycle, checklists can be used to monitor progress towards the achievement of the quality factor.

The Model would involve measuring three types of values:

(*a*) Quality Factor Metrics

(*b*) Quality Indicators

(*c*) Measures of Quality Drivers

The COQUAMO Model is illustrated hereunder:

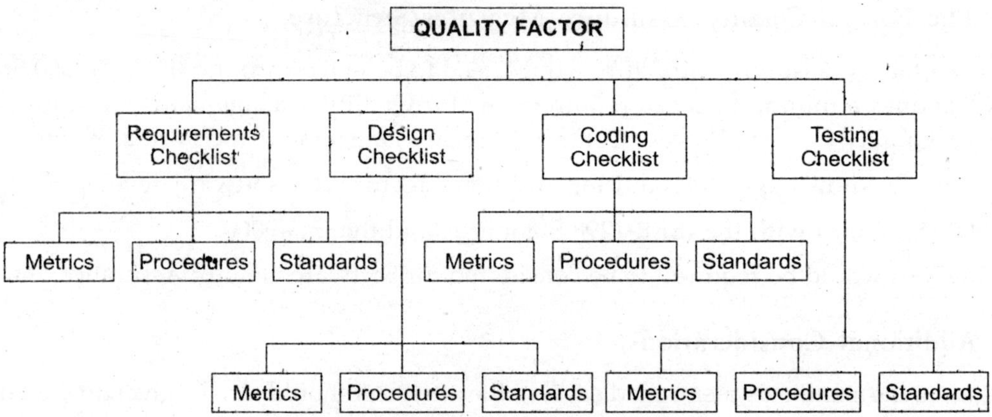

Fig. 6.2 *Constructive Quality Model*

6.1.7.3 "TickIT" Initiative

TickIT focuses on software development, as this is the component that gives an Information System its power and flexibility. Yet unfortunately, it is also the source of many of the problems.

The fundamental objective of the TickIT Initiative is to ensure that developers can deliver quality. The TickIT guide contains structured guidance for the application of ISO 9001. It also includes the ISO-9000.3 document which explains how ISO-9001 can be applied to software.

The TickIT Initiative has two components:

(*a*) A Quality Management Certification Scheme for the Software and IT industries.

(*b*) An Awareness Programme to raise the level of understanding of what quality is and how it may be achieved among the professionals within the industry.

The TickIT is about the certification of a Quality Management System within the context of an organisational commitment to Total Quality Management. Certification should result from delivering quality.

(*c*) TickIT Certification Scheme is a sector scheme.

(*d*) TickIT promotes certification within the context of Total Quality Management (TQM).

TickIT TQM Model, continuous improvement of the Quality Management System results from three long term driving components which work on the Quality Management System, the three Driving Components are:

1. Management Commitment for improvement.
2. Motivation for improvement.
3. Measurement for improvement.

6.2 GROWTH OF INTERNATIONAL INFORMATION SYSTEMS

Multinational companies, international companies and virtual global cooperation's need international information system.

- **Multinational Companies :** Multinational Companies are those that operate in several countries. Example would be Microsoft, IBM Coca-Cola and SAP/AG. Multinational organizations may have sales offices in several countries or may conduct operations in location where factory workers are plenty and inexpensive where highly skilled employees are available at low salaries, or where there is a need to be close to the market.
- **International Companies :** International companies are those that do business with other companies in different companies. Foe example, Toyota Motors Company, Japan works with many suppliers in the United States.
- **Virtual Qlobal Corporations :** Virtual global corporations are joint ventures whose business partners ate located in different countries. The partners from a company for the specific purpose producing a product or service. Such companies can be temporary, with a one-time mission or they can be permanent.

Benefits of International Information Systems

Regardless of its structure a company with global operations relies heavily on I.T. Major benefits of international information system are as follows:

Effective communication at a reasonable cost is necessary. The partners are far from each other, yet they need to work together, make decisions, monitor transactions and provide controls. Business partners communicate through email, EDI, and extranets. Communication is even more critical if the partners speak different languages. Intelligent IT system can provide automatic translation.

Effective collaboration is needed to overcome differences in distance, time, language and culture. Collaboration can be enabled with groupware software, group decision support system, and extranets and teleconferencing devices.

Organizations accesses each other's databases and frequently work on the same projects while their members are in different locations. Information technologies such as video teleconferencing and screen sharing are useful for this purpose.

6.3 ETHICAL AND SOCIAL DIMENSIONS

6.3.1 Introduction

In our earlier discussions, we have noted how I.T. has changed and is changing the rules of competition. But as the rules of competition changed and application of computers increased exponential speed, it has also given rise to a number of ethical and social dilemmas. It is proposed to discuss some of the illustrative, ethical and social dilemmas/dimensions of I.T. Information Systems Applications in the following paragraphs.

6.3.2 What is Ethics/Ethical?

While 'Ethics' means "the system or code of morals of a particular person, religion, group or professions", "Ethical" means "having to do with ethics or morality of or conforming to moral standards conforming to the standards of conduct of given profession or group".

A person's ethics, according to Griffin(1990) are formulated through the operation of five key process in the individual's environment viz,

1. Family Influences
2. Peer Influences
3. Experiences
4. Values and Morals
5. Situational Factors

6.3.3 Ethical Issues Related to Systems

Ethics is a branch of philosophy that deals with what is considered to be right and wrong. There are many definitions of ethics, such as "codes of morals of a particular profession", "the standards of conduct of a given profession", "agreement among people to do the right and to avoid the wrong". In one of the oldest codes of ethics, the Ten Commandments, Clear specifications are given about what an individual should and should not do. Over the years, philosophers have proposed many ethical guidelines. It is important to realize that what is unethical is not necessarily illegal.

A framework for Ethics

Many companies and professional organizations develop their own codes of ethics. A code of ethics is a collection of principles intended as a guide for members of a company or an organization. The diversity of IT application and the increased use of the technology have created a variety of ethical issues. Prof. R.O. Masson & others categorise ethical issues into four types: privacy, accuracy, property and accessibility.

1. **Privacy issues** : Collection, storage and dissemination of information about individuals.
   - What information about oneself should an individual be required to revel to others?
   - What kind of surveillance can be employer use on its employees?
   - What thing can people keep to themselves and not to be forced to revel others?
   - What information about individuals should be kept in databases and how secure is the information there?
2. **Accuracy issues** : Authenticity, fidelity and accuracy of information collected and processes.
   - Who is responsible for authenticity, fidelity, and accuracy of information collected?
   - How can we ensure that errors in databases, data transmissions and data processing are accidental and not intentional?
   - Who is to be held accountable for errors in information and how should the injured party be compensated?
3. **Property issues** : Ownership and value of information.
   - Who owns the information?
   - What are the just and fair prices for its exchange?
   - How should one handle software privacy?
   - Under what circumstances can one use proprietary databases?
   - Can corporate computers be used for private purposes?
   - How should experts who contribute their knowledge to create expert system be compensated?
   - How should access to information channels be allocated?
4. **Accessibility issues**: Right to access information and payment of fees to access it.
   - Who is allowed to access information?
   - How much should be changed for permitting accessibility to information?
   - How can accessibility to computers be provided for employees for disabilities?

- Who will be provided with equipment needed for accessing information?
- What information does a person or an organization has a right or privilege to obtain and under what conditions and with what safeguards?

6.3.4 Ethical Dimensions

The Ethical Dimensions would broadly cover the following aspects :

1. Obligation to Management
2. Obligation to Society
3. Obligation to Employer
4. Obligations to Country.

Ethical Dilemmas

Some of the illustrative ethical dilemmas could be summarized as follows:

1. Inappropriate use of computers technology.
2. Inappropriate use of computer resources.
3. Inefficient programming logic.
4. Inefficient processing instructions.
5. Manipulation of records.
6. Deletion/Distortion of records.

In view of the enormous power of Information Technology, and the resultant 'Nuisance Value' (Hacking, for example), it is imperative that a professional Code of Conduct and Ethics be devised and globally implemented for the I.T. Professionals.

6.4 SOFTWARE TESTING

Software testing is a process of *verifying* and *validating* that a software application or program

1. Meets the business and technical requirements that guided its design and development, and
2. Works as expected.

Software testing also identifies important *defects*, flaws, or errors in the application code that must be fixed. The modifier "important" in the previous sentence is, well, important because defects must be categorized by severity.

During test planning we decide what an important defect is by reviewing the requirements and design documents with an eye towards answering the question "Important to whom?" Generally speaking, an important defect is one that from the customer's perspective affects the usability or functionality of the application. Using colors for a traffic lighting scheme in a desktop dashboard may be a no-brainer during requirements definition and easily implemented during development but in fact may not be entirely workable if during testing we discover that the primary business sponsor is color blind. Suddenly, it becomes an important defect.

The quality assurance aspect of software development—documenting the degree to which the developers followed corporate standard processes or best practices—is not addressed in this chapter because assuring quality is not a responsibility of the testing team. The testing team cannot improve quality; they can only measure it, although it can be argued that doing things like designing tests before coding begins will improve quality because the coders can then use that information while thinking about their designs and during coding and debugging. Software testing has three main purposes: verification, validation, and defect finding.

- The *verification* process confirms that the software meets its technical specifications. A "specification" is a description of a function in terms of a measurable output value given a specific input value under specific preconditions. A simple specification may be along the line of "a SQL query retrieving data for a single account against the multi-month account—summary table must return these eight fields <list> ordered by month within 3 seconds of submission."
- The *validation* process confirms that the software meets the business requirements. A simple example of a business requirement is "After choosing a branch office name, information about the branch's customer account managers will appear in a new window. The window will present manager identification and summary information about each manager's customer base: <list of data elements>." Other requirements provide details on how the data will be summarized, formatted and displayed.
- A *defect* is a variance between the expected and actual result. The defect's ultimate source may be traced to a fault introduced in the specification, design, or development (coding) phases.

6.5 TYPES OF SOFTWARE TESTING

There are many types of testing according to which phases it is used.

Each testing phase and each individual test should have specific *entry criteria* that must be met before testing can begin and specific *exit criteria* that must be met before the test or phase can be certified as successful. The entry and exit criteria are defined by the Test Coordinators and listed in the Test Plan. The V-Model of testing identifies five software-testing phases, each with a certain type of test associated with it.

Phase	Guiding Document	Test Type
Development Phase	Technical Design	Unit Testing
System and Integration Phase	Functional Design	System Testing Integration Testing
User Acceptance Phase	Business Requirements	User Acceptance Testing
Implementation Phase	Business Case	Product Verification Testing
Regression Testing applies to all Phases		

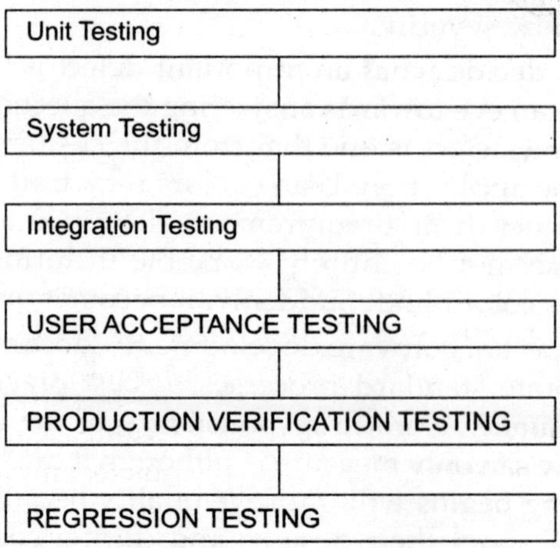

Fig. 6.3 *Types of Testing*

6.5.1 Unit Testing

A series of stand-alone tests are conducted during Unit Testing. Each test examines an individual component that is new or has been modified. A unit test is also called a module test because it tests the individual units of code that comprise the application.

Each test validates a single module that, based on the technical design documents, was built to perform a certain task with the expectation that it will behave in a specific way or produce specific results. Unit tests focus on functionality and reliability, and the entry and exit criteria can be the same for each module or specific to a particular module. Unit testing is done in a test environment prior to system integration. If a defect is discovered during a unit test, the severity of the defect will dictate whether or not it will be fixed before the module is approved.

Sample Entry and Exit Criteria for Unit Testing

Entry Criteria

- Business Requirements are at least 80% complete and have been approved to-date
- Technical Design has been finalized and approved
- Development environment has been established and is stable
- Code development for the module is complete

Exit Criteria

- Code has version control in place
- No known major or critical defects prevents any modules from moving to System Testing
- A testing transition meeting has been held and the developers signed off
- Project Manager approval has been received.

6.5.2 System Testing

System testing tests all components and modules that are new, changed, affected by a change, or needed to form the complete application. The system test may require involvement of other systems but this should be minimized as much as possible to reduce the risk of externally induced problems. Testing the interaction with other parts of the complete system comes in Integration Testing. The emphasis in system testing is validating and verifying the functional design specification and seeing how all the modules work together. For example, the system test for a new web interface that collects user input for addition to a database doesn't need to include the database's ETL application—processing can stop when the data is moved to the data staging area if there is one.

The first system test is often a smoke test. This is an informal quick-and-dirty run through of the application's major functions without bothering with details. The term comes from the hardware testing practice of turning on a new piece of equipment for the first time and considering it a success if it doesn't start smoking or burst into flame.

System testing requires many test runs because it entails feature-by-feature validation of behavior using a wide range of both normal and erroneous test inputs and data. The Test Plan is critical here because it contains descriptions of the test cases, the sequence in which the tests must be executed, and the documentation needed to be collected in each run.

When an error or defect is discovered, previously executed system tests must be rerun after the repair is made to make sure that the modifications didn't cause other problems. This will be covered in more detail in the section on *regression testing*.

Sample Entry and Exit Criteria for System Testing

Entry Criteria

- Unit Testing for each module has been completed and approved; each module is under version control
- An incident tracking plan has been approved
- A system testing environment has been established
- The system testing schedule is approved and in place

Exit Criteria

- Application meets all documented business and functional requirements
- No known critical defects prevent moving to the Integration Testing
- All appropriate parties have approved the completed tests
- A testing transition meeting has been held and the developers signed off

As part of system testing, conformance tests and reviews can be run to verify that the application conforms to corporate or industry standards in terms of portability, interoperability, and compliance with standards. For example, to enhance application portability a corporate standard may be that SQL queries must be written so that they work against both Oracle and DB2 databases.

6.5.3 Integration Testing

Integration testing examines all the components and modules that are new, changed, affected by a change, or needed to form a complete system. Where system testing tries to minimize outside factors, integration testing requires involvement of other systems and interfaces with other applications, including those owned by an outside vendor, external partners, or the customer. For example, integration testing for a new web interface that collects user input for addition to a database must include the database's ETL application even if a vendor hosts the database—the complete system must be tested end-to-end. In this example, integration testing doesn't stop with the database load; test reads must verify that it was correctly loaded.

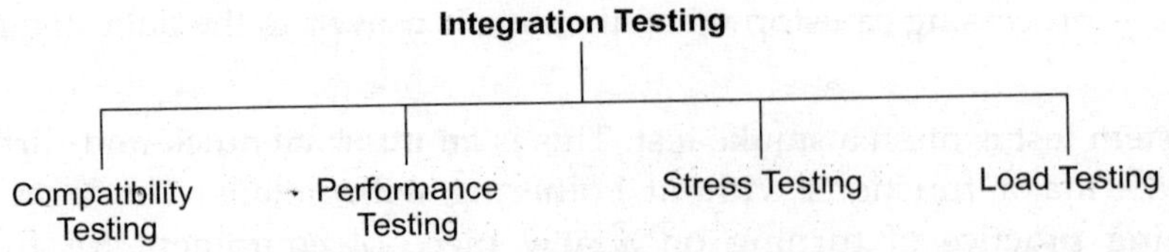

Fig. 6.4 *Types of Integration Testing*

Integration testing also differs from system testing in that when a defect is discovered, not all previously executed tests have to be rerun after the repair is made. Only those tests with a connection to the defect must be rerun, but retesting must start at the point of repair if it is before the point of failure. For example, the retest of a failed FTP process may use an existing data file instead of recreating it if up to that point everything else was OK.

Sample Entry and Exit Criteria for Integration Testing

Entry Criteria

- System testing has been completed and signed off
- Outstanding issues and defects have been identified and documented
- Test scripts and schedule are ready
- The integration testing environment is established

Exit Criteria

- All systems involved passed integration testing and meet agreed upon functionality and performance requirements
- Outstanding defects have been identified, documented, and presented to the business sponsor
- Stress, performance, and load tests have been satisfactorily conducted
- The implementation plan is final draft stage
- A testing transition meeting has been held and everyone has signed off.

Integration testing has a number of sub-types of tests that may or may not be used, depending on the application being tested or expected usage patterns.

Compatibility Testing : Compatibility tests insures that the application works with differently configured systems based on what the users have or may have. When testing a web interface, this means testing for compatibility with different browsers and connection speeds.

Performance Testing : Performance tests are used to evaluate and understand the application's scalability when, for example, more users are added or the volume of data increases. This is particularly important for identifying bottlenecks in high usage applications. The basic approach is to collect timings of the critical business processes while the test system is under a very low load (a 'quiet box' condition) and then collect the same timings with progressively higher loads until the maximum required load is reached. For a data retrieval application, reviewing the performance pattern may show that a change needs to be made in a stored SQL procedure or that an index should be added to the database design.

Stress Testing : Stress Testing is performance testing at higher than normal simulated loads. Stressing runs the system or application beyond the limits of its specified requirements to determine the load under which it fails and how it fails. A gradual performance slow-down leading to a non-catastrophic system halt is the desired result, but if the system will suddenly crash and burn it's important to know the point where that will happen. Catastrophic failure in production means beepers going off, people coming in after hours, system restarts, frayed tempers, and possible financial losses. This test is arguably the most important test for mission-critical systems.

Load Testing : Load tests are the opposite of stress tests. They test the capability of the application to function properly under expected normal production conditions and measure the response times for critical transactions or processes to determine if they are within limits specified in the business requirements and design documents or that they meet Service Level Agreements. For database applications, load testing must be executed on a current production-size database. If some database tables are forecast to grow much larger in the foreseeable future then serious consideration should be given to testing against a database of the projected size.

Performance, stress, and load testing are all major undertakings and will require substantial input from the business sponsors and IT staff in setting up a test environment and designing test cases that can be accurately executed.

Because of this, these tests are sometimes delayed and made part of the User Acceptance Testing phase. Load tests especially must be documented in detail so that the tests are repeatable in case they need to be executed several times to ensure that new releases or changes in database size do not push response times beyond prescribed requirements and Service Level Agreements.

6.5.4 User Acceptance Testing (UAT)

User Acceptance Testing is also called Beta testing, application testing, and end-user testing. Whatever you choose to call it, it's where testing moves from the hands of the IT department into those of the business users. Software vendors often make extensive use of Beta testing, some more formally than others, because they can get users to do it for free. By the time UAT is ready to start, the IT staff has resolved in one way or another all the defects they identified. Regardless of their best efforts, though, they probably don't find all the flaws in the application. A general rule of thumb is that no matter how bulletproof an application seems when it goes into UAT, a user somewhere can still find a sequence of commands that will produce an error.

To be of real use, UAT cannot be random users playing with the application. A mix of business users with varying degrees of experience and subject matter expertise need to actively participate in a controlled environment.

Representatives from the group work with Testing Coordinators to design and conduct tests that reflects activities and conditions seen in normal business usage. Business users also participate in evaluating the results. This insures that the application is tested in real-world situations and that the tests cover the full range of business usage. The goal of UAT is to simulate realistic business activity and processes in the test environment.

A phase of UAT called "Unstructured Testing" will be conducted whether or not it's in the Test Plan. Also known as guerilla testing, this is when business users bash away at the keyboard to find the weakest parts of the application. In effect, they try to break it. Although it's a free-form test, it's important that users who participate understand that they have to be able to reproduce the steps that led to any errors they find. Otherwise it's of no use.

A common occurrence in UAT is that once the business users start working with the application they find that it doesn't do exactly what they want it to do or that it does something that, although correct, is not quite optimal.

Investigation finds that the root cause is in the Business Requirements, so the users will ask for a change. During UAT is when change control must be most seriously enforced.

Suffice to say that scope creep is especially dangerous in this late phase and must be avoided.

Sample Entry and Exit Criteria for User Acceptance Testing

Entry Criteria

- Integration testing signoff was obtained
- Business requirements have been met or renegotiated with the Business Sponsor or representative

- UAT test scripts are ready for execution
- The testing environment is established
- Security requirements have been documented and necessary user access obtained.

Exit Criteria

- UAT has been completed and approved by the user community in a transition meeting
- Change control is managing requested modifications and enhancements
- Business sponsor agrees that known defects do not impact a production release—no remaining defects are rated 3, 2, or 1.

6.5.5 Production Verification Testing

Production verification testing is a final opportunity to determine if the software is ready for release. Its purpose is to simulate the production cutover as closely as possible and for a period of time simulate real business activity. As a sort of full dress rehearsal, it should identify anomalies or unexpected changes to existing processes introduced by the new application. For mission critical applications the importance of this testing cannot be overstated.

The application should be completely removed from the test environment and then completely reinstalled exactly as it will be in the production implementation. Then mock production runs will verify that the existing business process flows, interfaces, and batch processes continue to run correctly. Unlike parallel testing in which the old and new systems are run side-by-side, mock processing may not provide accurate data handling results due to limitations of the testing database or the source data.

Sample Entry and Exit Criteria for Production Verification Testing

Entry Criteria

- UAT testing has been completed and approved by all necessary parties
- Known defects have been documented
- Migration package documentation has been completed, reviewed, and approved by the production systems manager

Exit Criteria

- Package migration is complete
- Installation testing has been performed and documented and the results have been signed off
- Mock testing has been documented, reviewed, and approved
- All tests show that the application will not adversely affect the production environment
- A System Change Record with approvals has been prepared

Regression Testing

Regression testing is also known as validation testing and provides a consistent, repeatable validation of each change to an application under development or being modified. Each time a defect is fixed, the potential exists to inadvertently introduce new errors, problems, and defects. An element of uncertainty is introduced about ability of the application to repeat everything that went right up to the point of failure. Regression testing is the probably selective retesting of an application or system that has been modified to insure that no previously working components, functions, or features fail as a result of the repairs.

Regression testing is conducted in parallel with other tests and can be viewed as a quality control tool to ensure that the newly modified code still complies with its specified requirements and that unmodified code has not been affected by the change. It is important to understand that regression testing doesn't test that a specific defect has been fixed. Regression testing tests that the rest of the application up to the point or repair was not adversely affected by the fix.

Sample Entry and Exit Criteria for Regression Testing

Entry Criteria

- The defect is repeatable and has been properly documented
- A change control or defect tracking record was opened to identify and track the regression testing effort
- A regression test specific to the defect has been created, reviewed, and accepted

Exit Criteria

- Results of the test show no negative impact to the application.

EXERCISE

Short Answer Questions

1. What is quality assurance? Describe with the help of an example.
2. Describe Growth of International Information systems.
3. Describe various Ethical Issues related to systems.
4. Describe constructive quality model.
5. What is the role of management in assurance of software quality?
6. Describe formal quality assurance measures.

Long Answer Questions

1. Describe Multinational Companies.
2. What do you mean by International Companies?
3. Define Data security controls.
4. What are the Benefits of International Information systems?
5. What is ethics?
6. What are ethical dimensions?
7. Why software assurance is needed?

7

HTML

7.0 INTRODUCTION

HTML stands for **H**yper **T**ext **M**arkup **L**anguage. Hypertext means text stored in electronic form with cross — reference links between pages. HTML is the autoring language used to create documents on the world wide web. HTML makes documents readable across variety of computing platforms *i.e.*, computer systems operating on different operating systems.

Hyper : In the Electronic Form

Markup Text : Markup is the process of taking ordinary text and adding extra symbols. Each of the symbols used for markup in HTML is a command that tells a browser how to display the text.

Markup languages : Markup languages are a special type of computer language because they are solely concerned with classifying the parts of a document according to their function — in other words, indicating which part is the title of the document, which part is a subheading, which part is the name of the author, and so on.

SGML : SGML stands for Standard Generalized Markup Language. SGML is a formal system designed for building text markup languages. It is an internationally recognized standard for text information processing that provides an organized way to structure content for broad use. Documents marked according to rules outlined in SGML have two basic elements: the content and information about the content.

SGML is platform independent, requiring only a computer and the appropriate software to analyze the documents to make sense of the data. A piece of software that reads and analyzes a SGML document is called an SGML parser.

7.1 EVOLUTION OF HTML

One of the requirements for creating a usable, nonlinear information system like HTML is to make the system easy for non experts to understand and use. Berners Lee and his colleagues used SGML to describe the rules for hypertext markup language in a document type definition (DTD), the basis for the structure of documents on the World Wide Web.

Different Versions of HTML

HTML 0.0

Level 0, HTML offered a platform-independent means of marking data for interchange. The concept was that servers would store and supply data and clients would retrive and display it.

HTML 1.0

The original version of HTML was HTML 1.0. It had very limited features, which greatly limited what you could do in designing your web pages.

HTML 2.0

HTML 2.0 then arrived and included all the features of HTML 1.0 plus several new features for web page design. Until January, 1997, HTML 2.0 was the standard in web page design.

HTML 3.0

HTML 2.0 served its purpose very well, but many people designing web pages (called HTML authors or webmasters) wanted more control over their web pages and more ways to mark up their text and enhance the appearance of their websites. Netscape, the leading browser at that time, introduced new tags and attributes called the Netscape Extension Tags. Other browsers tried to duplicate them but Netscape did not fully specify their new tags and so these extension tags did not work in most other browsers. It led to considerable confusion and problems when HTML authors used these tags and attributes and then saw that they didn't work as expected in other browsers.

At about that time, an HTML working group, led by Dave Raggett, introduced the HTML 3.0 draft which included many new and useful enhancements to HTML. However, most browsers only implemented a few elements from this draft. The phrase "HTML 3.0 enhanced" quickly became popular on the web but it more often than not referred to documents containing browser specific tags (discussed below in "The Netscape Problem" section), instead of referring to documents adhering to the HTML 3.0 draft. This was one of the reasons why the draft was abandoned. HTML 3.0 is now an expired draft. Another reason why HTML 3.0 did not make it was because it was so "big". Future versions were now to be introduced in a more "modular" way so that browsers can implement them modular by modular or bit by bit.

HTML 3.2 (WILBUR)

As more browser-specific tags were introduced, it became obvious that a new standard was needed. For this reason, the Word Wide Web Consortium (W3C), founded in 1994 to develop common standards for the evolution of the World Wide Web, drafted the WILBUR standard, which later became known as HTML 3.2. HTML 3.2 captures the recommended practice as of early 1996 and became the official standard in January, 1997. Most, if not all, popular browsers in use today fully support HTML 3.2.

HTML 4.0 (COUGAR)

In the early days, HTML 4.0 was code-named COUGAR. This version introduces new functionality, most of which comes from the expired HTML 3.0 draft. This version became a recommendation in December, 1997 and a standard as of April, 1998. Explorer has done a very good job in implementing the many features of HTML 4.0. Unfortunately, Netscape has not kept pace. The latest version of Netscape Communicator still does not recognize the many tags and attributes introduced with HTML 4.0. This means that a web page that involves HTML 4.0 specific tags will look great in Explorer but can look disastrous in Netscape.

XHTML 1.0

You would think that the next major version after HTML 4.0 would be HTML 5.0 and with it would come a bunch of new tags that would do all sorts of wonderful things. That would be a good guess — but it would also be a wrong guess. The next version of HTML after HTML 4 is XHTML.

XHTML stands for EXtensible HyperText Markup Language.

EXtensible

Hyper

Text

Markup

Language

XHTML 1.0 is not bringing with it a lot of new tags. The purpose of XHTML is to address the new browser technologies that is sweeping the world. Today web pages are being viewed in browsers through cell/mobile phones, cars, televisions, plus a host of hand-held wireless devices and communicators. Alternate ways to access the internet are continually being introduced. In many cases, these devices will not have the computing power of a desktop or notebook computer and so will not be able to accommodate poor or sloppy coding practices. XHTML is designed to address these technologies. XHTML also begins to address the need for those with disabilities (such as the blind and visually impaired) to access the internet. Thus web pages written in XHTML will allow them to be viewed on a wide range of browsers and internet platforms.

XHTML 1.0 is the result of the hard working World Wide Web Consortium (W3C) to bring some sort of standard to provide rich high quality web pages through these varied devices. XHTML became an official W3C recommendation in January, 2000. XHTML is now a web standard and is the next generation of HTML.

HTML is a Mark Up language that gives general guidelines for displaying of information. The format of display is specified by tags or markups. A tag is a key word enclosed within angle brackets (<….>) and has a special significance.

HTML is a language for describing how pages of text, graphics and other information are organized, formatted and linked together. HTML pages are the standard interface to the Internet. They can include animated graphics, sound and video, complete interactive programs. HTML is also the interface of choice for publishing presentations on CD/DVD. HTML pages can be viewed as web pages in any web browser like internet explorer, Netscape navigator, mosaic etc. A web browser is a computer program that interprets (HTML) commands to collect, arranges, and displays the parts of web pages.

World Wide Web Consortium (W3C)

Berners-Lee proposed founding a consortium to handle the problems of establishing standards for HTML and HTTP, test proposals to determine compliance and award a stamp of approval. So the World Wide Web Consortium (W3C) was founded in 1994 with a goal to develop common standards for the evolution of the World Wide Web.

The W3C is hosted by Massachusetts Institute of Technology in the USA, INFRIA in France and keio University.

Even with its academic background, the members of its committees are representatives of World Wide Web companies, including organizations such as Microsoft, Netscape, Sun Microsystems, IBM and Others.

Netscape and Microsoft are members of the W3C.

7.2 HTML AND THE WEB

HTML allows you to format text, add rules, graphics, sound and video and save it all in a text-only ASCll file that any computer can read.

HTML's key ingredient is in the first part of its name : **Hypertext.**

HTML documents can contain links to other HTML documents or to practically anything else on the internet. This means you can create several Web pages and have your users jump from one to another as needed. You can also create links to other organozations Web pages giving your users access to information held at other sites.

7.3 LIMITATIONS OF HTML

HTML does a good job of formatting Web pages for display. Its inadequacies lie in its ability to supply all the features we seek in an information application. A partial list of these inadequacies include searching, site management and link management.

The structure of HTML is dedicated to formatting pages. There is not enough structure in HTML to provide for the processing needs of an information application.

HTML lacks the capability to define new structures by defining relationships between classes.

7.4 STRUCTURE OF THE HTML

There are three basic levels to the structure of an HTML document.

- First is the document structure, which is divided into major sections — such as the head, body and script components.
- Second are the divisions within each of the major sections such as titles, meta data, divisions, paragraphs, forms and headings.
- The third level exists primarily within each of the major sections. It is the substructure of elements and their children, such as lists and list items, forms and form elements, and tables with table rows and data cells.

Let us start with HTML

Step I : Open any Text Editor like notepad, WordPad, ms word etc.

Step II : Write the first tag *i.e.*, HMTL.

Step III : Write Head — for writing Heading of the Page and then close the HEAD tag by /HTML.

Step IV : Write Title — for writing title of the Page and then close the Title tag by /Title.

Step V : Write Body Tag for writing main text & other material of the page. Then close Body tag by /Body.

Step VI : Close HTML tag (/HTML).

Step VII : Save the page with extension .htm or .html.

Step VIII : Open the page in any web browser like internet explorer or Netscape navigator.

For Example

```
<HTML>
<HEAD> ABES Engineering College, Ghaziabad(UP), India</HEAD>
<TITLE> Home Page of Mr. Anuranjan Misra </TITLE>
<BODY> Qualification : M. Tech(CSE) </BODY>
</HTML>
```

When we open this code in any web browse it looks like :

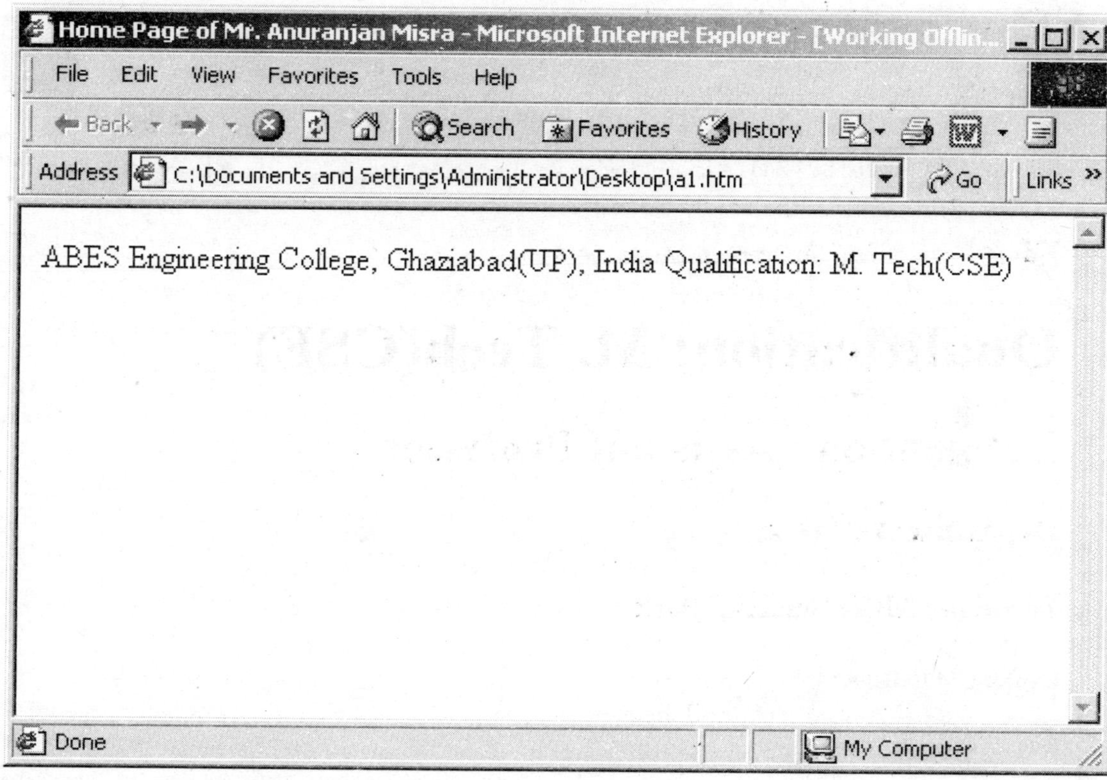

Every tag which is started must be closed by </Tag>

Various Tag(s) of HTML

1. **Headings :** Six types of heading available. They are <H1>, <H2>, <H3>, <H4>, <H5>, <H6>. For a big level 1 heading, put <H1> tag at the beginning and a </H1> tag at the end. For a slightly smaller level we put <H2> tag and close it by </H2> tag and so on. For example, in the previous example if we want to make qualification as heading the we write:

```
<HTML>
<HEAD> Home Page of Mr. Anuranjan Misra </HEAD>
<TITLE> ABES Engineering College, Ghaziabad(UP), India </TITLE>
<BODY><H1> Qualification : M. Tech(CSE) </H1>
<H2> Designation : Assistant Professor </H2>
<H3> Department : MCA </H3>
<H4> Location : MCA Building Block </H4>
<H5> Ranking of College : 1 </H5>
<H6> Ranking of Faculty : 1 </H6>
</BODY>
</HTML>
```

Then the web page looks like :

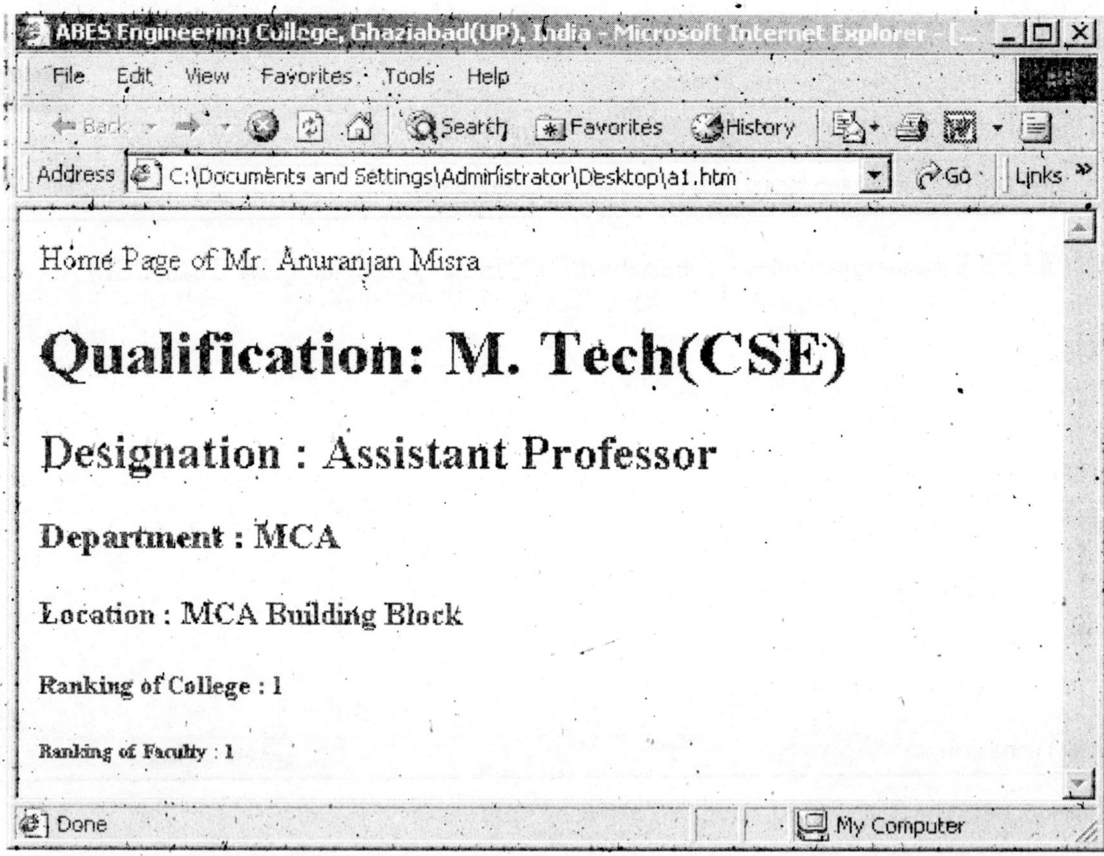

2. **Paragraph :** Unlike documents in most word processors, carriage returns in HTML files aren't significant. In fact, any amount of whitespace -- including spaces, linefeeds, and carriage returns -- are automatically compressed into a single space when your HTML document is displayed in a browser. So you don't have to worry about how long your lines of text are. Word wrapping can occur at any point in your source file without affecting how the page will be displayed.

Tag	Function
<HTML>............</HTML>	Contains the entire HTML document.
<HEAD>............</HEAD>	Contains the head of HTML document.
<TITLE>............</TITLE>	Contains the Title of HTML document.
<BODY>............</BODY>	Encloses the BODY of HTML document
<P>.........................</P>	Used for a paragraph. Closing </P> is optional
 	A line break.
<HR>	A horizontal rule line.
<H1>....................</H1>	First level heading.
<H2>....................</H2>	Second level heading.
<H3>....................</H3>	Third level heading.
<H4>....................</H4>	Forth level heading.
<H5>....................</H5>	Fifth level heading.
<H6>....................</H6>	Sixth level heading.

3. **Lists :** HTML supports unnumbered, numbered, and definition lists. You can nest lists too, but use this feature sparingly because too many nested items can get difficult to follow.

Unnumbered Lists

To make an unnumbered, bulleted list,

1. start with an opening list <UL> (for unnumbered list) tag
2. enter the <LI> (list item) tag followed by the individual item; no closing </LI> tag is needed
3. end the entire list with a closing list </UL> tag

Below is a sample three-item list:

```
<UL>
<LI> apples
<LI> bananas
<LI> mangoes
<LI> grapefruit
</UL>
```

The output is:

- apples
- bananas
- mangoes
- grapefruit

The <LI> items can contain multiple paragraphs. Indicate the paragraphs with the <P> paragraph tags.

Numbered Lists

A numbered list (also called an ordered list, from which the tag name derives) is identical to an unnumbered list, except it uses <OL> instead of <UL>. The items are tagged using the same <LI> tag. The following HTML code :

```
<OL>
<LI> oranges
<LI> peaches
<LI> grapes
</OL>
```

Produces this formatted output :

1. oranges
2. peaches
3. grapes

Definition Lists

A definition list (coded as <DL>) usually consists of alternating a definition term (coded as <DT>) and a definition definition (coded as <DD>). Web browsers generally format the definition on a new line and indent it.

The following is an example of a definition list:

```
<DL>
<DT> ABES
<DD> ABES, ABES is an engineering college
It is located on national highway no. 24
<DT> Ghaziabad
<DD> It is affiliated to UP technical University, Lucknow
</DL>
```

Nested Lists

Lists can be nested. You can also have a number of paragraphs, each containing a nested list, in a single list item.

Here is a sample nested list:

```
<UL>
<LI> A few New England states:
   <UL>
   <LI> Vermont
   <LI> New Hampshire
   <LI> Maine
</UL>
   <LI> Two Midwestern states:
   <UL>
   <LI> Michigan
   <LI> Indiana
   </UL>
</UL>
```

The nested list is displayed as

- A few New England states:
    - Vermont
    - New Hampshire
    - Maine
- Two Midwestern states:
    - Michigan
    - Indiana

Preformatted Text

Use the<PRE> tag (which stands for "preformatted") to generate text in a fixed-width font. This tag also makes spaces, new lines, and tabs significant -- multiple spaces are displayed as multiple spaces, and lines break in the same locations as in the source HTML file. This is useful for program listings, among other things.

Extended Quotations

Use the <BLOCKQUOTE> tag to include lengthy quotations in a separate block on the screen. Most browsers generally change the margins for the quotation to separate it from surrounding text.

In the example:

<P> What is Cryptology? </P>

<BLOCKQUOTE>

<P> Cryptology is the science underlying cryptography. Cryptanalysis is the science of 'breaking' or 'cracking' encryption schemes, *i.e.,* discovering the decryption key.

</P>

<P>—Anuranjan Misra …….. 2006 </P>

</BLOCKQUOTE>

the result is:

What is Cryptology?

Cryptology is the science underlying cryptography. Cryptanalysis is the science of 'breaking' or 'cracking' encryption schemes, i.e. discovering the decryption key.

— Anuranjan Misra …….. 2006

Forced Line Breaks/Postal Addresses

The <BR> tag forces a line break with no extra (white) space between lines. Using <P> elements for short lines of text such as postal addresses results in unwanted additional white space. For example, with

:

Anuranjan Mishra, Assistant Professor

ABES Engineering College, Near Lal Kua

Vijay Nagar , Ghaziabad

The output is :

Anuranjan Mishra, Assistant Professor

ABES Engineering College, Near Lal Kua

Vijay Nagar , Ghaziabad

Horizontal Rules

The <HR> tag produces a horizontal line the width of the browser window. A horizontal rule is useful to separate major sections of your document.

You can vary a rule's size (thickness) and width (the percentage of the window covered by the rule). Experiment with the settings until you are satisfied with the presentation. For example:

<HR SIZE=4 WIDTH="50%">

displays as :

Character Formatting

HTML has two types of styles for individual words or sentences: logical and physical. *Logical styles* tag text according to its meaning, while *physical styles* indicate the specific appearance of a section. For example, in the preceding sentence, the words "logical styles" was tagged as "emphasis." The same effect (formatting those words in italics) could have been achieved via a different tag that tells your browser to "put these words in italics."

Logical Versus Physical Styles

If physical and logical styles produce the same result on the screen, why are there both?

In the ideal SGML universe, content is divorced from presentation. Thus SGML tags a level-one heading as a level-one heading, but does not specify that the level-one heading should be, for instance, 24-point bold Times centered. The advantage of this approach (it's similar in concept to style sheets in many word processors) is that if you decide to change level-one headings to be 20-point left-justified Helvetica, all you have to do is change the definition of the level-one heading in your Web browser. Indeed, many browsers today let you define how you want the various HTML tags rendered on-screen using what are called *cascading style sheets*, or CSS. CSS is more advanced than HTML, though, and will not be covered in this Primer.

Another advantage of logical tags is that they help enforce consistency in your documents. It's easier to tag something as <H1> than to remember that level-one headings are 24-point bold Times centered or whatever. For example, consider the <STRONG> tag. Most browsers render it in bold text. However, it is possible that a reader would prefer that these sections be displayed in red instead. (This is possible using a local cascading style sheet on the reader's own computer.) Logical styles offer this flexibility.

Of course, if you want something to be displayed in italics (for example) and do not want a browser's setting to display it differently, you should use physical styles. Physical styles, therefore, offer consistency in that something you tag a certain way will always be displayed that way for readers of your document.

Try to be consistent about which type of style you use. If you tag with physical styles, do so throughout a document. If you use logical styles, stick with them within a document. Keep in mind that future releases of HTML might not support certain logical styles, which could mean that browsers will not display your logical-style coding. (For example, the <DFN> tag -- short for "definition", and typically displayed in italics -- is not widely supported and will be ignored if the reader's browser does not understand it.)

Logical Styles

<DFN>

for a word being defined. Typically displayed in italics. (*NCSA Mosaic* is a World Wide Web browser.)

<EM>

for emphasis. Typically displayed in italics. (*Consultants cannot reset your password unless you call the help line.*)

<CITE>

for titles of books, films, etc. Typically displayed in italics. (*A Beginner's Guide to HTML*)

<CODE>

for computer code. Displayed in a fixed-width font. (The `<stdio.h>` header file)

<KBD>

for user keyboard entry. Typically displayed in plain fixed-width font. (Enter passwd to change your password.)

<SAMP>

for a sequence of literal characters. Displayed in a fixed-width font. (Segmentation fault: Core dumped.)

<STRONG>

for strong emphasis. Typically displayed in bold. (**NOTE**: Always check your links.)

<VAR>

for a variable, where you will replace the variable with specific information. Typically displayed in italics. (rm *filename* deletes the file.)

Physical Styles

<B>

bold text

<I>

italic text

<TT>

typewriter text, e.g., fixed-width font.

Escape Sequences (a.k.a. Character Entities)

Character entities have two functions:

- escaping special characters
- displaying other characters not available in the plain ASCII character set (primarily characters with diacritical marks)

Three ASCII characters -- the left angle bracket (<), the right angle bracket (>), and the ampersand (&) -- have special meanings in HTML and therefore cannot be used "as is" in text. (The angle brackets are used to indicate the beginning and end of HTML tags, and the ampersand is used to indicate the beginning of an escape sequence.) Double quote marks may be used as-is but a character entity may also be used (").

To use one of the three characters in an HTML document, you must enter its *escape sequence* instead:

Non-breaking space		
Copyright	©	©
Trademark	™	™
Registered	®	® or ®
Less Than	<	<
Greater Than	>	>
Ampersand	&	&
Quote	"	"
Apostrophe	'	'
Cent	¢	¢
Euro	€	€ or €
One quarter	¼	¼
One half	½	½
Three quarters	¾	¾
Degrees	°	°
Larger middle dot	•	•

7.5 LINKING

The chief power of HTML comes from its ability to link text and/or an image to another document or section of a document. A browser highlights the identified text or image with color and/or underlines to indicate that it is a *hypertext link* (often shortened to *hyperlink* or just *link*).

HTML's single hypertext-related tag is <A>, which stands for *anchor*. To include an anchor in your document:

1. start the anchor with <A (include a space after the A)
2. specify the document you're linking to by entering the parameter HREF="*filename*" followed by a closing right angle bracket (>)
3. enter the text that will serve as the hypertext link in the current document
4. enter the ending anchor tag: </A> (no space is needed before the end anchor tag)

Here is a sample hypertext reference in a file called US.html:

<A HREF="MaineStats.html">Maine</A>

This entry makes the word *Maine* the hyperlink to the document MaineStats.html, which is in the same directory as the first document.

Relative Pathnames Versus Absolute Pathnames

You can link to documents in other directories by specifying the *relative path* from the current document to the linked document. For example, a link to a file NYStats.html located in the subdirectory AtlanticStates would be:

<A HREF="AtlanticStates/NYStats.html">New York</A>

These are called *relative links* because you are specifying the path to the linked file relative to the location of the current file. You can also use the absolute pathname (the complete URL) of the file, but relative links are more efficient in accessing a server. They also have the advantage of making your documents more "portable" — for instance, you can create several web pages in a single folder on your local computer, using relative links to hyperlink one page to another, and then upload the entire folder of web pages to your web server. The pages on the server will then link to other pages on the server, and the copies on your hard drive will still point to the other pages stored there.

It is important to point out that UNIX is a case-sensitive operating system where filenames are concerned, while DOS and the MacOS are not. For instance, on a Macintosh, "DOCUMENT.HTML", "Document.HTML", and "document.html" are all the same name. If you make a relative hyperlink to "DOCUMENT.HTML", and the file is actually named "document.html", the link will still be valid. But if you upload all your pages to a UNIX web server, the link will no longer work. Be sure to check your filenames before uploading.

Pathnames use the standard UNIX syntax. The UNIX syntax for the parent directory (the directory that contains the current directory) is "..". (For more information consult a beginning UNIX reference text such as *Learning the UNIX Operating System* from O'Reilly and Associates, Inc.)

If you were in the NYStats.html file and were referring to the original document US.html, your link would look like this:

<A HREF="../US.html">United States</A>

In general, you should use relative links whenever possible because:

1. it's easier to move a group of documents to another location (because the relative path names will still be valid)
2. it's more efficient connecting to the server
3. there is less to type

However, use absolute pathnames when linking to documents that are not directly related. For example, consider a group of documents that comprise a user manual. Links within this group should be relative links. Links to other documents (perhaps a reference to related software) should use absolute pathnames instead. This way if you move the user manual to a different directory, none of the links would have to be updated.

URLs

The World Wide Web uses Uniform Resource Locators (URLs) to specify the location of files on other servers. A URL includes the type of resource being accessed (*e.g.*, Web, gopher, FTP), the address of the server, and the location of the file. The syntax is :

scheme://host.domain [:port]/path/filename

where *scheme* is one of

file

a file on your local system

ftp

a file on an anonymous FTP server

http

a file on a World Wide Web server

gopher

a file on a Gopher server

WAIS

a file on a WAIS server

news

a Usenet newsgroup

telnet

a connection to a Telnet-based service

The *port* number can generally be omitted. (That means unless someone tells you otherwise, leave it out.)

For example, to include a link to this primer in your document, enter:

<A HREF="http://www.ncsa.uiuc.edu/General/Internet/WWW/HTMLPrimer.html">

NCSA's Beginner's Guide to HTML</A>

This entry makes the text *NCSA's Beginner's Guide to HTML* a hyperlink to this document.

- There is also a mailto scheme, used to hyperlink email addresses, but this scheme is unique in that it uses only a colon (:) instead of :// between the scheme and the address.

Links to Specific Sections

Anchors can also be used to move a reader to a *particular section* in a document (either the same or a different document) rather than to the top, which is the default. This type of an anchor is commonly called a *named anchor* because to create the links, you insert HTML names within the document.

This guide is a good example of using named anchors in one document. The guide is constructed as one document to make printing easier. But as one (long) document, it can be time-consuming to move through when all you really want to know about is one bit of information about HTML. Internal hyperlinks are used to create a "table of contents" at the top of this document. These hyperlinks move you from one location in the document to another location in the same document.

7.6 LINKS BETWEEN SECTIONS OF DIFFERENT DOCUMENTS

Suppose you want to set a link from document A (documentA.html) to a specific section in another document (MaineStats.html).

Enter the HTML coding for a link to a named anchor:

documentA.html:

In addition to the many state parks, Maine is also home to

<a href="MaineStats.html#ANP">Acadia National Park</a>.

Think of the characters after the hash (#) mark as a tab within the MaineStats.html file. This tab tells your browser what should be displayed at the top of the window when the link is activated. In other words, the first line in your browser window should be the Acadia National Park heading.

Next, create the *named anchor* (in this example "ANP") in MaineStats.html:

<H2><A NAME="ANP">Acadia National Park</a></H2>

With both of these elements in place, you can bring a reader directly to the Acadia reference in MaineStats.html.

NOTE: You cannot make links to specific sections within a different document unless either you have write permission to the coded source of that document or that document already contains in-document named anchors. For example, you could include named anchors to this primer in a document you are writing because there are named anchors in this guide (use View Source in your browser to see the coding). But if this document did not have named anchors, you could not make a link to a specific section because you cannot edit the original file on NCSA's server.

Links to Specific Sections within the Current Document

The technique is the same except the filename is *omitted*.

For example, to link to the ANP anchor from within MaineStats, enter:

...More information about

<A HREF="#ANP">Acadia National Park</a>

is available elsewhere in this document.

Be sure to include the <A NAME=> tag at the place in your document where you want the link to jump to (<A NAME="ANP">Acadia National Park</a>).

Named anchors are particularly useful when you think readers will print a document in its entirety or when you have a lot of short information you want to place online in one file.

Mailto

You can make it easy for a reader to send electronic mail to a specific person or mail alias by including the mailto attribute in a hyperlink. The format is:

<A HREF="mailto:*emailinfo@host*">*Name*</a>

For example, enter:

<A HREF="mailto:*pubs@ncsa.uiuc.edu*">

NCSA Publications Group</a>

Inline Images

Most Web browsers can display inline images (that is, images next to text) that are in X Bitmap (XBM), GIF, or JPEG format. Other image formats are also being incorporated into Web browsers [*e.g.*, the Portable Network Graphic (PNG) format]. Each image takes additional time to download and slows down the initial display of a document. Carefully select your images and the number of images in a document.

To include an inline image, enter:

<IMG SRC=*ImageName*>

where *ImageName* is the URL of the image file.

The syntax for <IMG SRC> URLs is identical to that used in an anchor HREF. If the image file is a GIF file, then the filename part of *ImageName* must end with .gif. Filenames of X Bitmap images must end with .xbm; JPEG image files must end with .jpg or .jpeg; and Portable Network Graphic files must end with .png.

Image Size Attributes

You should include two other attributes on <IMG> tags to tell your browser the size of the images it is downloading with the text. The HEIGHT and WIDTH attributes let your browser set aside the appropriate space (in pixels) for the images as it downloads the rest of the file. (You can get the pixel size from your image-processing software, such as Adobe Photoshop. Some browsers will also display the dimensions of an image file in the title bar if the image is viewed by itself without an enclosing HTML document.)

For example, to include a self portrait image in a file along with the portrait's dimensions, enter:

<IMG SRC=SelfPortrait.gif HEIGHT=100 WIDTH=65>

NOTE: Some browsers use the HEIGHT and WIDTH attributes to stretch or shrink an image to fit into the allotted space when the image does not exactly match the attribute numbers. Not all browser developers think stretching/shrinking is a good idea, so don't plan on your readers having access to this feature. Check your dimensions and use the correct ones.

Aligning Images

You have some flexibility when displaying images. You can have images separated from text and aligned to the left or right or centered. Or you can have an image aligned with text. Try several possibilities to see how your information looks best.

Aligning Text with an Image

By default the bottom of an image is aligned with the following text, as shown in this paragraph. You can align images to the top or center of a paragraph using the ALIGN= attributes TOP and CENTER.

This text is aligned with the top of the image (<IMG SRC = "BarHotlist.gif" ALT="[HOTLIST]" ALIGN=TOP>). Notice how the browser aligns only one line and then jumps to the bottom of the image for the rest of the text.

And this text is centered on the image (<IMG SRC = "BarHotlist.gif" ALT="[HOTLIST]" ALIGN=CENTER>). Again, only one line of text is centered; the rest is below the image.

Images without Text

To display an image without any associated text (e.g., your organization's logo), make it a separate paragraph. Use the paragraph ALIGN= attribute to center the image or adjust it to the right side of the window as shown below:

<p ALIGN=CENTER>

<IMG SRC = "BarHotlist.gif" ALT="[HOTLIST]">

</p>

which results in:

The image is centered; this paragraph starts below it and left justified.

Alternate Text for Images

Some World Wide Web browsers — primarily the text-only browsers such as Lynx -- cannot display images. Some users turn off image loading even if their software can display images (especially if they are using a modem or have a slow connection). HTML provides a mechanism to tell readers what they are missing on your pages if they can't load images.

The ALT attribute lets you specify text to be displayed instead of an image. For example:

<IMG SRC="UpArrow.gif" ALT="Up">

where UpArrow.gif is the picture of an upward pointing arrow. With graphics-capable viewers that have image-loading turned on, you see the up arrow graphic. With a text-only browser or if image-loading is turned off, the word *Up* is shown in your window in place of the image.

You should try to include alternate text for each image you use in your document, which is a courtesy for your readers — or, for users who might be visually impaired, a necessity.

Images as Hyperlinks

Inline images can be used as hyperlinks just like plain text. The following HTML code:

<A HREF="hotlist.html"><IMG SRC="BarHotlist.gif" ALT="[HOTLIST]"></A>

Produces the following result:

(Note that this link doesn't actually go anywhere.) The blue border that surrounds the image indicates that it's a clickable hyperlink. You may not always want this border to be displayed, though. In this case you can use the BORDER attribute of the IMG tag to make the image appear as normal. Adding the BORDER attribute and setting it to zero:

<A HREF="hotlist.html"><IMG SRC="BarHotlist.gif" BORDER=0 ALT="[HOTLIST]"></A>

Produces the following result:

The BORDER attribute can also be set to non-zero values, whether or not the image is used as a hyperlink. In this case, the border will appear using the default text color for the web page. For instance, if you wanted to give your image a plain black border to help it stand out on the page, you might try this:

<IMG SRC="BarHotlist.gif" BORDER=6 ALT="[HOTLIST]">

And get the following result:

Background Graphics

Newer versions of Web browsers can load an image and use it as a background when displaying a page. Some people like background images and some don't. In general, if you want to include a background, make sure your text can be read easily when displayed on top of the image.

Background images can be a texture (linen finished paper, for example) or an image of an object (a logo possibly). You create the background image as you do any image.

However you only have to create a small piece of the image. Using a feature called tiling, a browser takes the image and repeats it across and down to fill your browser window. In sum you generate one image, and the browser replicates it enough times to fill your window. This action is automatic when you use the background tag shown below.

The tag to include a background image is included in the <BODY> statement as an attribute:

<BODY BACKGROUND="*filename*.gif">

Background Color

By default browsers display text in black on a gray background. However, you can change both elements if you want. Some HTML authors select a background color and coordinate it with a change in the color of the text.

Always preview changes like this to make sure your pages are readable. (For example, many people find red text on a black background difficult to read!) In general, try to avoid using high-contrast images or images that use the color of your text anywhere within the graphic.

You change the color of text, links, visited links, and active links (links that are currently being clicked on) using further attributes of the <BODY> tag. For example:

<BODY BGCOLOR="#000000" TEXT="#FFFFFF" LINK="#9690CC">

This creates a window with a black background (BGCOLOR), white text (TEXT), and silvery hyperlinks (LINK).

The six-digit number and letter combinations represent colors by giving their RGB (red, green, blue) value. The six digits are actually three two-digit numbers in sequence, representing the amount of red, green, or blue as a hexadecimal value in the range 00-FF. For example, 000000 is black (no color at all), FF0000 is bright red, 0000FF is bright blue, and FFFFFF is white (fully saturated with all three colors).

External Images, Sounds and Animations

You may want to have an image open as a separate document when a user activates a link on either a word or a smaller, inline version of the image included in your document. This is called an external image, and it is useful if you do not wish to slow down the loading of the main document with large inline images.

To include a reference to an external image, enter:

<A HREF="*MyImage.gif*">link anchor</A>

You can also use a smaller image as a link to a larger image. Enter:

<A HREF="*LargerImage.gif*"><IMG SRC="*SmallImage.gif*"></A>

The reader sees the SmallImage.gif image and clicks on it to open the LargerImage.gif file.

Use the same syntax for links to external animations and sounds. The only difference is the file extension of the linked file. For example,

<A HREF="AdamsRib.mov">link anchor</A>

specifies a link to a QuickTime movie. Some common file types and their extensions are:

plain text
: .txt

HTML document
: .html

GIF image
: .gif

TIFF image
: .tiff

X Bitmap image
: .xbm

JPEG image
: .jpg or .jpeg

PostScript file
: .ps

AIFF sound file
: .aiff

AU sound file
: .au

WAV sound file

.wav

QuickTime movie

.mov

MPEG movie

.mpeg or .mpg

Keep in mind your intended audience and their access to software. Most UNIX workstations, for instance, cannot view QuickTime movies.

7.7 TABLES

Before HTML tags for tables were finalized, authors had to carefully format their tabular information within <PRE> tags, counting spaces and previewing their output. Tables are very useful for presentation of tabular information as well as a boon to creative HTML authors who use the table tags to present their regular Web pages.

Think of your tabular information in light of the coding explained below. A table has heads where you explain what the columns/rows include, rows for information, cells for each item. In the following table, the first column contains the header information, each row explains an HTML table tag, and each cell contains a paired tag or an explanation of the tag's function.

Table Elements

Element	Description
<TABLE> ... </TABLE>	defines a table in HTML. If the BORDER attribute is present, your browser displays the table with a border.
<CAPTION> ... </CAPTION>	defines the caption for the title of the table. The default position of the title is centered at the top of the table. The attribute ALIGN= BOTTOM can be used to position the caption below the table. **NOTE:** Any kind of markup tag can be used in the caption.
<TR> ... </TR>	specifies a table row within a table. You may define default attributes for the entire row: ALIGN (LEFT, CENTER, RIGHT) and/or VALIGN (TOP, MIDDLE, BOTTOM). See Table Attributes at the end of this table for more information.
<TH> ... </TH>	defines a table header cell. By default the text in this cell is bold and centered. Table header cells may contain other attributes to determine the characteristics of the cell and/or its contents. See Table Attributes at the end of this table for more information.
<TD> ... </TD>	defines a table data cell. By default the text in this cell is aligned left and centered vertically. Table data cells may contain other attributes to determine the characteristics of the cell and/or its contents. See Table Attributes at the end of this table for more information.

Table Attributes

NOTE: Attributes defined within <TH> ... </TH> or <TD> ... </TD> cells override the default alignment set in a <TR> ... </TR>.

Attribute	Description
ALIGN (LEFT, CENTER, RIGHT)	Horizontal alignment of a cell.
VALIGN (TOP, MIDDLE, BOTTOM)	Vertical alignment of a cell.
COLSPAN=*n*	The number (*n*) of columns a cell spans.
ROWSPAN=*n*	The number (*n*) of rows a cell spans.
NOWRAP	Turn off word wrapping within a cell.

General Table Format

The general format of a table looks like this:

```
<TABLE>
<!— start of table definition —>

<CAPTION> caption contents </CAPTION>
<!— caption definition —>
<TR>
<!— start of header row definition —>
  <TH> first header cell contents </TH>
  <TH> last header cell contents </TH>
</TR>
<!— end of header row definition —>

<TR>
<!— start of first row definition —>
  <TD> first row, first cell contents </TD>
  <TD> first row, last cell contents </TD>
</TR>
<!— end of first row definition —>
<TR>
<!— start of last row definition —>
  <TD> last row, first cell contents </TD>
  <TD> last row, last cell contents </TD>
</TR>
<!— end of last row definition —>

</TABLE>
<!— end of table definition —>
```

You can cut-and-paste the above code into your own HTML documents, adding new rows or cells as necessary. The above example looks like this when rendered in a browser.

The <TABLE> and </TABLE> tags **must** surround the entire table definition. The first item inside the table is the CAPTION, which is optional. Then you can have any number of rows defined by the <TR> and </TR> tags. Within a row you can have any number of cells defined by the <TD>...</TD> or <TH>...</TH> tags. Each row of a table is, essentially, formatted independently of the rows above and below it. This lets you easily display tables like the one above with a single cell, such as Table Attributes, spanning columns of the table.

Tables for Nontabular Information

Some HTML authors use tables to present nontabular information. For example, because links can be included in table cells, some authors use a table with no borders to create "one" image from separate images. Browsers that can display tables properly show the various images seamlessly, making the created image seem like an *image map* (one image with hyperlinked quadrants).

Using table borders with images can create an impressive display as well. Experiment and see what you like.

Fill-out Forms

Web forms let a reader return information to a Web server for some action. For example, suppose you collect names and email addresses so you can email some information to people who request it. For each person who enters his or her name and address, you need some information to be sent and the respondent's particulars added to a data base.

This processing of incoming data is usually handled by a script or program written in Perl or another language that manipulates text, files, and information. If you cannot write a program or script for your incoming information, you need to find someone who can do this for you.

7.8 TROUBLESHOOTING

Avoid Overlapping Tags

Consider this example of HTML:

<B>This is an example of <I>overlapping</B>

HTML tags.</I>

The word *overlapping* is contained within both the <B> and <I> tags. A browser might be confused by this coding and might not display it the way you intend. The only way to know is to check each popular browser (which is time-consuming and impractical).

In general, avoid overlapping tags. Look at your tags and try pairing them up. Tags (with the obvious exceptions of elements whose end tags may be omitted, such as paragraphs) should be paired without an intervening tag in between. Look again at the example above. You cannot pair the bold tags without another tag in the middle (the first definition tag). Try matching your coding up like this to see if you have any problem areas that should be fixed before you release your files to a server.

Embed Only Anchors and Character Tags

HTML protocol allows you to embed links within other HTML tags:

<H1><A HREF="Destination.html">My heading</A></H1>

Do not embed HTML tags within an anchor:

<A HREF="Destination.html">

```
<H1>My heading</H1>
</A>
```

Although most browsers currently handle this second example, the official HTML specifications do not support this construct and your file will probably not work with future browsers. Remember that browsers can be forgiving when displaying improperly coded files. But that forgiveness may not last to the next version of the software! When in doubt, code your files according to the HTML specifications Character tags modify the appearance of the text within other elements:

```
<UL>
<LI><B>A bold list item</B>
<LI><I>An italic list item</I>
</UL>
```

Avoid embedding other types of HTML element tags. For example, you might be tempted to embed a heading within a list in order to make the font size larger:

```
<UL>
<LI><H1>A large heading</H1>
<LI><H2>Something slightly smaller</H2>
</UL>
```

Although some browsers handle this quite nicely, formatting of such coding is unpredictable (because it is undefined). For compatibility with all browsers, avoid these kinds of constructs. (The Netscape <FONT> tag, which lets you specify how large individual characters will be displayed in your window, is not currently part of the official HTML specifications.)

What's the difference between embedding a <B> within a <LI> tag as opposed to embedding a <H1> within a <LI>? Within HTML the semantic meaning of <H1> is that it's the main heading of a document and that it should be followed by the content of the document. Therefore it doesn't make sense to find a <H1> within a list.

Character formatting tags also are generally not additive. For example, you might expect that:

```
<B><I>some text</I></B>
```

would produce bold-italic text. On some browsers it does; other browsers interpret only the innermost tag.

Do the Final Steps

Validate your Code

When you put a document on a Web server, be sure to check the formatting and each link (including named anchors). Ideally you will have someone else read through and comment on your file(s) before you consider a document finished.

You can run your coded files through one of several on-line HTML validation service that will tell you if your code conforms to accepted HTML. If you are not sure your coding conforms to HTML specifications, this can be a useful teaching tool. Fortunately the service lets you select the level of conformance you want for your files (*i.e.*, strict, level 2, level 3). If you want to use some codes that are not officially part of the HTML specifications, this latitude is helpful.

Dummy Images

When an <IMG SRC> tag points to an image that does not exist, a dummy image is substituted by your browser software. When this happens during your final review of your files, make sure that the referenced image does in fact exist, that the hyperlink has the correct information in the URL, and that the file permission is set appropriately (world-readable). Then check online again!

Update your Files

If the contents of a file are static (such as a biography of George Washington), no updating is probably needed. But for documents that are time sensitive or covering a field that changes frequently, **remember to update your documents!**

Updating is particularly important when the file contains information such as a weekly schedule or a deadline for a program funding announcement. Remove out-of-date files or note why something that appears dated is still on a server (*e.g.*, the program requirements will remain the same for the next cycle so the file is still available as an interim reference).

Browsers Differ

Web browsers display HTML elements differently. Remember that not all codes used in HTML files are interpreted by all browsers. Any code a browser does not understand is usually ignored though.

You could spend a lot of time making your file "look perfect" using your current browser. If you check that file using another browser, it will likely display (a little or a lot) differently. Hence these words of advice: code your files using correct HTML. Leave the interpreting to the browsers and hope for the best.

Commenting your Files

You might want to include comments in your HTML files. Comments in HTML are like comments in a computer program--the text you enter is not used by the browser in any formatting and is not directly viewable by the reader just as computer program comments are not used and are not viewable. The comments are accessible if a reader views the source file, however.

Comments such as the name of the person updating a file, the software and version used in creating a file, or the date that a minor edit was made are the norm.

To include a comment, enter:

<!-- *your comments here* -->

7.9 FRAMES

Frames are like tables in that they allow you to arrange text and graphics into rows and columns. But unlike a table cell, any frame can contain links that change the contents of other frames or itself.

Attributes of Frame

SRC = ".." The URL of the document to be displayed in this frame.

Name ="..'' A name to be used for targeting this frame with the TARGET attribute in <A HREF> links.

<MARGINWIDTH> The amount of space(in pixels) to leave to the left and right side of a document within a frame.

<MARGINHIGHT> The amount of space(in pixels) to leave to the above and below of a document within a frame.

SCROLLING ="..'' Determines whether a frame has scrollabars. Possible values are YES, NO and AUTO.

NORESIZE Prevents the user resizing this frame with the mouse.

<NOFRAMES> .... </NOFRAMES> Provides an alternative document body in <FRAMESET> documents for browsers that do not support frames.

<IFRAME> .... </IFRAME> Creates an inline frame.

7.10 FRAMESET

A frameset document is an HTML page that instructs the web browser to split its window into multiple frames, and specifies which web page should be displayed in each frame.

ROWS = " ..'' - Splits the window or frameset vertically into a number of rows specified by a number(such as 6), a percentage of the total window width (such as 30%) or as an asterisk(*) indicating that a frame should take up all remaining space or divide the space evenly between frames.

COLS = " .. " Works similar to ROWS, except that the window or frameset is split horizontally into columns.

FRAMESPACING = "..'' Space between frames, in pixels.

FRAMEBORDER = " ..'' Specifies whether to display a border for the frames.

BORDER = " .. " Defines a Single frame within a <FRAMESET>

7.11 HTML FORMS

HTML enables us to create forms. This is where our websites can become more than just a nice advertising brochure. Forms allow us to build more dynamic websites that allow our users to interact with it.

An HTML form is made up of any number of *form elements*. These elements enable the user to do things such as enter information or make a selection from a preset options.

In HTML, a form is defined using the <form></form> tags. The actual form elements are defined between these two tags.

The *Input* Tag

This is the most commonly used tag within HTML forms. It allows you to specify various types of user input fields such as text, radio buttons, checkboxes etc.

Text

Text fields are used for when you want the user to type text or numbers into the form.

```
<input type="text" />
```

This results in:

Bottom of Form

Radio Buttons

Radio buttons are used for when you want the user to select *one* option from a pre-determined set of options.

```
<input type="radio" name="lunch" value="pasta" /><br /> <input type="radio" name="lunch" value="rissotto" />
```

This results in:

■ ⊙

■ ⊙

Bottom of Form

Checkboxes

Checkboxes are similar to radio buttons, but enable the user to make multiple selections..

```
<input type="checkbox" name="lunch" value="pasta" /><br /> <input type="checkbox" name="lunch" value="rissotto" />
```

This results in:

☐

☐

Submit

The submit button allows the user to actually submit the form.

```
<input type="submit" />
```

This results in:

Submit Query

Select Lists

A select list is a dropdown list with options. This allows the user to select one option from a list of pre-defined options.

The select list is created using the select in conjunction with the option tag.

```
<select>
  <option value ="sydney">Sydney</option>
  <option value ="melbourne">Melbourne</option>
```

```
  <option value ="cromwell">Cromwell</option>
  <option value ="queenstown">Queenstown</option>
</select>
```

This results in:

Form Action

Usually when a user submits the form, you need the system to do something with the data. This is where the *action* page comes in. The action page is the page that the form is submitted to. This page could contain advanced scripts or programming that inserts the form data into a database or e-mails an administrator etc.

Creating an action page is outside the scope of this tutorial. In any case, many web hosts provide scripts that can be used for action page functionality, such as emailing the webmaster whenever the form has been completed. For now, we will simply look at how to submit the form to the action page.

You nominate an action page with the action attribute.

Example HTML Code:

```
<form action="/html/tags/html_form_tag_action.cfm" method="get">
First name:
<input type="text" name="first_name" value="" maxlength="100" />
<br />
Last name:
<input type="text" name="last_name" value="" maxlength="100" />
<input type="submit" value="Submit" />
</form>
```

This results in:

Top of Form

First name: name:

Last name:

Bottom of Form

Oh, one last thing. You may have noticed the above example uses a method attribute. This attribute specifies the HTTP method to use when the form is submitted.

Possible values are:

- get (the form data is appended to the URL when submitted)
- post (the form data is not appended to the URL)

Providing this attribute is optional. If you don't provide it, the method will be *post*.

HTML INTERVIEW QUESTIONS AND ANSWERS

1. *What is HTML?*

Solution: HTML, or Hyper Text Markup Language, is a Universal language, which allows an individual using special code to create web pages to be viewed on the Internet.

2. *What is a tag?*

Solution: In HTML, a tag tells the browser what to do. When you write an HTML page, you enter tags for many reasons — to change the appearance of text, to show a graphic, or to make a link to another page.

3. *What is the simplest HTML page?*

Solution:
```
<HTML>
<HEAD>
<TITLE>This is my page title! </TITLE>
</HEAD>
<BODY>
This is my message to the world!
</BODY>
</HTML>
```
Browser Display:

This is my message to the world!

4. *How do I create frames? What is a frameset?*

Solution: Frames allow an author to divide a browser window into multiple (rectangular) regions. Multiple documents can be displayed in a single window, each within its own frame. Graphical browsers allow these frames to be scrolled independently of each other, and links can update the document displayed in one frame without affecting the others.

You can't just "add frames" to an existing document. Rather, you must create a frameset document that defines a particular combination of frames, and then display your content documents inside those frames. The frameset document should also include alternative non-framed content in a NOFRAMES element.The HTML 4 frames model has significant design flaws that cause usability problems for web users. Frames should be used only with great care.

5. *How can I include comments in HTML?*

Solution: Technically, since HTML is an SGML application, HTML uses SGML comment syntax. However, the full syntax is complex, and browsers don't support it in its entirety anyway. Therefore, use the following simplified rule to create HTML comments that both have valid syntax and work in browsers: An HTML comment begins with "<!—", ends with "—>", and does not contain "—" or ">" anywhere in the comment The following are examples of HTML comments:

* <!— This is a comment. —>

* <!— This is another comment,
and it continues onto a second line. —>

* <!——>

Do not put comments inside tags (*i.e.*, between "<" and ">") in HTML markup.

6. *What is a Hypertext link?*

Solution: A hypertext link is a special tag that links one page to another page or resource. If you click the link, the browser jumps to the link's destination.

7. *How comfortable are you with writing HTML entirely by hand?*

Solution: Very. I don't usually use WYSIWYG. The only occasions when I do use Dreamweaver are when I want to draw something to see what it looks like, and then I'll usually either take that design and hand-modify it or build it all over again from scratch in code. I have actually written my own desktop HTML IDE for Windows (it's called Less Than Slash) with the intention of deploying it for use in web development training. If has built-in reference features, and will autocomplete code by parsing the DTD you specify in the file. That is to say, the program doesn't know anything about HTML until after it parses the HTML DTD you specified. This should give you some idea of my skill level with HTML.

8. *What is everyone using to write HTML?*

Solution: Everyone has a different preference for which tool works best for them. Keep in mind that typically the less HTML the tool requires you to know, the worse the output of the HTML. In other words, you can always do it better by hand if you take the time to learn a little HTML.

9. *What is a DOCTYPE? Which one do I use?*

Solution: According to HTML standards, each HTML document begins with a DOCTYPE declaration that specifies which version of HTML the document uses. Originally, the DOCTYPE declaration was used only by SGML-based tools like HTML validators, which needed to determine which version of HTML a document used (or claimed to use).

Today, many browsers use the document's DOCTYPE declaration to determine whether to use a stricter, more standards-oriented layout mode, or to use a "quirks" layout mode that attempts to emulate older, buggy browsers.

10. *Can I nest tables within tables?*

Solution: Yes, a table can be embedded inside a cell in another table. Here's a simple example:

```
<table>
<tr>
<td>this is the first cell of the outer table</td>
<td>this is the second cell of the outer table,
with the inner table embedded in it
<table>
<tr>
<td>this is the first cell of the inner table</td>
<td>this is the second cell of the inner table</td>
</tr>
</table>
</td>
</tr>
</table>
```

The main caveat about nested tables is that older versions of Netscape Navigator have problems with them if you don't explicitly close your TR, TD, and TH elements. To avoid problems, include every </tr>, </td>, and </th> tag, even though the HTML specifications don't require them. Also, older versions of Netscape Navigator have problems with tables that are nested extremely deeply (*e.g.*, tables nested ten deep). To avoid problems, avoid nesting tables more than a few deep. You may be able to use the ROWSPAN and COLSPAN attributes to minimize table nesting. Finally, be especially sure to validate your markup whenever you use nested tables.

11. *How do I align a table to the right (or left)?*

Solution: You can use <TABLE ALIGN="right"> to float a table to the right. (Use ALIGN="left" to float it to the left.) Any content that follows the closing </TABLE> tag will flow around the table. Use <BR CLEAR="right"> or <BR CLEAR="all"> to mark the end of the text that is to flow around the table, as shown in this example:

The table in this example will float to the right.

<table align="right">...</table>

This text will wrap to fill the available space to the left of (and if the text is long enough, below) the table.

<br clear="right">

This text will appear below the table, even if there is additional room to its left.

12. *How can I use tables to structure forms?*

Solution: Small forms are sometimes placed within a TD element within a table. This can be a useful for positioning a form relative to other content, but it doesn't help position the form-related elements relative to each other.

To position form-related elements relative to each other, the entire table must be within the form. You cannot start a form in one TH or TD element and end in another. You cannot place the form within the table without placing it inside a TH or TD element. You can put the table inside the form, and then use the table to position the INPUT, TEXTAREA, SELECT, and other form-related elements, as shown in the following example.

```
<FORM ACTION="[URL]">
<TABLE BORDER="0">
<TR>
<TH>Account:</TH>
<TD><INPUT TYPE="text" NAME="account"></TD>
</TR>
<TR>
<TH>Password:</TH>
<TD><INPUT TYPE="password" NAME="password"></TD>
</TR>
<TR>
<TD> </TD>
<TD><INPUT TYPE="submit" NAME="Log On"></TD>
```

</TR>
</TABLE>
</FORM>

13. *How do I center a table?*

Solution: In your HTML, use

```
<div class="center">
<table>...</table>
</div>
```

In your CSS, use

```
div.center {
text-align: center;
}
div.center table {
margin-left: auto;
margin-right: auto;
text-align: left;
}
```

14. *How do I use forms?*

Solution: The basic syntax for a form is: <FORM ACTION="[URL]">...</FORM>

When the form is submitted, the form data is sent to the URL specified in the ACTION attribute. This URL should refer to a server-side (*e.g.*, CGI) program that will process the form data. The form itself should contain

* at least one submit button (i.e., an <INPUT TYPE="submit" ...> element),

* form data elements (*e.g.*, <INPUT>, <TEXTAREA>, and <SELECT>) as needed, and

* additional markup (*e.g.*, identifying data elements, presenting instructions) as needed.

15. *How can I check for errors?*

Solution: HTML validators check HTML documents against a formal definition of HTML syntax and then output a list of errors. Validation is important to give the best chance of correctness on unknown browsers (both existing browsers that you haven't seen and future browsers that haven't been written yet).

HTML checkers (linters) are also useful. These programs check documents for specific problems, including some caused by invalid markup and others caused by common browser bugs. Checkers may pass some invalid documents, and they may fail some valid ones.

All validators are functionally equivalent; while their reporting styles may vary, they will find the same errors given identical input. Different checkers are programmed to look for different problems, so their reports will vary significantly from each other. Also, some programs that are called validators (*e.g.*, the "CSE HTML Validator") are really linters/checkers. They are still useful, but they should not be confused with real HTML validators.

When checking a site for errors for the first time, it is often useful to identify common problems that occur repeatedly in your markup. Fix these problems everywhere they occur (with an automated process if possible), and then go back to identify and fix the remaining problems.

Link checkers follow all the links on a site and report which ones are no longer functioning. CSS checkers report problems with CSS style sheets.

16. *Do I have to memorize a bunch of tags?*

Solution: No. Most programs that help you write HTML code already know most tags, and create them when you press a button. But you should understand what a tag is, and how it works. That way you can correct errors in your page more easily.

17. *How do I make a form so it can be submitted by hitting ENTER?*

Solution: The short answer is that the form should just have one <INPUT TYPE=TEXT> and no TEXTAREA, though it can have other form elements like checkboxes and radio buttons.

18. *How do I set the focus to the first form field?*

Solution: You cannot do this with HTML. However, you can include a script after the form that sets the focus to the appropriate field, like this:

```
<form id="myform" name="myform" action=...>
<input type="text" id="myinput" name="myinput" ...>
</form>
<script type="text/javascript">
document.myform.myinput.focus();
</script>
```

A similar approach uses <body onload=...> to set the focus, but some browsers seem to process the ONLOAD event before the entire document (*i.e.*, the part with the form) has been loaded.

19. *How can I eliminate the extra space after a </form> tag?*

Solution: HTML has no mechanism to control this. However, with CSS, you can set the margin-bottom of the form to 0. For example:

```
<form style="margin-bottom:0;" action=...>
```

You can also use a CSS style sheet to affect all the forms on a page:

```
form { margin-bottom: 0 ; }
```

20. *How can I use tables to structure forms?*

Solution: Small forms are sometimes placed within a TD element within a table. This can be a useful for positioning a form relative to other content, but it doesn't help position the form-related elements relative to each other.

To position form-related elements relative to each other, the entire table must be within the form. You cannot start a form in one TH or TD element and end in another. You cannot place the form within the table without placing it inside a TH or TD element. You can put the table inside the form, and then use the table to position the INPUT, TEXTAREA, SELECT, and other form-related elements, as shown in the following example.

```
<form action="[URL]">
<table border="0">
```

```
<tr>
<th scope="row">
<label for="account">Account:</label>
</th>
<td>
<input type="text" name="account" id="account">
</td>
</tr>
<tr>
<th scope="row">
<label for="password">Password:
</th>
<td>
<input type="password" name="password" id="password">
</td>
</tr>
<tr>
<td> </td>
<td><input type="submit" name="Log On"></td>
</tr>
</table>
</form>
```

MULTIPLE CHOICE QUESTIONS

1. Intrepret this statement: <strong>Michelle</strong>
   (*a*) It makes Michelle strong
   (*b*) It highlights Michelle as being strong
   (*c*) It will print out Michelle in bold font

2. Tables can be nested (table inside of another table).
   (*a*) True (*b*) False

3. Which is correct?
   (*a*) <b>Click Here<b> (*b*) <strong>Click Here<strong>
   (*c*) <b>Click Here</b> (*d*) </strong>Click Here</strong>

4. Which of the following is a two sided tag?
   (*a*) DT (*b*) LI (*c*) DD (*d*) DL

5. The Browser applies the feature of a tag until it encounters_____tag.
   (*a*) Quit (*b*) Closing (*c*) Exit (*d*) Anti
   (*e*) Deactivate

6. _______are the HTML codes that control the apearance of the document contents
   (*a*) Tags (*b*) Codas (*c*) Slashes (*d*) Properties
   (*e*) Code

7. What are the genral syntax for inline image?
   (*a*) src=img (*b*) src=image (*c*) img=file (*d*) img src=file
   (*e*) image src=file
8. An HTML_____takes text in one format and changes it to HTML code.
   (*a*) Browser (*b*) Editor (*c*) Converter (*d*) Processor
   (*e*) Parser
9. To create a link to an anchor, you use the______property in A tag.
   (*a*) Name (*b*) Tag (*c*) Link (*d*) Href
10. HTML Tags are case sensitive.
   (*a*) True (*b*) False
11. Relative path make your hypertext links______.
   (*a*) Portable (*b*) Discrete (*c*) Uniform
12. A_____structure starts with a general topic that includes link to more specific topics.
   (*a*) Hierarchical (*b*) Linear (*c*) Mixed
13. Which of the following path is supported by HTML?
   (*a*) Ralative (*b*) Deferernced (*c*) Absolute and Relative
14. You cannot designate an inline image as a hypertext link.
   (*a*) True (*b*) False
15. Because each computer differs in terms of what fonts it can display, each individual browser determines how text is to be displayed.
   (*a*) True (*b*) False
16. You do not have to connect to the internet to verify changes to a Web page on your computer.
   (*a*) True (*b*) False
17. You can combine structures *e.g*, linear and hierarchical.
   (*a*) True (*b*) False
18. What is HTML stands for?
   (*a*) Hypertext Mailing List (*b*) Hypertext Mark Language
   (*c*) Hypertext Markup Language
19. What is the tag for an inline frmae?
   (*a*) Iframe (*b*) Inframe (*c*) Frame (*d*) Inlineframe
20. Within the MAP tag, you use the AREA tag to specify the areas of the image that will act as a hotspot.
   (*a*) True (*b*) False
21. Can you create an e-mail form with auto responder using form action method=mailto: youdomainname.com?
   (*a*) Yes (*b*) No
22. What is the most widely use e-mail form script?
   (*a*) ASP (*b*) PHP (*c*) Perl CGI (*d*) JSP
23. There are_____color names recognized by all version of HTML.
   (*a*) 6 (*b*) 8 (*c*) 256 (*d*) 16
24. Software programs, like your Web browser, use a mathemathical approach to define color.
   (*a*) True (*b*) False

25. If you want to increase the font size by 2 relative to the sorounding text, you enter +2 in the tag.

(*a*) True (*b*) False

26. What operator makes converts 00110011 into 11001100?

(*a*) ~ (*b*) ! (*c*) & (*d*) |

27. The default statement of a switch is always executed.

(*a*) True (*b*) False

28. H1 is the smallest header tag.

(*a*) True (*b*) False

29. The page title is inside the____tag.

(*a*) Body (*b*) Head (*c*) Division (*d*) Table

30. _____refers to the way the GIF file is saved by the graphics software.

(*a*) Dithering (*b*) Interlacing (*c*) Balancing

Answers of Multiple Choice Questions

1. (*c*),	**2.** (*a*),	**3.** (*c*),	**4.** (*d*),	**5.** (*d*),
6. (*a*),	**7.** (*d*),	**8.** (*c*),	**9.** (*d*),	**10.** (*b*),
11. (*a*),	**12.** (*a*),	**13.** (*c*),	**14.** (*b*),	**15.** (*a*),
16. (*a*),	**17.** (*a*),	**18.** (*c*),	**19.** (*a*),	**20.** (*a*),
21. (*b*),	**22.** (*b*),	**23.** (*d*),	**24.** (*a*),	**25.** (*a*),
26. (*a*),	**27.** (*b*),	**28.** (*b*),	**29.** (*b*),	**30.** (*b*).

EXERCISE

1. What do you mean by HTML?
2. Define SGML.
3. What are the benefits of HTML?
4. How we insert an image in our documents.
5. Write an HTML code for scrolling to a location in the same documents.
6. How do you create frames in HTML?
7. What are the steps for creating lists.
8. How you can insert table captions and header in HTML?
9. How would you create image links including am image in a link?
10. What are the application areas of forms?
11. How would you create forms in HTML?
12. How do you create check box, password and pull down menus?
13. How would you define frame set and write a code for nesting frameset?
14. Write a code in HTML for linked frames.

8

DHTML

CSS (Cascading Style Sheets) allows web authors to apply styles to their web pages. More importantly, CSS enables them to do this independently of the HTML that makes up each web page.

Therefore, as a web author, you can code your HTML without having to be concerned with what each HTML element is going to look like. You can change the look later using CSS.

8.0 INTRODUCTION

With CSS, you can define all your common styles in an external Style Sheet. This way, if you want to change every occurrence of a style throughout your site, you only need to update one place.

8.0.1 What is CSS?

CSS is a language that you can use to define styles against any HTML element. These styles are set using CSS *properties*.For example, you can set font properties (size, colors, style etc), background images, border styles, and much more.

Cascading Style Sheets, level 1 (CSS1) became a W3C Recommendation in December 1996. It describes the CSS language as well as a simple visual formatting model. CSS2, which became a W3C recommendation in May 1998, builds on CSS1 and adds support for media-specific style sheets (e.g. printers and aural devices), downloadable fonts, element positioning and tables.

As of this writing, CSS3 is currently under development.

8.1 CSS ADVANTAGES

HTML has its limitations when it comes to layout. Sure, you have 6 different levels of headings and 6 different sizes of fonts. You also have tables, and you have control over alignment etc. These are good enough to get a reasonable looking document that shows the true structure of information. However, it's a far cry from some of the excellent layout & design that we see in magazines and printed brochures etc.

CSS helps us achieve such layouts.

With CSS, you have much better control over the layout of your web pages. You can specify exactly how big a font will be, exactly where an element will be on a page, what the page will look like when printed, and much more.

CSS can also save you a lot of time, particularly when maintaining a large site. Also, the World Wide Web Consortium (W3C) recommends that web developers use CSS tags instead of HTML tags wherever possible. The W3C are gradually phasing out quite a few of these HTML tags.

8.1.1 Advantages of CSS

- **CSS saves time :** When most of us first learn HTML, we get taught to set the font face, size, colour, style etc every time it occurs on a page. This means we find ourselves typing (or copying & pasting) the same thing over and over again. With CSS, you only have to specify these details once for any element. CSS will automatically apply the specified styles whenever that element occurs.
- **Pages load faster :** Less code means faster download times.
- **Easy maintenance :** To change the style of an element, you only have to make an edit in one place.
- **Superior styles to HTML :** CSS has a much wider array of attributes than HTML.

8.1.2 Disadvantages of CSS

- **Browser compatibility :** Browsers have varying levels of compliance with Style Sheets. This means that some Style Sheet features are supported and some aren't. To confuse things more, some browser manufacturers decide to come up with their own proprietary tags.

  Fortunately, browser compatibility is becoming less of an issue as the latest browser versions are much more standards-compliant than their earlier counterparts.

8.2 CSS SYNTAX

The CSS syntax consists of a set of rules. These rules have 3 parts: a selector, a property, and a value.

You don't need to remember this in order to code CSS. Once you start coding CSS, you'll do so without thinking "this is a selector" or "that is a property". This should begin to make sense once you study the examples on this page.

Syntax:

```
selector { property: value }
```

The selector is often the HTML element that you want to style. For example:

```
h1 { color: blue }
```

This code tells the browser to render all occurences of the HTML *h1* element in blue.

8.2.1 Grouping Selectors

You can apply a style to many selectors if you like. Just separate the selectors with a comma.

```
h1,h2,h3,h4,h5,h6 { color: blue }
```

8.2.2 Applying Multiple Properties

To apply more than one property separate each declaration with a semi-colon.

```
h1 { color:blue; font-family:arial,helvetica,"sans serif" }
```

8.2.3 Readability

You can make your CSS code more readable by spreading your style declarations across multiple lines. You can also indent your code if you like. This doesn't affect how your code is rendered - it just makes it easier for you to read.

```
h1 {
        color:blue;
        font-family:arial,helvetica,"sans serif";
        font-size:150%;
}
```

8.3 IMPLEMENTING CSS

There are 4 ways of implementing CSS: declare *inline*, *embed* into the head of your document, link to an *external* CSS file, *import* a CSS file.

8.3.1 Inline CSS

Style sheet information is applied to the **current** element. Instead of defining the style once, then applying the style against all instances of an element (say the <P> tag), you only apply the style to the instance you want the style to apply to.

For example:

```
<P style="color:#ff9900">
CSS tutorial.
</p>
```

8.3.2 Embedded CSS

You embed CSS information into an HTML document using the 'style' element. You do this by embedding the CSS information within <style>...</style> tags in the head of your document.

For example, place the following code between the <head>...</head> tags of your HTML document:

```
<style type="text/css" media=screen>
p {color:#ff9900;}
</style>
```

8.3.3 External CSS

An external style sheet is a separate file where you can declare all the styles that you want to use throughout your website. You then link to the external style sheet from all your HTML pages. This means you only need to set the styles for each element once. If you want to update the style of your website, you only need to do it in one place.

For example:

1. Type the following into a plain text file, and save with a .css extension (*i.e.* external_style_sheet.css).
2. p {font-family: georgia, serif; font-size: x-small;}
3. h1 {color: #000099; }
4. Add the following between the <head>...</head> tags of all HTML documents that you want to reference the external style sheet.
5. <link rel="stylesheet" href="external_style_sheet.css" type="text/css">

8.3.4 Imported CSS

You can use the *@import* rule to import rules from other style sheets.

Add either of the following between the <head>...</head> tags of all HTML documents that you want to import a style sheet into.

```
@import "imported_style_sheet.css";
@import url("imported_style_sheet.css");
```

8.4 CSS CLASS

In CSS, classes allow you to apply a style to a given *class* of an element. To do this, you link the element to the style by declaring a style for the class, then assigning that class to the element.

8.4.1 CSS Class Syntax

You declare a CSS class by using a dot (.) followed by the class name. You make up the class name yourself. After the class name you simply enter the properties/values that you want to assign to your class.

```
.class-name { property:value; }
```

If you want to use the same class name for multiple elements, but each with a different style, you can prefix the dot with the HTML element name.

```
html-element-name.class-name { property:value; }
```

8.4.2 CSS Class Example

```
<head>
  <style type="text/css">
  h1.css-section { color:#000099 }
  p.css-section { color:#999999; }
  </style>
  </head>
  <body>
  <h1 class="css-section">CSS Class</h1>
  <p class="css-section">CSS classes can be very useful</p>
  </body>
```

This results in:

CSS Class

CSS classes can be very useful

8.4.3 Cascading Rules of Classes

If you have already applied a style to an element, the element will first use those styles, then the ones defined in the class.

8.5 CSS ID

IDs allow you to assign a unique identifier to an HTML element. This allows you to define a style that can only be used by the element you assign the ID to.

8.5.1 CSS ID Syntax

The syntax for declaring a CSS ID is the same as for classes - except that instead of using a dot, you use a hash (#).

```
#id-name { property:value; }
```

Again, similar to classes, if you want to use the same id name for multiple elements, but each with a different style, you can prefix the hash with the HTML element name.

```
html-element-name#id-name { property:value; }
```

8.5.2 CSS ID Example

```
<head>
  <style type="text/css">
  h1#css-section { color:#000099 }
  p#css-section { color:#999999; }
  </style>
```

```
</head>
<body>
<h1 id="css-section">CSS ID</h1>
<p id="css-section">CSS IDs can be very useful</p>
</body>
```

This results in:

CSS ID

CSS IDs can be very useful

8.5.3 IDs vs Classes

Given classes and IDs are very similar, you may be wondering which one to use. This depends on the situation.

When to use classes

You should use classes when your style needs to be applied multiple times on the same page. For example, you might have many *h1* elements that need the same style applied.

When to use IDs

You should use IDs if only one element on the page should have the style applied, and/or you need a unique identifier for that element. For example, you might assign an ID to a *div* tag which contains your left menu. The styles for this ID could contain the position, background-color, float properties, size etc. You probably wouldn't want any other element on the page to use this particular style.

Another useful thing about IDs is that you can use the Document Object Model (DOM) to refer to them. This enables you to use JavaScript/DHTML techniques to build a much more interactive web site.

8.6 CSS FONT

CSS font properties enable you to change the look of your text. For example, you can assign a font family, apply bold or italic formatting, change the size and more.

8.6.1 CSS Font Family

```
<p style="font-family:georgia,garamond,serif;">This text is rendered in either georgia, garamond, or the default serif font (depending on which font the user's system has).</p>
```

This results in:

This text is rendered in either georgia, garamond, or the default serif font (depending on which font the user's system has).

8.6.2 CSS Font Size

Enables you to set the size of the text.

<p **style="font-size:20px;"**>This text is using a font size of 20 pixels.</p>

This results in:

This text is using a font size of 20 pixels.

CSS Font Size Adjust

This property enables you to adjust the x-height to make fonts more legible.

<p **style="font-size-adjust:0.58;"**>This text is using a font-size-adjust value.</p>

This results in:

This text is using a font-size-adjust value.

CSS Font Stretch

This property relies on the user's computer to have an expanded or condensed version of the font being used.

<p **style="font-stretch:ultra-expanded;"**>If your computer has an expanded version of the font being used, this text will be stretched.</p>

This results in:

If your computer has an expanded version of the font being used, this text will be stretched.

CSS Font Style

<p **style="font-style:italic;"**>This text is in italics.</p>

This results in:

This text is in italics.

CSS Font Variant

Enables you to set your text to use small caps.

<p **style="font-variant:small-caps;"**>This Text Is Using Small Caps.</p>

This results in:

This Text Is Using Small Caps.

CSS Font Weight

Enables you to set your text to bold.

<p **style="font-weight:bold;"**>This text is bold.</p>

This results in:

This text is bold.

CSS Font Property

The *font* property is a shorthand property that enables you to set all font properties in one go.

<p **style="font:italic small-caps bold 20px georgia,garamond,serif;"**>The styles for this text has been specified with the 'font' shorthand property.</p>

This results in:

The styles for this text has been specified with the 'font' shorthand property.

8.7 CSS TEXT

Apart from the various CSS font properties, there are other properties that can assist in styling your text. For example, you can change the color of text, align text, add decoration properties and more.

In CSS, text can be styled using the properties listed below.

CSS Text Color

<p **style="color:olive;"**>This CSS text color is olive</p>

This results in:

This CSS text color is olive

CSS Text Align

<p **style="text-align:right;"**>This CSS text is aligned right</p>

This results in:

This CSS text is aligned right

CSS Text Indent

Indents the first line of the paragraph.

<p **style="text-indent:50px;"**>This text is indented by 50 pixels. What this means is that the first line of the paragraph will be indented by 50 pixels, but the following lines will not be indented. The text will need to wrap before you can see the indent - hence all this text!</p>

This results in:

This text is indented by 50 pixels. What this means is that the first line of the paragraph will be indented by 50 pixels, but the following lines will not be indented. The text will need to wrap before you can see the indent - hence all this text!

CSS Letter Spacing

<p **style="letter-spacing:5px;"**>This text has letter spacing applied</p>

This results in:

T h i s   t e x t   h a s   l e t t e r   s p a c i n g   a p p l i e d

CSS Word Spacing

<p **style="word-spacing:50px;"**>This text has word spacing applied</p>

This results in:

This text has word spacing applied

CSS Text Decoration

<p style="text-decoration:overline;">This text has a line over the top</p>

<p style="text-decoration:line-through;">This text has a line through the middle</p>

<p style="text-decoration:underline;">This text has a line underneath</p>

<a style="text-decoration:none;" a href="/css/properties/css_text-decoration.cfm" >

This hyperlink has no underline</a>

<p style="text-decoration:blink;">This text is blinking</p>

This results in:

This text has a line over the top

~~This text has a line through the middle~~

This text has a line underneath

This hyperlink has no underline

This text is blinking

CSS Text Transform

<p style="text-transform:uppercase;">This text has been transformed to uppercase</p>

<p style="text-transform:lowercase;">THIS TEXT HAS BEEN TRANSFORMED TO LOWERCASE</p>

<p style="text-transform:capitalize;">this text has been capitalized.</p>

This results in:

THIS TEXT HAS BEEN TRANSFORMED TO UPPERCASE

THIS TEXT HAS BEEN TRANSFORMED TO LOWERCASE

this text has been capitalized.

CSS Text Direction

<p **style="direction:rtl;"**>This text is running from right to left. This can be useful for languages where the text runs from right to left. Not so useful for english though...</p>

This results in:

This text is running from right to left. This can be useful for languages where the text runs from right to left. Not so useful for english though...

CSS Unicode-bidi

Use this in conjunction with the *direction* property to determine the direction of the text. Possible values: *normal, embed, bidi-override,* and *inherit.*

<p style="direction:rtl;**unicode-bidi:bidi-override;**">This text is running from right to left. This can be useful for languages where the text runs from right to left. Not so useful for english though...</p>

This results in:

This text is running from right to left. This can be useful for languages where the text runs from right to left. Not so useful for english though...

CSS Text Shadow

<p **style="text-shadow:4px 4px 8px blue;"**>If your browser supports the CSS text-shadow property, this text will have a shadow.</p>

This results in:

If your browser supports the CSS text-shadow property, this text will have a shadow.

CSS White Space

Tells the browser how to handle white space. Possible values: *normal, pre,* and *nowrap.*

<p **style="white-space:pre;"**>This text has a line break
and the white-space pre setting tells the browser to honor it
just like the HTML pre tag.</p>

This results in:

This text has a line break
and the white-space pre setting tells the browser to honor it
just like the HTML pre tag.

8.8 CSS BACKGROUND CODE

The following CSS background codes demonstrate the various CSS properties you can use to style the background of any HTML element.

CSS Background Color

<p **style="background-color:yellow;"**>This text has a background color applied.</p>

This results in:

This text has a background color applied.

CSS Background Image

<p style="height:100px;**background-image:url(/pix/smile.gif)**;">This text has a background image applied. </p>

This results in:

This text has a background image applied.

CSS Background Repeat

Determines whether the background image repeats (tiles) or not.

<p style="height:100px;background-image:url(/pix/smile.gif);**background-repeat:no-repeat;**">This background image does not repeat. </p>

This results in:

This background image does not repeat.

CSS Background Position

Determines the position of the background image.

<p style="height:100px;background-image:url(/pix/smile.gif);background-repeat:no-repeat;**background-position:100px;**">This background image is positioned 100 pixels in from the left. </p>

This results in:

This background image is positioned 100 pixels in from the left.

CSS Background Attachment

Determines whether or not the background image scrolls with the outer container.

<p style="height:100px;width:150px;overflow:scroll;background-image:url(/pix/smile.gif); **background-attachment:fixed;**">This background image is fixed - it doesn't scroll with its outer container. This example uses the CSS overflow property to force the box to scroll when there's too much text to fit in the box. </p>

This results in:

This background image is fixed - it doesn't scroll with its outer container. This example uses the CSS overflow property to force the box to scroll when there's too much text to fit in the box.

Shorthand Code

You can use the *background* property to set all the background properties at once. For example:

<p style="height:100px;width:150px;overflow:scroll;**background:url(/pix/smile.gif) repeat fixed;**">This paragraph tag has been styled using the 'background' property, which is shorthand for setting multiple properties for an HTML element. </p>

This results in:

This paragraph tag has been styled using the 'background' property, which is shorthand for setting multiple properties for an HTML element.

8.9 CSS BORDER

The following CSS border codes demonstrate the various CSS properties you can use to apply styles to the border of any HTML element.

CSS allows you to set styles for the border of any HTML element. It also provides you with a way of setting border styles for one or more sides of an element.

Setting Borders on All Sides

To set border styles for all sides of an element, you use the *border-width, border-style,* and *border-color* properties. You can also use the *border* property to set all properties at once.

'border-width', 'border-style', and 'border-color'

<p **style="border-width:1px;border-style:solid;border-color:blue;"**>This text has border styles applied using the border-width, border-style, and border-color properties.</p>

This results in:

This text has border styles applied using the border-width, border-style, and border-color properties.

The 'border' Property

The 'border' property is shorthand for setting border-width, border-style, and border-color.

<p **style="border:1px solid blue;"**>This text has border styles applied using the border property.</p>

This results in:

This text has border styles applied using the border property.

Border Styles

Borders can have the following styles.

<p style="border:4px **solid** blue;">This text has a border style of 'solid'.</p>
<p style="border:4px **dotted** blue;">This text has a border style of 'dotted'.</p>
<p style="border:4px **dashed** blue;">This text has a border style of 'dashed'.</p>
<p style="border:4px **double** blue;">This text has a border style of 'double'.</p>
<p style="border:4px **groove** blue;">This text has a border style of 'groove'.</p>
<p style="border:4px **ridge** blue;">This text has a border style of 'ridge'.</p>
<p style="border:4px **inset** blue;">This text has a border style of 'inset'.</p>
<p style="border:4px **outset** blue;">This text has a border style of 'outset'.</p>
<p style="border:4px **hidden** blue;">This text has a border style of 'hidden'.</p>

This results in:

This text has a border style of 'solid'.

This text has a border style of 'dotted'.

This text has a border style of 'dashed'.

This text has a border style of 'double'.

This text has a border style of 'groove'.

This text has a border style of 'ridge'.

This text has a border style of 'inset'.

This text has a border style of 'outset'.

This text has a border style of 'hidden'.

Setting Borders for Each Side

If you don't want the border settings to be applied to all four sides, or if you want each side to have different styles applied, you can use the following properties:

Explicit Properties

- border-bottom-color
- border-bottom-style
- border-bottom-width
- border-left-color
- border-left-style
- border-left-width
- border-right-color
- border-right-style
- border-right-width
- border-top-color
- border-top-style
- border-top-width

Example:

<p style="border-bottom-width:4px;border-bottom-style:double;border-bottom-color:blue;">This text has a bottom border.</p>

This results in:

This text has a bottom border.

Shorthand Properties

The following properties provide you with a more concise way of specifying border properties for each side.

- border-bottom
- border-left
- border-right

- border-top

Example:

<p **style="border-bottom:4px double blue;"**>This text has a bottom border.</p>

This results in:

This text has a bottom border.

8.10 CSS MARGIN

The following CSS margin codes demonstrate the various CSS properties you can use to apply styles to the border of any HTML element.

Margins define the space around the element. CSS margins are specified in a similar way to borders - they can be set individually for each side, or all sides at once.

Setting Margins on all Sides

<div style="border:1px solid blue;">

<p style="border:1px solid orange;**margin:20px**;">

This text has a margin of 20 pixels on all four sides.

It is nested within a div with a border to make it easier to see the effect of the margin.

</p>

</div>

This results in:

This text has a margin of 20 pixels on all four sides. It is nested within a div with a border to make it easier to see the effect of the margin.

Setting Margins for Each Side

If you don't want the margin settings to be applied to all four sides, or if you want each side to have different margins applied, you can use the following properties:

- margin-bottom
- margin-left
- margin-right
- margin-top

Example:

<p style="border:1px solid orange;**margin-left:60px**;">This text has a left margin of 60 pixels.</p>

This results in:

This text has a left margin of 60 pixels

8.11 CSS PADDING

Padding defines the space between the element's border and its content. CSS padding is specified just like margins - they can be set individually for each side, or all sides at once.

Setting Padding on All Sides

<p style="border:1px solid orange;**padding:20px;**">

This text has padding of 20 pixels on all four sides.

</p>

This results in:

This text has padding of 20 pixels on all four sides.

Setting Padding for Each Side

If you don't want the padding settings to be applied to all four sides, or if you want each side to have different padding, you can use the following properties:

- padding-bottom
- padding-left
- padding-right
- padding-top

Example:

<p style="border:1px solid orange;**padding-left:60px;**">This text has left padding of 60 pixels.</p>

This results in:

This text has left padding of 60 pixels.

8.12 CSS LISTS

CSS includes a number of list properties to help you style your HTML lists.

List Style Type

Determines what the bullet looks like.

<ul **style="list-style-type:circle;"**>

<li>List item one</li>

<li>List item two</li>

</ul>

This results in:

- List item one
- List item two

List Style Image

```
<ul style="list-style-image:url(/pix/printer_icon.gif);">
  <li>List item one</li>
  <li>List item two</li>
  </ul>
```

This results in:

- List item one
- List item two

List Style Position

Determines whether the bullet is located inside the list's containing box or outside.

```
<ul style="list-style-position:inside;">
<li>List item one</li>
<li>List item two</li>
</ul>
<ul style="list-style-position:outside;">
<li>List item one</li>
<li>List item two</li>
</ul>
```

This results in:

- List item one
- List item two
- List item one
- List item two

List Style

The list-style property is shorthand for setting the list properties.

```
<ul style="list-style:square inside;">
<li>List item one</li>
<li>List item two</li>
</ul>
```

This results in:

- List item one
- List item two

Marker Offset

Used in conjunction with *display:marker*, marker-offset specifies the nearest border edges of the marker box and its associated principal box.

```
<ul>
<li style="display:marker;marker-offset:10px;">List item one</li>
<li>List item two</li>
</ul>
```

This results in:

- List item one
- List item two

At the time of writing, browser support for marker-offset was limited.

8.13 CSS HEIGHT AND WIDTH

CSS includes height and width properties to help you specify the size of your elements.

'height' and 'width' Properties

Applies to all HTML elements except non-replaced inline elements, table columns and column groups.

Can use a fixed height (*i.e.* pixels) or a percentage height.

```
<div style="background-color:orange;height:125px;width:75px;">
This div has height and width applied.
</div>
```

This results in:

This div has height and width applied.

'max-height' and 'max-width' Properties

Enables you to constrain the height and/or width of an element to a maximum value.

```
<div style="background-color:orange;max-height:125px;max-width:75px;">
This div has max-height and max-width applied.
</div>
```

This results in:

This div has max-height and max-width applied.

'min-height' and 'min-width' Properties

Enables you to constrain the height and/or width of an element to a minimum value.

```
<div style="background-color:orange;min-height:125px;min-width:75px;">
This div has min-height and min-width applied.
</div>
```

This results in:

This div has min-height and min-width applied.

8.14 CSS POSITIONING

The term "CSS positioning" refers to using CSS to position elements on your HTML page. CSS allows you to position any element precisely where you want it. You can specify whether you want the element positioned *relative* to its natural position in the page or *absolute* based on its parent element.

Absolute positioning can be very useful for creating advanced layouts and cool visual effects such as overlapping elements to present a layered effect.

Relative Positioning

To perform relative positioning in CSS you use *position:relative;* followed by the desired offset from either *top, right, bottom* or left

```
<div style="position:relative;left:80px;background-color:yellow;">
This div has relative positioning.
</div>
```

This results in

This div has relative positioning.

This example offsets the element 80 pixels from the left of where it would have been. If we had specified top, it would appear 80 pixels below where it would have been. It's important to note that other elements are not affected by this element's offset. Therefore, overlapping may occur.

Absolute Positioning

To perform absolute positioning in CSS you use *position:absolute;* followed by the desired offset.

```
<div style="position:absolute;top:100px;left:60px;background-color:yellow;">
This div is absolutely positioned 100 pixels from the top and 60 pixels from the left of its containing block.
</div>
```

Fixed Positioning

Fixed positioning allows you to fix the position of an element to a particular spot on the page - regardless of scrolling.

```
<div style="position:fixed;top:100px;left:60px;width:180px;background-color:red;">
This div is using a fixed position of 100 pixels from the top and 60 pixels from the left of its containing block.

When this page scrolls, this box will remain in a fixed position - it won't scroll with the rest of the page.

Go on - SCROLL!
</div>
```

8.15 CSS FLOAT

The CSS float property enables you to determine where to position an element relative to the other elements on the page. When you use the float property, other elements will simply wrap around the element you applied the float to.

Example code:

```
<div style="width:300px;">
<h1 style="float:left;margin-right:10px;">CSS float</h1>
<p>If your browser supports the CSS float Property, this text will be flowing around the heading.
If this does not seem to work, it could be a browser compatibility thing...</p>
</div>
```

This results in:

CSS Float

If your browser supports the CSS float Property, this text will be flowing around the heading. If this does not seem to work, it could be a browser compatibility thing...

8.16 CSS LAYERS

In CSS, layers refer to applying the *z-index* property to elements that overlap with each other.

The z-index property, when used in conjunction with the *position* property, enables you to specify which element should appear on top in the event of an overlap. An overlap can easily occur when using the position property, and this is often desirable when creating advanced layouts.

Example code:

```
<div style="background-color:red;
width:100px;
height:100px;
position:relative;
top:10px;
left:80px;
z-index:2;">
</div>
<div style="background-color:yellow;
width:100px;
height:100px;
position:relative;
```

```
top:-60px;
left:35px;
z-index:1;">
</div>
```

This results in:

- << Previous
- **Summary >>**

CSS INTERVIEW QUESTIONS AND ANSWERS

1. *What is CSS?*

Solution: CSS stands for Cascading Style Sheets and is a simple styling language which allows attaching style to HTML elements. Every element type as well as every occurrence of a specific element within that type can be declared an unique style, e.g., margins, positioning, color or size.

2. *CSS is a web standard that describes style for XML/HTML documents.*

Solution: CSS is a language that adds style (colors, images, borders, margins…) to your site. It's really that simple. CSS is not used to put any content on your site, it's just there to take the content you have and make it pretty. First thing you do is link a CSS-file to your HTML document. Do this by adding this line:

```
<link rel="stylesheet" href="style.css"
type="text/css">
```

The line should be placed in between your <head> and </head> tags. If you have several pages you could add the exact same line to all of them and they will all use the same stylesheet, but more about that later. Let's look inside the file "style.css" we just linked to.

```
h1 {
font-size: 40px;
height: 200px;
}
.warning {
color: Red;
font-weight: bold;
}
#footer {
background-color: Gray;
}
```

Cascading Style Sheets (CSS) is a simple mechanism for adding style (e.g., fonts, colors, spacing) to Web documents. This is also where information meets the artistic abilities of a web-designer. CSS helps you spice up your web-page and make it look neat in wide variety of aspects.

3. *What are Cascading Style Sheets?*

Solution: A Cascading Style Sheet (CSS) is a list of statements (also known as rules) that can assign various rendering properties to HTML elements. Style rules can be specified for a single element occurrence, multiple elements, an entire document, or even multiple documents at once. It is possible to specify many different rules for an element in different locations using different methods. All these rules are collected and merged (known as a "cascading" of styles) when the document is rendered to form a single style rule for each element.

4. *How do I center block-elements with CSS1?*

Solution: There are two ways of centering block level elements:

1. By setting the properties margin-left and margin-right to auto and width to some explicit value:

   BODY {width: 30em; background: cyan;}

   P {width: 22em; margin-left: auto; margin-right: auto}

   In this case, the left and right margins will each be four ems wide, since they equally split up the eight ems left over from (30em - 22em). Note that it was not necessary to set an explicit width for the BODY element; it was done here to keep the math clean.

   Another example:

   TABLE {margin-left: auto; margin-right: auto; width: 400px;}

   In most legacy browsers, a table's width is by default determined by its content. In CSS-conformant browsers, the complete width of any element (including tables) defaults to the full width of its parent element's content area. As browser become more conformant, authors will need to be aware of the potential impact on their designs.

5. *If background and color should always be set together, why do they exist as separate properties?*

Solution: There are several reasons for this. First, style sheets become more legible — both for humans and machines. The background property is already the most complex property in CSS1 and combining it with color would make it even more complex. Second, color inherits, but background doesn't and this would be a source of confusion.

6. *What is class?*

Solution: Class is a group of 1) instances of the same element to which an unique style can be attached or 2) instances of different elements to which the same style can be attached.

1. The rule P {color: red} will display red text in all paragraphs. By classifying the selector P different style can be attached to each class allowing the display of some paragraphs in one style and some other paragraphs in another style.
2. A class can also be specified without associating a specific element to it and then attached to any element which is to be styled in accordance with it's declaration. All elements to which a specific class is attached will have the same style.

   To classify an element add a period to the selector followed by an unique name. The name can contain characters a-z, A-Z, digits 0-9, period, hyphen, escaped characters, Unicode characters 161-255, as well as any Unicode character as a numeric code, however, they cannot start with a dash or a digit. (Note: in HTML the value of the CLASS attribute can contain more characters). (Note: text between /* and */ are my comments).

CSS

```
P.name1 {color: red} /* one class of P selector */
P.name2 {color: blue} /* another class of P selector */
.name3 {color: green} /* can be attached to any element */
```

HTML

```
<P class=name1>This paragraph will be red</P>
<P class=name2>This paragraph will be blue</P>
<P class=name3>This paragraph will be green</P>
<LI class=name3>This list item will be green</LI>
```

It is a good practice to name classes according to their function than their appearance; e.g., P.fotnote and not P.green. In CSS1 only one class can be attached to a selector. CSS2 allows attaching more classes, e.g.:

P.name1.name2.name3 {declaration} <P class="name1 name2 name2">This paragraph has three classes attached</P>

7. *What is grouping ?*

Solution: Grouping is gathering (1) into a comma separated list two or more selectors that share the same style or (2) into a semicolon separated list two or more declarations that are attached to the same selector (2).

1. The selectors LI, P with class name .first and class .footnote share the same style, e.g.:
   LI {font-style: italic}
   P.first {font-style: italic}
   .footnote {font-style: italic}
   To reduce the size of style sheets and also save some typing time they can all be grouped in one list.
   LI, P.first, .footnote {font-style: italic}
2. The declarations {font-style: italic} and {color: red} can be attached to one selector, e.g.:
   H2 {font-style: italic}
   H2 {color: red}
   and can also be grouped into one list:
   H2 {font-style: italic; color: red}

8. *What is external Style Sheet? How to link?*

Solution: External Style Sheet is a template/document/file containing style information which can be linked with any number of HTML documents. This is a very convenient way of formatting the entire site as well as restyling it by editing just one file. The file is linked with HTML documents via the LINK element inside the HEAD element. Files containing style information must have extension .css, e.g., style.css. <HEAD> <LINK REL=STYLESHEET HREF="style.css" TYPE="text/css"> </HEAD>

9. *Is CSS case sensitive?*

Solution: Cascading Style Sheets (CSS) is not case sensitive. However, font families, URLs to images, and other direct references with the style sheet may be.

The trick is that if you write a document using an XML declaration and an XHTML doctype, then the CSS class names will be case sensitive for some browsers.

It is a good idea to avoid naming classes where the only difference is the case, for example:

div.myclass { ...}

div.myClass { ... }

If the DOCTYPE or XML declaration is ever removed from your pages, even by mistake, the last instance of the style will be used, regardless of case.

10. *Three selectors: h1, .warning and #footer, what they do ?*

Solution: An element points at a HTML-tag somewhere on your page. In the example above we want to style the <h1>-tag. Note that using an element like that affects all tags with that name, so using p { margin-left: 100px; } gives all <p>-tags a left-margin.

Using a class is just as simple. When writing .your_class you style all tags with a class with the name "your_class". In the example above we have .warning which will style e.g., <div class="warning"> and <em class="warning">, that is, any element with the class warning. Classes are used when you want to style just a few of your tags in a way, perhaps you want some of your links red? Add a class to all those links.

You need one more building block: the id. This time you style an element with the attribute "id" set to the id you have chosen. Ids work exactly like classes except for one thing; you can only have one id with a certain name in each of your HTML documents. In the example above we style <div id="footer">. If you look at the example it does make sense: a HTML document may contain several warnings but only one footer. Ids should be used when you want to style just one specific tag.

Using those three building blocks will take you far but when you get to more advanced layouts you might want to combine the building blocks into more advanced selectors. Just to give you two examples of what you can do: em.warning to style only those <em>-tags with the class .warning set. You can also use #footer a to style only the links that are nested inside the tag with id "footer".

Each of the selectors has a set of declarations tied to them. Each declaration has a property, describing what we want to change and a value, what we should change it to. An example: a { color: Blue; font-size: 3em; }. You have the selector a there, so all links in your document will be styled. We have two declarations: color: Blue and font-size: 3em;. Lastly each declaration consists of two parts: the property color and the value Blue.

there is a LOT of things you can style and play with. Additionally (close to) all tags are equal in CSS, so you can set e.g. borders and colors of any element just like you could with a table if you used only HTML.

11. *What are Style Sheets?*

Solution: Style Sheets are templates, very similar to templates in desktop publishing applications, containing a collection of rules declared to various selectors (elements).

12. *What is CSS rule 'ruleset'?*

Solution: There are two types of CSS rules: ruleset and at-rule. Ruleset identifies selector or selectors and declares style which is to be attached to that selector or selectors. For example P {text-indent: 10pt} is a CSS rule. CSS rulesets consist of two parts: selector, e.g., P and declaration, e.g., {text-indent: 10pt}.

P {text-indent: 10pt} - CSS rule (ruleset)

{text-indent: 10pt} - CSS declaration

text-indent - CSS property

10pt - CSS value

13. *What is embedded style? How to link?*

Solution: Embedded style is the style attached to one specific document. The style information is specified as a content of the STYLE element inside the HEAD element and will apply to the entire document.

```
<HEAD>
<STYLE TYPE="text/css">
<!—
P {text-indent: 10pt}
—>
</STYLE>
</HEAD>
```

Note: The styling rules are written as a HTML comment, that is, between <!— and —> to hide the content in browsers without CSS support which would otherwise be displayed.

14. *What is ID selector?*

Solution: ID selector is an individually identified (named) selector to which a specific style is declared. Using the ID attribute the declared style can then be associated with one and only one HTML element per document as to differentiate it from all other elements. ID selectors are created by a character # followed by the selector's name. The name can contain characters a-z, A-Z, digits 0-9, period, hyphen, escaped characters, Unicode characters 161-255, as well as any Unicode character as a numeric code, however, they cannot start with a dash or a digit.

```
#abc123 {color: red; background: black}
<P ID=abc123>This and only this element can be identified as abc123 </P>
```

15. *What is contextual selector?*

Solution: Contextual selector is a selector that addresses specific occurrence of an element. It is a string of individual selectors separated by white space, a search pattern, where only the last element in the pattern is addressed providing it matches the specified context.

```
TD P CODE {color: red}
```

The element CODE will be displayed in red but only if it occurs in the context of the element P which must occur in the context of the element TD.

TD P CODE, H1 EM {color: red}

The element CODE will be displayed in red as described above AND the element EM will also be red but only if it occurs in the context of H1

P .footnote {color: red}

Any element with CLASS footnote will be red but only if it occurs in the context of P

P .footnote [lang]{color: red}

Any element with attribute LANG will be red but only if it is classed as "footnote" and occurs in the context of P

16. *How do I have a background image that isn't tiled?*

Solution: Specify the background-repeat property as no-repeat. You can also use the background property as a shortcut for specifying multiple background-* properties at once. Here's an example:

BODY {background: #FFF url(watermark.jpg) no-repeat;}

17. *What does \ABCD (and \ABCDE) mean?*

Solution: CSS allows Unicode characters to be entered by number. For example, if a CLASS value in some Russian document contains Cyrillic letters EL PE (Unicode numbers 041B and 041F) and you want to write a style rule for that class, you can put that letter into the style sheet by writing:

.\041B\041F {font-style: italic;}

This works on all keyboards, so you don't need a Cyrillic keyboard to write CLASS names in Russian or another language that uses that script.

The digits and letters after the backslash (\) are a hexadecimal number. Hexadecimal numbers are made from ordinary digits and the letters A to F (or a to f). Unicode numbers consist of four such digits.

If the number starts with a 0, you may omit it. The above could also be written as:

.\41B\41F {font-style: italic;}

But be careful if the next letter after the three digits is also a digit or a letter a to f! This is OK: .\41B-\41F, since the dash (-) cannot be mistaken for a hexadecimal digit, but .\41B9\41F is only two letters, not three.

Four digits is the maximum, however, so if you write:

.\041B9\041F {font-style: italic;}

18. *Three selectors: h1, .warning and #footer, what they do ?*

Solution: An element points at a HTML-tag somewhere on your page. In the example above we want to style the <h1>-tag. Note that using an element like that affects all tags with that name, so using p { margin-left: 100px; } gives all <p>-tags a left-margin.

Using a class is just as simple. When writing .your_class you style all tags with a class with the name "your_class". In the example above we have .warning which will style e.g., <div class="warning"> and <em class="warning">, that is, any element with the class warning. Classes are used when you want to style just a few of your tags in a way, perhaps you want some of your links red? Add a class to all those links.

You need one more building block: the id. This time you style an element with the attribute "id" set to the id you have chosen. Ids work exactly like classes except for one thing; you can only have one id with a certain name in each of your HTML documents. In the example above we style <div id="footer">. If you look at the example it does make sense: a HTML document may contain several warnings but only one footer. Ids should be used when you want to style just one specific tag.

Using those three building blocks will take you far but when you get to more advanced layouts you might want to combine the building blocks into more advanced selectors. Just to give you two examples of what you can do: em.warning to style only those <em>-tags with the class.warning set. You can also use #footer a to style only the links that are nested inside the tag with id "footer.

Each of the selectors has a set of declarations tied to them. Each declaration has a property, describing what we want to change and a value, what we should change it to. An example: a {color: Blue; font-size: 3em;}. You have the selector a there, so all links in your document will be styled. We have two declarations: color: Blue and font-size: 3em;. Lastly each declaration consists of two parts: the property color and the value Blue.

there is a LOT of things you can style and play with. Additionally (close to) all tags are equal in CSS, so you can set e.g., borders and colors of any element just like you could with a table if you used only HTML.

19. *What are Style Sheets?*

Solution: Style Sheets are templates, very similar to templates in desktop publishing applications, containing a collection of rules declared to various selectors (elements).

20. *What is CSS rule 'ruleset'?*

Solution: There are two types of CSS rules: ruleset and at-rule. Ruleset identifies selector or selectors and declares style which is to be attached to that selector or selectors. For example P {text-indent: 10pt} is a CSS rule. CSS rulesets consist of two parts: selector, e.g., P and declaration, e.g., {text-indent: 10pt}.

P {text-indent: 10pt} - CSS rule (ruleset)

{text-indent: 10pt} - CSS declaration

text-indent - CSS property

10pt - CSS value

MULTIPLE CHOICE QUESTIONS

1. What does CSS stand for?

(*a*) Creative Style Sheets
(*b*) Computer Style Sheets
(*c*) Cascading Style Sheets
(*d*) Cascade Style Sheets

(*e*) Colorful Style Sheets

2. Where in an HTML document is the correct place to refer to an external style sheet?
   (*a*) In the <body> section (*b*) At the end of the document
   (*c*) At the top of the document (*d*) In the <head> section
   (*e*) Between head and body
3. Which HTML tag is used to define an internal style sheet?
   (*a*) css (*b*) text/style (*c*) style (*d*) script
4. Which HTML attribute is used to define inline styles?
   (*a*) font (*b*) styles (*c*) css (*d*) text
   (*e*) style
5. Which is the correct CSS syntax?
   (*a*) body {color: black} (*b*) body:color=black
   (*c*) {body:color=black(body} (*d*) {body;color:black}
6. How do you insert a comment in a CSS file?
   (*a*) /* this is a comment */ (*b*) ' this is a comment
   (*c*) // this is a comment // (*d*) // this is a comment
7. Which property is used to change the background color?
   (*a*) bgcolor: (*b*) background-color:
   (*c*) color:
8. How do you add a background color for all "<h1>" elements?
   (*a*) all.h1 {background-color:#FFFFFF} (*b*) h1.all {background-color:#FFFFFF}
   (*c*) h1 {background-color:#FFFFFF}
9. How do you change the text color of an element?
   (*a*) text-color: (*b*) color: (*c*) text-color= (*d*) font-color:
10. Which CSS property controls the text size?
    (*a*) font-style (*b*) text-style (*c*) font-size (*d*) text-size
11. What is the correct CSS syntax for making all the <p> elements bold?
    (*a*) p {text-size:bold} (*b*) p {font-weight:bold}
    (*c*) style:bold (*d*) p{font:bold}
12. How do you display hyperlinks without an underline?
    (*a*) a {decoration:no underline} (*b*) a {text-decoration:no underline}
    (*c*) a {underline:none} (*d*) a {text-decoration:none}
13. How do you make each word in a text start with a capital letter?
    (*a*) text-transform:uppercase (*b*) text-transform:capitalize
    (*c*) You can't do that with CSS
14. How do you change the font of an element?
    (*a*) fon-face: (*b*) font-family: (*c*) f: (*d*) font-style:
15. How do you make the text bold?
    (*a*) font:b (*b*) style:bold
    (*c*) font-weight:bold
16. How do you display a border like this: The top border = 10 pixels, The bottom border = 5 pixels, The left border = 20 pixels, The right border = 1pixel?

(*a*) border-width:10px 20px 5px 1px
(*b*) border-width:10px 1px 5px 20px
(*c*) border-width:10px 5px 20px 1px
(*d*) border-width:5px 20px 10px 1px

17. How do you change the left margin of an element?
(*a*) padding: (*b*) indent: (*c*) margin: (*d*) text-indent:

18. To define the space between the element's border and content, you use the padding property, but are you allowed to use negative values?
(*a*) Yes (*b*) No

19. How do you make a list that lists its items with squares?
(*a*) type: square
(*b*) list-style-type: square
(*c*) list-type: square
(*d*) style-list: square

20. What is the correct HTML for referring to an external style sheet?
(*a*) <link rel="stylesheet" type="text/css" href="mainstyle.css">
(*b*) <style src="mainstyle.css">
(*c*) <stylesheet>mainstyle.css</stylesheet>
(*d*) <link url="stylesheet" type="text/css" href="mainstyle.css">

21. Which HTML tag is used to define an internal style sheet?
(*a*) <script> (*b*) <css> (*c*) <stylesheet> (*d*) <style>

22. Which HTML attribute is used to define inline styles?
(*a*) styles (*b*) class (*c*) font (*d*) style

23. What is the correct CSS syntax for making all the <p> elements bold?
(*a*) p {font-weight:bold}
(*b*) p {text-size:bold}
(*c*) <p style="text-size:bold">
(*d*) <p style="font-size:bold">

24. How do you make each word in a text start with a capital letter?
(*a*) text-transform:capitalize
(*b*) ext-transform:uppercase
(*c*) You can't do that with CSS

25. How do you change the left margin of an element?
(*a*) left-margin: (*b*) margin: (*c*) margin-left: (*d*) text-indent:

26. What are the three methods for using style sheets with a web page
(*a*) Dreamweaver, GoLive or FrontPage
(*b*) Inline, embedded or document level and external
(*c*) Handcoded, Generated or WYSIWYG

Answers of Multiple Choice Questions

1. (*c*),	**2.** (*d*),	**3.** (*c*),	**4.** (*e*),	**5.** (*a*),
6. (*a*),	**7.** (*b*),	**8.** (*c*),	**9.** (*b*),	**10.** (*c*),
11. (*b*),	**12.** (*d*),	**13.** (*b*),	**14.** (*b*),	**15.** (*c*),
16. (*b*),	**17.** (*e*),	**18.** (*b*),	**19.** (*b*),	**20.** (*a*),
21. (*d*),	**22.** (*d*),	**23.** (*a*),	**24.** (*b*),	**25.** (*c*),
26. (*b*).				

EXERCISE

1. What do you mean by style sheets?
2. What are the different ways for creating Style Sheet?
3. Apply a style rule to <H1> tag by specifying it in the style attributes.
4. How will you group style rules?
5. What are the padding properties?
6. What are the font properties?
7. What are the Box properties?
8. What are simple selectors?
9. What are HTML selectors?
10. What are class selectors?
11. What is the difference between ID and class selectors?
12. What are contextual selectors?
13. What is the procedure for linking a Style sheet?
14. What are text properties?
15. What are color and Background properties?
16. What are embedding style sheet?

9

JavaScript

9.0 INTRODUCTION

JavaScript enables you to build interactivity into your web pages. Using JavaScript, you can create drop down menus, add validation to your forms, display the date, and much more.

9.1 WHAT IS JAVASCRIPT?

JavaScript is a scripting language that enables web developers/designers to build more functional and interactive websites.

Common uses of JavaScript include:

- Alert messages
- Popup windows
- Dynamic dropdown menus
- Form validation
- Displaying date/time

JavaScript usually runs on the *client-side* (the browser's side), as opposed to *server-side* (on the web server). One benefit of doing this is performance. On the client side, JavaScript is loaded into the browser and can run as soon as it is called. Without running on the client side, the page would need to refresh each time you needed a script to run.

9.1.1 What do I Need to Create JavaScript?

You can create JavaScript using the same equipment you use when creating HTML. That is:

- Computer
- Text editor. For example, Notepad (for Windows), Pico (for Linux), or Simpletext (Mac). You could use a HTML editor if you like but it's not needed.
- Web Browser. For example, Internet Explorer or Firefox. You will need to ensure JavaScript is enabled within your browser's settings (this is normally enabled by default).

9.1.2 How to Enable JavaScript?

To view webpages with JavaScript, you need to ensure your browser has JavaScript enabled. Generally speaking, you can still view the webpage without JavaScript, but you will not be able to take advantage of the JavaScript functionality.

How do I check if my browser has JavaScript enabled?

You normally do this by checking your browser's *options*. This will depend on the browser you're using. Instructions for some of the more common browsers are below:

Internet Explorer (6.0):

1. Go to *Tools* from the top menu
2. Select *Internet Options*
3. Click on the *Security* tab
4. Click *Custom Level*
5. Scroll down until you see the *Scripting* section
6. Ensure that the *Active Scripting* option is set at *Enabled*
7. Click *OK*

Netscape Navigator (4.8):

1. Go to *Edit* from the top menu
2. Select *Preferences*
3. Select *Advanced*
4. Select *Scripts and Plugins*
5. Check the *Enable JavaScript* checkbox
6. Click *OK*

Mozilla Firefox (1.0):

1. Go to *Tools* from the top menu
2. Select *Options*
3. Select *Web Features* from the left menu
4. Ensure the *Enable JavaScript* option is checked
5. Click *OK*

Mozilla Firefox (1.5):

1. Go to *Tools* from the top menu
2. Select *Options*
3. Click on the *Content* button
4. Ensure that the *Enable JavaScript* option is checked
5. Click *OK*

Apple Safari (1.0):

1. Go to *Safari* from the top menu
2. Select *Preferences*
3. Select *Security*
4. Ensure that the *Enable JavaScript* option is checked
5. Click *OK*

9.1.3 How do I Disable JavaScript?

You simply go through the steps above but ensure the JavaScript options are not checked/selected.

If you're developing web pages with JavaScript, it's good practice to view your website with JavaScript disabled. This will show you what your website will look like to users who choose to disable JavaScript.

Other Browsers?

Most (if not all browsers) give you the option to enable/disable JavaScript. If your browser is not listed above, the steps above will give you some idea of how to find it. Just look for something called *tools, options, preferences* or something similar.

9.2 JAVASCRIPT SYNTAX

JavaScript syntax refers to a set of rules that determine how the language will be written (by the programmer) and interpreted (by the browser).

The JavaScript syntax is loosely based on the Java syntax. Java is a full blown programming environment and JavaScript could be seen as a sub-set of the Java syntax. Having said this, that is where the similarities end - Java and JavaScript are two totally different things.

In learning JavaScript you will become familiar with terms such as *variables, functions, statements, operators, data types, objects* etc.

Example Code

```
<script type="text/javascript">
<!--
        document.write("JavaScript is not Java");
-->
</script>
```

This results in:

JavaScript is not Java

The above example is how you write text to a web page using JavaScript.

Explanation of Code

- The <script> tags tell the browser to expect a script in between them. You specify the language using the type attribute. The most popular scripting language on the web is JavaScript.

- The bits that look like HTML comments tag (<-- -->) are just that - HTML comment tags. These are optional but recommended. They tell browsers that don't support JavaScript (or with JavaScript disabled) to ignore the code in between. This prevents the code from being written out to your website users.
- The part that writes the actual text is only 1 line (document.write("JavaScript is not Java");). This is how you write text to a web page in JavaScript. This is an example of using a JavaScript function (also known as *method*).

Where to Put Your Scripts?

You can place your scripts in any of the following locations:

- Between the HTML document's head tags.
- Within the HTML document's body (i.e. between the body tags).
- In an external file (and link to it from your HTML document).

9.3 TYPES OF POPUPS

JavaScript has three different types of popup box available for you to use. Here they are:

Alert

Displays a message to the user. Example:

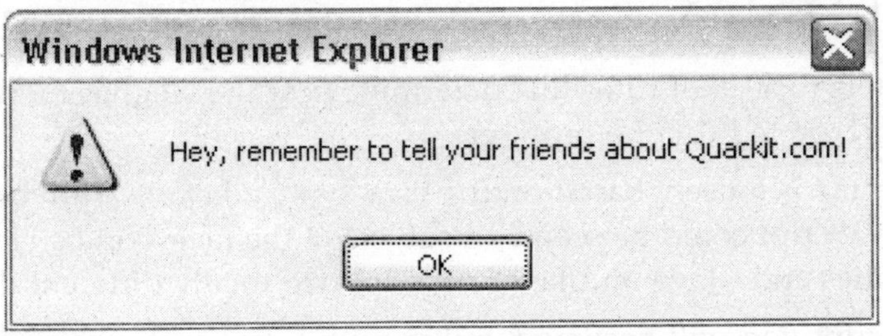

Confirm

Asks the user to confirm something. Often, this is in conjunction with another (potentially significant) action that the user is attempting to perform. Example:

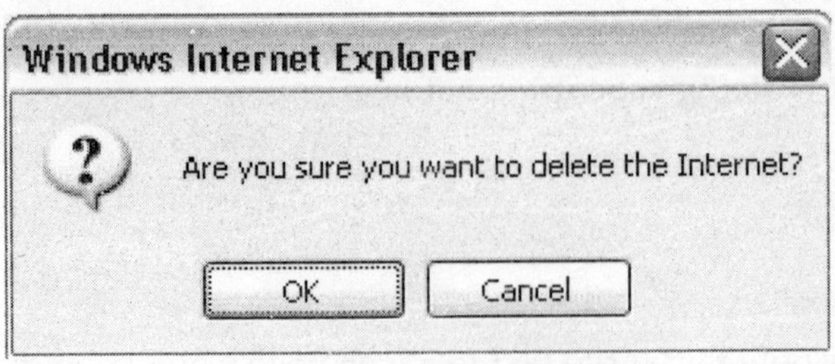

Prompt

Prompts the user for information. Example:

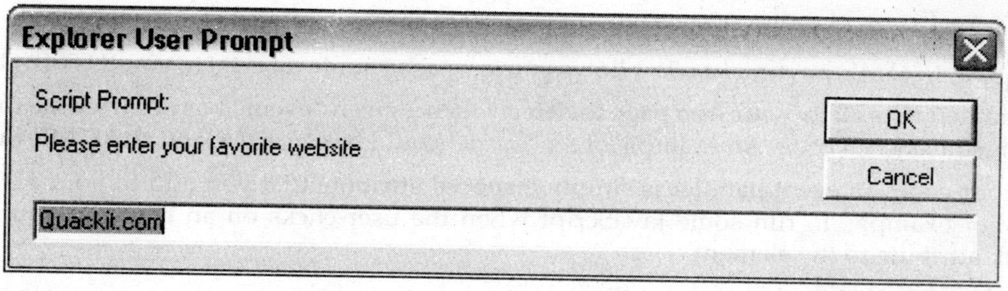

Popup Code

Here's the syntax for specifying popup boxes, along with some examples.

Type of Popup	Syntax	Example Code	Example Display
Alert	alert("Message");	alert("See the book on web technology");	
Confirm	confirm("Message");	confirm("Are you sure you want to delete the Internet?");	
Prompt	prompt("Message", "Default response");	prompt(Read the bokk on web technology very carefully);	

Note that the user's browser determines what the popup box actually looks like. This is because our popup code is simply telling the browser to "display this type of popup with this message". It is up to the browser to render the correct type of popup with the specified message.

9.4 INTEGATING JAVASCRIPT WITH HTML

You will have noticed that the (above) example popups didn't appear as soon as you loaded this page. They only appeared after you clicked the relevant button. This is because I placed code into each HTML button, so that when it was clicked, it triggered off our JavaScript.

This is a very common way of using JavaScript on the web. By "attaching" JavaScript to our HTML elements, we can make our pages much more responsive to our users' actions.

Standalone JavaScript

First, let's look at what a standalone piece of JavaScript looks like.

```
<script type="text/javascript">
<!--
        alert('Hey, remember to tell your friends about Quackit.com!');
-->
</script>
```

If we place the above JavaScript between the 'head' tags (or 'body' tags), it will run as soon as we load the page.

Now this is fine - as long as you want it to run as soon as the page loads!

But, what if you don't want it to run as soon as the page loads? What if you only want it to run when a user clicks on a button?

Easy! This is where you need to use an "event handler".

What's an Event Handler?

In JavaScript/HTML, an *event handler* allows you to attach your JavaScript to your HTML elements.

Event handlers allow your web page to detect when a given "event" has occurred, so that it can run some JavaScript code. An example of an "event" could be say, a click on an HTML element.

In your code, an event handler is simply a special attribute that you add to your HTML element. For example, to run some JavaScript when the user clicks on an element, you add the onClick attribute to the element.

The examples below demonstrate this for you.

Adding JavaScript to an HTML Element

Here's a basic example of adding JavaScript to an HTML element. In this case, when the user clicks on our button, a JavaScript alert box is displayed. This is done by adding an onClick attribute and placing the JavaScript alert box code into it.

When you use JavaScript like this, you don't need to use script tags (like we did above). Simply place your JavaScript within the event handler and it will work.

Code:

<input type="button" **onClick="alert('Hey, remember to tell your friends about Quackit.com!');"** value="Click Me!" />

Result:

JavaScript "On Double Click"

You could just have easily used another event to trigger the same JavaScript. For example, you could run JavaScript only when the double clicks the HTML element. We can do this using the onDblClick event handler.

Code:

<input type="button" **onDblClick="alert('Hey, remember to tell your friends about Quackit.com!');"** value="Double Click Me!" />

Result:

There are plenty of other event handlers you can use within your JavaScript/HTML code. In total, there are 18 event handlers (as listed by the W3C).

Complex Code

Once you become well versed in JavaScript, you'll be able to write some complex programs using lots of code. When this happens, you'll want to place your code into a "function". We'll cover functions later but, for now, understand that you'll be able to call your function just like we call the JavaScript alert() function in the above examples - using event handlers.

ns this in more detaExternal JavaScript File

You can place all your scripts into an external file (with a .js extension), then link to that file from within your HTML document. This is handy if you need to use the same scripts across multiple HTML pages, or a whole website.

To link to an external JavaScript file, you add a src attribute to your HTML script tag and specify the location of the external JavaScript file.

Linking to an External JavaScript File

<script style="text/javascript" **src="external_javascript.js"**></script>

Contents of Your External JavaScript File

The code in your .js file should be no different to the code you would normally have placed in between the script tags. But remember, you don't need to create script tag again — it is already on the HTML page calling the external file!

9.5 JAVASCRIPT OPERATORS

JavaScript operators are used to perform an operation. There are different types of operators for different uses.

Below is a listing of JavaScript operators and a brief description of them. Don't worry if you don't understand all of them at this stage - just bookmark this page for reference and return whenever you need to.

Arithmetic Operators

Operator	Description
+	Addition
–	Subtraction
*	Multiplication
/	Division
%	Modulus (remainder of a division)
++	Increment
--	Decrement

Assignment Operators

Operator	Description
=	Assign
+=	Add and assign. For example, x+=y is the same as x=x+y.
-=	Subtract and assign. For example, x-=y is the same as x=x-y.
*=	Multiply and assign. For example, x*=y is the same as x=x*y.
/=	Divide and assign. For example, x/=y is the same as x=x/y.
%=	Modulus and assign. For example, x%=y is the same as x=x%y.

Comparison Operators

Operator	Description
==	Is equal to
===	Is identical (is equal to and is of the same type)
!=	Is not equal to

!==	Is not identical
>	Greater than
>=	Greater than or equal to
<	Less than
<=	Less than or equal to

Logical/boolean Operators

Operator	Description
&&	and
||	or
!	not

String Operators

In JavaScript, a *string* is simply a piece of text.

Operator	Description
=	Assignment
+	Concatenate (join two strings together)
+=	Concatenate and assign

9.6 JAVASCRIPT VARIABLES

Like other programming languages, JavaScript variables are a container that contains a value - a value that can be changed as required.

For example, you could prompt your website users for their first name. When they enter their first name you could store it in a variable called say, firstName. Now that you have the user's first name assigned to a variable, you could do all sorts of things with it like display a personalised welcome message back to the user for example. By using a variable to store the user's first name, you can write one piece of code for all your users.

Declaring JavaScript Variables

First, you need to declare your variables. You do this using the var keyword. You can declare one variable at a time or more than one. You can also assign values to the variables at the time you declare them.

Different Methods of Declaring JavaScript Variables

```
// declaring one javascript variable
var firstName;

// declaring multiple javascript variables
var firstName, lastName;

// declaring and assigning one javascript variable
```

```
var firstName = 'Homer';

// declaring and assigning multiple javascript variables
var firstName = 'Homer', lastName = 'Simpson';
```

Using JavaScript Variables

Although there are many uses for JavaScript variables, here is a quick and dirty example:

```
<script language="javascript" type="text/javascript" >

<!-- hide me
var firstName = prompt("What's your first name?", "");
// end hide -->

<!-- hide me
document.write(firstName);
// end hide -->

</script>
```

The above example opens a JavaScript prompt, prompting the user for their first name. It will then write the name to the page (in practice, you would output the name somewhere between the <body></body> tags).

I suspect you can find a much better use for your javascript variables but this simply to demonstrate how easily you can store data inside a variable - data that could change at any moment.

Rules for JavaScript Variables

- Can contain any letter of the alphabet, digits 0-9, and the underscore character.
- No spaces
- No punctuation characters (*e.g.*, comma, full stop, etc)
- The first character of a variable name cannot be a digit.
- JavaScript variables' names are case-sensitive. For example *firstName* and *FirstName* are two different variables.

9.7 JAVASCRIPT FUNCTIONS

In JavaScript, you will use functions a lot. A function (also known as a *method*) is a self-contained piece of code that performs a particular "function". You can recognise a function by its format - it's a piece of descriptive text, followed by open and close brackets.

Sometimes there will be text in between the brackets. This text is known as an *argument*. An argument is passed to the function to provide it with further info that it needs to process. This info could be different depending on the context in which the function is being called.

Arguments can be extremely handy, such as allowing your users to provide information (say via a form) that is passed to a function to process. For example, your users could enter their name into a form, and the function would take that name, do some processing, then present them with a personalised message that includes their name.

A function doesn't actually do anything until it is called. Once it is called, it takes any arguments, then performs it's function (whatever that may be).

Writing a Function in JavaScript

It's not that hard to write a function in JavaScript. Here's an example of a JavaScript function.

Write the function:

```
<script type="text/javascript">
<!--
function displayMessage(firstName) {
   alert("Hello " + firstName + ", hope you like JavaScript functions!")
}
//-->
</script>
```

Call the function:

```
<form>
First name:
<input type="input" name="yourName" />
<input
 type="button"
 onclick="displayMessage(form.yourName.value)"
 value="Display Message" />
</form>
```

This should work like this:

Top of Form

First name:

Bottom of Form

Explanation of code

Writing the function:

1. We started by using the *function* keyword. This tells the browser that a function is about to be defined
2. Then we gave the function a name, so we made up our own name called "displayMessage". We specified the name of an argument ("firstName") that will be passed in to this function.
3. After the function name came a curly bracket {. This opens the function. There is also a closing bracket later, to close the function.
4. In between the curly brackets we write all our code for the function. In this case, we use JavaScript's built in alert() function to pop up a message for the user.

Calling the function:

1. We created an HTML form with an input field and submit button
2. We assigned a name ("yourName") to the input field
3. We added the onclick *event handler* to the button. This event handler is called when the user clicks on the button (more about event handlers later). This is where we call our JavaScript function from. We pass it the value from the form's input field. We can reference this value by using "form.yourName.value".

9.8 JAVASCRIPT EVENTS

There are 18 event handlers that you can use to link your HTML elements to a piece of JavaScript.

When you write a JavaScript function, you will need to determine when it will run. Often, this will be when a user does something like click or hover over something, submit a form, double clicks on something etc.

These are examples of *events*.

Using JavaScript, you can respond to an event using event handlers. You can attach an event handler to the HTML element for which you want to respond to when a specific event occurs.

For example, you could attach JavaScript's onMouseover event handler to a button and specify some JavaScript to run whenever this event occurs against that button.

The HTML 4 specification refers to these as intrinsic events and defines 18 as listed below:

Event Handler	Event that it Handles
onBlur	User has left the focus of the object. For example, they clicked away from a text field that was previously selected.
onChange	User has changed the object, then attempts to leave that field (*i.e.*, clicks elsewhere).
onClick	User clicked on the object.
onDblClick	User clicked twice on the object.
onFocus	User brought the focus to the object (*i.e.*, clicked on it/tabbed to it)
onKeydown	A key was pressed over an element.
onKeyup	A key was released over an element.
onKeypress	A key was pressed over an element then released.
onLoad	The object has loaded.
onMousedown	The cursor moved over the object and mouse/pointing device was pressed down.
onMouseup	The mouse/pointing device was released after being pressed down.
onMouseover	The cursor moved over the object (*i.e.*, user hovers the mouse over the object).
onMousemove	The cursor moved while hovering over an object.
onMouseout	The cursor moved off the object
onReset	User has reset a form.
onSelect	User selected some or all of the contents of the object. For example, the user selected some text within a text field.
onSubmit	User submitted a form.
onUnload	User left the window (*i.e.*, user closes the browser window).

The events in the above table provide you with many opportunities to trigger some JavaScript from within your HTML code.

I encourage you to bookmark this page as a reference - later on you may need a reminder of which events you can use when solvingJavaScript If Statements

When you write code, you will often need to use *conditional statements*.

A conditional statement refers to a piece of code that does one thing based on one condition, and another based on another condition. In fact, you could have as many conditions as you like.

JavaScript If statements are an example of conditional statements. With If statements, you can tell the browser to execute a piece of code only **if** a given condition is true.

Example If Statement:

```
<script type="text/javascript">
<!--
var myColor = "Blue";

if (myColor == "Blue") {
        document.write("Just like the sky!");
    }
//-->
</script>
```

The resulting output:

Just like the sky!

Explanation of Code

We first declare a variable called "myColor" and set the value to "Blue". We then use a JavaScript if statement to test if the value of the variable is "Blue". If it is, we output some text to the user.

9.9 TO CREATE A JAVASCRIPT IF STATEMENT

<the do statements, if JavaScript a construct>

1. Start with the word "if"
2. Between open and closed brackets, write the actual condition that is being tested (*i.e.* if something is equal to something else).
3. Between open and closed **curly** brackets (or braces), specify what will happen if the condition is satisfied.

JavaScript If Else Statement

The above code is OK if you only want to display something when the condition is true. But what if you want to display something when the condition isn't true. For example, what if the variable "myColor" was equal to, say, "red"?

This is where an If Else statement comes in handy. The "Else" part is what we're interested in here. The "Else" is what tells the browser what to do if the condition is not true.

Example If Else statement:

```
<script type="text/javascript">
<!--
var myColor = "Red";

if (myColor == "Blue") {
        document.write("Just like the sky!");
        }
else {
        document.write("Didn't pick blue huh?");
}
//-->
</script>
```

The resulting output:

Didn't pick blue huh?

Explanation of Code

The first part of this code is the same as the previous example. The second part is where we specify what to do if the condition is not true. . Therefore, you write "else" followed by what you want to occur, surrounded by curly braces.

1. Write an if statement (as per first example)
2. Follow this with the word "else"
3. Between open and closed **curly** brackets (or braces), specify what to do next.

JavaScript If Else If Statement

The If Else If statement is more powerful than the previous two. This is because you can specify many different outputs based on many different conditions - all within the one statement. You can also end with an "else" to specify what to do if none of the conditions are true.

Example If Else If Statement:

```
<script type="text/javascript">
<!--
var myColor = "Red";

if (myColor == "Blue") {
        document.write("Just like the sky!");
        }
else if (myColor = "Red") {
        document.write("Just like shiraz!");
}
else {
        document.write("Suit yourself then...");
```

```
}
//-->
</script>
```

The resulting output:

Just like shiraz!

Explanation of Code

We started with an "if" and ended with an "else", however, in the middle, we used an "else if" statement to specify what to do if the "myColor" variable was equal to Red. This statement looks exactly like the "if" statement - just with an "else" prepended to it.

By the way, we could have specified as many "else if" conditions as we liked.

If you do have many "else if" conditions, you might consider using a JavaScript "Switch" statement. The Switch statement is explained in the next lesson. a particular coding issue.

JavaScript Switch Statement

In the previous lesson about JavaScript If statements, we learned that we can use an If Else If statement to test for multiple conditions, then output a different result for each condition.

For example, if the variable "myColor" was equal to "Blue", we could output one message. If it is "Red" we could output another etc

Another way of doing this is to use the JavaScript Switch statement. An advantage of using the switch statement is that it uses less code, which is better if you have a lot of conditions that you need to check for.

Example Switch Statement:

Here, we will re-write the last example in the previous lesson into a switch statement.

```
<script type="text/javascript">
<!--
var myColor = "Red";

switch (myColor)
{
case "Blue":
        document.write("Just like the sky!");
        break
case "Red":
        document.write("Just like shiraz!");
        break
default:
        document.write("Suit yourself then...");
}
//-->
</script>
```

The resulting output:

Just like shiraz!

Explanation of Code

We started by declaring a variable called "myColor" and setting it to "Red". We then opened a switch statement, passing in the variable we want to test (myColor). This is followed by a set of "cases" within curly braces. We add a "default" condition, which is only executed if none of the above cases are true. It's important to use "break" after each case - this prevents the code from running into the next case.

1. We started by declaring a variable called "myColor" and setting it to "Red"
2. We then opened a switch statement, passing in the variable we want to test (myColor)
3. This is followed by a set of "cases" within curly braces. It's important to use "break" after each case - this prevents the code from running into the next case.

Prior to the closing bracket, we add a "default" condition, which is only executed if none of the above caJavaScript While Loop

In JavaScript and most other languages, "loops" enable your program to continuously execute a block of code for a given number of times, or while a given condition is true.

The JavaScript While loop executes code **while** a condition is true.

For example, you could make your program display a the value of a counter while the count is less than or equal to say, 10.

Example While Statement:

```
<script type="text/javascript">
<!--
var myBankBalance = 0;
while (myBankBalance <= 10) {
document.write("My bank balance is $" + myBankBalance + " ");
myBankBalance ++;
}
//-->
</script>
```

The resulting output:

Right now, my bank balance is $0

Right now, my bank balance is $1

Right now, my bank balance is $2

Right now, my bank balance is $3

Right now, my bank balance is $4

Right now, my bank balance is $5

Right now, my bank balance is $6

Right now, my bank balance is $7

Right now, my bank balance is $8
Right now, my bank balance is $9
Right now, my bank balance is $10

Explanation of Code

1. We started by declaring a variable called "myBankBalance" and setting it to 0
2. We then opened a while loop, inserting our condition between brackets. Our condition checks if the current value of the myBankBalance variable is less than or equal to 10.
3. This is followed by code to execute while the condition is true. In this case, we are simply, outputting the current value of myBankBalance, preceded by some text. This code is placed within curly braces.
4. We then increment the value by 1.
5. When the browser reaches the closing curly brace, if the condition is still true, it goes back to the first curly brace and executes the code again. Of course, by now, the myBankBalance variable has been incremented by 1. If the condition is not true (*i.e.*, the variable is greater than 10), it exits from the loop.
6. Ses are true

9.10 JAVASCRIPT FOR LOOP

We know that "loops" enable your program to continuously execute a block of code for a given number of times, or while a given condition is true.

In that lesson, we saw that the While loop executes code **while** a condition is true.

In this lesson, we will see that the JavaScript For loop executes code **for** a specified number of times.

Therefore, we could rewrite the example from the previous lesson to use a for loop.

Example for Statement:

```
<script type="text/javascript">
<!--
var myBankBalance = 0;
for (myBankBalance = 0; myBankBalance <= 10; myBankBalance++)
{
document.write("My bank balance is $" + myBankBalance + " ");
}
//-->
</script>
```

The resulting output:
My bank balance is $0
My bank balance is $1
My bank balance is $2

My bank balance is $3

My bank balance is $4

My bank balance is $5

My bank balance is $6

My bank balance is $7

My bank balance is $8

My bank balance is $9

My bank balance is $10

Explanation of Code

1. We started by declaring a variable called "myBankBalance" and setting it to 0
2. We then opened a for loop with our condition between brackets. Our condition sets a value to our variable, checks if the current value of the variable is less than or equal to 10, then increments the value by 1.
3. This is followed by code to execute while the condition is true. In this case, we are simply, outputting the current value of myBankBalance, preceded by some text. This code is placed within curly braces.
4. When the browser reaches the closing curly brace, if the condition is still true, it goes back to the first curly brace and executes the code again. Of course, by now, the myBankBalance variable has been incremented by 1. If the condition is not true (i.e., the variable is greater than 10), it exits from the loop.

JavaScript Try... Catch

The more JavaScript you code the more errors you'll encounter. This is a fact of life in any programming environment. Nobody's perfect and, once your scripts become more complex, you'll find there are sometimes scenarios that result in an error that you didn't think of.

JavaScript errors on web pages can scare your visitors away. How many times have you encountered a web page with errors, only to click the "back" button?

OK, so you can't always prevent errors from occuring, but you can do something about them. The JavaScript "Try... Catch" statement helps you handle errors in a "nice" way.

To use the Try... Catch statement, you take any code you think could potentially result in an error, and wrap it within the "try" statement. You then code what you want to happen in the event of an error and wrap that in a "catch" statement.

Code without a Try... Catch Statement:

```
<script type="text/javascript">
<!--
document.write("My bank balance is $" + myBankBalance);
//-->
</script>
```

The above code will result in an error. This is because the variable "myBankBalance" hasn't been declared yet.

Code with a Try... Catch Statement:

```
<script type="text/javascript">
<!--
try
{
document.write("My bank balance is $" + myBankBalance);
}
catch(err)
{
document.write("Sorry, an error has occurred");
document.write("...but hey, don't let that stop you!");
}
//-->
</script>
```

The resulting output:

Sorry, an error has occurred...but hey, don't let that stop you!

The above code will hide the error and present something more user friendly to the user. This is because the code with the error was wrapped inside a "try" statement. And, because there was an error, the browser outputs whatever is between the "catch" statement.

9.11 JAVASCRIPT ESCAPE CHARACTERS

When working with strings, you'll notice there are some characters that always seem to break your program. These include apostrophes, ampersands, double quotes etc.

When working with these characters, you need to use what is known as an "escape character". An escape character enables you to output characters you wouldn't normally be able to, usually because the browser will interpret it differently to what you intended.

In JavaScript, the backslash (\) is an escape character.

As an example, let's say I want to display the following text: They call it an "escape" character. Let's try that **without** an escape character:

Without an Escape Character:

```
<script type="text/javascript">
<!--
document.write("They call it an "escape" character");
//-->
</script>
```

The above code won't work as intended because, as soon as the browser encounters the first double quote, it will think that the string has finished. Further, it will result in an error because it will be expecting the closing bracket.

Code with an Escape Character:

```
<script type="text/javascript">
<!--
document.write("They call it an \"escape\" character");
//-->
</script>
```

The resulting output:

They call it an "escape" character

The above Code will Display the JavaScript Void(0)

Sometimes, you may need to call some JavaSript from within a link. Normally, when you click a link, the browser loads a new page (or refreshes the same page).

This might not always be desirable. For example, you might only want to dynamically update a form field when the user clicks a link.

To prevent the load from refreshing, you could use the JavaScript void() function and pass a parameter of 0 (zero).

Example of Void(0):

We have a link that should only do something (*i.e.*, display a message) upon two clicks (*i.e.*, a double click). If you click once, nothing should happen. We can specify the double click code by using JavaScript's "ondblclick" method. To prevent the page reloading upon a single click, we can use "JavaScript:void(0);" within the anchor link.

Code:

```
<a href="JavaScript:void(0);" ondblclick="alert('Well done!')">Double Click Me!</a>
```

Result:

Double Click Me!

Same Example, but without Void(0):

Look at what would happen if we didn't use "JavaScript:void(0);" within the anchor link...

Code:

```
<a href="" ondblclick="alert('Well done!')">Double Click Me!</a>
```

Result:

Double Click Me!

Did you notice the page refresh as soon you clicked the link. Even if you double clicked and triggered the "ondbclick" event, the page still reloads!

Note: Depending on your browser, your browser might have redirected you to the "/javascript/tutorial/" index page. Either way, JavaScript's "void()" method will prevent this from happening.

Void(0) can become useful when you need to call another function that may have otherwise resulted in an unwanted page refresh.

ouble quotes as intended.

9.12 JAVASCRIPT COOKIES

Cookies are small text files that sit on your hard disk. Cookies are created when you visit websites that use cookies to store information that they need (or prefer). Websites often use cookies to personalise the user experience — such as remembering your name (assuming you supplied it previously) or remembering the items in your shopping cart from previous visits.

Despite the many misconceptions about cookies being malicious, they are quite harmless. Cookies can't give your personal details to other websites, or transmit a virus or anything like that. A cookie can only be read by the server that created it. Websites normally use cookies to make its users' lives easier, not harder.

Creating Cookies in JavaScript

```
document.cookie =
"myContents=Quackit JavaScript cookie experiment;
        expires=Fri, 19 Oct 2007 12:00:00 UTC; path=/";
```

Now check your cookies folder to see if the cookie was created. Alternatively, write code to read the cookie.

Note: If the cookie wasn't created, check the expiry date - it needs to be a date in the future.

You can update this value by using the same code with a different value. If you want to add a second value, simply use a different variable name (for example "myContents2=").

Reading Cookies in JavaScript

```
document.write(document.cookie);
```

You simply reference the cookie using document.cookie. The only problem with the above code is that it outputs the equals sign and everything before it (i.e., "myContents="). To stop this from happening, try the following code:

```
document.write(document.cookie.split("=")[1])
```

Deleting Cookies in JavaScript

To delete a cookie, you can use the same code you used to create it but this time, set the expiry date in the past:

```
document.cookie =
"myContents=Quackit JavaScript cookie experiment;
        expires=Fri, 14 Oct 2005 12:00:00 UTC; path=/";
```

Once you are comfortable with JavaScript and cookies, you can do things like use the getDate() function to set the date at a date in the future (say, 6 months), creating a function for setting and naming your cookies etc.

- << Previous
- Next Lesson >>

9.13 JAVASCRIPT DATE AND TIME

JavaScript provides you with the ability to access the date and time of your users' local computer, which can be quite useful at times. Displaying the current date and time in a nice user friendly way using JavaScript is not quite as simple as you might like. You need to massage the data a little. You can do this using a bunch of JavaScript date and time functions.

Displaying the Current Date

Typing this code...

```
var currentDate = new Date()
var day = currentDate.getDate()
var month = currentDate.getMonth()
var year = currentDate.getFullYear()
document.write("<b>" + day + "/" + month + "/" + year + "</b>")
```

Results in this...

27/3/2009

Displaying the Current Time

Typing this code...

```
var currentTime = new Date()
var hours = currentTime.getHours()
var minutes = currentTime.getMinutes()
if (minutes < 10)
minutes = "0" + minutes

document.write("<b>" + hours + ":" + minutes + " " + "</b>")
```

Results in this...

14:59

You may have noticed that we had to add a leading zero to the minutes part of the date if it was less than 10. By default, JavaScript doesn't display the leading zero. Also, you might have noticed that the time is being displayed in 24 hour time format. This is how JavaScript displays the time. If you need to display it in AM/PM format, you need to convert it.

Displaying the Current Time in AM/PM Format

Typing this code...

```
var currentTime = new Date()
var hours = currentTime.getHours()
var minutes = currentTime.getMinutes()

var suffix = "AM";
```

```
if (hours >= 12) {
suffix = "PM";
hours = hours - 12;
}
if (hours == 0) {
hours = 12;
}

if (minutes < 10)
minutes = "0" + minutes

document.write("<b>" + hours + ":" + minutes + " " + suffix + "</b>")
```

Results in this...

2:59 PM

JavaScript Date and Time Functions

For a full list of JavaScript date and time functions, see JavaScript Date and Time Functions

9.14 JAVASCRIPT ARRAYS

What is an Array?

Arrays are a fundamental part of most programming languages and scripting languages. Arrays are simply an ordered stack of data items with the same data type. Using arrays, you can store multiple values under a single name. Instead of using a separate variable for each item, you can use one array to hold all of them.

For example, say you have three Frequently Asked Questions that you want to store and write to the screen. You could store these in a simple variable like this:

```
faqQuestion1 = "What is an array?"
faqQuestion2 = "How to create arrays in JavaScript?"
faqQuestion3 = "What are two dimensional arrays?"
```

This will work fine. But one problem with this approach is that you have to write out each variable name whenever you need to work with it. Also, you can't do stuff like loop through all your variables. That's where arrays come into play. You could put all your questions into one array.

Visualizing Arrays

Arrays can be visualized as a stack of elements.

Array	
0	What are JavaScript arrays?
1	How to create arrays in JavaScript?
2	What are two dimensional arrays?

Note: Some languages start arrays at zero, other start at one. JavaScript arrays start at zero.

Creating Arrays in JavaScript

Most languages use similar syntax to create arrays. JavaScript arrays are created by first assigning an array object to a variable name...

```
var array_name = new Array(number_of_elements)
```

then by assigning values to the array...

```
array_name[0] = "Array element"
```

So, using our prior example, we could write:

```
var faq = new Array(3)
faq[0] = "What are JavaScript arrays"
faq[1] = "How to create arrays in JavaScript?"
faq[2] = "What are two dimensional arrays?"
```

Accessing Arrays in JavaScript

You can access an array element by referring to the name of the array and the element's index number.

Displaying Array Elements

```
document.write(faq[1])
```

The above code displays the second element of the array named *faq* (JavaScript array index numbers begin at zero). In this case, the value would be *How to create arrays in JavaScript?*

Modifying the Contents of an Array

You can modify the contents of an array by specifying a value for a given index number:

```
faq[1] = "How to modify an array?"
```

In this case, the value of the second element of this array would now be *How to modify an array?*

Two Dimensional Arrays

So far we've only discussed one dimensional arrays. You can also create two dimensional arrays, which can be much more powerful than one dimensional arrays. Two dimensional arrays are covered in the next lesson.

Two Dimensional Arrays

Visualizing Two Dimensional Arrays

Whereas, one dimensional arrays can be visualized as a stack of elements, two dimensional arrays can be visualized as a multicolumn table or grid.

For example, we could create a two dimensional array that holds three columns of data; a question, an answer, and a topic.

Two Dimensional Array			
0	Arrays	What is an array?	An ordered stack of data
1	Arrays	How to create arrays?	Assign variable name to array object, then assign values to the array.
2	Arrays	What are two dimensional arrays?	An ordered grid of data

Creating Two Dimensional Arrays

Generally, creating two dimensional arrays is very similar to creating one dimensional arrays. Some languages allow you to create two dimensional arrays simply by adding an index item, however JavaScript doesn't support two dimensional arrays.

JavaScript, does however, allow you to simulate a two dimensional array. You can do this by creating an "array of an array".

To do this, you create an array, loop through the array, and for each element, you create another array. Then, you simply add an index for each column of your grid. In JavaSript this would look something like this:

```
var faq = new Array(3)

for (i=0; i <3; i++)
faq[i]=new  Array(3)

faq[0][1] = "Arrays"
faq[0][2] = "What is an array?"
faq[0][3] = "An ordered stack of data"
faq[1][1] = "Arrays"
faq[1][2] = "How to create arrays?"
faq[1][3] = "Assign variable name to array object,
            then assign values to the array."
faq[2][1] = "Arrays"
faq[2][2] = "What are two dimensional arrays?"
faq[2][3] = "An ordered grid of data"
```

JAVASCRIPT INTERVIEW QUESTIONS AND ANSWERS

1. *What is JavaScript?*

Solution: JavaScript is a general-purpose programming language designed to let programmers of all skill levels control the behavior of software objects. The language is used most widely today in Web browsers whose software objects tend to represent a variety of HTML elements in a document and the document itself. But the language can be—and is—used with other kinds of objects in other environments. For example, Adobe Acrobat Forms uses JavaScript as its underlying scripting language to glue together objects that are unique to the forms generated by Adobe Acrobat. Therefore, it is important to distinguish JavaScript, the language, from the objects it can communicate with in any particular environment. When used for Web documents, the scripts go directly inside the HTML documents and are downloaded to the browser with the rest of the HTML tags and content.

2. *How is JavaScript different from Java?*

Solution: JavaScript was developed by Brendan Eich of Netscape; Java was developed at Sun Microsystems. While the two languages share some common syntax, they were developed independently of each other and for different audiences. Java is a full-fledged programming language tailored for network computing; it includes hundreds of its own objects, including objects for creating user interfaces that appear in Java applets (in Web browsers) or standalone Java applications. In contrast, JavaScript relies on whatever environment it's operating in for the user interface, such as a Web document's form elements.

JavaScript was initially called LiveScript at Netscape while it was under development. A licensing deal between Netscape and Sun at the last minute let Netscape plug the "Java" name into the name of its scripting language. Programmers use entirely different tools for Java and JavaScript. It is also not uncommon for a programmer of one language to be ignorant of the other. The two languages don't rely on each other and are intended for different purposes. In some ways, the "Java" name on JavaScript has confused the world's understanding of the differences between the two. On the other hand, JavaScript is much easier to learn than Java and can offer a gentle introduction for newcomers who want to graduate to Java and the kinds of applications you can develop with it.

3. *What's relationship between JavaScript and ECMAScript?*

Solution: ECMAScript is yet another name for JavaScript (other names include LiveScript). The current JavaScript that you see supported in browsers is ECMAScript revision

4. *How do you submit a form using Javascript?*

Solution: Use document.forms[0].submit();

(0 refers to the index of the form - if you have more than one form in a page, then the first one has the index 0, second has index 1 and so on).

5. *How do we get JavaScript onto a web page?*

Solution: You can use several different methods of placing javascript in you pages.

You can directly add a script element inside the body of page.

1. For example, to add the "last updated line" to your pages, In your page text, add the following:

```
<p>blah, blah, blah, blah, blah.</p>
<script type="text/javascript" >
<!-- Hiding from old browsers
document.write("Last Updated:" +
document.lastModified);
document.close();
// -->
</script>
<p>yada, yada, yada.</p>
```

(**Note:** the first comment, "<--" hides the content of the script from browsers that don't understand javascript. The "// -->" finishes the comment. The "//" tells javascript that this is a comment so javascript doesn't try to interpret the "-->". If your audience has much older browsers, you should put this comments inside your javascript. If most of your audience has newer browsers, the comments can be omitted. For brevity, in most examples here the comments are not shown.)

The above code will look like this on Javascript enabled browsers,

2. Javascript can be placed inside the <head> element

Functions and global variables typically reside inside the <head> element.

```
<head>
<title>Default Test Page</title>
<script language="JavaScript" type="text/javascript">
var myVar = "";
function timer(){setTimeout('restart()',10);}
document.onload=timer();
</script>
</head>
```

Javascript can be referenced from a separate file

Javascript may also a placed in a separate file on the server and referenced from an HTML page. (Don't use the shorthand ending "<script ... />). These are typically placed in the <head> element.

```
<script type="text/javascript" SRC="myStuff.js"></script>
```

6. *How to read and write a file using javascript?*

Solution: I/O operations like reading or writing a file is not possible with client-side javascript. However , this can be done by coding a Java applet that reads files for the script.

7. *How to detect the operating system on the client machine?*

Solution: In order to detect the operating system on the client machine, the navigator.app Version string (property) should be used.

8. *How can JavaScript make a Web site easier to use? That is, are there certain JavaScript techniques that make it easier for people to use a Web site?*

Solution: JavaScript's greatest potential gift to a Web site is that scripts can make the page more immediately interactive, that is, interactive without having to submit every little thing to the server for a server program to re-render the page and send it back to the client. For example, consider a top-level navigation panel that has, say, six primary image map links into subsections of the Web site. With only a little bit of scripting, each map area can be instructed to pop up a more detailed list of links to the contents within a subsection whenever the user rolls the cursor atop a map area. With the help of that popup list of links, the user with a scriptable browser can bypass one intermediate menu page. The user without a scriptable browser (or who has disabled JavaScript) will have to drill down through a more traditional and time-consuming path to the desired content.

9. *How can JavaScript be used to improve the "look and feel" of a Web site? By the same token, how can JavaScript be used to improve the user interface?*

Solution: On their own, Web pages tend to be lifeless and flat unless you add animated images or more bandwidth-intensive content such as Java applets or other content requiring plug-ins to operate (ShockWave and Flash, for example).

Embedding JavaScript into an HTML page can bring the page to life in any number of ways. Perhaps the most visible features built into pages recently with the help of JavaScript are the so-called image rollovers: roll the cursor atop a graphic image and its appearance changes to a highlighted version as a feedback mechanism to let you know precisely what you're about to click on. But there are less visible yet more powerful enhancements to pages that JavaScript offers.

Interactive forms validation is an extremely useful application of JavaScript. While a user is entering data into form fields, scripts can examine the validity of the data—did the user type any letters into a phone number field?, for instance. Without scripting, the user has to submit the form and let a server program (CGI) check the field entry and then report back to the user. This is usually done in a batch mode (the entire form at once), and the extra transactions take a lot of time and server processing power. Interactive validation scripts can check each form field immediately after the user has entered the data, while the information is fresh in the mind.

Another helpful example is embedding small data collections into a document that scripts can look up without having to do all the server programming for database access. For instance, a small company could put its entire employee directory on a page that has its own search facility built into the script. You can cram a lot of text data into scripts no larger than an average image file, so it's not like the user has to wait forever for the data to be downloaded.

Other examples abound, such as interactive tree-structure tables of contents. More modern scriptable browsers can be scripted to pre-cache images during the page's initial download to make them appear lickety-split when needed for image swapping. I've even written some multi-screen interactive applications that run entirely on the client, and never talk to the server once everything is downloaded.

10. *What are JavaScript types?*

Solution: Number, String, Boolean, Function, Object, Null, Undefined.

11. *How do you convert numbers between different bases in JavaScript?*

Solution: Use the parseInt() function, that takes a string as the first parameter, and the base as a second parameter. So to convert hexadecimal 3F to decimal, use parseInt ("3F", 16);

12. *How to create arrays in JavaScript?*

Solution: We can declare an array like this

var scripts = new Array();

We can add elements to this array like this

scripts[0] = "PHP";

scripts[1] = "ASP";

scripts[2] = "JavaScript";

scripts[3] = "HTML";

Now our array scrips has 4 elements inside it and we can print or access them by using their index number. Note that index number starts from 0. To get the third element of the array we have to use the index number 2 . Here is the way to get the third element of an array.

```
document.write(scripts[2]);
```

We also can create an array like this

```
var no_array = new Array(21, 22, 23, 24, 25);
```

13. *How do you target a specific frame from a hyperlink?*

Solution: Include the name of the frame in the target attribute of the hyperlink. <a href="mypage.htm" target="myframe">>My Page</a>

14. *What is a fixed-width table and its advantages?*

Solution: Fixed width tables are rendered by the browser based on the widths of the columns in the first row, resulting in a faster display in case of large tables. Use the CSS style table-layout:fixed to specify a fixed width table.

If the table is not specified to be of fixed width, the browser has to wait till all data is downloaded and then infer the best width for each of the columns. This process can be very slow for large tables.

Example of using Regular Expressions for syntax checking in JavaScript

```
...
var re = new RegExp("^(&[A-Za-z_0-9]{1,}=[A-Za-z_0-9]{1,})*$");
var text = myWidget.value;
var OK = re.test(text);
if( ! OK ) {
alert("The extra parameters need some work.\r\n Should be something like: \"&a=1&c=4\"");
}
```

15. *Where are cookies actually stored on the hard disk?*

Solution: This depends on the user's browser and OS.

In the case of Netscape with Windows OS,all the cookies are stored in a single file called

cookies.txt

c:\Program Files\Netscape\Users\username\cookies.txt

In the case of IE,each cookie is stored in a separate file namely username@website.txt.

c:\Windows\Cookies\username@Website.txt

16. *How to add Buttons in JavaScript?*

Solution: The most basic and ancient use of buttons are the "submit" and "clear", which appear slightly before the Pleistocene period. Notice when the "GO!" button is pressed it submits itself to itself and appends the name in the URL.

```
<form action="" name="buttonsGalore" method="get">
Your Name: <input type="text" name="mytext" />
<br />
<input type="submit" value="GO!" />
<input type="reset" value="Clear All" />
</form>
```

Another useful approach is to set the "type" to "button" and use the "onclick" event.

```
<script type="text/javascript">
function displayHero(button) {
alert("Your hero is \""+button.value+" \".");
}
</script>
<form action="" name="buttonsGalore" method="get">
<fieldset style="margin: 1em; text-align: center;">
<legend>Select a Hero</legend>
<input type="button" value="Agamemnon" onclick="displayHero(this)" />
<input type="button" value="Achilles" onclick="displayHero(this)" />
<input type="button" value="Hector" onclick="displayHero(this)" />
<div style="height: 1em;" />
</fieldset>
</form>
```

17. *What can javascript programs do?*

Solution: Generation of HTML pages on-the-fly without accessing the Web server. The user can be given control over the browser like User input validation Simple computations can be performed on the client's machine The user's browser, OS, screen size, etc. can be detected Date and Time Handling

18. *How to set a HTML document's background color?*

Solution: document.bgcolor property can be set to any appropriate color.

19. *How can JavaScript be used to personalize or tailor a Web site to fit individual users?*

Solution: JavaScript allows a Web page to perform "if-then" kinds of decisions based on browser version, operating system, user input, and, in more recent browsers, details about the screen size in which the browser is running. While a server CGI program can make some of those same kinds of decisions, not everyone has access to or the expertise to create CGI programs. For example, an experienced CGI programmer can examine information about the browser whenever a request for a page is made; thus a server so equipped might serve up one page for Navigator users and a different page for Internet Explorer users. Beyond browser and operating system version, a CGI program can't know more about the environment. But a JavaScript-enhanced page can instruct the browser to render only certain content based on the browser, operating system, and even the screen size.

Scripting can even go further if the page author desires. For example, the author may include a preference screen that lets the user determine the desired background and text color combination. A script can save this information on the client in a well-regulated local file called a cookie. The next time the user comes to the site, scripts in its pages look to the cookie info and render the page in the color combination selected previously. The server is none the wiser, nor does it have to store any visitor-specific information.

20. *Are you concerned that older browsers don't support JavaScript and thus exclude a set of Web users? individual users?*

Solution: Fragmentation of the installed base of browsers will only get worse. By definition, it can never improve unless absolutely everyone on the planet threw away their old browsers and upgraded to the latest gee-whiz versions. But even then, there are plenty of discrepancies between the scriptability of the latest Netscape Navigator and Microsoft Internet Explorer.

The situation makes scripting a challenge, especially for newcomers who may not be aware of the limitations of earlier browsers. A lot of effort in my books and ancillary material goes toward helping scripters know what features work in which browsers and how to either workaround limitations in earlier browsers or raise the compatibility common denominator.

Designing scripts for a Web site requires making some hard decisions about if, when, and how to implement the advantages scripting offers a page to your audience. For public Web sites, I recommend using scripting in an additive way: let sufficient content stand on its own, but let scriptable browser users receive an enhanced experience, preferably with the same HTML document.

MULTIPLE CHOICE QUESTIONS

1. You are a junior web designer. Your company assigns you to work on a JavaScript project. Which of the following are the advantages of using JavaScript for form validation?
   (*a*) Conservation of client CPU resources (*b*) Increased validity of form submission
   (*c*) Conservation of bandwidth (*d*) Increase end-user satisfaction
   (*e*) Either BCD
2. Your company assigns you to work on a JavaScript project. With the DATE object, which of the following allows you to call a function based on an elapsed time?
   (*a*) setElapsedTime() (*b*) Timeout() (*c*) setTimeout() (*d*) setTime()
3. You are working on a JavaScript project. What is used to restart the inner most loop?
   (*a*) Abort (*b*) Breakloop (*c*) Stop (*d*) Continue label
4. You work on a JavaScript project. Which of the following correctly describe the relationships of JavaScript and "objects"?
   (*a*) JavaScript is Object-oriented
   (*b*) JavaScript is Object-based
   (*c*) JavaScript is Object-driven
   (*d*) JavaScript has no relationship with objects
5. You work on a JavaScript project. How do you prompt users with messages and at the same time requesting user inputs?
   (*a*) Alert() (*b*) Display() (*c*) Prompt() (*d*) Confirm()
6. Which of the following is the correct syntax of FOR?
   (*a*) for (increment; initialize; test) (*b*) for (initialize; test), increment
   (*c*) for (initialize; test; increment) (*d*) for (test; initalize; increment)
7. In your JavaScript code, how do you find out which character occurs at the 5th position in a string "How are you"?
   (*a*) Substring() (*b*) String() (*c*) Stringlength() (*d*) CharAt()
8. Which of the following do you use for a multi-way branch?
   (*a*) If (*b*) Ifthen (*c*) Ifelse (*d*) switch
   (*e*) for

9. You want to design a form validation mechanism. Using string methods, which of the following are the steps involved ?
   (*a*) Check for the presence of certain characters
   (*b*) Check the position of substrings
   (*c*) Test the length of data
   (*d*) Check the variable type of the strings
   (*e*) Either ABC
10. Which of the following is the minimum browser version that supports JavaScript
    (*a*) Navigator v2.0 (*b*) Mozilla V1.5 (*c*) IE 2.0 (*d*) Navigator V1.0
11. Under which of the following conditions will you need to include semi colons on a line of code?
    (*a*) When you have multiple statements on multiple lines
    (*b*) When you have multiple statements on a line
    (*c*) When you have single statement on multiple lines
    (*d*) When you have single statement on a line
12. Which of the following are the valid JavaScript versions?
    (*a*) Version 1.2 (*b*) Version 1.1 (*c*) Version 1.3 (*d*) Version 1.4
    (*e*) All of the above
13. Which of the following languages will you consider as being similar to JavaScript?
    (*a*) C (*b*) C++ (*c*) Pascal (*d*) PHP
    (*e*) Either A & C
14. You plan the coding of your project. When must the object references be ready?
    (*a*) at run time (*b*) at compile time (*c*) at debug time (*d*) at code time
15. Which of the following correctly describe cookies ?
    (*a*) Often referred to as "persistent cookies"
    (*b*) Often referred to as "persistent HTML"
    (*c*) Small memory-resident pieces of information sent from a server to the client
    (*d*) Small memory-resident pieces of information sent from a client to the server
    (*e*) Either AB&C
16. A program written by JavaScript is driven by
    (*a*) Events (*b*) Classes (*c*) Objects (*d*) DLL
    (*e*) Components
17. What are JavaScript relations with the underlying operating platform?
    (*a*) Platform dependent (*b*) Platform linkage
    (*c*) Platform independent (*d*) Platform binding
18. When you plan for the JavaScript variable names, the first character must be?
    (*a*) Underscore (*b*) Comma (*c*) Hyphen (*d*) Letter
    (*e*) Either A&D
19. Which of the following correctly describe JavaScript as a language?
    (*a*) It is based on object creation (*b*) It focuses on component building
    (*c*) It focuses on logic flow (*d*) It emphasis on SCRIPTING
20. When authoring web page with Javascript, why should you explicitly include the window object into your codes?
    (*a*) this is a good practice (*b*) this is REQUIRED
    (*c*) this ensures browser compatibility (*d*) this ensures OS compatibility

21. Inside which HTML element do we put the JavaScript?
(*a*) <scripting> (*b*) <javascript> (*c*) <script> (*d*) <js>

22. What is the correct JavaScript syntax to write "Hello World"?
(*a*) response.write("Hello World") (*b*) document.write("Hello World")
(*c*) ("Hello World") (*d*) echo("Hello World")

23. How do you call a function named "myFunction"?
(*a*) call function myFunction (*b*) myFunction()
(*c*) call myFunction()

24. How do you write a conditional statement for executing some statements only if "i" is equal to 5?
(*a*) if i==5 then (*b*) if i=5 then (*c*) if (i==5) (*d*) if i=5

25. How do you write a conditional statement for executing some statements only if "i" is NOT equal to 5?
(*a*) if (i <> 5) (*b*) if (i != 5) (*c*) if =! 5 then (*d*) if <> 5

26. How many different kind of loops are there in JavaScript?
(*a*) Two. The "for" loop and the "while" loop
(*b*) Four. The "for" loop, the "while" loop, the "do...while" loop, and the "loop...until" loop
(*c*) One. The "for" loop

27. How does a "for" loop start?
(*a*) for (i = 0; i <= 5) (*b*) for (i = 0; i <= 5; i++)
(*c*) for i = 1 to 5 (*d*) for (i <= 5; i++)

28. What is the correct way to write a JavaScript array?
(*a*) var txt = new Array(1:"tim",2:"shaq",3:"kobe")
(*b*) var txt = new Array="tim","shaq","kobe"
(*c*) var txt = new Array("tim","shaq","kobe")

29. How do you round the number 8.25, to the nearest whole number?
(*a*) Math.rnd(8.25) (*b*) Math.round(8.25)
(*c*) round(8.25) (*d*) rnd(8.25)

30. How do you find the largest number of 6 and 8?
(*a*) Math.max(6,8) (*b*) top(6,8) (*c*) ceil(6,8) (*d*) Math.ceil(6,8)

31. What is the correct JavaScript syntax for opening a new window called "window5" ?
(*a*) new("http://www.ex-designz.net","window5")
(*b*) window.open("http://www.ex-designz.net","window5")
(*c*) open.newwindow("http://www.ex-designz.net","window5")
(*d*) new.window("http://www.ex-designz.net","window5")

32. How do you put a message in the browser's status bar?
(*a*) window.status = "put your message here"
(*b*) statusbar = "put your message here"
(*c*) status("put your message here")
(*d*) window.status("put your message here")

33. How do you find the client's browser name?
(*a*) browser.name (*b*) navigator.appName
(*c*) client.navName

34. You define an array using

(*a*) var myarray = new Array(); (*b*) var myarray = array new;

(*c*) var new Array() = myarray; (*d*) var new array = myarray;

35. Onclick is equivalent to which two events in sequence

(*a*) onmouseover and onmousedown (*b*) onmousedown and onmouseout

(*c*) onmousedown and onmouseup (*d*) onmouseup and onmouseout

36. Which best describe void?

(*a*) A method (*b*) A function (*c*) An operator (*d*) A statement

37. Which property would you use to redirect visitor to another page?

(*a*) window.location.href (*b*) document.href

(*c*) java.redirect.url (*d*) link.redirect.href

38. Which of the following JavaScript statements use arrays?

(*a*) setTimeout("a["+i+"]",1000) (*b*) k = a & i

(*c*) k = a(i)

Answers of Multiple Choice Questions

1. (*e*),	**2.** (*d*),	**3.** (*d*),	**4.** (*b*),	**5.** (*c*),
6. (*c*),	**7.** (*d*),	**8.** (*d*),	**9.** (*e*),	**10.** (*a*),
11. (*b*),	**12.** (*e*),	**13.** (*e*),	**14.** (*a*),	**15.** (*e*),
16. (*a*),	**17.** (*c*),	**18.** (*e*),	**19.** (*d*),	**20.** (*a*),
21. (*c*),	**22.** (*d*),	**23.** (*b*),	**24.** (*c*),	**25.** (*b*),
26. (*a*),	**27.** (*b*),	**28.** (*c*),	**29.** (*b*),	**30.** (*a*),
31. (*b*),	**32.** (*a*),	**33.** (*b*),	**34.** (*a*),	**35.** (*c*),
36. (*c*),	**37.** (*a*),	**38.** (*a*).		

EXERCISE

1. What do you understand by JavaScript?
2. What is the difference between Java and JavaScript?
3. Is JavaScript a scripting or an object oriented language?
4. How you can dynamically changing the document's background color using JavaScript?
5. How you can change image using JavaScript?
6. What are JavaScript dialog boxes?
7. Write a JavaScript program to display random image.
8. Write a JavaScript program to display a clock.
9. What are the attributes of <Script> tag.?
10. How do you link documents in JavaScript program?
11. Write a JavaScript program for a calculator.

10

VBScript

10.0 INTRODUCTION

VBScript is a subset of the Visual Basic Programming language. The result of the slimming down process is a very small language that is easy to use. JavaScript can do all that VBScript can do and far more. So why use VBScript instead of JavaScript? Because VBScript is much easier to learn than JavaScript.

For example:

```
<HTML>
<HEAD>
<TITLE> "VBScript Demo"</TITLE>
<SCRIPT LANGUAGE="VBScript">
<!—
'Your Script goes here.
YourName = InputBox("What is your name?")
MsgBox "YourName"
'or you can display YourName like this:
Document.Write "<H1>"
Document.Write YourName
Document.Write "<\/H1>"
- ->
</SCRIPT>
</HEAD>
</BODY>
</HTML>
```

10.1 VBSCRIPT VS JAVASCRIPT SYNTAX

	VBScript	JavaScript
Arrays	Declaration (e.g., Dim, Static) Lbound, Ubound ReDim, Erase	new Array() new Object()
Assignment	=	=
Comments	REM Single Quote (')	// /* comment */

Control Flow	Do ....Loop
	For ...Next, For Each ...Next
	While ...Wend
	If ... Then ...Else
		do {
		statements
		} while (condition)
		
		for (expression; condition; [expression]){
		statements
		}
		
		for (variable in object) {
		statements
		}
		
		while (condition) {
		statements
		}
		
		if (condition) {
		statements1
		}
		else {
		statements2
		}
		
		switch (expression){
		case label :
		statement;
		break;
		case label :
		statement;
		break;
		...
		default : statement;
		}

Error Trapping	On Error Err Object	window.onError = handler-func window.onError(message,url,line)

Control flow

Literals	Empty Nothing Null True, False User Defined Literals(e.g., 123.456, "test")	NaN null true, false User Defined Literals(e.g., 123.456, "test")
Operators	Arithmetic +, -, *, /, \, ^, Mod, Negation (-) Strings concatenation (&) Comparison =, <, >, <>, <=, >=, Is Logical Not, And, Or, Xor, Eqv, Imp	Arithmetic +, ++, -, --, *, / % String + += Logical && | | ! Bitwise & ^ | ~ << >> >>> Assignment = += -= *= /= %= &= ^= |= <<= >>= >>>= Comparison == |= > >= < <= Special ?: , delete new this typeof void
Options	Option Explicit	N/A
Declaring Procedures	Functions Sub	function function-name(arg1, arg2, ... argN)
Calling Procedures:	Call	function function-name(arg1, arg2, ... argN) { statements; }
Exiting Procedures	Exit Function Exit Sub	
Parameters for Procedures	ByVal, ByRef	
Procedure-level	Dim	var variable-name
Variables	Static	
Module level Variables	Private dim	var variable-name

When one uses Option Explicit it forces the user to declare all variables. If one tries to use a variable without declaring it an error is generated. If one doesn't use Option Explicit one is free to use variables without declaring them, however, this is bad programming practice as it is easy to misspell a variable and produce faulty code.

10.2 VBSCRIPT VS JAVASCRIPT OPERATIONS

	VBScript	JavaScript
Divide & return an integer value	\	**N/A**
Exponentiation	^	**N/A**
Modulas	**MOD**	%
String Concatenation	**+ or &**	+
Left Shift	**N/A**	<<
Right Shift	**N/A**	>>
Bitwise AND	**AND**	&
Bitwise OR	**OR**	|
Bitwise XOR	**XOR**	^

Bitwise complement	**NOT**	~
Not equal to	<>	!=
Evaluation AND	**AND**	&&
Evaluation OR	**OR**	||
Evaluation XOR	**XOR**	**N/A**

10.3 VBSCRIPT FUNCTIONS

A Function is usually passed a list of variables, performs action upon these variables and returns a value.

```
Function Name(arguments)
code body of function
End Function
```

10.4 WORKING WITH STRINGS

Trim, Ltrim, Rtrim:

```
MyString = "This is a Test"
NewString = Trim(MyString) 'NewString = "This is a Test"
NewString = Ltrim(MyString) 'NewString = "This is a test"
NewString = Rtrim(MyString) 'NewString = "This is a test"
```

Len:

```
MyString = "Test this string"
l = Len(MyString) ' l = 16
```

Mid:

```
NewString = Mid(MyString,1,1) ' NewString = "T"
NewString = Mid(MyString,6,4) ' NewString = "this"
```

Left:

```
MyString = "Test this string"
NewString = Left(MyString,3) ' NewString = "Tes"
```

Right:

```
MyString = "Test this string"
NewString = Right(MyString,4) ' NewString = "ring"
```

For example to count the number of spaces in MyString:

```
<HTML>
<HEAD>
<TITLE> "VBScript Demo"</TITLE>
<SCRIPT LANGUAGE="VBScript">
<!--

Dim MyString, SpaceCount, Length, Position
MyString = "This is my test string"
SpaceCount = 0
Length = Len(MyString)
```

```
For Position = 1 to Length
If Mid(MyString, Position, 1) = Chr(32) Then ' Chr(32) equals the space character.
SpaceCount = SpaceCount + 1
End If
Next
MsgBox SpaceCount
'SpaceCount would equal 4
-->
</SCRIPT>
</HEAD>
</BODY>
</HTML>
```

InStr and InStrRev. Syntax is: Instr([start,] OriginalString, SubString[, Compare])

Start defines the start of the search and is optional, Compare lets you defining whether the search should be case sensitive and is also optional.

```
MyString = "This is a test"
Position = InStr(MyString, "s") 'Position = 4
Position = InStrRev(MyString, "s") 'Position = 13
Position = InStr(5, MyString, "s") 'Position = 7
```

10.5 ARRAYS

Fixed Arrays

A one-dimensional array is a way to group items so that you can refer to each item individually by means of its Index:

```
Dim MyButton(4)
```

This means that you have five elements in an array, MyButton(0) to MyButton(4).

Dynamic Arrays

```
Dim MyButtons()
NumberOfButtons = InputBox("How many Buttons")
ReDim MyButtons(NumberOfButtons)
```

Format

```
MsgBox FormatDatTime(Now, vbGeneralDate) ' 15/6/98 5:15:20 PM
```

vbLongDate Monday, June 15, 1998

vbShortDate 15/6/98

vbLongTime 5:15;20 PM

vbShortTime 17:15 (24-hour clock)

10.6 ACTIVEX

10.6.1 ActiveX Control Pad

ActiveX Control Pad available free from Microsoft combines a simple HTML editor with some very powerful features for working with ActiveX Controls. The key is that ActiveX Control Pad will let you do the following: Specify the type of ActiveX control, such as command button or text box that you want to insert.

- Set the controls initial properties.
- Properties include the background colour of the control, the height of the control, the font in which the text is displayed etc.

ActiveX Control Pad comes with a tool named Script Wizard. Script Wizard will generate code automatically when you give it directions, however, it only generates the code for the controls used. If you need additional operability you will have to add the code by hand.

10.6.2 Visual Basic 5 Control Creation Edition (VB5CCE)

Visual Basic 5 Control Creation Edition is another way in which you can create your own ActiveX controls and again it is available from Microsoft and again its free. VB5CCE can create full blown ActiveX controls as 32-bit OCX's.

QUESTIONS WITH ANSWERS

1. *What is VBScript?*

Solution: VBScript is the name given to Microsoft's Visual Basic Scripting Edition. It is a subset of the Visual Basic for Applications (VBA) language although it has a few features that haven't yet been introduced into VBA. It can also be used to program Windows95 and Windows NT by using the Microsoft Windows Scripting Host.

2. *How do I get VBScript?*

Solution: VBScript is part of Internet Explorer version 4 or later for the Windows platform. This means that millions of people have VBScript and don't even know it!

3. *Where can I find more information on VBScript?*

Solution: Have a look at VBScript at Microsoft. This site has a list of non-Microsoft sites that you might find useful. It also contains information about VBScript news groups.

4. *How does VBScript compare to JavaScript?*

Solution: JavaScript is a language designed by Netscape Communications for programming Web pages. Thus VBScript and JavaScript are designed to do the same job. In my opinion JavaScript has a much steeper learning curve than VBScript since JavaScript uses syntax similar to the cryptic C programming language.

EXERCISE

1. What do you understand by VbScript?
2. What is the difference between VbScript and JavaScript?
3. Discuss VbScript vs JavaScript operations?
4. How we define arrays in VbScript?
5. Describe active x controls in brief.

11

XML

11.0 INTRODUCTION

XML stands for eXtensible Markup Language. The XML specification was created by the World Wide Web Consortium (W3C), the body that sets standards for the web.

Features/Benefits of XML

XML has been widely adopted since its creation and with good reason. Some of the key features and benefits of XML include:

- **Easy data exchange :** One of the great things about XML is that it can allow easy sharing of data between different applications - even if these applications are written in different languages and reside on different platforms.
- **Self-describing data :** When you look at an XML document, it is very easy to figure out what's going on.
- **Create your own languages :** XML allows you to specify your own markup language for your own specific purpose.

How to Start XML ?

```
<?xml version="1.0" encoding="UTF-8"?>
<tutorials>
  <tutorial>
    <name>Enter Name</name>
      </tutorial>
  <tutorial>
    <name>ABES Ghaziabad</name>
    <url>http://www.abes.ac.in </url>
  </tutorial>
</tutorials>
```

I'll be explaining what this is all about in the coming lessons.

Difference between XML and HTML

If you're familiar with HTML, you might notice that XML looks similar to HTML. Like XML, HTML is also a markup language. In fact, HTML stands for Hypertext Markup Language. Markup languages are used for describing how a document's contents should be interpreted.

HTML

HTML includes over 100 pre-defined tags to allow the author to specify how each piece of content should be presented to the end user.

XML

XML allows you to create your own tags to describe the data between them. You're not particularly interested in how the data will be presented. Your main focus is ensuring that the data is well organised within descriptive tags (or elements).

11.1 XML VIEWERS

While you can view XML documents with a simple text editor, there are free XML viewers that present the contents in a more readable form. XML viewers interpret the document so it will display the XML document using any styles that have been applied using XSLT or CSS. It will also warn you if something doesn't look right, or if it doesn't validate correctly.

Most modern browsers include XML support, so it's quite possible that your own browser is able to display the contents of XML files.

You open an XML file in your browser the same way you open any other file in your browser. If it's a local file you can type the full path into the address bar. Otherwise, if it's available over the web, you can type the URL into the address bar.

Notepad

You can use a text editor such as Notepad to create or view a simple XML file. Here's what `this XML file` looks like in Notepad:

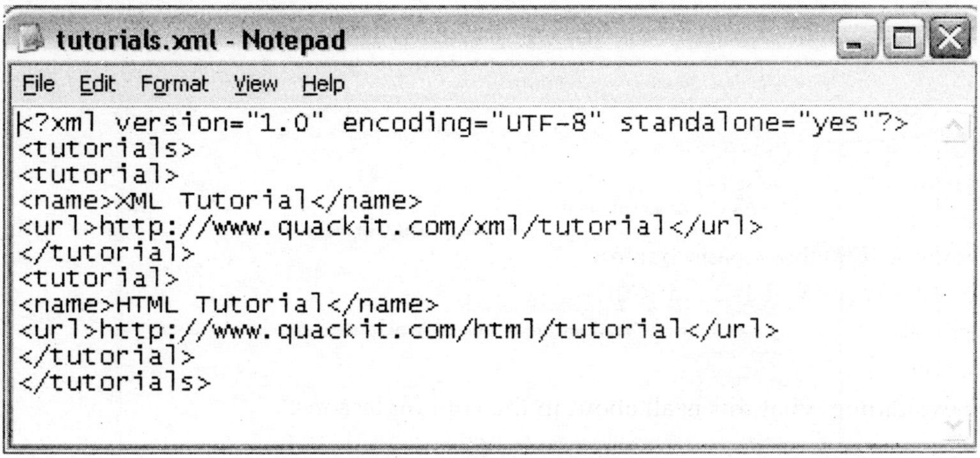


```
<?xml version="1.0" encoding="UTF-8" standalone="yes"?>
<tutorials>
<tutorial>
<name>XML Tutorial</name>
<url>http://www.quackit.com/xml/tutorial</url>
</tutorial>
<tutorial>
<name>HTML Tutorial</name>
<url>http://www.quackit.com/html/tutorial</url>
</tutorial>
</tutorials>
```

Firefox

Here's how the above XML file appears in Firefox 2.0. Notice the difference between Notepad and Firefox. Firefox actually attempts to interpret the document. It even warns us if it thinks something could be out of place (such as a missing stylesheet).

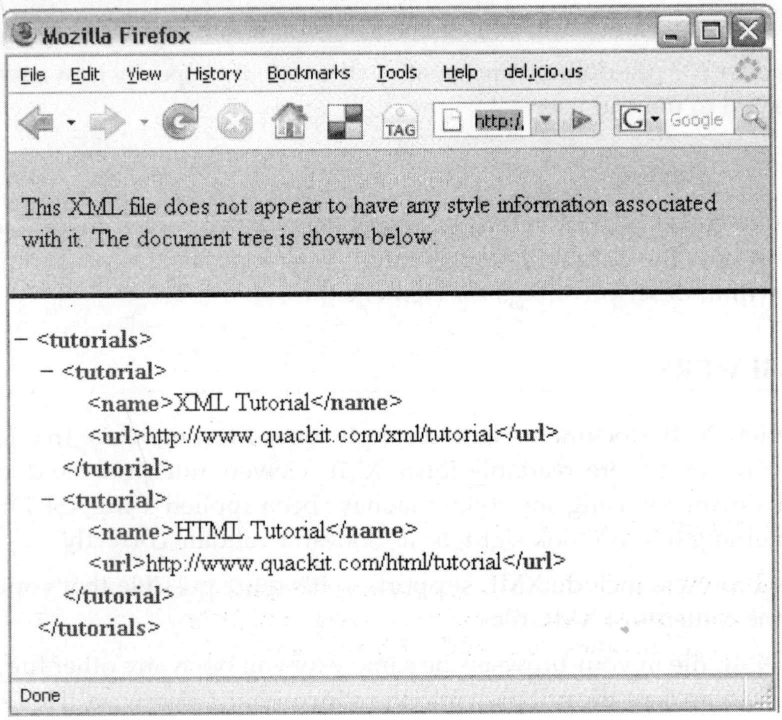

Internet Explorer

Here's how the same XML file appears in Internet Explorer 6.0

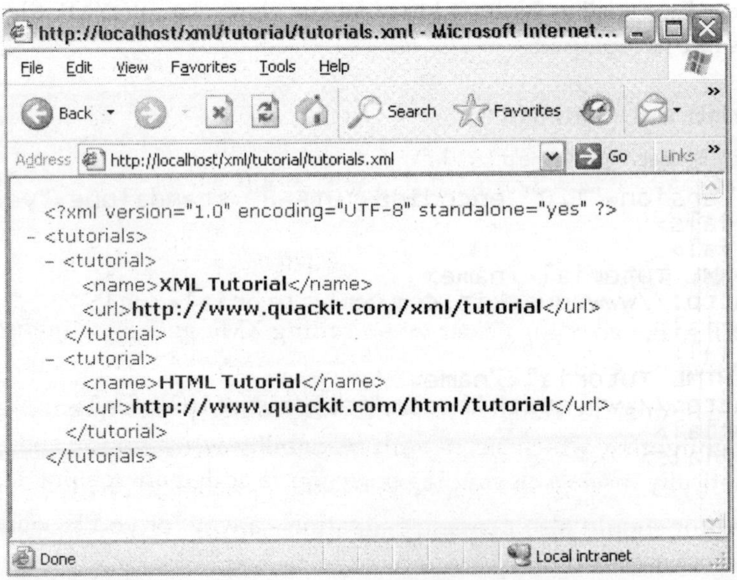

Displaying Errors

If your XML document contains an error, your XML viewer should display a message indicating the error. In this file, I have purposely included an error.

Below is how the error is reported in Internet Explorer.

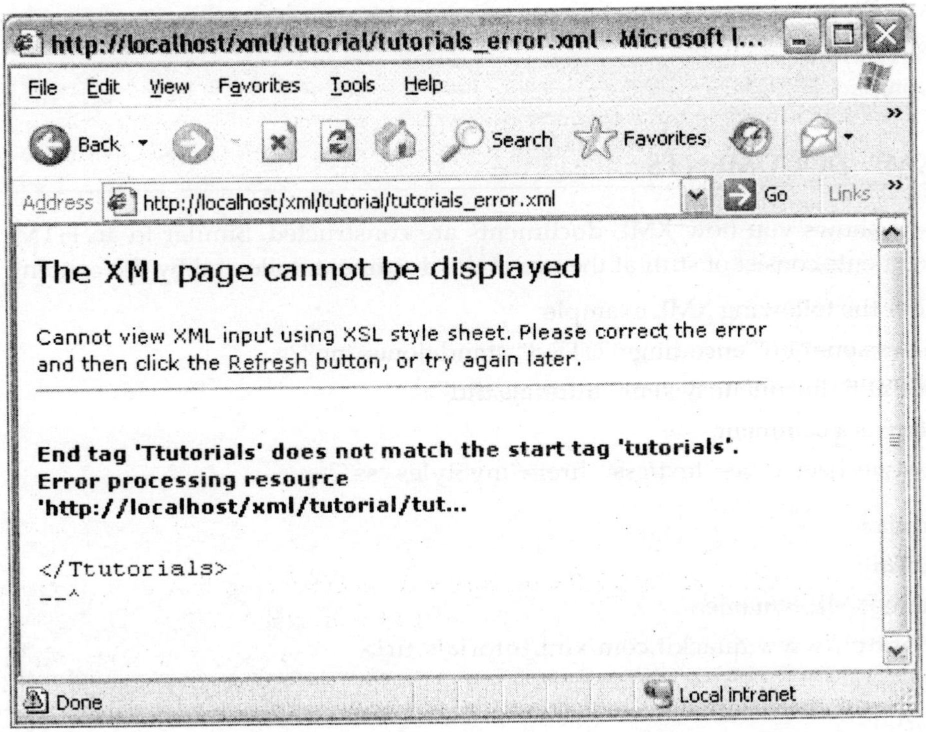

Adding Styles

Once you start adding styles to your XML, you'll see a huge difference in how your XML documents appear with an XML viewer.

11.2 XML EDITORS

You can create XML documents using a simple text editor such as Notepad, WordPad, vi, emacs, or SimpleText etc. Text editors are OK, but if you're serious about creating XML, you'd be better off finding an XML editor.

Benefits of an XML Editor

An XML editor will make your life easier when coding XML and more importantly, it will help prevent you from making errors.

XML editors are similar to HTML editors (or any other programming editor) in that they provide syntax highlighting which helps with readability when you're coding. They'll also do things like automatically insert a closing tag once you're added an opening tag.

A good XML editor should also provide validation - a way for you to validate that the documents you create are well formed.

Examples of XML Editors

Here are some XML editors you might find useful:

- XML Notepad
- XML Cooktop
- XML Pro
- XML Spy
- eNotepad

11.3 XML DOCUMENTS

This lesson shows you how XML documents are constructed. Similar to an HTML document, XML documents consist of stuff at the top of the document, followed by the content.

Consider the following XML example:

```
<?xml version="1.0" encoding="UTF-8" standalone="no"?>
<!DOCTYPE document system "tutorials.dtd">
<!— Here is a comment —>
<?xml-stylesheet type="text/css" href="myStyles.css"?>

<tutorials>
  <tutorial>
    <name>XML l</name>
    <url>http://www.quackit.com/xml/tutorial</url>
  </tutorial>
  <tutorial>
    <name>HTML </name>
    <url>http://www.quackit.com/html/tutorial</url>
  </tutorial>
</tutorials>
```

Document Type Definition (DTD)

The DTD defines the rules of your XML document. Although XML itself has rules, the rules defined in a DTD are specific to your own needs. More specifically, the DTD allows you to specify the names of the elements that are allowed in the document, which elements are allowed to be nested inside other elements, and which elements can only contain data.

The DTD is used when you validate your XML document. Any application that uses the document must stop processing if the document doesn't adhere to the DTD.

Comments

XML comments begin with <!-- and end with -->. Similar to HTML comments, XML comments allow you to write stuff within your document without it being parsed by the processor.

Processing Instructions

Processing instructions begin with <? and end with ?>. Processing instructions are instructions for the XML processor.

White Space

White space is simply blank space created by carriage returns, line feeds, tabs, and/or spaces. White space doesn't affect the processing of the document, so you can choose to include whitespace or not.

Speaking of white space, there is a special attribute (xml:whitespace) that you can use to preserve whitespace within your elements .

Elements and Content

This is where the document's content goes. It consists of one or more elements, nested within a single root element.

Root Element Opening Tag

All XML documents must have one (and only one) root element. All other elements must be nested inside this root element. In other words, the root element must contain all other elements within the document. Therefore, the first tag in the document will always be the opening tag of the root element (the closing tag will always be at the bottom of the document).

Child Elements and Content

These are the elements that are contained within the root element. Elements are usually represented by an opening and closing tag. Data and other elements reside between the opening and closing tag of an element.

Although most elements contain an opening and closing tag, XML allows you to use *empty elements*. An empty element is one without a closing tag. You might be familiar with some empty elements used in HTML such as the `<img>` element or the `<br>` element. In XML, you must close empty elements with a forward slash before the > symbol. For example, `<br />`.

Elements can also contain one or more attributes. An *attribute* is a name/value pair, that you place within an opening tag, which allows you to provide extra information about an element. You may be familiar with attributes in HTML. For example, the HTML img tag requires the `src` attribute which specifies the location of an image (eg, `<img src="myImage.gif" />`).

Root Element Closing Tag

The last tag of the document will always be the closing tag of the root element. This is because all other elements are nested inside the root element.

11.4 XML SYNTAX

XML syntax refers to the rules that determine how an XML application can be written. The XML syntax is very straight forward, and this makes XML very easy to learn. Below are the main points to remember when creating XML documents.

Well-formedness

The W3C specifies that all XML documents must be *well-formed*. Specifically, a textual object is a well-formed XML document if:

- Taken as a whole, it matches the production labeled document
- It meets all the well-formedness constraints given the XML specification
- Each of the parsed entities which is referenced directly or indirectly within the document is well-formed

If this all sounds confusing, don't worry too much. Basically, all you need to do is ensure you build your XML applications correctly!

XML Declaration

If you include an XML declaration, it must be the first item in your document. The XML declaration uses the `<?xml?>` element.

Example:

```
<?xml version="1.0" encoding="UTF-8" standalone="no"?>
```

One Root Element Only

Each XML document must have one root element and no more. All other elements must be contained within the root element.

Example:

```
<root>
  <child>Data</child>
  <child>More Data</child>
</root>
```

XML Markup

Generally speaking, an XML document consists of *markup* and *data*. Markup is provided in the form of tags and attributes. Data is the text that goes in between the tags or is provided within their attributes.

```
<?xml version="1.0" encoding="UTF-8" standalone="no"?>
<!DOCTYPE document system "tutorials.dtd">
<student>
<name> Enter Name</name>
<roll>Enter Roll No.</roll>
</student>
```

11.5 XML ELEMENTS

XML elements are represented by tags. Elements usually consist of an opening tag and a closing tag, but they can consist of just one tag. Opening tags consist of <, followed by the element name, and ending with >. Closing tags are the same but have a forward slash inserted between the less than symbol and the element name.

Example:

```
<tag>Data</tag>
```

Empty elements are closed by inserting a forward slash before the greater than symbol.

Example of empty tag:

```
<tag />
```

Syntax Rules are Given Below:

All Elements Must be Closed Properly

If you're familiar with HTML, you will know that some HTML tags don't need to be closed. In XML however, you must close all tags. This is usually done in the form of a closing tag where you repeat the opening tag, but place a forward slash before the element name (*i.e.*, `</child>`). If you are using an empty element (i.e., one with no closing tag), you need to place a forward slash before the greater than symbol at the end of the tag (*i.e.*, `<child />`).

Example for opening/closing tags:

```
<child>Data</child>
```

Example for empty elements:

```
<child attribute="value" />
```

Tags are Case Sensitive

All tags must be written using the correct case. XML sees `<tutorial>` as a different tag to `<Tutorial>`

Wrong:

```
<Tutorial>XML</tutorial>
```

Right:

```
<Tutorial>XML</Tutorial>
<tutorial>XML</tutorial>
<TUTORIAL>XML</TUTORIAL>
```

Elements Must be Nested Properly

You can place elements inside other elements but you need to ensure each element's closing tag doesn't overlap with any other tags.

Wrong:

```
<tutorial>
<name>XML</tutorial>
</name>
```

Right:

```
<tutorial>
<name>XML</name>
</tutorial>
```

Element Names

You can use any name you like for your elements as long as they adhere to the following rules:

- Element names can contain any character (including letters and numbers)
- Element names must not contain spaces
- Element names must not begin with a number or punctuation character (for example a comma or semi-colon etc)
- Element names must not start with the letters *xml* (whether lowercase, uppercase, or mixed case)

You should using a colon (:) in your element names, as this is reserved for another purpose.

11.6 XML ATTRIBUTES

XML elements can also contain attributes. You use attributes within your elements to provide more information about the element. These are represented as name/value pairs.

Example:

```
<tag attribute="value">Data</tag>
```

It's important to remember the following syntax rules when using attributes.

Quotes

You must place quotation marks around the attribute's value.

```
<tutorials type="Web">
  <tutorial>
    <name>XML</name>
  </tutorial>
</tutorials>
```

Shorthand is Prohibited

Attributes must contain a value. Some HTML coders like to use shorthand, where if you provide the attribute name without a value, it will equal true. This is not allowed in XML.

```
<tutorials published="true">
  <tutorial>
    <name>XML</name>
  </tutorial>
</tutorials>
```

11.7 XML WITH CSS

To refresh your memory, here's what a raw XML file looks like in Firefox:

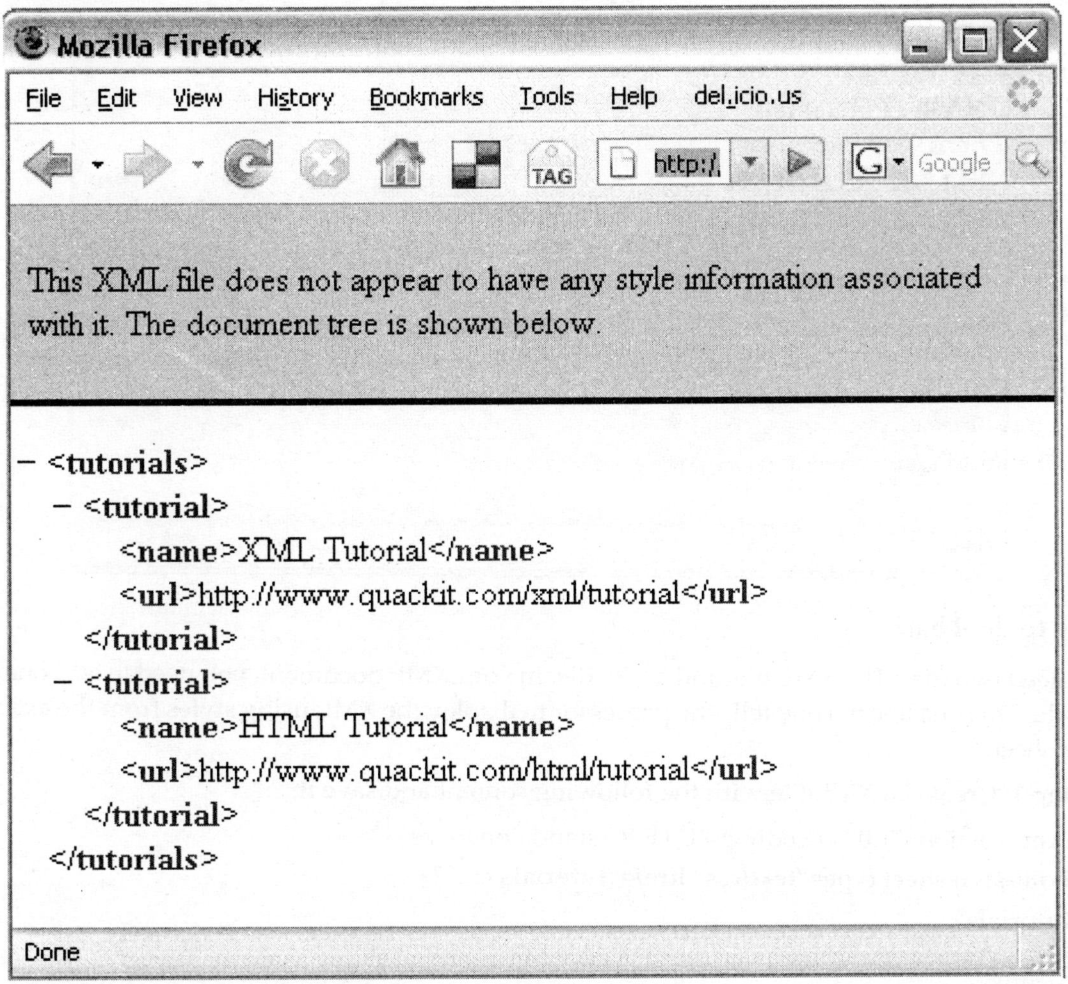

You might notice that, apart from some basic formatting, it doesn't look much different to viewing the file in a text editor such as Notepad. This is to be expected because the browser doesn't know anything about how our tags/elements should appear so it just displays it as is. Actually, Firefox even provides us with a message stating that the document has no style information associated with it.

In order to change this, we need to specify some styles that stipulate how our XML should be displayed. We can do this using Cascading Style Sheets (CSS).

Applying CSS

This XML document has been styled using CSS. If your browser supports XML and CSS, it should look something like this:

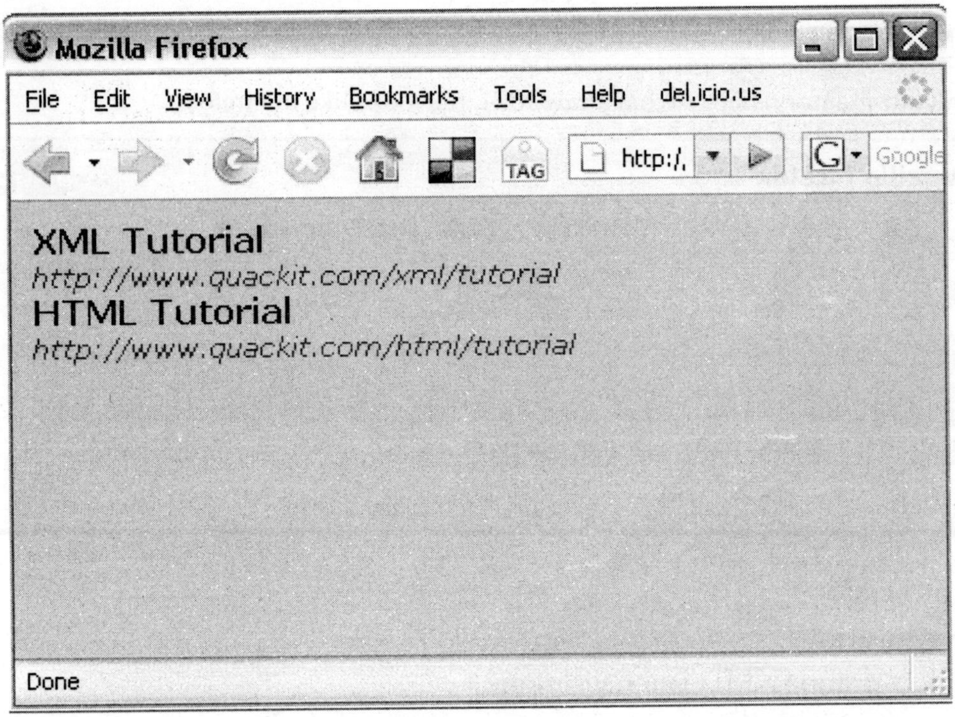

How to do That?

You need two files: The XML file, and a CSS file. In your XML document, you need to add one line of code. This one line of code tells the processor to display the XML using styles from the external style sheet.

Step 1: Create an XML file with the following content and save it:

```
<?xml version="1.0" encoding="UTF-8" standalone="yes"?>
<?xml-stylesheet type="text/css" href="tutorials.css"?>
<tutorials>
<tutorial>
<name>XML Tutorial</name>
<url>http://www.quackit.com/xml/tutorial</url>
</tutorial>
<tutorial>
<name>HTML Tutorial</name>
<url>http://www.quackit.com/html/tutorial</url>
</tutorial>
</tutorials>
```

In order to style our XML document, we can simply add those elements to our style sheet, followed by the styles we want to be applied to that element. If we don't need to style an element, we can omit it from the style sheet.

Step 2: Create a file with the following content and save it as *tutorials.css* into the same directory as the XML file.

```
tutorials
{
margin:10px;
background-color:#ccff00;
font-family:verdana,helvetica,sans-serif;
}
name
{
display:block;
font-weight:bold;
}
url
{
display:block;
color:#636363;
font-size:small;
font-style:italic;
}
```

Now, when you view your XML file in a browser, it should be styled using the styles from the CSS file.

11.8 XML AND XSL

Applying styles improved the look of our document when viewing it with a browser.

XML also has it's own styles language - *XSL*. XSL stands for *Extensible Styles Language* and is a very powerful language for applying styles to XML documents. XSL has two parts - a *formatting* language and a *transformation* language.

The formatting language allows you to apply styles similar to what CSS does. Browser support for the XSL formatting language is limited at this stage.

The transformation language is known as XSLT (XSL Transformations). XSLT allows you to transform your XML document into another form. For example, you could use XSLT to dynamically output some (or all) of the contents of your XML file into an HTML document containing other content.

XSLT Example

Using our previous XML example, imagine if we wanted to add a heading and some text to the top of the document when we output our XML document. Something like this:

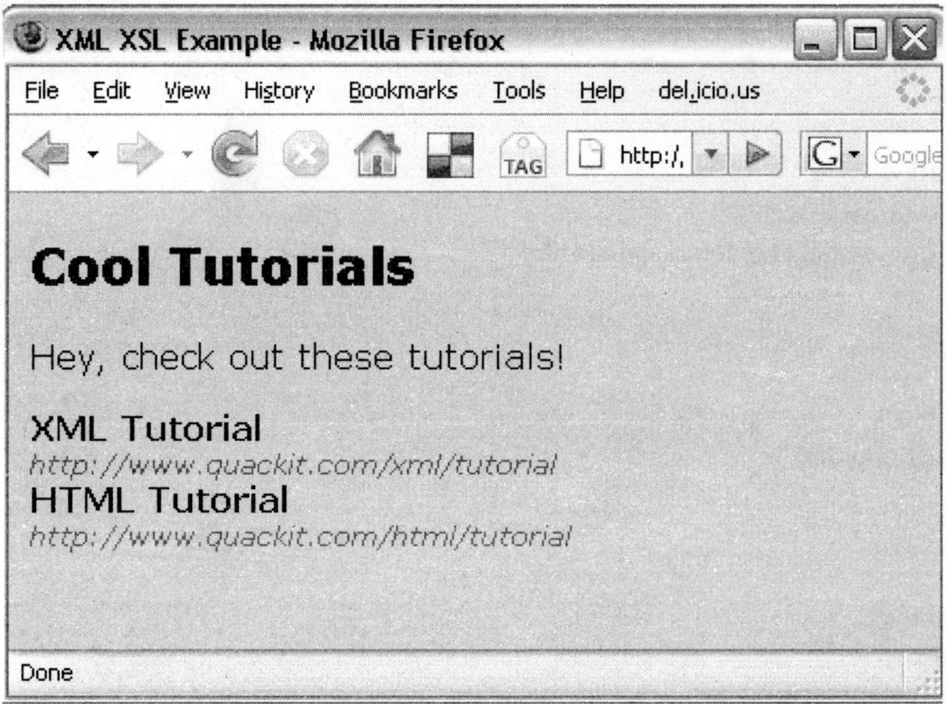

The only problem is, the heading and the text isn't in the XML file. Well, this is where XSLT comes in. Using XSLT, all we need to do is create a style sheet that transforms the XML into HTML and adds the heading/text.

How to do This?

Instead of linking to a CSS file, we will link to a XSL file.

Step 1: Create an XML file with the following content and save it.

```
<?xml version="1.0" encoding="UTF-8" standalone="yes"?>
<?xml-stylesheet type="text/xsl" href="tutorials.xsl"?>
<tutorials>
<tutorial>
<name>XML Tutorial</name>
<url>http://www.quackit.com/xml/tutorial</url>
</tutorial>
<tutorial>
<name>HTML Tutorial</name>
<url>http://www.quackit.com/html/tutorial</url>
</tutorial>
</tutorials>
```

Step 2: Create a file with the following content and save it as *tutorials.xsl* into the same directory as the XML file.

```
<?xml version="1.0"?>
<xsl:stylesheet version="1.0" xmlns:xsl="http://www.w3.org/1999/XSL/Transform">
<xsl:template match="/">
<html>
<head>
<title>XML XSL Example</title>
<style type="text/css">
body
{
margin:10px;
background-color:#ccff00;
font-family:verdana,helvetica,sans-serif;
}
.tutorial-name
{
display:block;
font-weight:bold;
}
.tutorial-url
{
display:block;
color:#636363;
font-size:small;
font-style:italic;
}
</style>
</head>
<body>
<h2>Cool Tutorials</h2>
<p>Hey, check out these tutorials!</p>
<xsl:apply-templates/>
</body>
</html>
</xsl:template>
<xsl:template match="tutorial">
<span class="tutorial-name"><xsl:value-of select="name"/></span>
<span class="tutorial-url"><xsl:value-of select="url"/></span>
</xsl:template>
</xsl:stylesheet>
```

I don't expect you to understand all this code just yet. I'll be explaining that later on - I've written a whole section on XSLT. But, it does give you an hint of what's to come in this tutorial. In the above XSL file, I'm using XSLT and XPath - both of which are explained later in this tutorial.

11.9 XML NAMESPACE

In XML, a *namespace* is used to prevent any conflicts with element names.

Because XML allows you to create your own element names, there's always the possibility of naming an element exactly the same as one in another XML document.

Example Name Conflict

Imagine we have an XML document containing a list of books. Something like this:

```
<books>
 <book>
  <title>The Dream Saga</title>
  <author>Matthew Mason</author>
 </book>
 ...
</books>
```

And imagine we want to combine it with the following HTML page:

```
<html>
 <head>
  <title>Cool Books</title>
 </head>
 <body>
 <p>Here's a list of cool books...</p>
 (XML content goes here)
 </body>
</html>
```

11.10 XML LOCAL NAMESPACE

When we defined the namespace, we defined it against the root element. This meant that the namespace was to be used for the whole document, and we prefixed all child elements with the same namespace.

You can also define namespaces against a child node. This way, you could use multiple namespaces within the same document if required.

Example Local Namespace

Here, we apply the namespace against the *title* element only:

```
<books>
  <book>
    <bk:title xmlns:bk="http://somebooksite.com/book_spec">
     The Dream Saga
    </bk:title>
    <author>Matthew Mason</author>
  </book>
  ...
</books>
```

Multiple Namespaces

You could also have multiple namespaces within your XML document. For example, you could define one namespace against the root element, and another against a child element.

Example:

```
<bk:books xmlns:bk="http://somebooksite.com/book_spec">
  <bk:book>
    <bk:title>The Dream Saga</bk:title>
    <bk:author>Matthew Mason</bk:author>
    <pub:name xmlns:pub="http://somepublishingsite.com/spec">
     Sid Harta Publishers
    </pub:name>
    <pub:email>author@sidharta.com.au</pub:email>
  </bk:book>
  ...
</bk:books>
```

11.11 XML DEFAULT NAMESPACE

You can also use what is known as a *default namespace* within your XML documents. A default namespace is one where you don't apply a prefix. You can also define namespaces against a child node. This way, you could use multiple namespaces within the same document if required.

Example Default Namespace

Here, we define the namespace without a prefix:

```
<books xmlns="http://somebooksite.com/book_spec">
  <book>
    <title>The Dream Saga</title>
    <author>Matthew Mason</author>
  </book>
  ...
</books>
```

When you define the namespace without a prefix, all descendant elements are assumed to belong to that namespace, unless specified otherwise (*i.e.*, with a local namespace).

11.12 XML ENTITIES

XML entities allow you to use text to refer to a data item, instead of using the data item itself.

You can use entities to represent:

- Characters that would otherwise cause problems for the XML processor
- Large blocks of data that need to be repeated throughout the document
- Characters that you can't type on your keyboard (*i.e.*, ©)

Problematic Characters

Some characters have a special meaning in XML. For example, the less than sign (<) marks the beginning of a tag. And, of course, the greater than sign (>) marks the end of the tag. When the XML processor parses the document, it looks for these characters (and others) to determine how to interpret the document.

This is fine, as long as your data doesn't contain any of these characters. But what if it does? What if your data contains say, a less than sign?

Imagine you had the following text within an element: *10 < 5*. When the XML processor encounters the <, it will assume it's the start of an opening tag. Problem is, it's not.

In order to include characters such as < and & etc, you need to use their *entity reference* instead of the character itself.

Entity Syntax

You start an entity reference using the & character and close it using the ; character.

Example:

<

The above entity reference represents the following character:

<

Predefined Entity References

There are 5 predefined entity references in XML. These are:

Entity Reference	Character
<	<
>	>
&	&
"	"
'	'

11.13 XML CREATING ENTITIES

To create your own entity, you simply define the entity in your DTD. Once you've defined the entity in your DTD, you are ready to use it within your XML document.

Note: We will be covering DTDs later so don't be too concerned if you don't know what a DTD is yet.

Defining your Entity

You define your entity using the <!ENTITY> element using the following syntax:

<!ENTITY *name definition*>

Here, `name` is the entity's name. `definition` is the entity's definition.

Using your Entity

Whenever you need to use your entity, you simply write the entity's name, surrounded by an ampersand (&) and a semi-colon (&).

&entity_name;

Example

Imagine you have some text that you want to repeat at the bottom of all your documents. Let's say the text goes something like "Thank you, please come again!".

Instead of typing all that text out every time you need to use it, you could create an entity called say, "footer". That way, you just need to include *&footer;* whenever you want to include that text. Now, if you ever need to change the text you only need to change it in one place - the definition.

```
<?xml version="1.0"?>
<!DOCTYPE tutorials [
<!ENTITY footer "Thank you, please come again!">
<]>
<tutorials>
  <tutorial>
    <name>XML Tutorial</name>
    <url>http://www.quackit.com/xml/tutorial</url>
    <footer>&footer;</footer>
  </tutorial>
  <tutorial>
    <name>HTML Tutorial</name>
    <url>http://www.quackit.com/html/tutorial</url>
    <footer>&footer;</footer>
  </tutorial>
</tutorials>
```

11.14 XML CDATA

In XML, a *CDATA section* is used to escape a block of text that would otherwise be parsed as markup.

Why are CDATA Sections Useful?

You might occasionally find that your data contains large blocks of text with lots of potentially problematic characters. For example, your data could contain a programming script. Many progamming scripts contain characters such as less than/greater than signs, ampersands etc, which would cause problems for the XML processor.

CDATA allows you to escape the whole block of text. This eliminates the need to go through the whole script, individually replacing all the potentially problematic characters. The XML processor knows to escape all data between the CDATA tags.

CDATA Syntax

You declare a CDATA section using `<![CDATA[` as the opening tag, and `]]>` as the closing tag.

Example:

```
<root>
 <child>
 <![CDATA[
   Text you want to escape goes here...
 ]]>
 </child>
</root>
```

CDATA Section Example

```
<?xml version="1.0"?>
<!DOCTYPE html PUBLIC "-//W3C//DTD XHTML 1.0 Transitional//EN"
"http://www.w3.org/TR/xhtml1/DTD/xhtml1-transitional.dtd">
<html  xmlns="http://www.w3.org/1999/xhtml">
<head>
<title>Displaying the Time</title>

<script  type="text/javascript">
<![CDATA[
 var currentTime = new Date()
 var hours = currentTime.getHours()
 var minutes = currentTime.getMinutes()

 var suffix = "AM";
 if (hours >= 12) {
 suffix = "PM";
 hours = hours - 12;
 }
 if (hours == 0) {
 hours = 12;
```

```
}
if (minutes < 10)
minutes = "0" + minutes
document.write("<b>" + hours + ":" + minutes + " " + suffix + "</b>")
]]>
</script>
</head>
<body>
<h1>Displaying the Time</h1>
</body>
t
```

XML INTERVIEW QUESTIONS AND ANSWERS

1. *What is XML?*

Solution: XML is the Extensible Markup Language. It improves the functionality of the Web by letting you identify your information in a more accurate, flexible, and adaptable way.

It is extensible because it is not a fixed format like HTML (which is a single, predefined markup language). Instead, XML is actually a metalanguage—a language for describing other languages—which lets you design your own markup languages for limitless different types of documents. XML can do this because it's written in SGML, the international standard metalanguage for text document markup (ISO 8879).

2. *What is a markup language?*

Solution: A markup language is a set of words and symbols for describing the identity of pieces of a document (for example 'this is a paragraph', 'this is a heading', 'this is a list', 'this is the caption of this figure', etc). Programs can use this with a style sheet to create output for screen, print, audio, video, Braille, etc.

Some markup languages (*e.g.*, those used in word processors) only describe appearances ('this is italics', 'this is bold'), but this method can only be used for display, and is not normally re-usable for anything else.

3. *Where should I use XML?*

Solution: Its goal is to enable generic SGML to be served, received, and processed on the Web in the way that is now possible with HTML. XML has been designed for ease of implementation and for interoperability with both SGML and HTML.

Despite early attempts, browsers never allowed other SGML, only HTML (although there were plugins), and they allowed it (even encouraged it) to be corrupted or broken, which held development back for over a decade by making it impossible to program for it reliably. XML fixes that by making it compulsory to stick to the rules, and by making the rules much simpler than SGML.

But XML is not just for Web pages: in fact it's very rarely used for Web pages on its own because browsers still don't provide reliable support for formatting and transforming it. Common uses for XML include:

Information identification because you can define your own markup, you can define meaningful names for all your information items. Information storage because XML is portable and non-proprietary, it can be used to store textual information across any platform. Because it is backed by an international standard, it will remain accessible and processable as a data format. Information structure XML can therefore be used to store and identify any kind of (hierarchical) information structure, especially for long, deep, or complex document sets or data sources, making it ideal for an information-management back-end to serving the Web. This is its most common Web application, with a transformation system to serve it as HTML until such time as browsers are able to handle XML consistently. Publishing

The original goal of XML as defined in the quotation at the start of this section. Combining the three previous topics (identity, storage, structure) means it is possible to get all the benefits of robust document management and control (with XML) and publish to the Web (as HTML) as well as to paper (as PDF) and to other formats (*e.g.*, Braille, Audio, etc) from a single source document by using the appropriate style sheets. Messaging and data transfer

XML is also very heavily used for enclosing or encapsulating information in order to pass it between different computing systems which would otherwise be unable to communicate. By providing a lingua franca for data identity and structure, it provides a common envelope for inter-process communication (messaging). Web services

Building on all of these, as well as its use in browsers, machine-processable data can be exchanged between consenting systems, where before it was only comprehensible by humans (HTML). Weather services, e-commerce sites, blog newsfeeds, AJAX sites, and thousands of other data-exchange services use XML for data management and transmission, and the web browser for display and interaction.

4. *Why is XML such an important development?*

Solution: It removes two constraints which were holding back Web developments:

1. dependence on a single, inflexible document type (HTML) which was being much abused for tasks it was never designed for;
2. the complexity of full SGML, whose syntax allows many powerful but hard-to-program options.

XML allows the flexible development of user-defined document types. It provides a robust, non-proprietary, persistent, and verifiable file format for the storage and transmission of text and data both on and off the Web; and it removes the more complex options of SGML, making it easier to program for.

5. *Describe the role that XSL can play when dynamically generating HTML pages from a relational database.*

Solution: Even if candidates have never participated in a project involving this type of architecture, they should recognize it as one of the common uses of XML. Querying a database and then formatting the result set so that it can be validated as an XML document allows developers to translate the data into an HTML table using XSLT rules. Consequently, the format of the resulting

HTML table can be modified without changing the database query or application code since the document rendering logic is isolated to the XSLT rules.

6. *What is SGML?*

Solution: SGML is the Standard Generalized Markup Language (ISO 8879:1986), the international standard for defining descriptions of the structure of different types of electronic document. There is an SGML FAQ from David Megginson at http://math.albany.edu:8800/hm/sgml/cts-faq.htmlFAQ; and Robin Cover's SGML Web pages are at http://www.oasis-open.org/cover/general.html. For a little light relief, try Joe English's 'Not the SGML FAQ' at http://www.flightlab.com/~joe/sgml/faq-not.txtFAQ.

SGML is very large, powerful, and complex. It has been in heavy industrial and commercial use for nearly two decades, and there is a significant body of expertise and software to go with it.

XML is a lightweight cut-down version of SGML which keeps enough of its functionality to make it useful but removes all the optional features which made SGML too complex to program for in a Web environment.

7. *Aren't XML, SGML, and HTML all the same thing?*

Solution: Not quite; SGML is the mother tongue, and has been used for describing thousands of different document types in many fields of human activity, from transcriptions of ancient Irish manuscripts to the technical documentation for stealth bombers, and from patients' clinical records to musical notation. SGML is very large and complex, however, and probably overkill for most common office desktop applications.

XML is an abbreviated version of SGML, to make it easier to use over the Web, easier for you to define your own document types, and easier for programmers to write programs to handle them. It omits all the complex and less-used options of SGML in return for the benefits of being easier to write applications for, easier to understand, and more suited to delivery and interoperability over the Web. But it is still SGML, and XML files may still be processed in the same way as any other SGML file (see the question on XML software).

HTML is just one of many SGML or XML applications-the one most frequently used on the Web.

Technical readers may find it more useful to think of XML as being SGML— rather than HTML++.

8. *Who is responsible for XML?*

Solution: XML is a project of the World Wide Web Consortium (W3C), and the development of the specification is supervised by an XML Working Group. A Special Interest Group of co-opted contributors and experts from various fields contributed comments and reviews by email.

XML is a public format: it is not a proprietary development of any company, although the membership of the WG and the SIG represented companies as well as research and academic institutions. The v1.0 specification was accepted by the W3C as a Recommendation on Feb 10, 1998.

9. *Why is XML such an important development?*

Solution: It removes two constraints which were holding back Web developments:

1. dependence on a single, inflexible document type (HTML) which was being much abused for tasks it was never designed for;

2. the complexity of full question A.4, SGML, whose syntax allows many powerful but hard-to-program options.

XML allows the flexible development of user-defined document types. It provides a robust, non-proprietary, persistent, and verifiable file format for the storage and transmission of text and data both on and off the Web; and it removes the more complex options of SGML, making it easier to program for.

10. *Give a few examples of types of applications that can benefit from using XML.*

Solution: There are literally thousands of applications that can benefit from XML technologies. The point of this question is not to have the candidate rattle off a laundry list of projects that they have worked on, but, rather, to allow the candidate to explain the rationale for choosing XML by citing a few real world examples. For instance, one appropriate answer is that XML allows content management systems to store documents independently of their format, which thereby reduces data redundancy. Another answer relates to B2B exchanges or supply chain management systems. In these instances, XML provides a mechanism for multiple companies to exchange data according to an agreed upon set of rules. A third common response involves wireless applications that require WML to render data on hand held devices.

11. *What is DOM and how does it relate to XML?*

Solution: The Document Object Model (DOM) is an interface specification maintained by the W3C DOM Workgroup that defines an application independent mechanism to access, parse, or update XML data. In simple terms it is a hierarchical model that allows developers to manipulate XML documents easily Any developer that has worked extensively with XML should be able to discuss the concept and use of DOM objects freely. Additionally, it is not unreasonable to expect advanced candidates to thoroughly understand its internal workings and be able to explain how DOM differs from an event-based interface like SAX.

12. *What is SOAP and how does it relate to XML?*

Solution: The Simple Object Access Protocol (SOAP) uses XML to define a protocol for the exchange of information in distributed computing environments. SOAP consists of three components: an envelope, a set of encoding rules, and a convention for representing remote procedure calls. Unless experience with SOAP is a direct requirement for the open position, knowing the specifics of the protocol, or how it can be used in conjunction with HTTP, is not as important as identifying it as a natural application of XML.

13. *Why not just carry on extending HTML?*

Solution: HTML was already overburdened with dozens of interesting but incompatible inventions from different manufacturers, because it provides only one way of describing your information.

XML allows groups of people or organizations to question C.13, create their own customized markup applications for exchanging information in their domain (music, chemistry, electronics, hill-walking, finance, surfing, petroleum geology, linguistics, cooking, knitting, stellar cartography, history, engineering, rabbit-keeping, question C.19, mathematics, genealogy, etc).

HTML is now well beyond the limit of its usefulness as a way of describing information, and while it will continue to play an important role for the content it currently represents, many new applications require a more robust and flexible infrastructure.

14. *Why should I use XML?*

Solution: Here are a few reasons for using XML (in no particular order). Not all of these will apply to your own requirements, and you may have additional reasons not mentioned here (if so, please let the editor of the FAQ know!).

- XML can be used to describe and identify information accurately and unambiguously, in a way that computers can be programmed to 'understand' (well, at least manipulate as if they could understand).
- XML allows documents which are all the same type to be created consistently and without structural errors, because it provides a standardised way of describing, controlling, or allowing/disallowing particular types of document structure. [Note that this has absolutely nothing whatever to do with formatting, appearance, or the actual text content of your documents, only the structure of them.]
- XML provides a robust and durable format for information storage and transmission. Robust because it is based on a proven standard, and can thus be tested and verified; durable because it uses plain-text file formats which will outlast proprietary binary ones.
- XML provides a common syntax for messaging systems for the exchange of information between applications. Previously, each messaging system had its own format and all were different, which made inter-system messaging unnecessarily messy, complex, and expensive. If everyone uses the same syntax it makes writing these systems much faster and more reliable.
- XML is free. Not just free of charge (free as in beer) but free of legal encumbrances (free as in speech). It doesn't belong to anyone, so it can't be hijacked or pirated. And you don't have to pay a fee to use it (you can of course choose to use commercial software to deal with it, for lots of good reasons, but you don't pay for XML itself).
- XML information can be manipulated programmatically (under machine control), so XML documents can be pieced together from disparate sources, or taken apart and re-used in different ways. They can be converted into almost any other format with no loss of information.
- XML lets you separate form from content. Your XML file contains your document information (text, data) and identifies its structure: your formatting and other processing needs are identified separately in a stylesheet or processing system. The two are combined at output time to apply the required formatting to the text or data identified by its structure (location, position, rank, order, or whatever).

15. *Can you walk us through the steps necessary to parse XML documents?*

Solution: Superficially, this is a fairly basic question. However, the point is not to determine whether candidates understand the concept of a parser but rather have them walk through the process of parsing XML documents step-by-step. Determining whether a non-validating or validating parser is needed, choosing the appropriate parser, and handling errors are all important aspects to this process that should be included in the candidate's response.

16. *Give some examples of XML DTDs or schemas that you have worked with.*

Solution: Although XML does not require data to be validated against a DTD, many of the benefits of using the technology are derived from being able to validate XML documents against business or technical architecture rules. Polling for the list of DTDs that developers have worked with provides insight to their general exposure to the technology. The ideal candidate will have knowledge of several of the commonly used DTDs such as FpML, DocBook, HRML, and RDF, as well as experience designing a custom DTD for a particular project where no standard existed.

17. *Using XSLT, how would you extract a specific attribute from an element in an XML document?*

Solution: Successful candidates should recognize this as one of the most basic applications of XSLT. If they are not able to construct a reply similar to the example below, they should at least be able to identify the components necessary for this operation: xsl:template to match the appropriate XML element, xsl:value-of to select the attribute value, and the optional xsl:apply-templates to continue processing the document.

Extract Attributes from XML Data

Example 1.

```
<xsl:template match="element-name">
Attribute Value:
<xsl:value-of select="@attribute"/>
<xsl:apply-templates/>
</xsl:template>
```

18. *When constructing an XML DTD, how do you create an external entity reference in an attribute value?*

Solution: Every interview session should have at least one trick question. Although possible when using SGML, XML DTDs don't support defining external entity references in attribute values. It's more important for the candidate to respond to this question in a logical way than the candidate know the somewhat obscure answer.

19. *How would you build a search engine for large volumes of XML data?*

Solution: The way candidates answer this question may provide insight into their view of XML data. For those who view XML primarily as a way to denote structure for text files, a common answer is to build a full-text search and handle the data similarly to the way Internet portals handle HTML pages. Others consider XML as a standard way of transferring structured data between disparate systems. These candidates often describe some scheme of importing XML into a relational or object database and relying on the database's engine for searching. Lastly, candidates that have worked with vendors specializing in this area often say that the best way the handle this situation is to use a third party software package optimized for XML data.

20. *Does XML replace HTML?*

Solution: No. XML itself does not replace HTML. Instead, it provides an alternative which allows you to define your own set of markup elements. HTML is expected to remain in common use for some time to come, and the current version of HTML is in XML syntax. XML is designed to make the writing of DTDs much simpler than with full SGML. (See the question on DTDs for what one is and why you might want one.)

21. *Do I have to know HTML or SGML before I learn XML?*

Solution: No, although it's useful because a lot of XML terminology and practice derives from two decades' experience of SGML.

Be aware that 'knowing HTML' is not the same as 'understanding SGML'. Although HTML was written as an SGML application, browsers ignore most of it (which is why so many useful things don't work), so just because something is done a certain way in HTML browsers does not mean it's correct, least of all in XML.

22. *What is the difference between XML and C or C++ or Java ?*

Solution: C and C++ (and other languages like FORTRAN, or Pascal, or Visual Basic, or Java or hundreds more) are programming languages with which you specify calculations, actions, and decisions to be carried out in order:

```
mod curconfig[if left(date,6) = "01-Apr",
t.put "April googlel!",
f.put days('31102005','DDMMYYYY') -
days(sdate,'DDMMYYYY')
" more shopping days to Samhain"];
```

XML is a markup specification language with which you can design ways of describing information (text or data), usually for storage, transmission, or processing by a program. It says nothing about what you should do with the data (although your choice of element names may hint at what they are for):

```
<part num="DA42" models="LS AR DF HG KJ"
update= "2001-11-22">
<name>Camshaft end bearing retention circlip</name>
<image drawing="RR98-dh37" type="SVG" x="476"
y="226"/> <maker id="RQ778">Ringtown Fasteners Ltd</maker>
<notes>Angle-nosed insertion tool <tool
id="GH25"/> is required for the removal
and replacement of this part.</notes>
</part>
```

On its own, an SGML or XML file (including HTML) doesn't do anything. It's a data format which just sits there until you run a program which does something with it.

23. *Does XML replace HTML?*

Solution: No. XML itself does not replace HTML. Instead, it provides an alternative which allows you to define your own set of markup elements. HTML is expected to remain in common use for some time to come, and the current version of HTML is in XML syntax. XML is designed to make the writing of DTDs much simpler than with full SGML. (See the question on DTDs for what one is and why you might want one.)

24. *Do I have to know HTML or SGML before I learn XML?*

Solution: No, although it's useful because a lot of XML terminology and practice derives from two decades' experience of SGML.

Be aware that 'knowing HTML' is not the same as 'understanding SGML'. Although HTML was written as an SGML application, browsers ignore most of it (which is why so many useful things don't work), so just because something is done a certain way in HTML browsers does not mean it's correct, least of all in XML.

25. *Does XML let me make up my own tags?*

Solution: No, it lets you make up names for your own element types. If you think tags and elements are the same thing you are already in considerable trouble: read the rest of this question carefully.

MULTIPLE CHOICE QUESTIONS

1. What does XML stand for?
   (*a*) eXtensible Markup Language (*b*) X-Markup Language
   (*c*) Example Markup Language (*d*) eXtra Modern Link
2. Which of the following is (are) a valid XML name(s)?
   (*a*) 1-2-4_6 (*b*) :3:-3:5:-7 (*c*) ;123456 (*d*) 3:4;-7
3. DOM 2 doesn't provide mechanism for interrogating and modifying the namespace for a document.
   (*a*) True (*b*) False
4. The DOM specification describes how strings are to be manipulated by the DOM by defining the datatype _______. It is encoded using _______ encoding scheme.
   (*a*) DOMString, UTF-8 (*b*) DOMString, Unicode
   (*c*) UNICODEString, Unicode (*d*) String, Unicode
5. An MNC receives at its headquarter from its subsidiaries, XML documents containing various reports of that subsidiary. These reports need to be displayed to the person responsible at the headquarter for that subsidiary in a user-friendly manner (allowing searches through the document) and the person is allowed to make any changes/comments that he/she desires. Once the user is done with all the changes/comments the information needs to be fed into the central database. Which of the following is MOST appropriate for processing these XML documents?
   (*a*) DOM (*b*) SAX (*c*) CSS (*d*) XSL
6. Which of the following is an XML-based service IDL that defines the service interface and its implementation characteristics.
   (*a*) UDDI (*b*) WSDL (*c*) SOAP (*d*) Path
7. Which statement about XML is true?
   (*a*) Elements may nest but not overlap
   (*b*) Quoting attributes is optional
   (*c*) Elements may have multiple attributes with the same name
8. What is the correct declaration syntax for the version of XML document?
   (*a*) <?xml version="1.0" /> (*b*) <?xml version="1.0"?>
   (*c*) <xml version="1.0" />
9. How is an empty element field defined?
   (*a*) <name></name (*b*) <name />
   (*c*) <name/> (*d*) All of the above
10. XML document must be valid?
    (*a*) True (*b*) False
11. Every XML document must be well formed
    (*a*) True (*b*) False
12. Every XML document must have an associated DTD or schema
    (*a*) True (*b*) False
13. XML preserves white spaces
    (*a*) True (*b*) False

14. For the XML parser to ignore a certain section of your XML document, which syntax is correct?

(*a*) <![CDATA[Text to be ignored]]>

(*b*) <xml:CDATA[Text to be ignored]>

(*c*) <PCDATA> Text to be ignored </PCDATA>

(*d*) <CDATA> Text to be ignored </CDATA>

15. What is a correct way of referring to a stylesheet called "style.xsl"?

(*a*) <stylesheet type="text/xsl" href="style.xsl" />

(*b*) <link type="text/xsl" href="style.xsl" />

(*c*) <?xml-stylesheet type="text/xsl" href="style.xsl" ?>

16. Which is not a correct name for an XML element?

(*a*) <first name> (*b*) <age>

(*c*) <NAME>

17. What does DTD stand for?

(*a*) Document Type Definition (*b*) Dynamic Type Definition

(*c*) Direct Type Definition

18. What makes XML more powerful than HTML?

(*a*) Not as much coding is needed

(*b*) Its ability to adapt to new uses

(*c*) The fact that its supported by all of the major software vendors

19. Unlike most other markup languages, including HTML, XML allows you to do what?

(*a*) Create new tags

(*b*) Exchange information over the Web

(*c*) Put your tags in any order, with closing tags optional

20. In what year did the World Wide Web Consortium release its draft of XML?

(*a*) 1994 (*b*) 1995 (*c*) 1996 (*d*) 1997

21. What organization presented the first version of Standardized Generalized Markup Language (SGML) in 1980?

(*a*) Internet Engineering Task Force (IETF)

(*b*) IEEE

(*c*) American National Standards Institute (ANSI)

(*d*) OASIS

22. You can use XSL Transformation (XSLT) to convert database files described by XML to Structured Query Language (SQL) statements, which creates the tables, indexes and views that the XML data describes.

(*a*) True (*b*) False

Answers of Multiple Choice Questions

1. (*a*),	**2.** (*b*),	**3.** (*b*),	**4.** (*b*),	**5.** (*a*),
6. (*b*),	**7.** (*a*),	**8.** (*b*),	**9.** (*d*),	**10.** (*a*),
11. (*a*),	**12.** (*b*),	**13.** (*a*),	**14.** (*a*),	**15.** (*c*),
16. (*a*),	**17.** (*a*),	**18.** (*b*),	**19.** (*a*),	**20.** (*c*),
21. (*c*),	**22.** (*a*).			

EXERCISE

1. What do you understand by XML?
2. Why we use XML?
3. Where HTML runs out of stream?
4. What are Naming rules in XML?
5. What do you mean by entity declarations?
6. What is Element Control model?
7. What are the procedures for checking well formedness of a document?
8. What do you mean by Object model?
9. What is DOM?
10. What is SAX?
11. What is the difference between SAX and DOM?

12

Active Server Pages

12.0 INTRODUCTION

Active Server Pages (ASP) is a server-side scripting technology that can be used to create dynamic and interactive Web applications. An ASP page is an HTML page that contains server-side scripts that are processed by the Web server before being sent to the user's browser. For designing a powerful website ASP uses XML, COM and HTML. Server-side scripts run when a browser requests an .asp file from the Web server. ASP is called by the Web server, which processes the requested file from top to bottom and executes any script commands. It then formats a standard Web page and sends it to the browser.

To run ASP script on your computer; you must have IIS(Internet Information Server). If IIS is not loaded in your computer then you must have administrator right to load it and make the setting. If you did not customize your installation of IIS, C:\InetPub\WWWroot was created as default directory. Let us make a web directory to run the file. Let it be abc. So now you save your files in C:\InetPub\WWWroot\abc.

12.1 WRITE AND RUN AN ASP PAGE

The best way to learn about ASP pages is to write your own. To create an ASP page, use a text editor to insert script commands into an HTML page. Saving the page with an .asp file name extension tells the Web server how to process the script commands. To view the results of a script, request the page using a Web browser. VBScript is the default scripting language for ASP, we have used Vbscript in the most of examples.

In HTML, you use brackets as delimiters around the tags:

<example>

In VBScript, you use the percent sign with brackets as delimiters around the tags:

<%example%>

You can put many tags inside one pair of VBScript delimiters:

<%example, samples%>

Example 1

This example displays the words "Hello World". To run this example, cut and paste it into an empty file and save it in the C:\Inetpub\Wwwroot\Abc directory as Example1.asp. Make sure to save your file with an .asp extension. Some text editors automatically change the file name extension to .txt when the **Text Document** option is selected in the **Save** dialog box. To prevent this, select the **All Files(*.*)** option. Exit your text editor as the server may not be able to display an HTML page that is open in a text editor. View your page with your browser by typing **http://<Your Server Name>/Abc/Example1.asp** in the address bar.

When running Example 1, the page is processed by the Web server in the following sequence:

1. Assigns the text "Hello World" to the variable FirstVar.
2. Uses HTML to make an HTML page.
3. Uses <%FirstVar%> to print out the value of the variable FirstVar.
4. Ends the HTML page.

```
<%@ Language=VBScript %>
<html>
<head>
<title>Example 1</title>
</head>
<body>
<%
FirstVar = "Hello world!"
%>
<%=FirstVar%>
</body>
</html>
```

Example 2

This example incorporates a FOR loop in the ASP page. The FOR loop is a statement that prints "Hello World" 10 times. To create Example 2, use the file from Example 1 and add the FOR loop code as shown in the following code sample. Save the file as Example2.asp. View it in your browser.

```
<%@ Language=VBScript %>
<html>
<head>
<title>Example 2</title>
</head>
<body>
<%
FirstVar = "Hello world!"
%>
<%FOR i=1 TO 10%>
```

```
<%=FirstVar%>
<%NEXT%>
</body>
</html>
```

Example 3

In this example, a time stamp is added to the ASP page. The word *time* is a function; it is a predefined VBScript function variable containing the current time. There are more than 90 functions in VBScript. Add the code for **time** shown in the following code sample to Example2.asp and save it as Example3.asp. View it in your browser.

```
<%@ Language=VBScript %>
<html>
<head>
<title>Example 3</title>
</head>
<body>
<%
FirstVar = "Hello world!"
%>
The time is: <%=time%> <BR>
<%FOR i=1 TO 10%>
<%=FirstVar%>
<%NEXT%>
</body>
</html>
```

Example 4

This example displays the message "Good Morning Everyone" if the hour is between 4:00 A.M. and 6:00 P.M. It displays the message "Good Night Everyone" if the hour is between 6:00 P.M. and 4:00 A.M. Add the IF THEN statement in the code shown below to Example3.asp and save it as Example4.asp.

```
<%@ Language=VBScript %>
<html>
<head>
<title>Example 4</title>
</head>
<body>
<%IF Hour(time)>18 OR Hour(time)<4 THEN%>
Good Night Everyone.
<%ELSE%>
Good Morning Everyone.
<%END IF%>
</body>
</html>
```

12.2 SEND INFORMATION BY USING FORMS

- A common use of intranet and Internet server applications is to process a form submitted by a browser. With ASP, you can embed scripts written in VBScript directly into an HTML file to process the form. ASP processes the script commands and returns the results to the browser.

Button Example

In this example, there are three input lines that use "buttons," and two default buttons-RESET and SUBMIT. The **Post** method is used to send data from the client browser to the Web server. Open your text editor, create a new file, and paste in the following code. Save the file as **Button.htm** and view the page in your browser.

```
<html>
<head>
<title>Button Form</title>
</head>
<body>
<FORM NAME="Button Example" METHOD="POST" ACTION="abc/button.htm">
Computer Programming Experience:
<P>
<INPUT TYPE="button" NAME="choice" VALUE="Less than 1">Less
than 1 year.<BR>
<INPUT TYPE="button" NAME="choice" VALUE="1 to 5">1-5 years.<BR>
<INPUT TYPE="button" NAME="choice" VALUE="More than 5">More
than 5 years.
</P>
<P><INPUT TYPE="reset" VALUE="Clear Form">
<INPUT TYPE="submit" VALUE="Submit">
</P>
</form>
</body>
</html>
```

Text example

In this example, you create text fields in a form. Open a new file in your text editor, paste in the following code, and save the file as Text.htm:

```
<html>
<head>
<title>Text Form</title>
```

```
</head>
<body>
<FORM NAME="Text Example" FORM METHOD="POST" ACTION="abc/text.htm">
<TABLE>
<TR>
<TD ALIGN="RIGHT" VALIGN="MIDDLE">Name?
<TD ALIGN="LEFT">
<INPUT TYPE="text" NAME="name" VALUE=""
      SIZE="20" MAXLENGTH="150">
<TR>
<TD ALIGN="RIGHT" VALIGN="MIDDLE">Company?
<TD ALIGN="LEFT">
<INPUT TYPE="text" NAME="company" VALUE=""
      SIZE="25" MAXLENGTH="150">
<TR>
<TD ALIGN="RIGHT" VALIGN="MIDDLE">
Email Address?
<TD ALIGN="LEFT">
<INPUT TYPE="text" NAME="email" VALUE=""
      SIZE="25" MAXLENGHT="150">
</TABLE>
<INPUT TYPE="reset">
<INPUT TYPE="Submit" NAME="Submit" VALUE="Submit">
</form>
</body>
</html>
```

12.3 CREATE A GUEST BOOK

Guest books allow visitors to your site a chance to give you feedback. Information such as the visitor's name, e-mail address, and comments can be available to you.

12.3.1 Create the Guest Book Database

You must first create an Access database called Guestbook.mdb and save it in the C:\Inetpub\Wwwroot\Abc directory. The database must have the fields with the properties described in the following table.

Field Name	Data Type and General Properties
ID	AutoNumber, Field Size=Long Integer, New Values=Increment, Indexed=Yes(No Duplicates)
TB1	Text, Field Size=255, Required=No, Allow Zero Length=Yes, Indexed=No

TB2	Text, Field Size=255, Required=No, Allow Zero Length=Yes, Indexed=No
TB3	Text, Field Size=255, Required=No, Allow Zero Length=Yes, Indexed=No
TB4	Text, Field Size=255, Required=No, Allow Zero Length=Yes, Indexed=No
MB1	Memo, Required=No, Allow Zero Length=Yes

After you create the database, you need to create a data source name (DSN) connection to the database so your ASP application can interact with it. The DSN must be created on the Web server that is running the ASP application. If you move the ASP application to a different Web server, you have to re-create the DSN on the new Web server. The following procedure describes how to create a DSN on Windows NT and Windows 2000.

1. In the ODBC Data Source Administrator, select the ODBC icon.
2. Select **File DSN**.
3. Select **Add**, select **Microsoft Access Driver,** and click **Next**.
4. Type in a descriptive name for your file DSN (Guestbook) and click **Next**.
5. Click **Finish**, click **Select**, specify the location of the database file, and select **OK**.
6. Click **OK** twice. After you specify the location of the database file, the ODBC Data Source Administrator creates a file DSN for it.

Now that you have created the database and the DSN, paste the following code into a file named Guestbook.asp and place it in the C:\Inetpub\Wwwroot\Abc directory.

```
<% @Language=VBScript %>
<html dir=ltr>
<head>
<TITLE>Guest Book</TITLE>
</head>
<body bgcolor="#FFFFFF" text="#000000">
<%
IF request.form ("Message")="True" THEN
strTB1=request.form("To")
strTB2=request.form("EMailAdd")
strTB3=request.form("CC")
strTB4=request.form("Subject")
strMB1=request.form("Memo")
IF strMB1 = "" THEN
iLenMB1=255
ELSE
iLenMB1 = Len(strMB1)
ENDIF
'Connects to the Access driver and Access database in the Inetpub
'directory where the database is saved
strProvider = "Driver={Microsoft Access Driver (*.mdb)};
DBQ=C:\Inetpub\Wwwroot\Abc\guestbook.mdb;"
```

```
'Creates an instance of an Active Server component
set objConn = server.createobject("ADODB.Connection")
'Opens the connection to the data store
objConn.Open strProvider
'Instantiate Command object and use ActiveConnection property to
'attach connection to Command object
set cm = Server.CreateObject("ADODB.Command")
cm.ActiveConnection = objConn
'Define SQL query
cm.CommandText ="INSERT INTO Guestbook (TB1,TB2,TB3,TB4,MB1)
VALUES (?,?,?,?,?)"
'Define query parameter configuration information for guestbook fields
set objparam=cm.createparameter(, 200, , 255, strTB1)
cm.parameters.append objparam
set objparam=cm.createparameter(, 200, , 255, strTB2)
cm.parameters.append objparam
set objparam=cm.createparameter(, 200, , 255, strTB3)
cm.parameters.append objparam
set objparam=cm.createparameter(, 200, , 255, strTB4)
cm.parameters.append objparam
set objparam=cm.createparameter(, 201, , iLenMB1, strMB1)
cm.parameters.append objparam
cm.execute
response.write("Thank you!")
ELSE%>
<h1>Guestbook</h1>
<!--Post information to Guestbook form -->
<form name=guestbook.asp action="guestbook.asp" method="POST">
<p>To</p>
<p><input type="Text" name="To"></p>
<p>Email Address</p>
<p><input type="Text" name="EmailAdd"></p>
<p> CC</p>
<p><input type="Text" name="CC"></p>
<p>Subject</p>
<p><input type="Text" name="Subject"></p>
<p>Message</p>
<p><textarea name="Memo" rows=6 cols=70></textarea></p>
<input type="HIDDEN" name="Message" value="True">
<input type="submit" value="Submit information">
```

```
</form>
<%End if%>
</body>
</html>
```

12.4 VIEW THE DATABASE IN A BROWSER

Using a database in web application to make it very powerful, useful, dynamic and you can easily update the data.

```
<% @Language=VBScript %>
<html dir=ltr>
<head>
<title>View Guest Book</title>
</head>
<body bgcolor="#FFFFFF" text="#000000">
<%
'This section makes it possible for visitors to sort the data in the
columns in ascending order.
if request.form("sort")<> "" THEN
StrSort=request.form("sort")
ELSE
StrSort="TB1 ASC"
END IF
strQuery="SELECT * FROM Guestbook ORDER BY " &StrSort
'Database path statement describing the driver to use and the
path to the desired database.
strProvider = "Driver=Microsoft Access Driver (*.mdb); DBQ=C:\Inetpub\Wwwroot\Abc\
guestbook.mdb;"
IF Request("ID") <> "" THEN
strIDNum=Request("ID")
'Creates an instance of an Active server component
set objConn = server.createobject("ADODB.Connection")
'Opens the connection to the data store
objConn.Open strProvider
'Instantiate Command object and use ActiveConnection property to
'attach connection to Command object
set cm = Server.CreateObject("ADODB.Command")
cm.ActiveConnection = objConn
'Define SQL query
cm.CommandText = "DELETE FROM Guestbook WHERE ID = " &strIDNum
```

```
cm.Execute
ENDIF
'Instantiate a Recordset object and open a recordset using
'the Open method
Set rst = Server.CreateObject("ADODB.recordset")
rst.Open strQuery, strProvider
%>
<h1>Guest Book</h1>
<form name=viewdb.asp action=viewdb.asp method=post>
<table border=1 cellspacing=3 cellpadding=3 rules=box>
<%
ON ERROR RESUME NEXT
IF rst.EOF THEN
Response.Write "There are no entries in the database."
ELSE%>
<tr>
<%
'Deletes rows from the database, this cannot be undone
Response.Write "<td width=200><center>Delete Record</center></td>"
FOR i = 1 to rst.Fields.Count -1
Response.Write "<td width=200><input name=sort value=" & rst(i).Name
& " type=submit></td>"
NEXT
WHILE NOT rst.EOF %>
<tr>
<%
Response.Write "<td align=left valign=top bgcolor='#ffffff'>
<a href=viewdb.asp?id=" & rst(0) & ">Delete</a></td>"
FOR i = 1 to rst.fields.count - 1
Response.Write "<td align=left valign=top bgcolor='#ffffff'>" & rst(i)
&"</td>"
NEXT
rst.MoveNext
WEND
ENDIF
%>
</table>
</form>
</body>
</html>
```

12.5 DISPLAY AN EXCEL SPREADSHEET IN ASP

Let us discuss a technique that can be used to display a Microsoft Excel spreadsheet in a Web page. There are several standard server components supplied with IIS. One of these is the ActiveX® Data Objects (ADO) component, which is used as a connection mechanism to provide access to data. In the database earlier, we used ADO. We use it again here to show you how to view and edit a spreadsheet with a Web browser.

To prepare your Excel spreadsheet for display in an Active Server Page:

1. Create a spreadsheet using either Excel 98 or Excel 2000 and save it as ASPTOC.xls in the C:\Inetpub\Wwwroot\directory.

   Note: Do not include any special formatting or column labels when creating the spreadsheet.
2. Highlight the rows and columns on the spreadsheet that you want displayed in the Web page.
3. On the **Insert** menu, choose **Name,** and select **Define**.
4. If there are any names listed, select them and select **Delete.**
5. Type a name for the workbook, select **Add,** and select **OK**.

To display the spreadsheet in a Web page, you must create a DSN for the spreadsheet. The process is the same as it was for the database lesson earlier in this module. The only difference is that you must select the **{Microsoft Excel Driver (*.xls)}** option for the DSN.

Once you have created the spreadsheet and named the table in the spreadsheet, and also created a DSN for the spreadsheet, you are ready to create the page that displays the contents. Paste the following code into a new file and name it ASPTOC.asp. Save it in the C:\Inetpub\Wwwroot\Abc directory and view the page in your browser.

```
<%@Language=VBScript %>
<html>
<head>
<title> Displaying An Excel Spreadsheet in an Web Page </title>
</head>
<body bgcolor="#FFFFFF" text="#000000" >
<h1>ASP Table of Contents</h1>
<%
'Creates an instance of an Active Server Component
Set oConn = Server.CreateObject("ADODB.Connection")
'Connects to the Excel driver and the Excel spreadsheet
'in the directory where the spreadsheet was saved
strConn = "Driver={Microsoft Excel Driver (*.xls)}; DBQ=C:\Inetpub\Wwwroot\Abc\ASPTOC.xls;"
'Opens the connection to the data store
oConn.Open strConn
'Selects the records from the Excel spreadsheet
strCmd = "SELECT * from `ASPTOC`"
Set oRS = Server.CreateObject("ADODB.Recordset")
```

```
'Opens the recordset
oRS.Open strCmd, oConn
'Prints the cells and rows in the table
Response.Write "<table border=1><tr><td>"
'Gets records in spreadsheet as a string and prints them in the table
Response.Write oRS.GetString (, , "</tr><td>", "</td></tr><tr><td>",
NBSPACE)
%>
</body>
</html>
```

12.6 ROTATE AD INFORMATION

Let us discuss how to take advantage of the Ad Rotator component installed with ASP by describing how to use this component to rotate advertisements on your Web pages. The Ad Rotator component selects an advertisement for your Web page each time the user refreshes or loads the Web page. Two files are required to set up the Ad Rotator component: an Ad Rotator Include file and an ad images data file. By setting up these two files, this component can be called by any ASP page on your site. Changes to the ad parameters are not done on all the sites containing the ad, but to the ad images data file. This saves lots of time if the ad appears on numerous pages within your Website. Now we describes the following:

Write an Ad Rotator Include File. Creates the ad-image links on any page that calls this file.

Create an Ad Image Data File. Specifies global ad-display data and information specific to each ad.

Test the Ad Rotator. Uses an ASP page that calls the Ad Rotator logic Include file and the image data file to display and rotate ads.

12.6.1 Write an Ad Rotator Include File

Include files are used to store information that will be used by more than one ASP or HTML file. By creating an Ad Rotator Include file, when changes need to be made to specific information, you only need to change the information in one location.

Open a new file in your text editor, paste in the following script, and save the file as Adrotatorlogic.inc:

```
<%
Function getAd()
Dim load
'Create an instance of the AdRotator component
Set load=Server.CreateObject("MSWC.AdRotator")
'Set the target frame, if any. This is the frame
'where the URL will open up. If the HTML page does
```

```
'not find the target name, the URL will be opened
'in a new window.
load.TargetFrame = "Target = new"
'Get a random advertisement from the text file.
getAd = load.GetAdvertisement("adimagedata.txt")
End Function
%>
```

12.6.2 Create an Ad Images Data File

An ad images data file is created to provide information about the ads to be displayed. By placing the data in one text file, when changes need to be made, you only need to change the data in one location. The ASP page (with the logic in the Include file) sends data in the ad images data file to the Ad Rotator component. The component then selects an ad for display.

The data file is divided into two sections that are separated by an asterisk (*). The first section provides information common to all the ads to be displayed. The second section lists data relevant to each ad.

- The following outlines the structure of an ad images data file:
- **REDIRECTION**. URL, the path and name of the ASP file that redirects browsers that select ad images.
- **WIDTH**. The width of ad images in pixels. Default is 440.
- **HEIGHT**. The height of ad images in pixels. Default is 60.
- **BORDER**. The border thickness around ad images. Default is 1.
- *. Separates the first section from the second section.
- **AdURL**. Virtual path and filename of the image file containing the advertisement.
- **AdHomeURL**. URL to jump to when this link is selected. To indicate there is no link, use a hyphen.
- **Text**. Text to display if browser does not support graphics.
- **Impressions**. An integer indicating the relative weight, or probability, that this ad will be selected for display. For example, if two ads were displayed, one with an impression of 3 and the other with 7, then the one with 3 would have a 30 percent probability of being selected, while the other would have a 70 percent probability.

Open a new file in your text editor, paste in the following script, and save the file as Adimagedata.txt:

```
REDIRECT adrotatorredirect.asp
WIDTH 250
HEIGHT 60
BORDER 0
* ' separates the general data from the image information
images/windows_logo.gif
http://www.microsoft.com/windows
Microsoft Windows
2
```

```
images/office_logo.gif
http://www.microsoft.com/office
Office 2000
3
```

12.6.3 Test the Ad Rotator

To test the system, you will need an ASP page that calls the Ad Rotator Include file and the ad images data file, and then displays the ads. First, you will need test ad images stored on your site.

Acquire and store the ad images as follows:

1. Create a directory named Images in the abc folder: C:\Inetpub\Wwwroot\Abc\Images.

Open a new file in your text editor, paste in the following script, and save the file as Displayad.asp:

```
<%@ Language="VBScript" %>
<!—Call the Include file, which in turn -->
<!—calls the ad images data text file-->
<!—#include file="adrotatorlogic.inc"-->
<html>
<head>
<title>Test Ad Display Page</title>
</head>
<body>
<h1>Test Ad Display Page</h1>
<!—Display the ad banner-->
<p><%=getAd()%></p>
<p>The space above should contain an image displaying either the
  Microsoft Windows family logo or the Microsoft Office
  family logo.</p>
<ul>
<li type="disc">This indicates that Displayad.asp, Adrotatorlogic.inc,
  and Adimagedata.txt are working together to correctly display the
  images.</li>
<li type="disc">Repeatedly refreshing the page should result in the
  Windows and Office logos displaying in random order.</li>
<li type="disc">After you save Adrotatorredirect.asp, clicking on the
  displayed image should cause a new window to open, displaying the
  home page corresponding to the displayed logo.</li>
<li type="disc">After you add the hit counter script to this page,
  under "Statistics" you should see the number of page hits since
  the script was added.</li>
```

```
</ul>
<br><br><br><br><br>
<h3>Statistics</h3>
<% Set pageCount = Server.CreateObject("MSWC.PageCounter") %>
<!—Increment the counter-->
<% pageCount.PageHit %>
<p>You are visitor number <% =pageCount.Hits %> to this Web page.</p>
</body>
</html>
```

12.6.4 Redirect Users from Ad Links

When a user clicks the ad, the browser appends a query string to the request to the server. Then, the server directs the user's browser to the ad's URL.

Open a new file in your text editor, paste in the following script, and save the file as Adrotatorredirect.asp:

```
<%@Language=VBScript %>
<html>
<head>
<title>Redirection Page</title>
</head>
<body>
<%
'Set the response buffer on
Response.Buffer = True
Dim lsURL
'Obtain the URL from the query string
lsURL = Request.QueryString("URL")
'Clear the response and redirect to URL
Response.Clear()
Response.Redirect(lsURL)
%>
</body>
</html>
```

To check your work, use Displayad.asp. When you click on an ad, you should see a new window displaying an appropriate ad-related Web page.

12.6.5 Count Page Hits

To know how many hits your Web pages get. For this use cointer in your web application or directly use Hits() function in your web application.

- **Hits()**. This displays the number of hits for a Web page. The default is the current page.
- **PageHit()**. This increments the hit count for the current page.
- **Reset()**. This resets the hit count for a page to zero. The default is the current page.

An in-use sample of this script can be seen at the bottom of the Displayad.asp script. To place a page hit counter on a Web page, place the following script where you want the counter displayed on the page:

```
<% Set pageCount = Server.CreateObject("MSWC.PageCounter") %>
<% pageCount.PageHit %>
You are visitor number <% =pageCount.Hits %> to this Website.
```

MULTIPLE CHOICE QUESTIONS — CLIENT SIDE ASP

1. In ASP, a request object retrieves info from a user by ________.
   (*a*) a collection of values sent as cookies in a HTTP header
   (*b*) a collection of data sent with a submitted form
   (*c*) from client variables described from within an object
   (*d*) from the OS module
   (*e*) A&B
2. Which of the following are ASP standard objects?
   (*a*) server (*b*) response (*c*) session (*d*) All of the above
3. Abandon is an ASP ________ object method.
   (*a*) server (*b*) session (*c*) request (*d*) response
4. In ASP, the Response Object is used to send output to the user from the server.
   (*a*) True (*b*) False
5. MapPath is an ASP ________ object method.
   (*a*) session (*b*) request (*c*) server (*d*) response
6. ASP is an acronym for what?
   (*a*) Active Server Protocol (*b*) ActiveX Server Pages
   (*c*) Active Setup Pages (*d*) Active Server Pages
   (*e*) Active Setup Protocol
7. ASP makes a website more interactive and dynamic.
   (*a*) True (*b*) False
8. How do you comment a line in ASP using VBScript?
   (*a*) <!-- Comment a line in ASP --> (*b*) < Comment a line in ASP >
   (*c*) 'Comment a line in ASP (*d*) <% Comment a line in ASP %>
9. Which is better in managing your code when writing with ASP or any other scripting code?
   (*a*) Break it up into smaller easier-to-manage files that can serve as subroutines and function calls.
   (*b*) Keep it nice and simple in one file and use subroutines and function calls.
10. My ASP page won't work is a common complaint for those new to ASP. Which of these can be the cause?
    (*a*) Syntax error such as missing parentheses, comma or quotation mark.
    (*b*) Comments in your code are not tagged properly as comments.

(c) Make sure function names have both opening and closing parentheses.
(d) Check to see that the web page is properly saved with the extension as .asp
(e) All of the above

11. You want to add ASP capability to your company's website. What is the first thing you would check?
(a) That all pages are saved in .asp extensions.
(b) Check that the web server has Microsoft FrontPage extensions installed.
(c) Make sure the web server is capable of hosting ASP pages.
(d) Check the coding and be sure the ASP code is surrounded with <% and %>
(e) All of the above

12. You have determined that your company's website is housed on a web server that cannot handle ASP. What would you do?
(a) Contact the ISP and have them switch the website to have ASP capability.
(b) Have your ISP install the Microsoft FrontPage extensions
(c) Develop a transition plan first that includes a step-by-step plan on every detail prior to contacting the ISP.
(d) All the above

13. Some say that JavaScript is easier to use than ASP and will run regardless of whatever operating system the web server is using (Unix, Linux, Windows 2000, etc). Then others say that ASP has advantages over JavaScript such as what?
(a) ASP does not depend upon which browser the viewer is using.
(b) ASP code does not show up in the source code; thus, the code is protected
(c) ASP does not download with the page to the viewer.
(d) ASP can easily interact with a database.
(e) All of the above

14. A feature of ASP is its ability to interact with a database. Which of these databases is the most popular to use with ASP?
(a) dBase
(b) Delimited text files
(c) Access (97 or 2000)
(d) Excel spreadsheets
(e) SQL

15. JavaScript is which?
(a) Client-side executable code (executes at the browser level)
(b) Server side executable code (runs at the server only)

16. ASP is which?
(a) Client-side executable code (executes at the browser level)
(b) Server side executable code (runs at the server only)

17. Client-side scripting code and server-side scripting code can coexist and can be used on the same page.
(a) True
(b) False

18. Variable are used to hold both numerical and text values. Which of these IS NOT a valid variable name?
(a) X
(b) X1
(c) 1X
(d) x1X

19. Which of these is OKAY to use for a variable name?

(*a*) employee salary
(*b*) 2nd_employee
(*c*) employee_hire_date
(*d*) date-of-birth
(*e*) date_of.birth

20. You have a long piece of code tracking employee salaries. In your opinion, which of these variables is the best (shortest yet most descriptiv(*e*) to use throughout the code to track the salaries of the managers? Keep in mind that you may try to analyze your

(*a*) manager_salaries
(*b*) SalariesOfManagers
(*c*) Salaries_Of_Managers
(*d*) mgmtSalary
(*e*) Salary1

21. ASP code is....

(*a*) a client-side executable code.
(*b*) a server-side executable code.
(*c*) a world-wide-web executable code.
(*d*) all of the above.

22. Which programming language is most commonly used to script ASP code?

(*a*) ASP
(*b*) JavaScript
(*c*) VBScript
(*d*) C++
(*e*) Perl

23. ASP pages can contain embedded HTML code.

(*a*) True
(*b*) False

24. What happens when a user types in a URL that requests an ASP page?

(*a*) Browser requests ASP code, server returns code, browser executes code into HTML form
(*b*) Browser requests ASP code, server executes ASP code and returns HTML document to browser
(*c*) Browser requests code, server returns code, Windows executes code since ASP is Microsoft code.

25. If the default pages in HTML are index.htm, default.html, etc, what are the default pages in ASP?

(*a*) index.asp
(*b*) default.asp
(*c*) home.asp
(*d*) Both A and B
(*e*) Both B and C

26. When writing ASP code, what are the correct delimiters to use?

(*a*) <!-- code -->
(*b*) < code >
(*c*) <% code >
(*d*) <% code %>

27. It is imperative when writing ASP code is to begin every file with which statement?

(*a*) <% Language=VBScript %>
(*b*) <% ASPLanguage = VBScript %>
(*c*) <%@ Language=VBScript %>

28. In order for you to execute ASP code on your computer, you need to be running web server software such as Personal Web Server.

(*a*) True
(*b*) False

29. ASP code can be written in any text editor such as Notepad.

(*a*) True
(*b*) False

Multiple Choice Questions—Server Side ASP

30. Thinking Question: ASP code can be written to show the current time. Is it possible to show a live, ticking clock using ASP?

(*a*) Yes, ASP will pull the time from the web server and feed it to the client browser.
(*b*) No, once the ASP script has finished executing, it cannot do any more after the page reaches the client browser.

31. Server-Side Includes (also known as SSI) allows you to do what?

(*a*) Allows you to include server executed code into any ASP application.

(*b*) Allows you to use one file in several different web pages.

(*c*) Allows you to use a piece of code more than once.

(*d*) All of the above

32. The include files can be written in which scripting language?

(*a*) HTML (*b*) JavaScript (*c*) VBScript (*d*) Perl

(*e*) All of the above

33. Changing an include file will affect all the pages that link to it such as a navigation bar. Suppose you want certain pages to display a certain navigation bar not available on other pages. Which is the BEST method to do this?

(*a*) Write a separate include file for those unique pages.

(*b*) Forget the include file. It is easier to just put the unique menu in using HTML code.

(*c*) Have the include file test for the type of page and then print out the correct menu.

34. An include file can be saved with a .asp extension.

(*a*) True (*b*) False

35. Which of these page extensions WILL NOT recognize and execute an include file?

(*a*) .shtml (*b*) .shtm (*c*) .stm (*d*) .html

(*e*) .asp

36. Which is the correct format of an include statement?

(*a*) <% '#include virtual="banner.asp" %>

(*b*) <!-- #include virtual="banner.asp" -->

(*c*) <-- #include virtual="banner.asp" -->

(*d*) <-- #include virtual="banner.asp" -->

37. An include file that contains ASP code can be saved with a .inc extension.

(*a*) True (*b*) False

38. Where would you place an include statement that has functions, subroutines and other configuration type of code?

(*a*) At the beginning to keep the code neat and tidy.

(*b*) Anywhere in the code where it is actually needed.

39. Lets say that your include file is a piece of code that will print out your navigation menu. Where would you place the include statement?

(*a*) At the beginning to keep the code neat and tidy

(*b*) Anywhere in the code where it is actually needed.

40. You are working on a file called index.asp and have put in the include statement below. Where is the include file actually located on the web server? ..<!-- #include file="config\ functions. asp" -->

(*a*) The include file is in the same directory as the file that is requesting it.

(*b*) The include file is in another directory away from the file that is requesting it.

41. When viewing the source code of a web page, the JavaScript code can be seen and copied; thus, the code is not secure. Since JavaScript and include statements are both written with the same HTML delimiters: <!-- and -->, this also means that the include st

(*a*) True (*b*) False

Answers of Multiple Choice Questions

1. (*e*)	2. (*d*)	3. (*b*)	4. (*a*)	5. (*c*)
6. (*d*)	7. (*a*)	8. (*c*)	9. (*a*)	10. (*e*)
11. (*c*)	12. (*c*)	13. (*e*)	14. (*c*)	15. (*a*)
16. (*b*)	17. (*a*)	18. (*c*)	19. (*c*)	20. (*d*)
21. (*b*)	22. (*c*)	23. (*a*)	24. (*b*)	25. (*d*)
26. (*d*)	27. (*a*)	28. (*a*)	29. (*a*)	30. (*b*)
31. (*d*)	32. (*e*)	33. (*c*)	34. (*a*)	35. (*d*)
36. (*b*)	37. (*a*)	38. (*a*)	39. (*b*)	40. (*a*)
41. (*b*).				

EXERCISE

1. What is ASP?
2. What is the procedure to run ASP?
3. What are the rules for writing ASP code?
4. What is the procedure to create the variable in ASP?
5. What are cookies?
6. What is the procedure for creating cookies?
7. What are application objects?
8. What 3is the procedure to include a file into ASP file?
9. What is session variable? How sessions are created and destroyed.
10. What is the procedure for lock and unlock in ASP?

13

INTRODUCTION TO PERL

13.0 CGI

Common Gateway Interface (CGI) is an important World Wide Web technology that enables a client web browser to request data from a program executed on the Web server. CGI specifies a standard for passing data between the client and the program.

Originally, CGI was invented by NCSA for the NCSA HTTPd web server in 1993. This web server used UNIX shell environment variables to store parameters passed from the web server execution environment before spawning the CGI program as a separate process.

The programming language Perl is well known as a language used for CGI, but one of the points of CGI is to be language-neutral. The Web server does not need to know anything about the language in question. In fact, CGI programs can be written in any scripting language or a full-fledged programming language, as long as that language can be executed on the system. Besides Perl, examples include Unix shell scripts, Python, Ruby, PHP, Tcl, C/C++, and Visual Basic.

An example of a CGI program is the one implementing a wiki: you hand it the name of an entry, and it will retrieve the source of that entry's page (if one exists), transform it into HTML, and send the result back to the browser. Or tell it that you want to edit a page. All wiki operations are managed by this one program.

Because this technology generally requires a fresh copy of the program to be executed for every CGI request, the workload could quickly overwhelm web servers, inspiring more efficient technologies such as mod_perl that allow script interpreters to be integrated directly into web servers as modules, thus avoiding the overhead of repeatedly loading and initializing language interpreters.

13.0.1 Data Communication on the Web

A Web client program (such as a web browser) can access data from many different servers, such as Gopher, FTP, NNTP (Usenet) or HTTP. The HTTP server was designed specifically for the Web, and employs a protocol (system of messages) that supports sending documents from the server to a browser, and that also support sending complex data *from* the client back *to* the server. There are several HTTP *methods* for doing this (in HTTP, *methods* is a technical term for the way in which data are sent between a client browser and server).

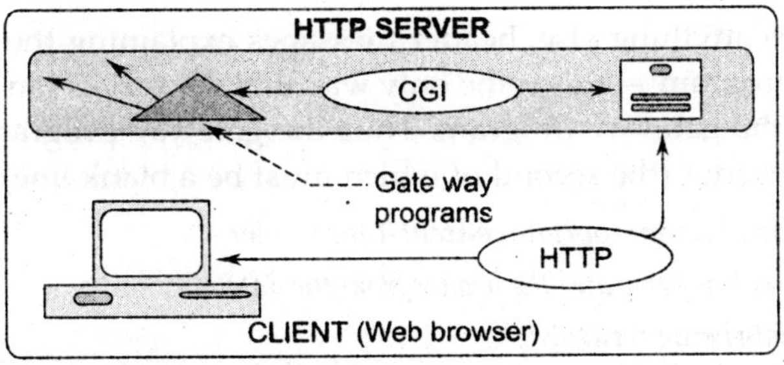

The most common methods are

- **GET** – the data are passed within the *query string* of the URL. For example, accessing the URL http://bla.bla.edu/stuff/program?query_string
sends the data included in query_string to the HTTP server running on the machine bla.bla.edu.
- **POST** – the data are sent as a *message body* that follows the request message sent by the client to the server. This is more complex than GET, but allows for more complex data.

The Common Gateway Interface, or CGI, is the mechanism used by most servers to process the client data.

13.0.2 Server Processing of Passed Data: Gateway Programs

In gateway program server cannot process data. It depends upon three things as follows:

- a second program to do process the data sent by the client,
- a mechanism by which the server can forward the data to this second program. Such secondary programs are called gateway programs, because they act as a gateway between the Web and other resources on the HTTP server machine, such as databases
- a way whereby this second program can return data to the client, so that the gateway program can return results of its analysis to the user.

13.0.3 The Common Gateway Interface

CGI (Common Gateway Interface) only worry about how data is send to the gateway and how data is returned to the gateway.

13.0.3.1 Sending Data to the Gateway Program

CGI (Common Gateway Interface) is the generic interface between the server and these server-side 'gateway' programs. The CGI specifies how data are sent to the gateway program (as environment variables or as data read, by the gateway program, from standard input) and what data are sent (in general, all the data sent by the client to the server, plus extra environment variables describing the status of the server).

13.0.3.2 Returning Data to the Client

To return data back to the client program (the user's web browsers) the gateway program just writes data to it's regular (standard) output. These data are sent back the the client, after some processing by the server to ensure they have the correct *message headers* describing the data and the state of the transaction. Of special note is the fact that the gateway program ***must*** write to standard output, before anything else, header messages explaining the MIME type of the data being returned by the program — this is the only way that the server can know what type of data are being returned by the gateway program. Thus the gateway program must, at the very list, print out a a two- line header (the second of which must be a blank line):

Content-type: text/html	*The appropriate content-type header*
	A blank line separates the header from the data
data	*The data being returned*

The preceeding was, of course, just a very cursory introduction to CGI. To become a proficient CGI developer you will need to learn:

- the details of HTML (so you can create valid FORMS, and so your gateway programs can return valid HTML documents as output);
- the details of the HTTP protocol (so you can return the correct HTTP headers from your gateway programs)
- the details of CGI protocol (you need to know the names of the different environment variables passed to the gateway programs; the contents of the variables, and the encoding schemes used to send client-data to the gateway program)
- how to write programs. Gateways are commonly written in perl or C, but you can use just about any programming language.

13.0.4 CGI Scripts

Web pages cannot interact directly with the reader. In fact, until JavaScript came along, Web pages had no way of interpreting reader reaction except through interaction with the server they were running on. This interaction is done through scripts and programs that use common gateway interface to create interactive programs on your Web pages.

13.0.4.1 Some Things to Remember About CGI Scripts

1. CGI is not the program itself

   CGI is simply the interface between the Web page or browser and the Web server that runs the program.
2. You must have CGI access to run programs on your Web page

   Many of the less expensive and free hosting providers do not allow CGI access on their servers. Contact your hosting provider for more information.
3. Any program or script that will run on your Web server, can be used as a CGI program Most people use Perl to write their CGI scripts, but other languages include C and C++, Tcl, and UNIX shell scripts.

13.0.4.2 Uses of CGI Scripts

Some of the most interesting uses of CGI are to create Web documents that depend on user interaction. There are scripts to take readers to random pages on the site, create pages specific to them based on form input, and generate pages based on databases of information.

CGI scripts are used to resolve form data, put that data in to databases, send the data out as an email message, and respond to the form entry with email or another Web page, and much more.

CGI scripts also are used for behind the scenes interaction with Web readers. They can set and read cookies, get and tabulate information such as browser and operating system, calculate hit counts, and monitor Web traffic.

13.0.4.3 *Advantages of CGI*

- Any browser can use the program (few expectations)
- CGI Scripts run on the external web server so they do not worry about the browser.
- The load of web server increases.

13.0.4.4 *Disadvantages of CGI*

The biggest drawback to CGI Scripts is that they can put a lot of load on a Web server. Poorly written programs can fall into endless loops tying up server processor time. The Web browser will time out (usually after around 5 minutes), but often the server will continue to run the program until a system administrator comes in and shuts off the faulty script. The browser based scripting tools mentioned above have the advantage of running off the reader's computer. They use the processor locally rather than on the Web server itself, and so are less intense on the Web server.

13.1 INTRODUCTION TO PERL

Perl is a *"Practical Extraction and Report Language"* freely available for Unix, MVS, VMS, MS/DOS, Macintosh, OS/2, Amiga, and other operating systems. Perl has powerful text-manipulation functions.Two types of programmers use Perl. System administrators like it for the way it glues together system commands to manipulate data and processes, and for its pattern-matching functions aids in system searches and reporting. People developing electronic forms for Unix Web servers find Perl easier to learn and use than C, and for their purposes Perl offers more built-in or publicly available functions such as easy data validation and simple databases.

13.2 STARTING PERL

Quite useful Perl programs can be short. Suppose we want to change the same text in many files. Instead of editing each possible file or constructing some cryptic find, awk, or sed commands, you could issue a single command:

Example: *Amazing Perl One-Liner That Substitutes Text In Multiple Files*

```
perl -e 's/gopher/World Wide Web/gi' -p -i.bak *.html
```

Example: *Global Substitution, The Scenic Route*

```
#!/usr/local/bin/perl -w
# File: go2www
# This Perl program in classic programming style changes
# the string "gopher" to "World Wide Web" in all files
# specified on the command line.
# 19950926 gkj
$original='gopher';
```

```
$replacement="World Wide Web";
$nchanges = 0;
# The input record separator is defined by Perl global
# variable $/. It can be anything, including multiple
# characters. Normally it is "\n", newline. Here, we
# say there is no record separator, so the whole file
# is read as one long record, newlines included.
undef $/;

# Suppose this program was invoked with the command
# go2www ax.html big.basket.html candle.html
# Then builtin list @ARGV would contain three elments
# ('ax.html', 'big.basket.html', 'candle.html')
# These could be accessed as $ARGV[0] $ARGV[1] $ARGV[2]
foreach $file (@ARGV) {
    if (! open(INPUT,"<$file") ) {
        print STDERR "Can't open input file $bakfile\n";
        next;
    }

    # Read input file as one long record.
    $data=<INPUT>;
    close INPUT;
    if ($data =~ s/$original/$replacement/gi) {
        $bakfile = "$file.bak";
        # Abort if can't backup original or output.
        if (! rename($file,$bakfile)) {
            die "Can't rename $file $!";
        }
        if (! open(OUTPUT,">$file") ) {
            die "Can't open output file $file\n";
        }
        print OUTPUT $data;
        close OUTPUT;
        print STDERR "$file changed\n";
        $nchanges++;
    }
    else { print STDERR "$file not changed\n"; }
}
print STDERR "$nchanges files changed.\n";
exit(0);
```

The Perl Creed is, "There is more than one way!" This noble freedom of expression however results in the first of the four **Perl Paradoxes:** *Perl programs are easy to write but not always easy to read.* For example, the following lines are equivalent!

```
if ($x == 0) {$y = 10;} else {$y = 20;}
$y = $x==0 ? 10 : 20;
$y = 20; $y = 10 if $x==0;
unless ($x == 0) {$y=20} else {$y=10}
if ($x) {$y=20} else {$y=10}
$y = (10,20)[$x != 0];
```

13.3 STORING AND RUNNING PERL PROGRAMS

Homework: Hello

To test your ability to store and run a Perl program, enter and execute something like this classic code:

```
#!/usr/local/bin/perl -w
if ($#ARGV >= 0) { $who = join(' ', @ARGV); }
else { $who = 'World'; }
print "Hello, $who!\n";
```

Here's How

Let us assume that the above lines are stored in a Unix file ~/bin/hello. (That's in your home directory, subdirectory bin, file hello.) You can then run the program by entering a command like:

```
perl ~/bin/hello
perl ~/bin/hello Citizens of Earth
perl hello                (If you're in the ~/bin directory.)
```

If you expect to use this program a lot and want to execute it as a command, then you need to do five things.

1. The first line of the program should after a "#!" specify the location of the perl command, typically as `#!/usr/local/bin/perl` or `#!/usr/bin/perl`, as illustrated in the preceding example program. This line can also give command options, like -w (warn of possible inconsistencies).
2. Set the execute permissions of the program file. To make the file executable (and readable and writable) by only yourself, use a Unix command like:

   ```
   chmod 700 ~/bin/hello
   ```

   To make it executable and readable by all enter a Unix command like the following:

   ```
   chmod a+rx ~/bin/hello
   ```

   You may also need to use chmod *a+x* on the directories ~ and ~/bin. See "man chmod" for details and the security implications. (The MU program "chweb" can make a file accessible to the Web server and yourself, but not to other users. See "man chweb" for details.)

3. Edit your file ~/.cshrc or ~/.login to make directory ~/bin part of the path Unix searches for executables, with a line like this:

```
set path = ($path ~/bin)
```

This takes effect the next time you start a default tcsh or csh shell (.cshrc file) or login (.login file). If you want it to take effect immediately, enter the above set path command at the Unix prompt or enter execute your .cshrc or .login file with the "source" command. If you are using sh, bash, ksh or some other shell, alter ~/.profile or some other file to set the path at login.

If a program you want to execute has just been newly created, then issue the csh/tcsh command "rehash" to rescan the path.

If you perform (1)–(5), then you can execute your program via a command like this:

```
hello
```

13.4 THE ELEMENTS

Perl's Three Data Structures

- **Scalars** can be numeric or character as determined by context:

```
123  12.4  5E-10  0xff  (hex)  0377  (octal)
'What you $see is (almost) what \n you get'  'Don\'t Walk'
"How are you?"  "Substitute values of $x and \n in \" quotes."
'date'  'uptime -u'  'du -sk $filespec | sort -n'
$x  $list_of_things[5]  $lookup{'key'}
```

Single-quotes ' ' allow no substitution except for \\ and \'. Double-quotes " " allow substitution of variables like $x and control codes like \n (newline). Back-quotes ` ` also allow substitution, then try to execute the result as a system command, returning as the final value whatever the system command outputs.

- **Arrays** of scalars (also called **lists**) are sequentially-arranged scalars:

```
('Sunday', 'Monday', 'Tuesday', 'Wednesday',
   'Thursday', 'Friday', 'Saturday')
(13,14,15,16,17,18,19)  equivalent to (13..19)
(13,14,15,16,17,18,19)[2..4]  equivalent to (15,16,17)
@whole_list
```

- **Associative arrays** (also called **hashes**) help you remember things:

```
$DaysInMonth{'January'} = 31;  $enrolled{'Joe College'} = 1;
$StudentName{654321} = 'Joe College';
$score{$studentno,$examno} = 89;
%whole_hash
```

Perl 5 allows combinations of these, such as lists of lists and associative arrays of lists.

Name Conventions

Scalar variables start with '$', even when referring to an array element. The variable name reference for a whole list starts with '@', and the variable name reference for a whole associative array starts with '%'.

Lists are indexed with square brackets enclosing a number, normally starting with [0]. In Perl 5, negative subscripts count from the end. Thus, `$things[5]` is the 6th element of array `@things`, and

```
('Sun','Mon','Tue','Wed','Thu','Fri','Sat')[1]
```

equals `'Mon'`.

Subroutines and **functions** are referenced with an initial '&', which is optional if reference is obviously a subroutine or function such as following the sub, do, and sort directives:

```
sub square { return $_[0] ** 2; }
print "5 squared is ", &square(5);
```

Filehandles don't start with a special character, and so as to not conflict with reserved words are most reliably specified as uppercase names: INPUT, OUTPUT, STDIN, STDOUT, STDERR, etc.

13.5 LITERALS AND OPERATORS

Example: Numbers and Characters

```
#!/usr/local/bin/perl
print '007',' has been portrayed by at least ', 004, ' actors. ';
print 7+3, ' ', 7*3, ' ', 7/3, ' ', 7%3, ' ', 7**3, ' ';
$x = 7;
print $x;
print ' Doesn\'t resolve variables like $x and backslashes \n. ';
print "Does resolve $x and backslash\n";
$y = "A line containing $x and ending with line feed.\n";
print $y;
$y = "Con" . "cat" . "enation!\n";
print $y;
```

This produces:

```
007 has been portrayed by at least 4 actors. 10 21
2.3333333333333335 1 343 7
Doesn't resolve variables like $x and backslashes \n. Does
resolve 7 and backslash
A line containing 7 and ending with line feed.
Concatenation!
```

Example: Comparisons

```
# The following "<<" variation of
# data input simplifies CGI forms.
$x = 'operator';
print <<THATSALL;
A common mistake: Confusing the assignment $x =
and the numeric comparison $x ==, and the character
```

```
comparison $x eq.
THATSALL
$x = 7;
if ($x == 7) { print "x is $x\n"; }
if ($x = 5) {
    print "x is now $x,",
     "the assignment is successful.\n";
}
$x = 'stuff';
if ($x eq 'stuff') {
    print "Use eq, ne, lt, gt, etc for strings.\n";
}
```

This produces:

```
A common mistake: Confusing the assignment operator =
and the numeric comparison operator ==, and the character
comparison operator eq.
x is 7
x is now 5, the assignment is successful.
Use eq, ne, lt, gt, etc for strings.
```

Example: Ordinary Arrays

```
@stuff = ('This', 'is', 'a', 'list.');
print "Lists and strings are indexed from 0.\n";
print "So \$stuff[1] = $stuff[1], ",
"and \$#stuff = $#stuff.\n";
print @stuff,"\n";
print join('...',@stuff),"\n";
splice(@stuff, 3, 0, ('fine', 'little'));
print join('...',@stuff),"\n";
```

This produces:

```
Lists and strings are indexed from 0.
So $stuff[1] = is, and $#stuff = 3.
Thisisalist.
This...is...a...list.
This...is...a...fine...little...list.
```

13.6 LOOPS AND I/O

Example: Command Line Values and Iterative Loops

```
print "$#ARGV is the subscript of the ",
     "last command argument.\n";
```

```
# Iterate on numeric subscript 0 to $#ARGV:
for ($i=0; $i <= $#ARGV; $i++) {
    print "Argument $i is $ARGV[$i].\n";
}
# A variation on the preceding loop:
foreach $item (@ARGV) {
    print "The word is: $item.\n";
}
# A similar variation, using the
# "Default Scalar Variable" $_ :
foreach (@ARGV) {
    print "Say: $_.\n";
}
```

Demonstration:

```
> perl example5.pl Gooood morning, Columbia!
2 is the subscript of the last command argument.
Argument 0 is Gooood.
Argument 1 is morning,.
Argument 2 is Columbia!.
The word is: Gooood.
The word is: morning,.
The word is: Columbia!.
Say: Gooood.
Say: morning,.
Say: Columbia!.
```

Example: Standard I/O

```
print STDOUT "Tell me something: ";
while ($input = <STDIN>) {
        print STDOUT "You said, quote: $input endquote\n";
        chop $input;
        print STDOUT "Without the newline: $input endquote\n";
        if ($input eq '') { print STDERR "Null input!\n"; }
        print STDOUT "Tell me more, or ^D to end:\n";
}
print STDOUT "That's all!\n";
```

Example: Perls, A Perl Shell, Calculator, & Learning Tool

```
#!/usr/local/bin/perl
for (;;) {
    print '(',join(', ',@ReSuLt),') ?';
    last unless $InPuT = <STDIN>;
```

```
        $? = ''; $@ = ''; $! = '';
        @ReSuLt = eval $InPuT;
        if ($?) { print 'status=',$?,' ' }
        if ($@) { print 'errmsg=',$@,' ' }
        if ($!) { print 'errno=',$!+0,': ',$!,' ' }
}
```

This reads a line from the terminal and executes it as a Perl program. The "for (;;) {...}" makes an endless loop. The "last unless" line might be equivalently specified:

```
$InPuT = <STDIN>;                  # Get line from standard input.
if (! defined($InPuT)) {last;}  # If no line, leave the loop.
```

The "eval" function in Perl evaluates a string as a Perl program. "$@" is the Perl error message from the last "eval" or "do".

Demonstration:

```
perls
() ?Howdy
(Howdy) ?2+5
(7) ?sqrt(2)
(1.4142135623730951) ?$x
() ?$x = sqrt(2)
(1.4142135623730951) ?$x + 5
(6.4142135623730949) ?1/0
errmsg=Illegal division by constant zero in file (eval) at line 2,
next 2 tokens "0;"
() ?system 'date'
Fri Sep 27 10:02:43 CDT 1996
(0) ?$x = 'date'
(Fri Sep 27 10:02:52 CDT 1996
) ?chop $x
(
) ?$x
(Fri Sep 27 10:02:52 CDT 1996) ?@y = split(/ /,$x)
(Fri, Sep, 27, 10:02:52, CDT, 1996) ?@y[1,2,5]
(Sep, 27, 1996) ?localtime()
(37, 4, 10, 27, 8, 96, 5, 270, 1) ?
() ?foreach (1..10) {print sqrt(),' '}
1 1.4142135623730951 1.7320508075688772 2 2.2360679774997898
2.4494897427831779 2.6457513110645907 2.8284271247461903 3
3.1622776601683795
() ?exit
```

Example: File I/O

```
#!/usr/local/bin/perl
# Function: Reverse each line of a file

# 1: Get command line values:
if ($#ARGV !=1) {
    die "Usage: $0 inputfile outputfile\n";
}
($infile,$outfile) = @ARGV;
if (! -r $infile) {
    die "Can't read input $infile\n";
}
if (! -f $infile) {
    die "Input $infile is not a plain file\n";
}

# 2: Validate files
# Or statements "||" short-circuit, so that if an early part
# evaluates as true, Perl doesn't bother to evaluate the rest.
# Here, if the file opens successfully, we don't abort:
open(INPUT,"<$infile") ||
    die "Can't input $infile $!";
if ( -e $outfile) {
    print STDERR "Output file $outfile exists!\n";
    until ($ans eq 'r' || $ans eq 'a' || $ans eq 'e' ) {
        print STDERR "replace, append, or exit? ";
        $ans = getc(STDIN);
    }
    if ($ans eq 'e') {exit}
}
if ($ans eq 'a') {$mode='>>'}
else {$mode='>'}
open(OUTPUT,"$mode$outfile") ||
    die "Can't output $outfile $!";
# 3: Read input, reverse each line, output it.
while (<INPUT>) {
    chop $_;
    $_ = reverse $_;
    print OUTPUT $_,"\n";
}
```

```
# 4: Done!
close INPUT,OUTPUT;
exit;
```

13.7 PIPE I/O AND SYSTEM CALLS

```
#!/usr/local/bin/perl
# Report on disk usage under specified files
# The Unix command "du -sk ..." (on BSD Unix, "du -s ...")
# produces a series of lines:
#    1942    bin
#    2981    etc
#    ...
# listing the K bytes used under each file or directory.
# It doesn't show other information, such as the
# modification date or owner.
# This program gets du's kbytes and filename, and merges
# this info with other useful information for each file.
#

$files = join(' ',@ARGV);

# The trailing pipe "|" directs command output
# into our program:

if (! open (DUPIPE,"du -sk $files | sort -nr |")) {
    die "Can't run du! $!\n";
}

printf "%8s %-8s %-16s %8s %s\n",
    'K-bytes','Login','Name','Modified','File';
while (<DUPIPE>) {
    # parse the du info:
    ($kbytes, $filename) = split;

    # Call system to look up file info like "ls" does:
    ($dev,$ino,$mode,$nlink,$uid,$gid,$rdev,
        $size,$atime,$mtime,$ctime)
        = stat($filename);

    # Call system to associate login & name with uid:
    if ($uid != $previous_uid) {
        ($login,$passwd,$uid,$gid,$quota,$comment,
            $realname,$dir,$shell) = getpwuid($uid);
```

```
        ($realname) = split(',',substr($realname,0,20));
        $previous_uid = $uid;
    }

    # Convert the modification-time to readable form:
    ($sec,$min,$hour,$mday,$mon,$myear) = localtime($mtime);
    $mmonth = $mon+1;
    printf "%8s %-8s %-16s %02s-%02d-%02d %s\n",
        $kbytes, $login, $realname,
        $myear, $mmonth, $mday, $filename;
}
```

Demonstration Output

```
K-bytes Login   Name              Modified File
  40788 c527100 Fred Flintstone   95-10-05 c527100
  32685 c565060 Peter Parker      95-10-05 c565060
  24932 c579818 Clark Kent        95-10-06 c579818
  15388 c576657 Lois Lane         95-10-06 c576657
   9462 c572038 Bruce Wayne       95-10-06 c572038
   8381 c517401 Eric McGregor     95-10-05 c517401
   7022 c594912 Asterisk de Gaul  95-10-05 c594912
```

13.8 MATCHING

Matching involves use of patterns called "regular expressions". This, as you will see, leads to Perl Paradox Number Four: *Regular expressions aren't.*

The =~ operator performs pattern matching and substitution. For example, if:

```
$s = 'One if by land and two if by sea';
```

then:

```
if ($s =~ /if by la/) {print "YES"}
else {print "NO"}
```

prints "YES", because the string $s matches the simple constant pattern "if by la".

```
if ($s =~ /one/) {print "YES"}
else {print "NO"}
```

prints "NO", because the string does not match the pattern. However, by adding the "i" option to ignore case, we would get a "YES" from the following:

```
if ($s =~ /one/i) {print "YES"}
else {print "NO"}
```

Patterns can contain a mind-boggling variety of special directions that facilitate very general matching. See *Perl Reference Guide* section 13, Regular Expressions. For example, a period matches any character (except the "newline" \n character).

```
if ($x =~ /l.mp/) {print "YES"}
```

would print "YES" for $x = "lamp", "lump", "slumped", but not for $x = "lmp" or "less amperes".

13.9 PARSING

When you include parenthesis ( ) in a matched string, the matching text in the parenthesis may subsequently be referenced via variables $1, $2, $3, ... for each left parenthesis encountered. These matches can also be assigned as sequential values of an array.

```
#!/usr/local/bin/perl -w
$s = 'There is 1 date 10/25/95 in here somewhere.';
print "\$s=$s\n";
$s =~ /(\d{1,2})\/(\d{1,2})\/(\d{2,4})/;
print "Trick 1: \$1=$1, \$2=$2, \$3=$3,\n",
      "           \$\`=",$`," \$\'=",$',"\n";

($mo, $day, $year) =
     ( $s =~ /(\d{1,2})\/(\d{1,2})\/(\d{2,4})/ );
print "Trick 2: \$mo=$mo, \$day=$day, \$year=$year.\n";

($wholedate,$mo, $day, $year) =
     ( $s =~ /((\d{1,2})\/(\d{1,2})\/(\d{2,4}))/ );
print "Trick 3: \$wholedate=$wholedate, \$mo=$mo, ",
    "\$day=$day, \$year=$year.\n";
```

Results of above:

```
$s=There is 1 date 10/25/95 in here somewhere.
Trick 1: $1=10, $2=25, $3=95,
           $'=There is 1 date $'= in here somewhere.
Trick 2: $mo=10, $day=25, $year=95.
Trick 3: $wholedate=10/25/95, $mo=10, $day=25, $year=95.
```

Note that when patterns are matched in an array context as in Tricks 2 and 3, $1, $2, ..., and $', $', and $& are not set.

Regular expressions are greedy. In the following example we try to match whatever is between "<" and ">" :

```
#!/usr/local/bin/perl -w
$s = 'Beware of <STRONG>greedy</strong> regular expressions.';
print "\$s=$s\n";
($m) = ( $s =~ /<(.*)>/ );
print "Try 1: \$m=$m\n";
($m) = ( $s =~ /<([^>]*)>/ );
print "Try 2: \$m=$m\n";
```

This results in:

```
$s=Beware of <STRONG>greedy</strong> regular expressions.
Try 1: $m=STRONG>greedy</strong
Try 2: $m=STRONG
```

13.10 SIMPLE CGI

Example: Server Status Report

Let's start with a CGI program that takes no input but produces output. The following Perl program reports the load on the Web server, using the standard Unix commands "hostname", "uptime", and "w". The output would look something like this:

What's Happening at sgi1

7:09pm up 1 day, 18:38, 4 users, load average: 0.08, 0.21, 0.53

```
c676828   q0   128.206.58.85   3 pico
c676828   ftp  UNKNOWN@128.20    -
ccgreg    q1   monad.missouri    tcsh
c552997   q5   mizzou-ts2.mis    telnet
```

Here's the program that produced it:

```
#!/usr/local/bin/perl
# Send error messages to the user, not system log
open(STDERR,'<&STDOUT'); $| = 1;
# Headers terminate by a null line:
print "Content-type: text/html\n\n";
$host = 'hostname';
chop $host;
$uptime = 'uptime';
$w = 'w -s -h';
print <<BUNCHASTUFF;
<HTML><HEAD>
<TITLE>$host Status</TITLE>
</HEAD><BODY>
<H1>What's Happening at $host</H1>
$uptime
<PRE>$w</PRE>
<HR>
</BODY></HTML>
BUNCHASTUFF
exit;
```

Suppose user "bitman" wants to store this program on MU's SHOWME and SGI webservers, which use the "Apache" server software, configured for "CGI anywhere". If bitman doesn't already have a web directory, he should create one with these Unix commands:

```
mkdir ~/www; chmod a+x ~ ~/www
```

Then the above program could be put in a file `~/www/status.cgi`, and that file made readable and executable:

```
chmod a+rx ~/www/status.cgi
```

On the SHOWME server, the program would then be referenced as: `http://www.missouri.edu/~bitman/status.cgi`

Example: Web Form

Here is the image of a World Wide Web Electronic Form:

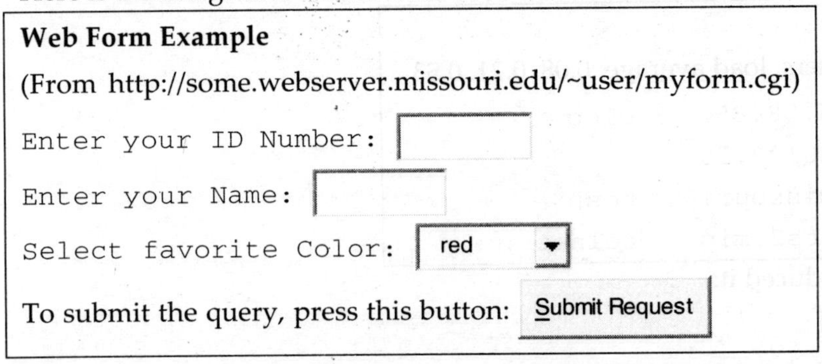

Perl Program to Generate and Process Form

Here is the Perl program that generates both the form and the response. It uses an external module called "cgi-lib.pl" that is available from network Perl archives such as http://cgi-lib.stanford.edu or a local copy.

```
#!/usr/local/bin/perl
# Send error messages to the user, not system log
open(STDERR,'<&STDOUT'); $| = 1
require "cgi-lib.pl"; # Get external subroutines
print &PrintHeader;

$script = $ENV{'SCRIPT_NAME'};
$webserver = $ENV{'SERVER_NAME'};

if (! &ReadParse(*input)) { &showform }
else { &readentries }
exit;

sub showform {
# If there is no input data, show the blank form

print <<EOF;
<HTML><HEAD>
```

```
<TITLE>Form Example, Part 1</TITLE>
</HEAD><BODY>
<H1>Web Form Example</H1>
<P>(From http://$webserver$script)
<FORM METHOD="POST"
  ACTION=$script>
<PRE>
Enter your ID Number:
<INPUT NAME=idnum>
Enter your Name:
<INPUT NAME=name>
Select favorite Color:
<SELECT NAME=color>
<OPTION>red<OPTION>green<OPTION>blue
</SELECT>
</PRE>
To submit the query, press this button:
<INPUT TYPE=submit VALUE="Submit Request">
</FORM>
</BODY></HTML>
EOF
} # End of sub showform #
sub readentries {
# Input data was detected. Echo back to form user.
print <<EOF;
<HTML><HEAD>
<TITLE>Form Example, Part 2</TITLE>
</HEAD><BODY>
<H1>Results of Form</H1>
<P>(From http://$webserver$script)
<P>Your ID Number is $input{'idnum'}, your name is $input{'name'},
and your favorite color is $input{'color'}.
<HR>
[<A HREF=$script>Try again</A>]
EOF
} # end of sub readentries #
```

13.11 TESTING PERL PROGRAMS

Use the compiler -w switch to warn about identifiers that are referenced only once, uninitialized scalars, redefined subroutines, undefined file handles, probable confusion of "==" and "eq", and other things. This can be coded in the magic cookie first line:

```
#!/usr/local/bin/perl -w
```

As you write your program, put in print statements to display variables as you proceed. Comment "#" them out when you feel you don't need to see their output.

CGI scripts require some special attention in testing.

MU's "showme" and "SGI" Web servers (www.missouri.edu and www.cclabs.missouri.edu) use the Apache "sucgi" facility. This causes CGI programs stored under your directory ~/www/ with file name ending ".cgi" to execute as your own ID. On some other Web server the script does not execute under your login ID! It executes under the ID of the Web server, typically as user "nobody".

Thus a script that works at the command line may fail under the Web server because:

- The path for executables or Perl library might be inappropriate. Print $ENV{'PATH'} and @INC to see if there's a difference. Fix it with Perl statements like:

  ```
  $ENV{'PATH'} .= ':~myid/bin:~myid/cgibin';
  push @INC,'~myid/lib/perl';
  ```

- File permissions give your ID access don't give the Web server appropriate access.

EXERCISE

1. What is the procedure to write a simple CGI script?
2. Write a code for using Submit buttons.
3. What is the difference between checkbox and radio buttons?
4. Write and explain a basic program in perl.
5. What is the syntax for declaring scalar variable?
6. What do you mean by interpolation?
7. What are array variables in perl?
8. How would you handle files in perl?
9. Explain string matching in perl.
10. What is the substitution an translation in perl?
11. What are control structures in perl?
12. Write a program to find sum of *n* numbers in perl?
13. Write a program to find the average of marks of five subjects in perl?
14. Write a program in perl to calculate simple interest.
15. Why does the output from the first few print statements run together?

16. Is it necessary to declare variables in Perl? Is it possible?

17. What do you guess that the "!" means, as in:

```
                if  (! open(OUTPUT,">$file") ) {
                        die "Can't open output file $file\n";
        }
```

18. What does the ">" probably mean here? Compare with "open(INPUT ...)".

19. What does "die" do?

20. Some languages use "IF ... THEN DO ... END; ELSE IF ... THEN DO ... END". How is this notated in Perl?

21. What does $nchanges++ do?

14

RMI AND COM/DCOM

14.0 COM AND DCOM

14.0.1 COM

COM stands for Component Object Model, and is a binary standard for getting pieces of code (components) to interact with each other. Since COM is a binary standard, it's language-independent, and we can write COM objects and clients in C, C++, Java, Visual Basic, and anything else that supports COM. Essentially it's a form of object-oriented programming, since one creates objects, then invokes methods on them

COM = OLE = ActiveX. (more or less)

COM (Component Object Model), OLE (formerly Object Linking and Embedding, now it's no longer an acronym), and ActiveX are the same thing. The only substantial difference that I'm aware of is that ActiveX objects are intended to be transfered across the networks (*i.e.*, the Internet), and so are optimized to be small in size.OLE is what grew out of inter-application data transfer (*i.e.*, how to get an Excel spreadsheet into a Word document), and tends to deal with those issues. COM is the architecture that underlies both ActiveX and OLE.

14.0.1.1 Reference Counting

Since COM was originally intended to be used in C++, we don't have garbage collection (yet -- COM+ is a new runtime component that may offer garbage collection), but we still need a way to keep track of when objects should be deallocated. Ideally, we'd like the objects to delete themselves, because multiple clients can use the same object, simultaneously, without knowing that the others are using it. If one client were to delete the object while the other clients were still trying to use the object, there would be massive problems. We solve this problem with reference counting -- the object itself keeps a count of the number of clients using it (who are refering to it, thus the name), and when that count is decremented to 0, it deletes itself. Each time a client starts using an object, it increments a private, internal reference count within the object (by calling the public AddRef method on that object). When the client is finished using on object, it decrements the private, internal count on the object (by calling the public Release method on that object). When the reference count is decremented to 0, the object calls delete on itself, and is removed from memory. It's a pretty snazzy way to solve the problem of trying to figure out when to delete the object, but can be tough to debug. Also, once the object has executed the delete this statement, the object should be careful to *not* access any member variables.

14.0.2 The Distributed Component Object Model (DCOM)

The Distributed Component Object Model (DCOM) is a protocol that enables software components to communicate directly over a network in a reliable, secure, and efficient manner. Previously called "Network OLE," DCOM is designed for use across multiple network transports, including Internet protocols such as HTTP. DCOM is based on the Open Software Foundation's DCE-RPC spec and will work with both Java applets and ActiveX components through its use of the Component Object Model (COM).

The Microsoft Distributed Component Object Moindexdel (DCOM) extends the Component Object Model (COM) to support communication among objects on different computers-on a Local Area Network (LAN), a Wide Area Network (WAN), or even the Internet.

14.0.2.1 DCOM Architecture

DCOM is an extension of the Component Object Model (COM). COM defines how components and their clients interact. This interaction is defined such that the client and the component can connect without the need of any intermediary system component. The client calls methods in the component without any overhead whatsoever. Fig. 14.1 illustrates this in the notation of the Component Object Model:

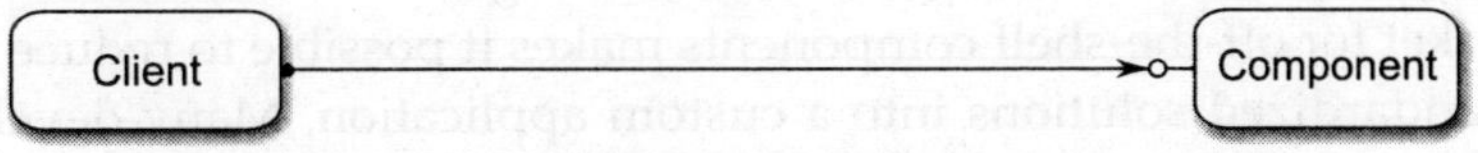

Fig. 14.1 *COM components in the same process*

In today's operating systems, processes are shielded from each other. A client that needs to communicate with a component in another process cannot call the component directly, but has to use some form of interprocess communication provided by the operating system. COM provides this communication in a completely transparent fashion: it intercepts calls from the client and forwards them to the component in another process. Fig. 14.2 illustrates how the COM/DCOM run-time libraries provide the link between client and component.

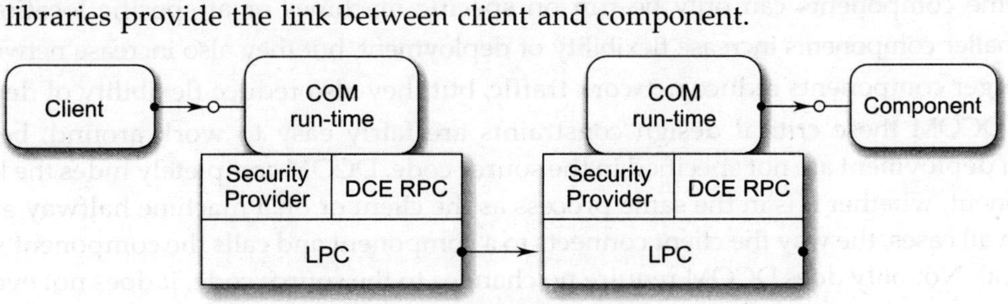

Fig. 14.2 *COM components in different processes*

When client and component reside on different machines, DCOM simply replaces the local interprocess communication with a network protocol. Neither the client nor the component is aware that the wire that connects them has just become a little longer.

Figure 14.3 shows the overall DCOM architecture: The COM run-time provides object-oriented services to clients and components and uses RPC and the security provider to generate standard network standard network packets that conform to the DCOM wire-protocol standard.

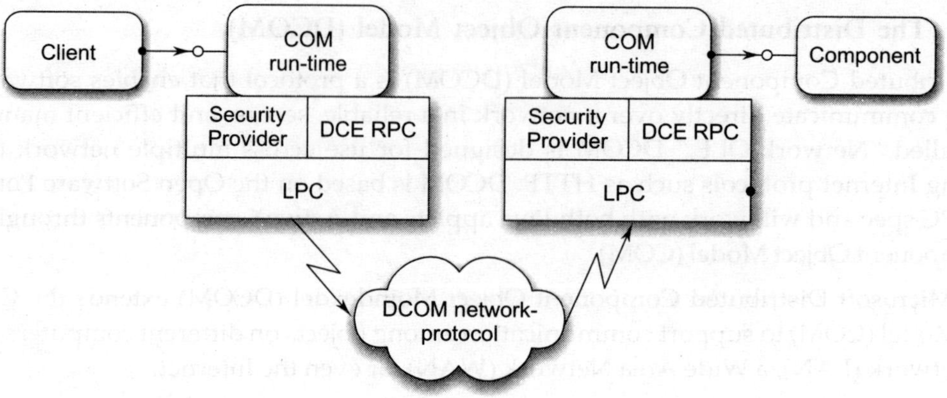

Fig. 14.3 *DCOM: COM components on different machines*

14.0.2.2 *Components and Reuse*

Most distributed applications are not developed from scratch and in a vacuum. Existing hardware infrastructure, existing software, and existing components, as well as existing tools, need to be integrated and leveraged to reduce development and deployment time and cost. DCOM directly and transparently takes advantage of any existing investment in COM components and tools. A huge market for off-the-shelf components makes it possible to reduce development time by integrating standardized solutions into a custom application. Many developers are familiar with COM and can easily apply their knowledge to DCOM-based distributed applications.

14.0.2.3 *Location Independence*

When you begin to implement a distributed application on a real network, several conflicting design constraints become apparent:

- Components that interact more should be "closer" to each other.
- Some components can only be run on specific machines or at specific locations.
- Smaller components increase flexibility of deployment, but they also increase network traffic.
- Larger components reduce network traffic, but they also reduce flexibility of deployment.

With DCOM these critical design constraints are fairly easy to work around, because the details of deployment are not specified in the source code. DCOM completely hides the location of a component, whether it is in the same process as the client or on a machine halfway around the world. In all cases, the way the client connects to a component and calls the component's methods is identical. Not only does DCOM require no changes to the source code, it does not even require that the program be recompiled. A simple reconfiguration changes the way components connect to each other.

DCOM's location independence greatly simplifies the task of distributing application components for optimum overall performance. Suppose, for example, that certain components must be placed on a specific machine or at a specific location. If the application has numerous small components, you can reduce network loading by deploying them on the same LAN segment, on the same machine, or even in the same process. If the application is composed of a smaller number of large components, network loading is less of a problem, so your can put them on the fastest machines available, wherever those machines are.

Figure 14.4 shows how the same "validation component" can be deployed on the client machine, when network-bandwidth between "client" machine and "middle-tier" machine is sufficient, and on the server machine, when the client is accessing the application through a slow network link.

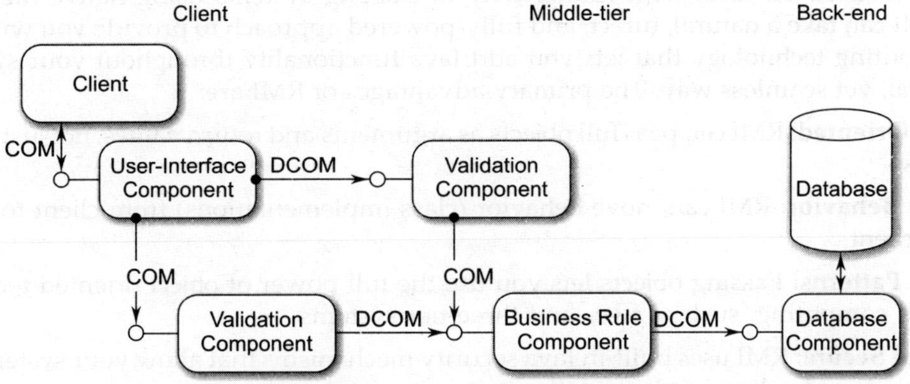

Fig. 14.4 *Location independence*

With DCOM's location independence, the application can combine related components into machines that are "close" to each other onto a single machine or even into the same process. Even if a larger number of small components implement the functionality of a bigger logical module, they can still interact efficiently among each other. Components can run on the machine where it makes most sense: user interface and validation on or close to the client, database-intensive business rules on the server close to the database.

14.1 INTRODUCTION TO RMI

Java Remote Method Invocation (RMI) allows you to write distributed objects using Java. This paper describes the benefits of RMI, and how you can connect it to existing and legacy systems as well as to components written in Java.

RMI provides a simple and direct model for distributed computation with Java objects. These objects can be new Java objects, or can be simple Java wrappers around an existing API. Java embraces the "Write Once, Run Anywhere model. RMI extends the Java model to be run everywhere."

Because RMI is centered around Java, it brings the power of Java safety and portability to distributed computing. You can move behavior, such as agents and business logic, to the part of your network where it makes the most sense. When you expand your use of Java in your systems, RMI allows you to take all the advantages with you.

RMI connects to existing and legacy systems using the standard Java native method interface JNI. RMI can also connect to existing relational database using the standard JDBC?? package. The RMI/JNI and RMI/JDBC combinations let you use RMI to communicate today with existing servers in non-Java languages, and to expand your use of Java to those servers when it makes sense for you to do so. RMI lets you take full advantage of Java when you do expand your use.

14.2 ADVANTAGES

At the most basic level, RMI is Java's remote procedure call (RPC) mechanism. RMI has several advantages over traditional RPC systems because it is part of Java's object oriented approach. Traditional RPC systems are language-neutral, and therefore are essentially least-common-denominator systems-they cannot provide functionality that is not available on all possible target platforms.

RMI is focused on Java, with connectivity to existing systems using native methods. This means RMI can take a natural, direct, and fully-powered approach to provide you with a distributed computing technology that lets you add Java functionality throughout your system in an incremental, yet seamless way. The primary advantages of RMI are:

Object Oriented: RMI can pass full objects as arguments and return values, not just predefined data types.

Mobile Behavior: RMI can move behavior (class implementations) from client to server and server to client.

Design Patterns: Passing objects lets you use the full power of object oriented technology in distributed computing, such as two- and three-tier systems.

Safe and Secure: RMI uses built-in Java security mechanisms that allow your system to be safe when users downloading implementations.

Easy to Write/Easy to Use: RMI makes it simple to write remote Java servers and Java clients that access those servers.

Connects to Existing/Legacy Systems: RMI interacts with existing systems through Java's native method interface JNI. Using RMI and JNI you can write your client in Java and use your existing server implementation.

Write Once, Run Anywhere: RMI is part of Java's "Write Once, Run Anywhere" approach. Any RMI based system is 100% portable to any Java Virtual Machine*, as is an RMI/JDBC system.

Parallel Computing: RMI is multi-threaded, allowing your servers to exploit Java threads for better concurrent processing of client requests.

The Java Distributed Computing Solution: RMI is part of the core Java platform starting with JDK?? 1.1, so it exists on every 1.1 Java Virtual Machine.

14.3 PASSING BEHAVIOR

Now we are going to describe how you can use RMI from one system to another.

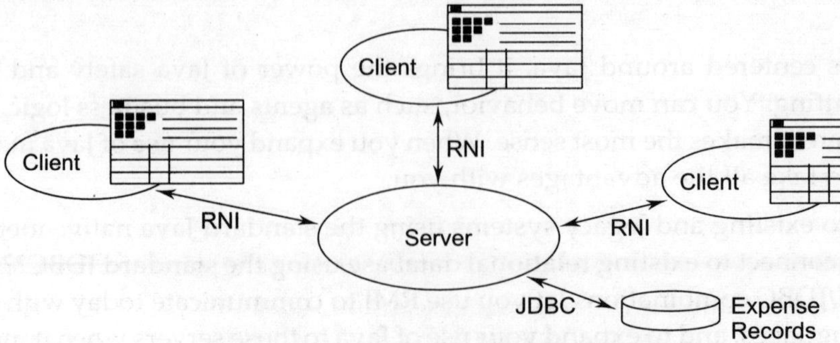

Fig. 14.5 *An expense reporting architecture*

Above Figure shows the general picture of such a dynamically configurable expense reporting system. A client displays a GUI (graphical user interface) to a user, who fills in the fields of the expense report. Clients communicate with the server using RMI. The server stores the expense reports in a database using JDBC, the Java relational database package. So far this may look like any multi-tier system, but there is an important difference-RMI can download behavior.

Suppose that the company's policies about expense reports change. Here is the remote interface that defines the methods the client can invoke on the server:

```
import java.rmi.*;
public interface ExpenseServer extends Remote {
    Policy getPolicy() throws RemoteException;
    void submitReport(ExpenseReport report)
        throws RemoteException, InvalidReportException;
}
```

The import statement imports the Java RMI package. All the RMI types are defined in the package java.rmi or one of its subpackages. The interface ExpenseServer is a normal Java interface with two interesting characteristics

It extends the RMI interface named Remote, which marks the interface as one available for remote invocation.

All its methods throw RemoteException, which is used to signal network and messaging failures. Remote methods can throw any other exception you like, but they must throw at least RemoteException so that you can handle error conditions that only arise in distributed systems. The interface itself supports two methods: getPolicy which returns an object that implements the Policy interface, and submitReport which submits a completed expense request, throwing an exception if the report is malformed for any reason.

The Policy interface itself declares a method that lets the client know if it is acceptable to add an entry to the expense report:

```
public interface Policy {
    void checkValid(ExpenseEntry entry)
        throws PolicyViolationException;
}
```

If the entry is a valid one-one that matches current policy-the method returns normally. Otherwise it throws an exception that describes the error. The Policy interface is local (not remote), and so will be implemented by an object local to the client-one that runs in the client's virtual machine, not across the network. A client would operate something like this:

```
Policy curPolicy = server.getPolicy();
start a new expense report
show the GUI to the user
while (user keeps adding entries) {
    try {
        curPolicy.checkValid(entry); // throws exception if not OK
        add the entry to the expense report
```

```
    } catch (PolicyViolationException e) {
        show the error to the user
    }
}
server.submitReport(report);
```

When the user asks the client software to start up a new expense report, the client invokes server.getPolicy to ask the server to return an object that embodies the current expense policy. Each entry that is added is first submitted to that policy object for approval. If the policy object reports no error, the entry is added to the report; otherwise the error will be displayed to the user who can take corrective action. When the user is finished adding entries to the report, the entire report is submitted. The server looks like this:

```
import java.rmi.*;
import java.rmi.server.*;
class ExpenseServerImpl
    extends UnicastRemoteObject
    implements ExpenseServer
{
    ExpenseServerImpl() throws RemoteException {
        // ...set up server state...
    }
    public Policy getPolicy() {
        return new TodaysPolicy();
    }
    public void submitReport(ExpenseReport report) {
        // ...write the report into the db...
    }
}
```

We import RMI's server package in addition to the basic package. The type UnicastRemoteObject defines the kind of remote object this server will be, in this case a single server as opposed to a replicated service (more on this later). The Java class ExpenseServerImpl implements the methods of the remote interface ExpenseServer. Clients on remote hosts can use RMI to send messages to ExpenseServerImpl objects.

The important method for this discussion is getPolicy, which simply returns an object that defines the current policy. Let's take a look at an example implementation of a policy:

```
public class TodaysPolicy implements Policy {
    public void checkValid(ExpenseEntry entry)
            throws PolicyViolationException
    {
            if (entry.dollars() < 20) {
                return; // no receipt required
            } else if (entry.haveReceipt() == false) {
```

```
            throw new PolicyViolationException;
        }
    }
}
```

TodaysPolicy checks to ensure that any entry without a receipt is less than $20. If the policy changes tomorrow so that only meals under $20 are exempt from the "receipts required" policy, you could provide a new implementation of policy:

```
public class TomorrowsPolicy implements Policy {
    public void checkValid(ExpenseEntry entry)
        throws PolicyViolationException
    {
        if (entry.isMeal() && entry.dollars() < 20) {
            return; // no receipt required
        } else if (entry.haveReceipt() == false) {
            throw new PolicyViolationException;
        }
    }
}
```

Write this class, install it on the server, and tell the server to start handing out TomorrowsPolicy objects instead of TodaysPolicy objects, and your entire system will start using the new policy. When the client invokes the server's getPolicy method, RMI on the client checks to see if the returned object is of a known type. The first time each client encounters a TomorrowsPolicy object, RMI will download the implementation for the policy before getPolicy returns. The client will, without effort, start enforcing the new policy.

RMI uses the standard Java object serialization mechanism to pass objects. Arguments that are references to remote objects are passed as remote references. If an argument to a method is a primitive type or a local (non-remote) object, a deep copy is passed to the server. Return values are handled in the same way, but in the other direction. RMI lets you pass and return full object graphs for local objects and references to remote objects.

14.4 COMPUTE SERVER

The server can pass the data in any direction and client gets the information from the server.

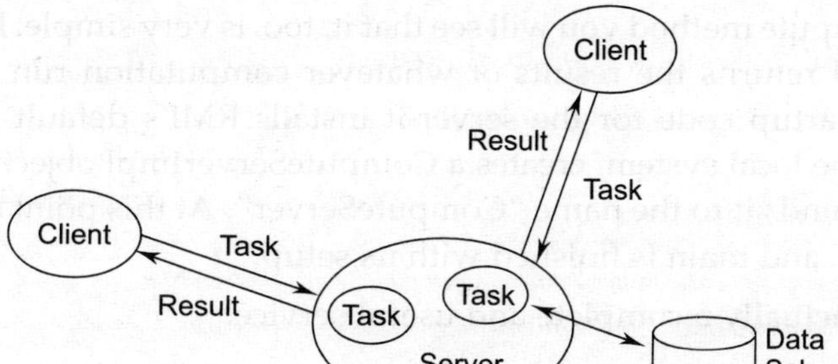

Fig. 14.6 *An computer server architecture*

Tasks are defined by a simple local (non-remote) interface:

```
public interface Task {
    Object run();
}
```

When run is invoked, it does some computation and returns an object that contains the results. This is purposefully completely generic-almost any computational task can be implemented under this interface. The remote interface Compute Server is equally simple:

```
import java.rmi.*;
public interface ComputeServer extends Remote {
    Object compute(Task task) throws RemoteException;
}
```

The only purpose of this remote interface is to allow a client to create a Task object and send it to the server for execution, returning the results. Here is a basic implementation of that server:

```
import java.rmi.*;
import java.rmi.server.*;
public class ComputeServerImpl
    extends UnicastRemoteObject
    implements ComputeServer
{
    public ComputeServerImpl() throws RemoteException { }
    public Object compute(Task task) {
        return task.run();
    }
    public static void main(String[] args) throws Exception {
        // use the default, restrictive security manager
        System.setSecurityManager(new RMISecurityManager());
        ComputeServerImpl server = new ComputeServerImpl();
        Naming.rebind("ComputeServer", server);
        System.out.println("Ready to receive tasks");
        return;
    }
}
```

If you look at the compute method you will see that it, too, is very simple. It just takes the object that is passed to it and returns the results of whatever computation run performs. The main method contains the startup code for the server-it installs RMI's default security manager to prevent any access to the local system, creates a ComputeServerImpl object for handling incoming requests, and then binds it to the name "ComputeServer". At this point the server is ready to receive tasks to execute, and main is finished with its setup.

As described this is actually a complete and useful service.

14.5 AGENTS

Because RMI lets you download behavior using Java implementations, you can write an agent system using RMI. In its simplest form it would look like this:

```
import java.rmi.*;
public interface AgentServer extends Remote {
    void accept(Agent agent)
        throws RemoteException, InvalidAgentException;
}
public interface Agent extends java.io.Serializable {
    void run();
}
```

Starting an agent would be a matter of creating a class that implemented the Agent interface, finding a server, and invoking accept with that agent object. The implementation for the agent would be downloaded to the server and run there. The accept method would start up a new thread for the agent, invoke its run method, and then return, letting the agent continue execution after the method returned. The agent could migrate to another host by invoking accept on a server running on that host, passing itself as the agent to be accepted, and then killing its thread on the original host.

14.6 OBJECT ORIENTED CODE REUSE AND DESIGN PATTERNS

Object oriented programming is a powerful technique for allowing code reuse. Many organizations are using object oriented programming to reduce the burden of creating programs and to increase the flexibility of their systems. RMI is object oriented at all levels-messages are sent to remote objects, and objects can be passed and returned.

All design patterns rely upon object oriented polymorphism-the ability of an object (such as Task) to have multiple implementations. The general part of the algorithm (such as the compute method) does not need to know which particular implementation is present, it need only know what to do with such an object when it gets one. In particular, the compute server is an example of the Command pattern, which lets you represent a request (task) as an object, letting it be dispatched.

This polymorphism is only available if the full objects, including implementations, can be passed between client and server. Traditional RPC systems, such as DCE and DCOM, and object based RPC systems, such as CORBA, cannot download and execute implementations because they cannot pass real objects as arguments, only data.

RMI passes full types, including implementations, so you can use object oriented programming-including design patterns-every where in your distributed computing solutions, not just in local computation.

14.7 CONNECTING TO AN EXISTING SERVER

It is commonly said that RMI works for "Java to Java," but this hides an important fact: Java connects quite well to existing and legacy systems using the native method interface called JNI.

You can use JNI with RMI as easily as with any other Java code. You can use JDBC with RMI to connect to existing relational databases. This means you can use RMI to connect two- and three-tier systems even if both sides are not written in Java. There are significant advantages to doing so, as we will discuss below. But first let's see how it can be done.

Let us suppose that you had an existing server that stored information on customer orders in a relational database. In any multi-tier system you would have to design a remote interface to let clients access the server-with RMI that would be a Remote interface:

```
import java.rmi.*;
import java.sql.SQLException;
import java.util.Vector;
public interface OrderServer extends Remote {
    Vector getUnpaid() throws RemoteException, SQLException;
    void shutDown() throws RemoteException;
    // ... other methods (getOrderNumber, getShipped, ...)
}
```

The package java.sql contains the JDBC package. Each remote method can be implemented by the server using JDBC calls onto the actual database or by native methods that use other database access mechanisms. The methods shown return a vector (list) of Order objects. Order is a class defined in your system to hold a customer's order.

In this section we will show how you can implement getUnpaid using JDBC and shutDown using JNI.

JDBC-Direct to the Database

Here is OrderServerImpl that uses JDBC to implement getUnpaid:

```
import java.rmi.*;
import java.rmi.server.*;
import java.sql.*;
import java.util.Vector;
public class OrderServerImpl
    extends UnicastRemoteObject
    implements OrderServer
{
    Connection db;              // connection to the db
    PreparedStatement unpaidQuery; // unpaid order query
    OrderServerImpl() throws RemoteException, SQLException {
        db = DriverManager.getConnection("jdbc:odbc:orders");
        unpaidQuery = db.prepareStatement("...");
    }
    public Vector getUnpaid() throws SQLException {
        ResultSet results = unpaidQuery.executeQuery();
        Vector list = new Vector();
```

```
        while (results.next())
            list.addElement(new Order(results));
        return list;
    }
    public native void shutDown();
}
```

Most of this is JDBC work. All types you see are part of JDBC or RMI except those that start with Order, which are part of your system. The constructor initializes the OrderServerImpl object, creating a Connection to a database that is specified in a jdbc URL. Given that connection, we use prepareStatement to define a query that will find all unpaid orders. Other queries could be defined here for other methods. The OrderServerImpl server runs on the same system as the database, possibly in the same process. (We will describe shutDown below).

When a getUnpaid method is invoked on the RMI server object OrderServerImpl, the precompiled query is executed, returning a JDBC ResultSet object that contains all the matching elements. We then create new Order objects for each item in the result set, putting each into a Vector object (Java's dynamically-sized array). When we are finished reading the results, we return the Vector to the client, who can then display the results to the user or do whatever else is appropriate.

14.8 JNI-NATIVE METHODS

RMI servers and clients can use native methods as a bridge to existing and legacy systems. You can use native methods to implement remote methods that are not direct database access, or which can be implemented more easily using existing code. The native interface JNI lets you write C and C++ code that implements Java methods and invokes methods on Java objects. Here is how shutDown could be implemented by a native method:

```
JNIEXPORT void JNICALL
Java_OrderServerImpl_shutDown(JNIEnv *env, jobject this)
{
    jclass cls;
    jfieldID fid;
    DataSet *ds;
    cls = (*env)->GetObjectClass(env, this);
    fid = (*env)->GetFieldID(env, cls, "dataSet", "J");
    ds = (DataSet *) (*env)->GetObjectField(env, this, fid);
    /* With a DataSet pointer we can use the original API */
    DSshutDown(ds);
}
```

This presumes that the existing server is referenced via a DataSet type defined by the existing server's API. A pointer to server's DataSet would be stored in a dataSet field. When the client invokes shutDown, this causes the shutDown method of the server to be invoked. Because the server implementation declares shutDown to be implemented with a native method, RMI will directly invoke this native method. The native method finds the dataSet field of the object, gets its value, and uses it to invoke the existing API function DSshutDown.

Sun is currently working in partnership with ILOG on a product called TwinPeaks. TwinPeaks will take existing C and C++ APIs and generate Java classes that wrap calls to that API in Java classes. This would allow you to invoke methods on arbitrary existing APIs from Java. When TwinPeaks is available it will make it possible to write methods like shutDown completely in Java instead of using JNI calls.

14.9 ARCHITECTURE

The RMI system is designed to provide a direct, simple foundation for distributed object oriented computing. The architecture is designed to allow for future expansion of server and reference types so that RMI can add features in a coherent way.

When a server is exported, its reference type is defined. In the examples above we exported the servers as UnicastRemoteObject servers, which are point-to-point unreplicated servers. The references for these objects are appropriate for this type of server. Different server types would have different reference semantics. For example, a MulticastRemoteObject would have reference semantics that allowed for a replicated service.

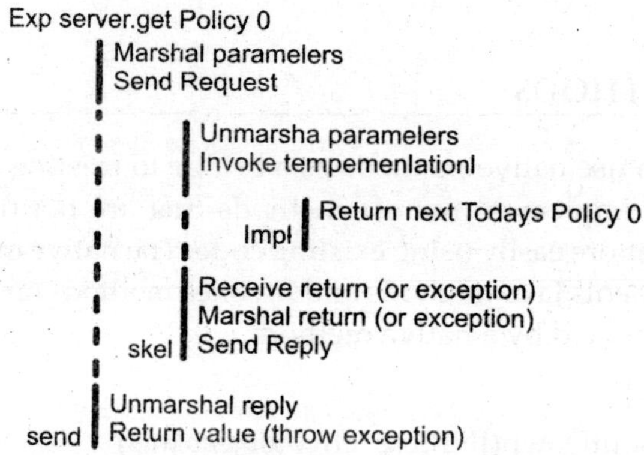

Fig. 14.7 *Stubs and skeleton*

When a client receives a reference to a server, RMI downloads a stub that translates calls on that reference into remote calls to the server. As shown in Figure 3, the stub marshals the arguments to the method using object serialization, and sends the marshalled invocation across the wire to the server. On the server side the call is received by the RMI system and connected to a skeleton, which is responsible for unmarshalling the arguments and invoking the server's implementation of the method. When the server's implementation completes, either by returning a value or by throwing an exception, the skeleton marshals the result and sends a reply to the client's stub. The stub unmarshals the reply and either returns the value or throws the exception as appropriate. Stubs and skeletons are generated from the server implementation, usually using the program rmic. Stubs use references to talk to the skeleton. This architecture allows the reference to define the behavior of communication. The references used for UnicastRemoteObject servers communicate with a single server object running on a particular host and port. With the stub/reference separation RMI will be able to add new reference types. A reference that dealt with replicated servers would multicast server requests to an appropriate set of replicants, gather in the responses, and return an appropriate result based on those multiple responses. Another reference type could activate the server if it was not already running in a virtual machine. The client would work transparently with any of these reference types.

14.10 SAFETY AND SECURITY

There are clear safety and security implications when you are executing RMI requests. RMI provides for secure channels between client and server and the isolation of downloaded implementations inside a security "sandbox" to protect your system from possible attacks by untrusted clients.

First it is important to define your security needs. If you are executing something like the ComputeServer inside a secure corporate network, you may simply need to be able to know who is using the compute cycles so you can track down anyone abusing the system. If you wanted to provide a commercial compute server you would need to protect against more malicious acts. These will affect the exact design of the interface-internally you may just require that each Task object come accompanied by a person's name and department number for tracking purposes. In the commercial case you would want tighter security, including a digitally signed identity and some contractual language that would let you kill off a rogue task that was consuming more than its allotted time.

You may need a secure channel between client and server. RMI lets you provide a socket factory that can create sockets of any type you need, including encrypted sockets. Starting with JDK 1.2, you will be able to specify requirements on the services provided for a server's sockets by giving a description of those requirements. This new technique will work in applets, where most browsers refuse permission to set the socket factory. The socket requirements can include encryption as well as other requirements.

Downloaded classes present security issues as well. Java handles security via a SecurityManager object, which passes judgement on all security-sensitive actions, such as opening files and network connections. RMI uses this standard Java mechanism by requiring that you install a security manager before exporting any server object or invoking any method on a server. RMI provides an RMISecurityManager type that is as restrictive as those used for applets (no file access, only connections to the originating host, and so forth). This will prevent downloaded implementations from reading or writing data from the computer, or connecting to other systems behind your firewall. You can also write and install your own security manager object to enforce different security constraints.

14.11 FIREWALLS

RMI provides a means for clients behind firewalls to communicate with remote servers. This allows you to use RMI to deploy clients on the Internet, such as in applets available on the World Wide Web. Traversing the client's firewall can slow down communication, so RMI uses the fastest successful technique to connect between client and server. The technique is discovered by the reference for UnicastRemoteObject on the first attempt the client makes to communicate with the server by trying each of three possibilities in turn:

Communicate directly to the server's port using sockets.

If this fails, build a URL to the server's host and port and use an HTTP POST request on that URL, sending the information to the skeleton as the body of the POST. If successful, the results of the post are the skeleton's response to the stub.

If this also fails, build a URL to the server's host using port 80, the standard HTTP port, using a CGI script that will forward the posted RMI request to the server.

Whichever of these three techniques succeeds first is used for all future communication with the server. If none of these techniques succeeds, the remote method invocation fails.

This three-stage back-off allows clients to communicate as efficiently as possible, in most cases using direct socket connections. On systems with no firewall, or with communication inside an enterprise behind a firewall, the client will directly connect to the server using sockets. The secondary communication techniques are significantly slower than direct communication, but their use enables you to write clients that can be used broadly across the Internet and Web.

14.12 RMI IN AN EVOLVING ENTERPRISE

You can use RMI today to connect between new Java applications (or applets) and existing servers. When you do this, you allow your organization to benefit incrementally from expanded Java use over time. When parts of your systems are rewritten in Java, RMI allows the benefits of Java to flow from the existing Java components into the new Java code. Consider the path of a single request in a two-tier system from the client to the server and back again:

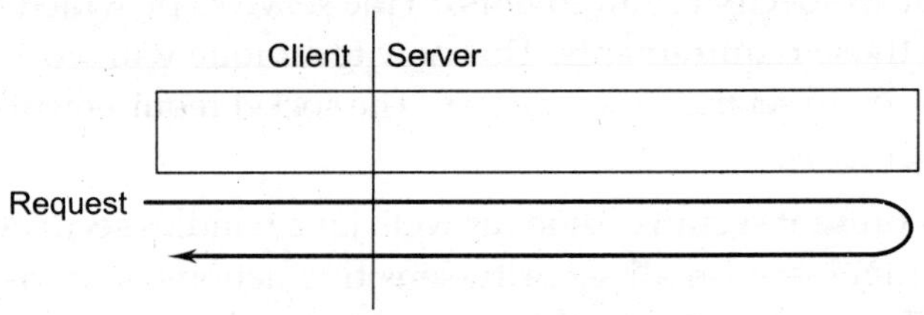

Using RMI means that you can get Java benefits throughout your system by using RMI as the transport between client and server, even if the server remains in non-Java code for some time. If you choose to rewrite some or all of your servers in Java, you will get leverage from your existing Java components. Some of the most important Java advantages you maintain are:

Object oriented code reuse. The ability to pass objects from client to server and server to client means that you can use design patterns and other object oriented programming techniques to enhance code reuse in your organization.

Passing behavior. The objects passed between client and server can be of types not previously seen by the other side. Implementations will be downloaded to execute the new behavior.

Type safety. Java objects are always type safe, preventing bugs that would occur if a programmer makes a mistake about the type of an object.

Security. Java Classes can be run in a secure fashion, allowing you to interact with clients that may be running in an untrusted environment. Here is that diagram showing a client written in Java using RMI to talk to the server. The "request" arrow has been shaded to show where you get Java's safety, object oriented, and other advantages:

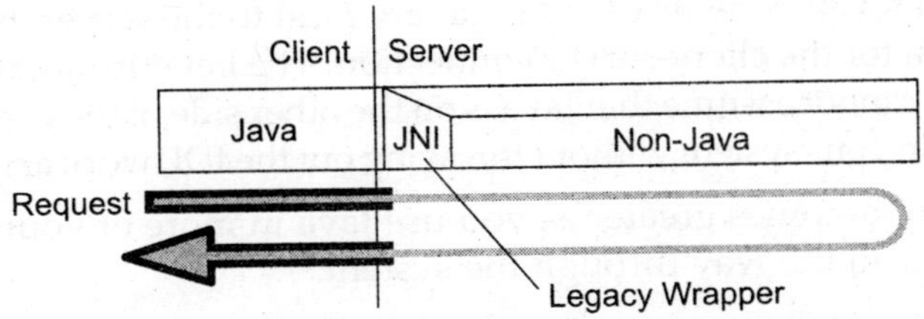

A small amount of Java code connects to a "legacy wrapper" that uses the existing server's API. The legacy wrapper is the bridge between Java and the existing API, as shown in the implementations of getUnpaid and shutDown above. In this diagram we show it written using JNI, but as shown above the legacy wrapper could use JDBC or, when it is available, TwinPeaks.

Contrast the above diagram with one in which a language neutral system using an interface definition language (commonly called an IDL) introduces a least-common-denominator connection between the client and server:

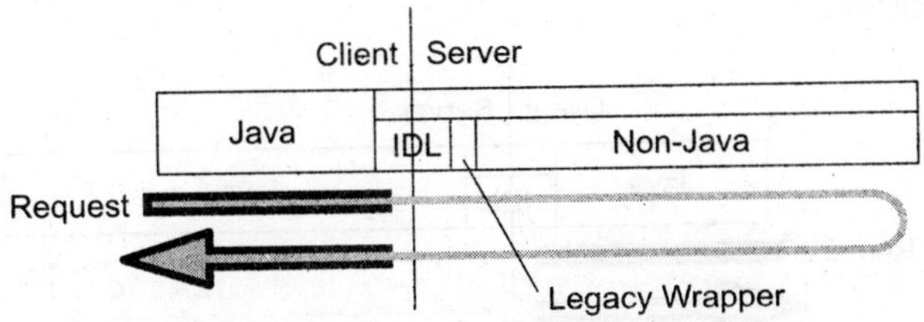

A legacy wrapper must still be written to connect the IDL-defined calls to the existing server API. But with an IDL-based approach the benefits of Java have been isolated on the client side-because the client's Java is reduced to the least common denominator before crossing to the server. Suppose you decide that rewriting some of the server in Java would be useful to you. This might be for any reason, such as wanting the improved reliability of a safe Java system, or because you want to reduce porting costs. Or possibly the vendor from whom you bought some of your server Implementation has provided an upgrade that takes advantage of Java. Here is how the RMI based picture now looks:

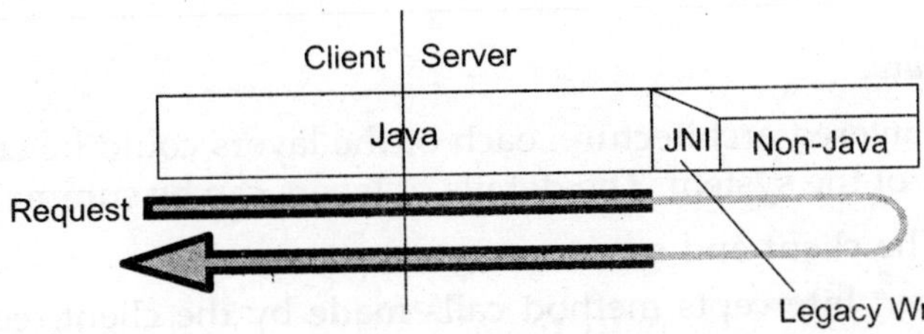

More of the request now benefits from having Java. The objects that you pass across the wire between client and server can now have more benefits to the overall system. You could, for example, start passing behavior across the same remote interfaces you have already defined to enhance the value of client and server. Compare this to the IDL-based approach:

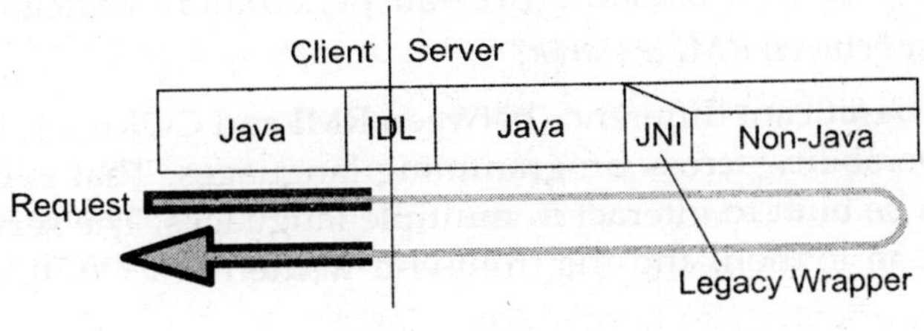

You would have achieved benefits of Java that are local to the server, but you cannot leverage expanded value of Java for the client-server connection. The benefits of Java are cut off at the IDL boundary because IDL cannot assume that Java is on the other side of the connection. You cannot get the full benefits of Java in your system without throwing out the IDL work and rewriting it using RMI.

This lost opportunity becomes greater as you use Java in more of your enterprise. Using RMI you get benefits of Java all the way through the system:

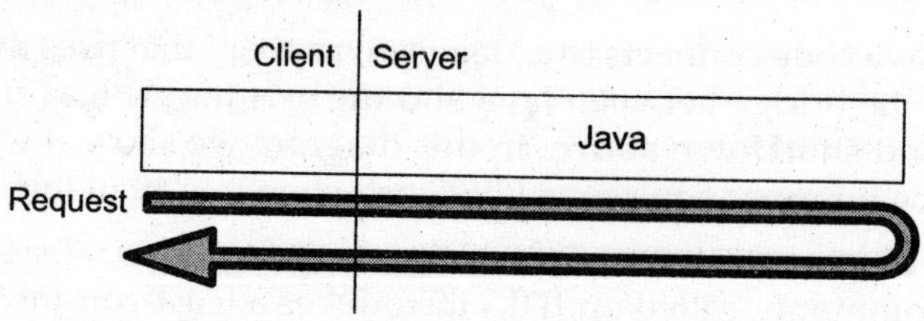

Using an IDL-based approach, rewriting the server in Java still only gives you localized benefit isolated to the server alone:

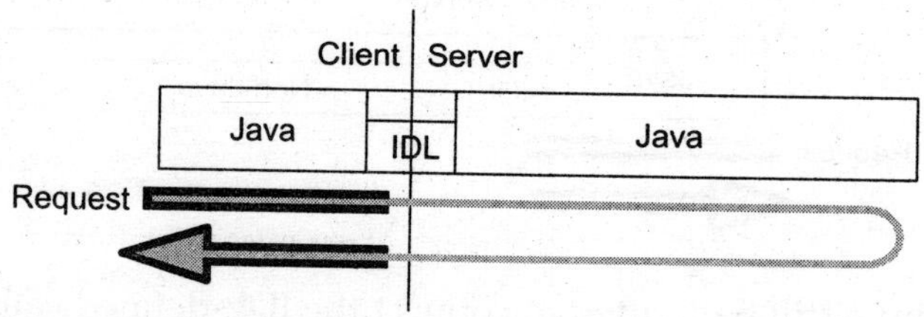

You can use RMI today to connect to your servers without rewriting it in Java. RMI is simple to use, so it is easy to create the server-side RMI class. The legacy wrapper is of similar complexity in either case. But if you use an IDL-based distributed system you will create isolated pockets of Java that share no benefits with each other. RMI lets you connect easily now, and as you decide to expand your use of Java, you will get expanded benefits from the synergy of having Java on both sides of the wire.

QUESTIONS WITH ANSWERS

1. *Explain RMI Architecture?*

Solution: RMI uses a layered architecture, each of the layers could be enhanced or replaced without affecting the rest of the system. The details of layers can be summarised as follows:

- *Application Layer*: The client and server program
- *Stub & Skeleton Layer*: Intercepts method calls made by the client/redirects these calls to a remote RMI service.
- *Remote Reference Layer*: Understands how to interpret and manage references made from clients to the remote service objects.
- *Transport layer*: Based on TCP/IP connections between machines in a network. It provides basic connectivity, as well as some firewall penetration strategies.

2. *What is the difference between RMI & Corba?*

Solution: The most significant difference between RMI and CORBA is that CORBA was made specifically for interoperability across programming languages. That is CORBA fosters the notion that programs can be built to interact in multiple languages. The server could be written in C++, the business logic in Python, and the front-end written in COBOL in theory. RMI, on the other hand is a total Java solution, the interfaces, the implementations and the clients--all are written in Java.

RMI allows dynamic loading of classes at runtime. In a multi-language CORBA environment, dynamic class loading is not possible. The important advantage to dynamic class loading is that it allows arguments to be passed in remote invocations that are subtypes of the declared types. In CORBA, all types have to be known in advance. RMI (as well as RMI/IIOP) provides support for polymorphic parameter passing, whereas strict CORBA does not. CORBA does have support for multiple languages which is good for some applications, but RMI has the advantage of being dynamic, which is good for other applications.

3. *What are the services in RMI ?*

Solution: An RMI "service" could well be any Java method that can be invoked remotely. The other service is the JRMP RMI naming service which is a lookup service.

4. *Does RMI-IIOP support code downloading for Java objects sent by value across an IIOP connection in the same way as RMI does across a JRMP connection?*

Solution: Yes. The JDK 1.2 support the dynamic class loading.

5. *How many types of protocol implementations does RMI have?*

Solution: RMI has at least three protocol implementations: Java Remote Method Protocol(JRMP), Internet Inter ORB Protocol(IIOP), and Jini Extensible Remote Invocation(JERI). These are alternatives, not part of the same thing, All three are indeed layer 6 protocols for those who are still speaking OSI reference model.

6. *Does RMI-IIOP support dynamic downloading of classes?*

Solution: No, RMI-IIOP doesn't support dynamic downloading of the classes as it is done with CORBA in DII (Dynamic Interface Invocation).Actually RMI-IIOP combines the usability of Java Remote Method Invocation (RMI) with the interoperability of the Internet Inter-ORB Protocol (IIOP). So in order to attain this interoperability between RMI and CORBA,some of the features that are supported by RMI but not CORBA and vice versa are eliminated from the RMI-IIOP specification.

7. *Does RMI-IIOP support code downloading for Java objects sent by value across an IIOP connection in the same way as RMI does across a JRMP connection?*

Solution: Yes. The JDK 1.2 support the dynamic class loading.

8. *Can RMI and Corba based applications interact ?*

Solution: Yes they can. RMI is available with IIOP as the transport protocol instead of JRMP.

EXERCISE

1. What is RMI server?
2. How will you design remote interface?
3. How will you implement remote interface?
4. Implement the server's main method.
5. How will you create a client program?
6. How will you built a JAR file of Interface Classes?
7. Explain COM in detail.
8. Explain DCOM in detail.
9. Differentiate COM and DCOM.

15

JavaBeans and EJB

15.0 INTRODUCTION

As software developers, we are constantly being asked to build applications in less time and with less money. And, of course, these applications are expected to be better and faster than ever before. Object-oriented techniques and component software environments are in wide use now, in the hope that they can help us build applications more quickly. Development tools like Microsoft's Visual Basic have made it easier to build applications faster by taking a building-block approach to software development. Such tools provide a visual programming model that allows you to include software components rapidly in your applications.

15.1 THE COMPONENT MODEL

Components are self-contained elements of software that can be controlled dynamically and assembled to form applications. But that's not the end of it. These components must also interoperate according to a set of rules and guidelines. They must behave in ways that are expected. It's like a society of software citizens. The citizens (components) bring functionality, while the society (environment) brings structure and order.

JavaBeans is Java's component model. It allows users to construct applications by piecing components together either programmatically or visually (or both). Support of visual programming is paramount to the component model; it's what makes component-based software development truly powerful.

The model is made up of an architecture and an API (Application Programming Interface). Together, these elements provide a structure whereby components can be combined to create an application. This environment provides services and rules, the framework that allows components to participate properly. This means that components are provided with the tools necessary to work in the environment, and they exhibit certain behaviors that identify them as such. One very important aspect of this structure is containment. A container provides a context in which components can interact. A common example would be a panel that provides layout management or mediation of interactions for visual components. Of course, containers themselves can be components.

15.1.1 Discovery and Registration

Class and interface discovery is the mechanism used to locate a component at run-time and to determine its supported interfaces so that these interfaces can be used by others. The component model must also provide a registration process for a component to make itself and its interfaces known. The component, along with its supported interfaces, can then be discovered at run-time. Dynamic (or late) binding allows components and applications to be developed independently. The dependency is limited to the "contract" between each component and the applications that use it; this contract is defined by interfaces that the component supports. An application does not have to include a component during the development process in order to use it at run-time; it only needs to know what the component is capable of doing. Dynamic discovery also allows developers to update components without having to rebuild the applications that use them.

This discovery process can also be used in a design-time environment. In this case, a development tool may be able to locate a component and make it available for use by the designer.

15.1.2 Raising and Handling of Events

An event is something of importance that happens at a specific point in time. An event can take place due to a user action such as a mouse click?when the user clicks a mouse button, an event takes place. Events can also be initiated by other means. Imagine the heating system in your house. It contains a thermostat that sets the desired comfort temperature, keeps track of the current ambient temperature, and notifies the boiler when its services are required. If the thermostat is set to keep the room at 70 degrees Fahrenheit, it will notify the boiler to start producing heat if the temperature dips below that threshold. Components will send notifications to other objects when an event takes place in which those objects have expressed an interest.

15.1.3 Persistence

Generally, all components have state. The thermostat component has state that represents the comfort temperature. If the thermostat were a software component of a computer-based heating control system, we would want the value of the comfort temperature to be stored on a non-volatile storage medium (such as the hard disk). This way if we shut down the application and brought it back up again, the thermostat control would still be set to 70 degrees. The visual representation and position of the thermostat relative to other components in the application would be restored as well.

Components must be able to participate in their container's persistence mechanism so that all components in the application can provide application-wide persistence in a uniform way. If every component were to implement its own method of persistence, it would be impossible for an application container to use components in a general way. This wouldn't be an issue if reuse weren't the goal. If we were building a monolithic temperature control system we might create an application-specific mechanism for storing state. But we want to build the thermostat component so that it can be used again in another application, so we have to use a standard mechanism for persistence.

15.1.4 Visual Presentation

The component environment allows the individual components to control most of the aspects of their visual presentation. For example, imagine that our thermostat component includes a display of the current ambient temperature. We might want to display the temperature in different fonts or colors depending on whether we are above, below, or at the comfort temperature. The component is free to choose the characteristics of its own visual presentation. Many of these characteristics will be properties of the component (a topic that will be discussed later). Some of these visual properties will be persistent, meaning that they represent some state of the control that will be saved to, and restored from, persistent storage.

15.1.5 Support of Visual Programming

Visual programming is a key part of the component model. Components are represented in toolboxes or palettes. The user can select a component from the toolbox and place it into a container, choosing its size and position. The properties of the component can then be edited in order to create the desired behavior. Our thermostat control might present some type of user interface to the application developer to set the initial comfort temperature. Likewise, the choice of font and color will be selectable in a similar way. None of these manipulations require a single line of code to be written by the application developer. In fact, the application development tool is probably writing the code for you. This is accomplished through a set of standard interfaces provided by the component environment that allow the components to publish, or expose, their properties. The development tool can also provide a means for the developer to manipulate the size and position of components in relation to each other. The container itself may be a component and allow its properties to be edited in order to alter its behavior.

15.1.6 The JavaBeans Architecture

JavaBeans is an architecture for both using and building components in Java. This architecture supports the features of software reuse, component models, and object orientation. One of the most important features of JavaBeans is that it does not alter the existing Java language. If you know how to write software in Java, you know how to use and create Beans. The strengths of Java are built upon and extended to create the JavaBeans component architecture.

Although Beans are intended to work in a visual application development tool, they don't necessarily have a visual representation at run-time (although many will). What this does mean is that Beans must allow their property values to be changed through some type of visual interface, and their methods and events should be exposed so that the development tool can write code capable of manipulating the component when the application is executed.

Creating a Bean doesn't require any advanced concepts. So before I go any further, here is some code that implements a simple Bean:

```
public class MyBean implements java.io.Serializable
{
  protected int theValue;
  public MyBean()
  {
  }

  public void setMyValue(int newValue)
  {
```

```
    theValue = newValue;
  }

  public int getMyValue()
  {
    return theValue;
  }
}
```

This is a real Bean named *MyBean* that has state (the variable theValue) that will automatically be saved and restored by the JavaBeans persistence mechanism, and it has a property named *MyValue* that is usable by a visual programming environment. This Bean doesn't have any visual representation, but that isn't a requirement for a JavaBean component.

JavaSoft is using the slogan "Write once, use everywhere." Of course "everywhere" means everywhere the Java run-time environment is available. But this is very important. What it means is that the entire run-time environment required by JavaBeans is part of the Java platform. No special libraries or classes have to be distributed with your components. The JavaBeans class libraries provide a rich set of default behaviors for simple components (such as the one shown earlier). This means that you don't have to spend your time building a lot of support for the Beans environment into your code.

The design goals of JavaBeans are discussed in Sun's white paper, "Java Beans: A Component Architecture for Java." This paper can be found on the JavaSoft web site at *http://splash.javasoft.com/beans/WhitePaper.html*. It might be interesting to review these goals before we move on to the technology itself, to provide a little insight into why certain aspects of JavaBeans are the way they are.

15.1.7 Compact and Easy

JavaBeans components are simple to create and easy to use. This is an important goal of the JavaBeans architecture.

15.1.8 Portable

Since JavaBeans components are built purely in Java, they are fully portable to any platform that supports the Java run-time environment. All platform specifics, as well as support for JavaBeans, are implemented by the Java virtual machine.

15.1.9 Leverages the Strengths of the Java Platform

JavaBeans uses the existing Java class discovery mechanism. This means that there isn't some new complicated mechanism for registering components with the run-time system.

15.1.10 Flexible Build-Time Component Editors

Developers are free to create their own custom property sheets and editors for use with their components if the defaults aren't appropriate for a particular component. It's possible to create elaborate property editors for changing the value of specific properties, as well as create sophisticated property sheets to house those editors.

Imagine that you have created a Sound class that is capable of playing various sound format files. You could create a custom property editor for this class that listed all of the known system sounds in a list. If you have created a specialized color type called PrimaryColor, you could create a color picker class to be used as the property editor for PrimaryColor that presented only primary colors as choices.

The JavaBeans architecture also allows you to associate a custom editor with your component. If the task of setting the property values and behaviors of your component is complicated, it may be useful to create a component wizard that guides the user through the steps. The size and complexity of your component editor is entirely up to you.

15.2 JAVABEANS OVERVIEW

"A Java Bean is a reusable software component that can be manipulated visually in a builder tool".

Well, if you have to sum it up in one sentence, this is as good as any. But it's pretty difficult to sum up an entire component architecture in one sentence. Beans will range greatly in their features and capabilities. Some will be very simple and others complex; some will have a visual aspect and others won't. Therefore, it isn't easy to put all Beans into a single category. Let's take a look at some of the most important features and issues surrounding Beans.

15.2.1 Properties, Methods and Events

Properties are attributes of a Bean that are referenced by name. These properties are usually read and written by calling methods on the Bean specifically created for that purpose. A property of the thermostat component mentioned earlier in the chapter could be the comfort temperature. A programmer would set or get the value of this property through method calls, while an application developer using a visual development tool would manipulate the value of this property using a visual property editor.

The methods of a Bean are just the Java methods exposed by the class that implements the Bean. These methods represent the interface used to access and manipulate the component. Usually, the set of public methods defined by the class will map directly to the supported methods for the Bean, although the Bean developer can choose to expose only a subset of the public methods.

Events are the mechanism used by one component to send notifications to another. One component can register its interest in the events generated by another. Whenever the event occurs, the interested component will be notified by having one of its methods invoked. The process of registering interest in an event is carried out simply by calling the appropriate method on the component that is the source of the event. In turn, when an event occurs a method will be invoked on the component that registered its interest. In most cases, more than one component can register for event notifications from a single source. The component that is interested in event notifications is said to be *listening* for the event.

15.2.2 Introspection

Introspection is the process of exposing the properties, methods, and events that a JavaBean component supports. This process is used at run-time, as well as by a visual development tool at design-time. The default behavior of this process allows for the automatic introspection of any Bean. A low-level reflection mechanism is used to analyze the Bean's class to determine its methods. Next it applies some simple design patterns to determine the properties and events that are supported. To take advantage of reflection, you only need to follow a coding style that matches the design pattern. This is an important feature of JavaBeans. It means that you don't have to do anything more than code your methods using a simple convention. If you do, your Beans will automatically support introspection without you having to write any extra code.

This technique may not be sufficient or suitable for every Bean. Instead, you can choose to implement a BeanInfo class which provides descriptive information about its associated Bean explicitly. This is obviously more work than using the default behavior, but it might be necessary to describe a complex Bean properly. It is important to note that the BeanInfo class is separate from the Bean that it is describing. This is done so that it is not necessary to carry the baggage of the BeanInfo within the Bean itself.

15.2.3 Customization

When you are using a visual development tool to assemble components into applications, you will be presented with some sort of user interface for customizing Bean attributes. These attributes may affect the way the Bean operates or the way it looks on the screen. The application tool you use will be able to determine the properties that a Bean supports and build a property sheet dynamically. This property sheet will contain editors for each of the properties supported by the Bean, which you can use to customize the Bean to your liking. The Beans class library comes with a number of property editors for common types such as float, boolean, and String. If you are using custom classes for properties, you will have to create custom property editors to associate with them.

In some cases the default property sheet that is created by the development tool will not be good enough. You may be working with a Bean that is just too complex to customize easily using the default sheet. Beans developers have the option of creating a customizer that can help the user to customize an instance of their Bean. You can even create smart wizards that guide the user through the customization process.

Customizers are also kept separate from the Bean class so that it is not a burden to the Bean when it is not being customized. This idea of separation is a common theme in the JavaBeans architecture. A Bean class only has to implement the functionality it was designed for; all other supporting features are implemented separately.

15.2.4 Persistence

It is necessary that Beans support a large variety of storage mechanisms. This way, Beans can participate in the largest number of applications. The simplest way to support persistence is to take advantage of Java Object Serialization. This is an automatic mechanism for saving and restoring the state of an object. Java Object Serialization is the best way to make sure that your Beans are fully portable, because you take advantage of a standard feature supported by the core Java platform. This, however, is not always desirable. There may be cases where you want your Bean to use other file formats or mechanisms to save and restore state.

15.2.5 Design-Time Vs Run-Time

JavaBeans components must be able to operate properly in a running application as well as inside an application development environment. At design-time the component must provide the design information necessary to edit its properties and customize its behavior. It also has to expose its methods and events so that the design tool can write code that interacts with the Bean at run-time. And, of course, the Bean must support the run-time environment.

- **Visibility :** There is no requirement that a Bean be visible at run-time. It is perfectly reasonable for a Bean to perform some function that does not require it to present an interface to the user; the Bean may be controlling access to a specific device or data feed. However, it is still necessary for this type of component to support the visual application builder. The component can have properties, methods, and events, have persistent state, and interact with other Beans in a larger application. An "invisibie" run-time Bean may be shown visually in the application development tool, and may provide custom property editors and customizers.
- **Multithreading :** The issue of multithreading is no different in JavaBeans than it is in conventional Java programming. The JavaBeans architecture doesn't introduce any new language constructs or classes to deal with threading. You have to assume that your code will be used in a multithreaded application. It is your responsibility to make sure your Beans are thread-safe. Java makes this easier than in most languages, but it still requires some careful planning to get it right. Remember, thread-safe means that your Bean has anticipated its use by more than one thread at a time and has handled the situation properly.
- **Security :** Beans are subjected to the same security model as standard Java programs. You should assume that your Bean is running in an untrusted applet. You shouldn't make any design decisions that require your Bean to be run in a trusted environment. Your Bean may be downloaded from the World Wide Web into your browser as part of someone else's applet. All of the security restrictions apply to Beans, such as denying access to the local file system, and limiting socket connections to the host system from which the applet was downloaded.

  If your Bean is intended to run only in a Java application on a single computer, the Java security constraints do not apply. In this case you might allow your Bean to behave differently. Be careful, because the assumptions you make about security could render your Bean useless in a networked environment.
- **Using Design Patterns :** The JavaBeans architecture makes use of patterns that represent standard conventions for names, and type signatures for collections of methods and interfaces. Using coding standards is always a good idea because it makes your code easier to understand, and therefore easier to maintain. It also makes it easier for another programmer to understand the purpose of the methods and interfaces used by your component. In the JavaBeans architecture, these patterns have even more significance. A set of simple patterns are used by the default introspection mechanism to analyze your Bean and determine the properties, methods, and events that are supported. These patterns allow the visual development tools to analyze your Bean and use it in the application being created. The following code fragment shows one such pattern:

```
public void setTemperatureColor(Color newColor)
{
```

```
    ...
}
public Color getTemperatureColor()
{
    ...
}
```

These two methods together use a pattern that signifies that the Bean contains a property named *TemperatureColor* of type Color. No extra development is required to expose the property.

15.3 JAVABEANS VS. ACTIVEX

JavaBeans is certainly not the first component architecture to come along. Microsoft's ActiveX technology is based upon COM, their component object model. ActiveX offers an alternative component architecture for software targeted at the various Windows platforms. So how do you choose one of these technologies over the other? Organizational, cultural, and technical issues all come into play when making this decision. ActiveX and JavaBeans are not mutually exclusive of each other?Microsoft has embraced Java technology with products like Internet Explorer and Visual J++, and Sun seems to have recognized that the desktop is dominated by Windows and has targeted Win32 as a strategic platform for Java. It is not in anyone's best interest to choose one technology to the exclusion of another. Both are powerful component technologies. I think we should choose a technology because it supports the work we are doing, and does so in a way that meets the needs of the customer.

The most important question is how Beans will be used by containers that are designed specifically to contain ActiveX controls. Certainly, all Beans will not also be ActiveX controls by default. To address the need to integrate Beans into the world of ActiveX, an ActiveX Bridge is available that maps the properties, methods, and events exposed by the Bean into the corresponding mechanisms in COM.

15.4 ENTERPRISE JAVABEANS

15.4.1 What is an EJB?

An Enterprise JavaBean (EJB) is a reusable, portable J2EE component. EJBs consist of methods that encapsulate business logic. For example, an EJB may have business logic that contains a method to update customer data in a database. A variety of remote and local clients can invoke this method. Additionally, EJBs run inside a container, allowing the developer to focus on the business logic contained in the bean without having to worry about complicated and error-prone issues such as transaction support, security, and remote object access. EJBs are developed as *POJOs*, or Plain Old Java Objects, and developers can use metadata annotations to specify to the container how these beans are to be managed.

15.4.2 Types of EJBs

EJBs consist of three main types: Session, Entity, and Message-Driven.

Session Beans

Session beans generally represent actions in the business process such as "process order." Session beans are classified based on the maintenance of the conversation state, either stateful or stateless.

Stateless session beans do not have an internal state. They do not keep track of the information that is passed from one method call to another. Thus, each invocation of a stateless business method is independent of its previous invocation.

For Example

```
import javax.ejb.Stateless.*;
/**
* A simple stateless session bean implementing the incrementValue() method of the *
CalculateEJB interface.
*/

@Stateless(name="CalculateEJB")
public class CalculateEJBBean
implements CalculateEJB
{
int value = 0;
public String incrementValue()
{
value++;
return "value incremented by 1";
}
}
```

Entity Beans

An entity bean is an object that manages persistent data, potentially uses several dependent Java objects, and can be uniquely identified by a primary key. Specify that a class is an entity bean by including the @Entity annotation. Entity beans represent persistent data from the database, such as a row in a customer table, or an employee record in an employee table. Entity beans are also sharable across multiple clients.

For Example

```
import javax.persistence.*;
import java.util.ArrayList;
import java.util.Collection;

@Entity
@Table(name = "EMPLOYEES")
public class Employee implements java.io.Serializable
{
```

```
private int empId;
private String eName;
private double sal;

@Id
@Column(name="EMPNO", primaryKey=true)
public int getEmpId()
{
return empId;
}

public void setEmpId(int empId)
{
this.empId = empId;
}

public String getEname()
{
return eName;
}

public void setEname(String eName)
{
this.eName = eName;
}

public double getSal()
{
return sal;
}

public void setSal(double sal)
{
this.sal = sal;
}

public String toString()
{
StringBuffer buf = new StringBuffer();
buf.append("Class:")
.append(this.getClass().getName()).append(" :: ").append(" empId:").append(getEmpId()) .ap-
pend(" ename:").append(getEname()).append("sal:").append(getSal());
return buf.toString();
}
}
```

Message Driven Beans

Message driven beans (MDBs) provide an easier method to implement asynchronous communication than by using straight Java Message Services (JMS). MDBs were created to receive asynchronous JMS messages. The container handles most of the setup processes that are required for JMS queues and topics. It sends all the messages to the interested MDB. An MDB allows J2EE applications to send asynchronous messages that can then be processed by the application. To specify that a bean is an MDB, implement the javax.jms.MessageListener interface and annotate the bean with @MessageDriven.

Message Driven Bean Example

```
import javax.ejb.MessageDriven;
import javax.ejb.ActivationConfigProperty;
import javax.ejb.Inject;
import javax.jms.*;
import java.util.*;
import javax.ejb.TimedObject;
import javax.ejb.Timer;
import javax.ejb.TimerService;
@MessageDriven(
activationConfig = {
@ActivationConfigProperty(propertyName="connectionFactoryJndiName", propertyValue="jms/
TopicConnectionFactory"),
@ActivationConfigProperty(propertyName="destinationName", propertyValue="jms/myTopic"),
@ActivationConfigProperty(propertyName="destinationType", propertyValue="javax.jms.Topic"),
@ActivationConfigProperty(propertyName="messageSelector", propertyValue="RECIPIENT
='MDB'")
}
)

/**
* A simple Message-Driven Bean that listens to the configured JMS Queue or Topic and gets
notified via an * invocation of it's onMessage() method when a message has been posted to the
Queue or Topic. The bean
* prints the contents of the message.
*/

public class MessageLogger implements MessageListener, TimedObject
{

@Inject javax.ejb.MessageDrivenContext mc;

public void onMessage(Message message)
{
```

```
System.out.println("onMessage() - " + message);
try
{
String subject = message.getStringProperty("subject");
String inmessage = message.getStringProperty("message");
System.out.println("Message received\n\tDate: " + new java.util.Date() + "\n\tSubject: " +
subject + "\n\tMessage: " + inmessage + "\n");
System.out.println("Creating Timer a single event timer");
TimerService ts = mc.getTimerService();
Timer timer = ts.createTimer(30000, subject);
System.out.println("Timer created by MDB at: " + new Date(System.currentTimeMillis()) +"
with info: "+subject);
}
catch (Throwable ex)
{
ex.printStackTrace();
}
}

public void ejbTimeout(Timer timer)
{
System.out.println("EJB 3.0: Timer with MDB");
System.out.println("ejbTimeout() called at: " + new Date(System.currentTimeMillis()));
return;
}
}
```

15.4.3 Utilizing EJBs

An EJB client is the application that accesses the bean. It does not necessarily reside on the client tier, but can be a stand-alone application, JSP, servlet, or another EJB. The client accesses the methods of an EJB through the remote or local interfaces of the bean, depending on whether the client resides in the same or a different JVM than the bean. These interfaces define the methods of the bean, while the bean class actually implements the methods. When a client accesses a method of the bean class, the container generates a proxy for the bean, called the remote or local object. The remote or local object receives the request, delegates it to the corresponding bean instance, and returns the results to the client. To invoke a bean's methods, a client finds the bean by using its name defined in the EJB deployment descriptor. In the following example, the client finds the bean named "Statelessejb" using the Context object.

EJB Client Example

```
import javax.naming.Context;
import javax.naming.InitialContext;
```

```
/**
* A simple bean client which calls methods on a stateless session bean.
*/

public class CalculateejbClient
{
public static void main(String [] args)
{
Context context = new InitialContext();
CalculateEJB myejb =
(CalculateEJB)context.lookup("java:comp/env/ejb/CalculateEJB");
myejb.incrementValue();
}
}
```

QUESTIONS WITH ANSWERS

1. *What are the different kinds of enterprise beans?*

Solution: Stateless session bean- An instance of these non-persistent EJBs provides a service without storing an interaction or conversation state between methods. Any instance can be used for any client.

Stateful session bean- An instance of these non-persistent EJBs maintains state across methods and transactions. Each instance is associated with a particular client.

Entity bean- An instance of these persistent EJBs represents an object view of the data, usually rows in a database. They have a primary key as a unique identifier. Entity bean persistence can be either container-managed or bean-managed.

Message-driven bean- An instance of these EJBs is integrated with the Java Message Service (JMS) to provide the ability for message-driven beans to act as a standard JMS message consumer and perform asynchronous processing between the server and the JMS message producer.

2. *What is Session Bean?*

Solution: A session bean is a non-persistent object that implements some business logic running on the server. One way to think of a session object is as a logical extension of the client program that runs on the server.

Session beans are used to manage the interactions of entity and other session beans,access resources, and generally perform tasks on behalf of the client.

There are two basic kinds of session bean: stateless and stateful.

Stateless session beans are made up of business methods that behave like procedures; they operate only on the arguments passed to them when they are invoked. Stateless beans are called stateless because they are transient; they do not maintain business state between method invocations.Each invocation of a stateless business method is independent from previous invocations. Because stateless session beans are stateless, they are easier for the EJB container to manage, so they tend to process requests faster and use less resources.

Stateful session beans encapsulate business logic and state specific to a client. Stateful beans are called "stateful" because they do maintain business state between method invocations, held in memory and not persistent. Unlike stateless session beans, clients do not share stateful beans. When a client creates a stateful bean, that bean instance is dedicated to service only that client. This makes it possible to maintain conversational state, which is business state that can be shared by methods in the same stateful bean.

3. *What is Entity Bean?*

Solution: The entity bean is used to represent data in the database. It provides an object-oriented interface to data that would normally be accessed by the JDBC or some other back-end API. More than that, entity beans provide a component model that allows bean developers to focus their attention on the business logic of the bean, while the container takes care of managing persistence,transactions, and access control.

There are two basic kinds of entity beans: container-managed ersistence (CMP) andbean-managed persistence (BMP).

Container-managed persistence beans are the simplest for the bean developer to create and the most difficult for the EJB server to support. This is because all the logic for synchronizing the bean's state with the database is handled automatically by the container. This means that the bean developer doesn't need to write any data access logic, while the EJB server is

supposed to take care of all the persistence needs automatically. With CMP, the container manages the persistence of the entity bean. Vendor tools are used to map the entity fields to the database and absolutely no database access code is written in the bean class.

The bean-managed persistence (BMP) enterprise bean manages synchronizing its state with the database as directed by the container. The bean uses a database API to read and write its fields to the database, but the container tells it when to do each synchronization operation and manages the transactions for the bean automatically. Bean-managed persistence gives the bean developer the flexibility to perform persistence operations that are too complicated for the container or to use a data source that is not supported by the container.

4. *What are the methods of Entity Bean?*

Solution: An entity bean consists of 4 groups of methods:

(*i*) **Create methods:** To create a new instance of a CMP entity bean, and therefore insert data into the database, the create() method on the bean's home interface must be invoked. They look like this: EntityBeanClass ejbCreateXXX(parameters), where EntityBeanClass is an Entity Bean you are trying to instantiate, ejbCreateXXX(parameters) methods are used for creating Entity Bean instances according to the parameters specified and to some programmer-defined conditions.

A bean's home interface may declare zero or more create() methods, each of which must have corresponding ejbCreate() and ejbPostCreate() methods in the bean class. These creation methods are linked at run time, so that when a create() method is invoked on the home interface, the container delegates the invocation to the corresponding ejbCreate() and ejbPostCreate() methods on the bean class.

(*ii*) **Finder methods:** The methods in the home interface that begin with "find" are called the find methods. These are used to query the EJB server for specific entity beans, based on the name of the method and arguments passed. Unfortunately, there is no standard query language defined for find methods, so each vendor will implement the find method differently. In CMP entity beans, the find methods are not implemented with matching methods in the bean class; containers implement them when the bean is deployed in a vendor specific manner. The deployer will use vendor specific tools to tell the container how a particular find method should behave. Some vendors will use object-relational mapping tools to define the behavior of a find method while others will simply require the deployer to enter the appropriate SQL command.

There are two basic kinds of find methods: single-entity and multi-entity. Single-entity find methods return a remote reference to the one specific entity bean that matches the find request. If no entity beans are found, the method throws an ObjectNotFoundException. Every entity bean must define the single-entity find method with the method name findByPrimaryKey(), which takes the bean's primary key type as an argument.

The multi-entity find methods return a collection (Enumeration or Collection type) of entities that match the find request. If no entities are found, the multi-entity find returns an empty collection.

(*iii*) **Remove methods:** These methods (you may have up to 2 remove methods, or don't have them at all) allow the client to physically remove Entity beans by specifying either Handle or a Primary Key for the Entity Bean.

(*iv*) **Home methods:** These methods are designed and implemented by a developer, and EJB specification doesn't have any requirements for them except the need to throw a RemoteException is each home method.

5. *What are the methods of Entity Bean?What is the difference between Container-Managed Persistent (CMP) bean and Bean-Managed Persistent(BMP) ?*

Solution: Container-managed persistence beans are the simplest for the bean developer to create and the most difficult for the EJB server to support. This is because all the logic for synchronizing the bean's state with the database is handled automatically by the container. This means that the bean developer doesn't need to write any data access logic, while the EJB server is supposed to take care of all the persistence needs automatically. With CMP, the container manages the persistence of the entity bean. A CMP bean developer doesn't need to worry about JDBC code and transactions, because the Container performs database calls and transaction management instead of the programmer. Vendor tools are used to map the entity fields to the database and absolutely no database access code is written in the bean class. All table mapping is specified in the deployment descriptor. Otherwise, a BMP bean developer takes the load of linking an application and a database on his shoulders.

The bean-managed persistence (BMP) enterprise bean manages synchronizing its state with the database as directed by the container. The bean uses a database API to read and write its fields to the database, but the container tells it when to do each synchronization operation and manages the transactions for the bean automatically. Bean-managed persistence gives the bean developer the flexibility to perform persistence operations that are too complicated for the container or to use a data source that is not supported by the container.BMP beans are not 100% database-independent, because they may contain database-specific code, but CMP beans are unable to perform complicated DML (data manipulation language) statements. EJB 2.0 specification introduced some new ways of querying database (by using the EJB QL - query language).

6. *What are the callback methods in Entity beans?*

Solution: The bean class defines create methods that match methods in the home interface and business methods that match methods in the remote interface. The bean class also implements a set of callback methods that allow the container to notify the bean of events in its life cycle. The callback methods are defined in the **javax.ejb.EntityBean** interface that is implemented by all entity beans.The EntityBean interface has the following definition. Notice that the bean class implements these methods.

```
public interface javax.ejb.EntityBean {
        public void setEntityContext();
        public void unsetEntityContext();
        public void ejbLoad();
        public void ejbStore();
        public void ejbActivate();
        public void ejbPassivate();
        public void ejbRemove();
}
```

The **setEntityContext()** method provides the bean with an interface to the container called the EntityContext. The EntityContext interface contains methods for obtaining information about the context under which the bean is operating at any particular moment. The EntityContext interface is used to access security information about the caller; to determine the status of the current transaction or to force a transaction rollback; or to get a reference to the bean itself, its home, or its primary key. The EntityContext is set only once in the life of an entity bean instance, so its reference should be put into one of the bean instance's fields if it will be needed later.

The **unsetEntityContext()** method is used at the end of the bean's life cycle before the instance is evicted from memory to dereference the EntityContext and perform any last-minute clean-up.

The **ejbLoad()** and **ejbStore()** methods in CMP entities are invoked when the entity bean's state is being synchronized with the database. The ejbLoad() is invoked just after the container has refreshed the bean container-managed fields with its state from the database. The ejbStore() method is invoked just before the container is about to write the bean container-managed fields to the database. These methods are used to modify data as it's being synchronized. This is common when the data stored in the database is different than the data used in the bean fields.

The **ejbPassivate()** and **ejbActivate()** methods are invoked on the bean by the container just before the bean is passivated and just after the bean is activated, respectively. Passivation in entity beans means that the bean instance is disassociated with its remote reference so that the container can evict it from memory or reuse it. It's a resource conservation measure the container employs to reduce the number of instances in memory. A bean might be passivated if it hasn't been used for a while or as a normal operation performed by the container to maximize reuse of resources. Some containers will evict beans from memory, while others will reuse instances for other more active remote references. The ejbPassivate() and ejbActivate() methods provide the bean with a notification as to when it's about to be passivated (disassociated with the remote reference) or activated (associated with a remote reference).

7. *What is software architecture of EJB?*

Solution: Session and Entity EJBs consist of (*iv*) and (*v*) parts respetively:

(*i*) A remote interface (a client interacts with it),

(*ii*) A home interface (used for creating objects and for declaring business methods),

(*iii*) A bean object (an object, which actually performs business logic and EJB-specific operations).

(*iv*) A deployment descriptor (an XML file containing all information required for maintaining the EJB) or a set of deployment descriptors (if you are using some container-specific features).

(*v*) A Primary Key class - is only Entity bean specific.

8. *Can Entity Beans have no create() methods?*

Solution: Yes. In some cases the data is inserted NOT using Java application, so you may only need to retrieve the information, perform its processing, but not create your own information of this kind.

9. *What is bean managed transaction?*

Solution: If a developer doesn't want a Container to manage transactions, it's possible to implement all database operations manually by writing the appropriate JDBC code. This often leads to productivity increase, but it makes an Entity Bean incompatible with some databases and it enlarges the amount of code to be written. All transaction management is explicitly performed by a developer.

10. *What are transaction attributes?*

Solution: The transaction attribute specifies how the Container must manage transactions for a method when a client invokes the method via the enterprise bean's home or component interface or when the method is invoked as the result of the arrival of a JMS message. (Sun's EJB Specification) Below is a list of transactional attributes:

(*i*) **NotSupported** - transaction context is unspecified.

(*ii*) **Required** - bean's method invocation is made within a transactional context. If a client is not associated with a transaction, a new transaction is invoked automatically.

(*iii*) **Supports** - if a transactional context exists, a Container acts like the transaction attribute is Required, else - like NotSupported.

(*iv*) **RequiresNew** - a method is invoked in a new transaction context.

(*v*) **Mandatory** - if a transactional context exists, a Container acts like the transaction attribute is Required, else it throws a javax.ejb.TransactionRequiredException.

(*vi*) **Never** - a method executes only if no transaction context is specified.

11. *What are transaction isolation levels in EJB?*

Solution:

(*i*) **Transaction_read_uncommitted**- Allows a method to read uncommitted data from a DB(fast but not wise).

(*ii*) **Transaction_read_committed**- Guarantees that the data you are getting has been committed.

(*iii*) **Transaction_repeatable_read** - Guarantees that all reads of the database will be the same during the transaction (good for read and update operations).

(*iv*) **Transaction_serializable**- All the transactions for resource are performed serial.

EXERCISE

1. What is the difference between objects and JavaBeans?
2. What are the development phases of JavaBeans?
3. Write down the various steps involved in creating JavaBeans?
4. What are the elements of JavaBeans?
5. What are the various types of JavaBeans?
6. Define BDK?
7. Differentiate between JavaBeans and EJB.
8. What are control beans?
9. What are container beans?
10. What do you mean by invisible runtime beans?
11. What do you mean by Accessor and mutator methods?
12. What is the manifest file?
13. What is JAR file?
14. What do you mean by EJB architecture?
15. What are the main factors of EJB?
16. What do you mean by EJB server?
17. What do you mean by EJB container?
18. What are interfaces?
19. What is the difference between Build and Execution phases?

16

SERVLETS

16.0 INTRODUCTION

Over the last few years, Java has become the predominant language for server-side programming. This is due in no small part to the Java Servlet API, which provides a standard way to extend web servers to support dynamic content generation. With the introduction of the J2EE specification for enterprise applications, servlets have taken over as the primary interface for thin-client applications. In terms of enterprise computing, servlets are a natural fit if you are using the Web as your deployment platform. You can take advantage of web browsers as universally available thin clients using the web server as middleware for running application logic. Under this model, the user makes a request of the web server, the server invokes a servlet designed to handle the request, the servlet fulfills the request, and the result is returned to the user for display in the web browser.

While this sounds like every other dynamic content technology (such CGI, ISAPI, ASP, PHP, and the like), servlets have some major advantages. For one, servlets are persistent between invocations, which dramatically improves performance relative to CGI-style programs. Servlets are also 100% portable across operating systems and servers, unlike any of the alternatives. Finally, servlets have access to all the APIs of the Java platform, so, for example, it is easy to create a servlet that interacts with a database, using the JDBC API.

16.1 GETTING A SERVLET ENVIRONMENT

You need a *servlet container* to run servlets. A servlet container uses a Java Virtual Machine* to run servlet code as requested by a web server. The servlet container is also responsible for managing other aspects of the servlet lifecycle: user sessions, class loading, servlet contexts, servlet configuration information, servlet persistence, and temporary storage.

There are a few varieties of servlet containers. Some are simply add-ons to existing web servers. The most popular of these is Apache/JServ, a Servlets 2.0 container that adds servlet capability to the Apache Web Server. Since interaction with servlets occurs almost exclusively through a web browser, these servlet engines aren't useful on their own. Other servlet engines include embedded web servers.

16.2 SERVLET BASICS

The Servlet API consists of two packages, javax.servlet and javax.servlet.http. The javax is there because servlets are a standard extension to Java, rather than a mandatory part of the API. This means that while servlets are official Java, Java virtual machine developers aren't required to include the classes for them in their Java development and execution environments. As mentioned already, however, the Servlet API is required for J2EE 1.3

16.3 THE SERVLET LIFE CYCLE

When a client makes a request involving a servlet, the server loads and executes the appropriate Java classes. Those classes generate content, and the server sends the content back to the client. In most cases, the client is a web browser, the server is a web server, and the servlet returns standard HTML. From the web browser's perspective, this isn't any different from requesting a page generated by a CGI script, or, indeed, standard HTML. On the server side, however, there is an important difference: persistence.* Instead of shutting down at the end of each request, the servlet can remain loaded, ready to handle subsequent requests. Figure below shows how this all fits together.

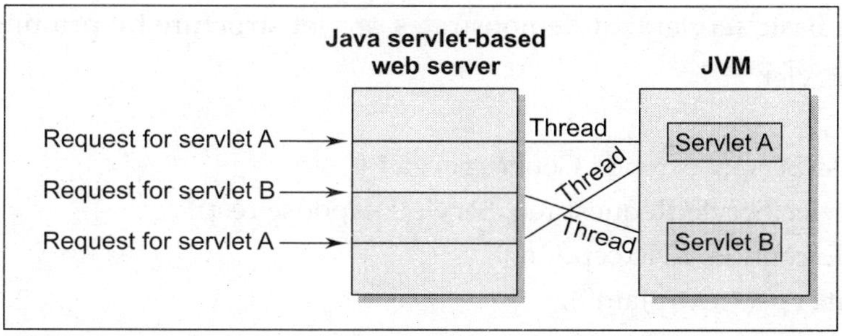

The servlet life cycle

The request-processing time for a servlet can vary, but it is typically quite fast when compared to a similar CGI program. The real performance advantage of a servlet, however, is that you incur most of the startup overhead only once. When a servlet loads, its init() method is called. You can use init() to create I/O-intensive resources, such as database connections, for use across multiple invocations. If you have a high-traffic site, the performance benefits can be quite dramatic. Instead of putting up and tearing down a hundred thousand database connections, the servlet just needs to create a connection once.

After the init() method runs, the servlet container marks the servlet as available. For each incoming connection directed at a particular servlet, the container calls the service() method on the servlet to process the request. The service() method can have access to all the resources created in the init() method. The servlet's destroy() method is called to clean up resources when the server shuts down.

Because servlets are persistent, you can actually remove a lot of filesystem and/or database accesses altogether. For example, to implement a page counter, you can simply store a number in a static variable, rather than consulting a file (or database) for every request. Using this technique, you need to read and write to the disk only occasionally to preserve state. Since a servlet remains active, it canperform other tasks when it is not servicing client requests, such as running a background processing thread (*i.e.*, where clients connect to the servlet to view a result) or even acting as an RMI host, enabling a single servlet to handle connections from multiple types of clients. For example, if you write an order processing servlet, it can accept transactions from both an HTML form and an applet using RMI.

The Servlet API includes numerous methods and classes for making application development easier. Most common CGI tasks require a lot of fiddling on the programmer's part; even decoding HTML form parameters can be a chore, to say nothing of dealing with cookies and session tracking. Libraries exist to help with these tasks, but they are, of course, decidedly nonstandard. You can use the Servlet API to handle most routine tasks, thus cutting development time and keeping things consistent for multiple developers on a project.

16.4 WRITING SERVLETS

The three core elements of the Servlet API are the javax.servlet.Servlet interface, the javax.servlet. GenericServlet class, and the javax.servlet.http. HttpServlet class. Normally, you create a servlet by subclassing one of the two classes, although if you are adding servlet capability to an existing object, you may find it easier to implement the interface.

The GenericServlet class is used for servlets that don't implement any particular communication protocol. Here's a basic servlet that demonstrates servlet structure by printing a short message:

```
import javax.servlet.*;
import java.io.*;
public class BasicServlet extends GenericServlet {
public void service(ServletRequest req, ServletResponse resp)
throws ServletException, IOException {
resp.setContentType("text/plain");
PrintWriter out = resp.getWriter();
// We won't use the ServletRequest object in this example
out.println("Hello.");
}
}
```

BasicServlet extends the GenericServlet class and implements one method: service(). Whenever a server wants to use the servlet, it calls the service() method, passing ServletRequest and ServletResponse objects. The servlet tells the server what type of response to expect, gets a PrintWriter from the response object, and transmits its output.

The GenericServlet class can also implement a *filtering servlet* that takes output from an unspecified source and performs some kind of alteration. For example, a filter servlet might be used to prepend a header, scan servlet output or raw HTML files for <DATE> tags and insert the current date, or remove <BLINK> tags. A more advanced filtering servlet might insert content from a database into HTML templates.

16.5 HTTP SERVLETS

The HttpServlet class is an extension of GenericServlet that includes methods for handling HTTP-specific data.* HttpServlet provides a number of methods, such as doGet(), doPost(), and doPut(), to handle particular types of HTTP requests (GET, POST, and so on). These methods are called by the default implementation of the service() method, which figures out what kind of request is being made and then invokes the appropriate method. Here's a simple HttpServlet:

```
import javax.servlet.*;
import javax.servlet.http.*;
import java.io.*;
public class HelloWorldServlet extends HttpServlet {
public void doGet(HttpServletRequest req, HttpServletResponse resp)
throws ServletException, IOException {
resp.setContentType("text/html");
PrintWriter out = resp.getWriter();
out.println("<HTML>");
out.println(
"<HEAD><TITLE>Have you seen this before?</TITLE></HEAD>");
out.println(
"<BODY><H1>Hello, World!</H1><H6>Again.</H6></BODY></HTML>");
}
}
```

HelloWorldServlet demonstrates many essential servlet concepts. First, HelloWorldServlet extends HttpServlet. This is standard practice for an HTTP servlet. HelloWorldServlet defines one method, doGet(), which is called whenever anyone requests a URL that points to this servlet.† The doGet() method is actually called by the default service() method of HttpServlet. The service()method is called by the web server when a request is made of HelloWorldServlet; the method determines what kind of HTTP request is being made and dispatches the request to the appropriate doXXX() method (in this case, doGet()). doGet() is passed two objects, HttpServletRequest and HttpServletResponse, that contain information about the request and provide a mechanism for the servlet to produce output, respectively.

The doGet() method itself does three things.

- It sets the output type to text/ html, which indicates that the servlet produces standard HTML as its output.
- It calls the getWriter() method of the HttpServletResponse parameter to get a java.io. PrintWriter that points to the client.
- It uses the stream to send some HTML back to the client.

If you define a doGet() method for a servlet, you may also want to override the getLastModified() method of HttpServlet. The server calls getLastModified() to find out if the content delivered by a servlet has changed. The default implementation of this method returns a negative number, which tells the server that the servlet doesn't know when its content was last updated, so the server is forced to call doGet() and return the servlet's output.

16.6 WEB APPLICATIONS

Now that we've seen a basic servlet, we can step back for a moment and talk about how servlets are integrated into the servlet container. Version 2.2 of the Servlet API popularized the concept of a web application installed within a web server. A web application consists of a set of resources, including servlets, static content, JSP files, and class libraries, installed within a particular path on a web server. This path is called the *servlet context,* and all servlets installed within the context are given an isolated, protected environment to operate in, without interference from (or the ability to interfere with) other software running on the server.

A servlet context directory tree contains several different types of resources. These include class files and JAR files (which aren't exposed to clients connecting via web browsers), JSP files (which are processed by the JSP servlet before being fed back to the client), and static files, such as HTML documents and JPEG images, which are served directly to the browser by the web server.

16.7 STRUCTURE OF WEB APPLICATIONS

On disk, a web application consists of a directory. The directory contains a subdirectory called *WEB-INF,* and whatever other content is required for the application. The *WEB-INF* directory contains a classes directory (containing application code), a lib directory (containing application JAR files), and a file called *web.xml.* The *web.xml* file contains all of the configuration information for the servlets within the context, including names, path mappings and initialization parameters and context-level configuration information.

The procedure for installing a web application into a servlet container varies from product to product, but it generally consists of selecting a context root and pointing the server to the directory containing the web application.

16.8 CONTEXT METHODS

Resources within a servlet context (such as HTML files, images, and other data) can be accessed directly via the web server. If a file called *index.html* is stored at the root of the */app* context, then it can be accessed with a request to */app/index.html*. Context resources can also be accessed via the ServletContext object, which is accessed via the getResource() and getResourceAsStream() methods. A full list of available resources can be accessed via the getResourcePaths() method. In this case, an InputStream containing the contents of the *index.html* file can be retrieved by calling getResourceAsStream("/index.html") on the ServletContext object associated with the */app* context.

The ServletContext interface provides servlets with access to a range of information about the local environment. The getInitParameter() and getInitParameterNames() methods allow servlets to retrieve context-wide initialization parameters. ServletContext also includes a number of methods that allow servlets to share attributes. The new setAttribute() method allows a servlet to set an attribute that can be shared by any other servlets that live in its ServletContext, and removeAttribute() allows them to be removed. The getAttribute() method, which previously allowed servlets to retrieve hardcoded server attributes, provides access to attribute values, while getAttributeNames() returns an Enumeration of all the shared attributes.

The servlet container is required to maintain a temporary working directory on disk for each servlet context. This directory is accessed by retrieving the javax. servlet.context.tempdir attribute, which consists of a java.io.File object pointing to the temporary directory. The temporary directory is exclusive to the context. The servlet container is not required to maintain its contents across restarts.

Version 2.1 of the Servlet API deprecated all methods related to accessing other servlets directly, due to the fact that they are inherently insecure. Thus, getServlet() and getServletNames() join the already deprecated getServlets(). The problem was that getServlet() incorrectly allowed one servlet to call another servlet's life-cycle methods, including init() and destroy().

16.9 SERVLET REQUESTS

When a servlet is asked to handle a request, it typically needs specific information about the request so that it can process the request appropriately. Most frequently, a servlet will retrieve the value of a form variable and use that value in its output. A servlet may also need access to information about the environment in which it is running. For example, a servlet may need to find out about the actual user who is accessing the servlet, for authentication purposes.

The ServletRequest and HttpServletRequest interfaces provide access to this kind of information. When a servlet is asked to handle a request, the server passes it a request object that implements one of these interfaces. With this object, the servlet can determine the actual request (e.g., protocol, URL, type), access parts of the raw request (e.g., headers, input stream), and get any client-specific request parameters (e.g., form variables, extra path information). For instance, the getProtocol() method returns the protocol used by the request, while getRemoteHost() returns the name of the client host. The interfaces also provide methods that let a servlet get information about the server (e.g., getServername(), getServerPort()). As we saw earlier, the getParameter() method provides access to request parameters such as form variables. There is also the getParameterValues() method, which returns an array of strings that contains all he values for a particular parameter. This array generally contains only one string, ut some HTML form elements (as well as non-HTTP oriented services) do allow ultiple selections or options, so the method always returns an array, even if it as a length of one.

HttpServletRequest adds a few more methods for handling HTTP-specific request data. For instance, getHeaderNames() returns an enumeration of the names of all the HTTP headers submitted with a request, while getHeader() returns a particular header value.

Example below shows a servlet that restricts access to users who are connecting via the HTTPS protocol, using Digest style authentication, and coming from a government site (a domain ending in *.gov*)..

Example : *Checking Request Information to Restrict Servlet Access*

```
import javax.servlet.*;
import javax.servlet.http.*;
import java.io.*;
public class SecureRequestServlet extends HttpServlet {
public void doGet(HttpServletRequest req, HttpServletResponse resp)
throws ServletException, IOException {
```

```
resp.setContentType("text/html");
PrintWriter out = resp.getWriter();
out.println("<HTML>");
out.println("<HEAD><TITLE>Semi-Secure Request</TITLE></HEAD>");
out.println("<BODY>");
String remoteHost = req.getRemoteHost();
String scheme = req.getScheme();
String authType = req.getAuthType();
if((remoteHost == null) || (scheme == null) || (authType == null)) {
out.println("Request Information Was Not Available.");
return;
}
if(scheme.equalsIgnoreCase("https") && remoteHost.endsWith(".gov")
&& authType.equals("Digest")) {
out.println("Special, secret information.");
}
else {
out.println("You are not authorized to view this data.");
}
out.println("</BODY></HTML>");
}
}
```

16.10 FORMS AND INTERACTION

The problem with creating a servlet like HelloWorldServlet is that it doesn't do anything we can't already do with HTML. If we are going to bother with a servlet at all, we should do something dynamic and interactive with it. In many cases, this means processing the results of an HTML form. To make our example less impersonal, let's have it greet the user by name. The HTML form that calls the servlet using a GET request might look like this:

```
<HTML>
<HEAD><TITLE>Greetings Form</TITLE></HEAD>
<BODY>
<FORM METHOD=GET ACTION="/servlet/HelloServlet">
What is your name?
<INPUT TYPE=TEXT NAME=username SIZE=20>
<INPUT TYPE=SUBMIT VALUE="Introduce Yourself">
</FORM>
</BODY>
</HTML>
```

This form submits a form variable named username to the URL */servlet/HelloServlet*. The HelloServlet itself does little more than create an output stream, read the username form variable, and print a nice greeting for the user. Here's the code:

```
import javax.servlet.*;
import javax.servlet.http.*;
import java.io.*;
public class HelloServlet extends HttpServlet {
public void doGet(HttpServletRequest req, HttpServletResponse resp)
throws ServletException, IOException {
resp.setContentType("text/html");
PrintWriter out = resp.getWriter();
out.println("<HTML>");
out.println("<HEAD><TITLE>Finally, interaction!</TITLE></HEAD>");
out.println("<BODY><H1>Hello, " + req.getParameter("username") +
"!</H1>");
out.println("</BODY></HTML>");
}
}
```

All we've done differently is use the getParameter() method of HttpServletRequest to retrieve the value of a form variable.* When a server calls a servlet, it can also pass a set of request parameters. With HTTP servlets, these parameters come from the HTTP request itself—in this case, in the guise of URLencoded form variables. Note that a GenericServlet running in a web server also has access to these parameters using the simpler ServletRequest object. When the HelloServlet runs, it inserts the value of the username form variable into the HTML output.

16.11 POST, HEAD AND OTHER REQUESTS

As mentioned earlier, doGet() is just one of a collection of enabling methods for HTTP request types. doPost() is the corresponding method for POST requests. The POST request is designed for posting information to the server, although in practice it is also used for long parameterized requests and larger forms, to get around limitations on the length of URLs.

If your servlet is performing database updates, charging a credit card, or doing anything that takes an explicit client action, you should make sure this activity is happening in a doPost() method. That's because POST requests aren't *idempotent*, which means that they aren't safely repeatable, and web browsers treat them specially. For example, a browser can't bookmark or, in some cases, reload a POST request. On the other hand, GET requests are idempotent, so they can safely be bookmarked, and a browser is free to issue the request repeatedly without necessarily consulting the user.

To create a servlet that can handle POST requests, all you have to do is override the default doPost() method from HttpServlet and implement the necessary functionality in it. If necessary, your application can implement different code in doPost() and doGet(). For instance, the doGet() method might display a postable data entry form that the doPost() method processes. doPost() can even call doGet() at the end to display the form again.

The less common HTTP request types, such as HEAD, PUT, TRACE, and DELETE, are handled by other doXXX() dispatch methods. A HEAD request returns HTTP headers only, PUT and DELETE allow clients to create and remove resources from the web server, and TRACE returns the request headers to the client. Since most servlet programmers don't need to worry about these requests, the HttpServlet class includes a default implementation of each corresponding doXXX() method that either informs the client that the request is unsupported or provides a minimal implementation. You can provide your own versions of these methods, but the details of implementing PUT or DELETE functionality go rather beyond our scope.

16.12 SERVLET RESPONSES

In order to do anything useful, a servlet must send a response to each request that is made to it. In the case of an HTTP servlet, the response can include three components: a status code, any number of HTTP headers, and a response body.

The ServletResponse and HttpServletResponse interfaces include all the methods needed to create and manipulate a servlet's output. We've already seen that you specify the MIME type for the data returned by a servlet using the setContentType() method of the response object passed into the servlet. With an HTTP servlet, the MIME type is generally text/html, although some servlets return binary data: a servlet that loads a GIF file from a database and sends it to the web browser should set a content type of image/gif while a servlet that returns an Adobe Acrobat file should set it to application/pdf.

ServletResponse and HttpServletResponse each define two methods for producing output streams, getOutputStream() and getWriter(). The former returns a ServletOutputStream, which can be used for textual or binary data. The latter returns a java.io.PrintWriter object, which is used only for textual output.The getWriter() method examines the content-type to determine which charset to use, so setContentType() should be called before getWriter().

HttpServletResponse also includes a number of methods for handling HTTP responses. Most of these allow you to manipulate the HTTP header fields. For example, setHeader(), setIntHeader(), and setDateHeader() allow you to set the value of a specified HTTP header, while containsHeader() indicates whether a certain header has already been set. You can use either the setStatus() or sendError() method to specify the status code sent back to the server. HttpServletResponse defines a long list of integer constants that represent specific status codes (we'll see some of these shortly). You typically don't need to worry about setting a status code, as the default code is 200 ("OK"), meaning that the servlet sent a normal response. However, a servlet that is part of a complex application structure (such as the file servlet included in the Java Web Server that handles the dispatching of HTML pages) may need to use a variety of status codes. Finally, the sendRedirect() method allows you to issue a page redirect. Calling this method sets the Location header to the specified location and uses the appropriate status code for a redirect.

16.13 REQUEST DISPATCHING

Request dispatching allows a servlet to delegate request handling to other components on the server. A servlet can either forward an entire request to another servlet or include bits of content from other components in its own output. In either case, this is done with a RequestDispatcher object that is obtained from the ServletContext via the getRequestDispatcher() method (also available via the HttpServletRequest object.) When you call this method, you specify the path to the servlet to which you are dispatching the request. The path should be relative to the servlet context. If you want to dispatch a request to the */servlet/TargetServlet* URI within the */app* context (which is accessed from a user's browser by */app/ servlet/TargetServlet*), request a dispatcher for */ servlet/TargetServlet*.

When you dispatch a request, you can set request attributes using the setAttribute() method of ServletRequest and read them using the getAttribute() method. A list of available attributes is returned by getAttributeNames(). All three of these methods were new in Version 2.1. Rather than taking only String objects (like parameters), an attribute may be any valid Java object.

RequestDispatcher provides two methods for dispatching requests: forward() and include(). To forward an entire request to another servlet, use the forward() method. When using forward(), the ServletRequest object is updated to include the new target URL. If a ServletOutputStream or PrintWriter has already been retrieved from the ServletResponse object, the forward() method throws an IllegalStateException.

The include() method of RequestDispatcher causes the content of the dispatchee to be included in the output of the main servlet, just like a server-side include. To see how this works, let's look at part of a servlet that does a keep-alive check on several different servers. The ServerMonitorServlet referenced in this example relies on the serverurl attribute to determine which server to display monitoring information for:

```
out.println("Uptime for our servers");
// Get a RequestDispatcher to the ServerMonitorServlet
RequestDispatcher d = getServletContext().
getRequestDispatcher("/servlet/ServerMonitorServlet");
req.setAttribute("serverurl", new URL("http://www1.company.com"));
d.include(req, res);
req.setAttribute("serverurl", new URL("http://www2.company.com"));
d.include(req, res);
```

16.14 ERROR HANDLING

Sometimes things just go wrong. When that happens, it's nice to have a clean way out. The Servlet API gives you two ways of to deal with errors: you can manually send an error message back to the client or you can throw a ServletException. The easiest way to handle an error is simply to write an error message to the servlet's output stream. This is the appropriate technique to use when the error is part of a servlet's normal operation, such as when a user forgets to fill in a required form field.

16.14.1 Status Codes

When an error is a standard HTTP error, you should use the sendError() method of HttpServletResponse to tell the server to send a standard error status code. HttpServletResponse defines integer constants for all the major HTTP status codes. Table 5-1 lists the most common status codes. For example, if a servlet can't find a file the user has requested, it can send a 404 ("File

Not Found") error and let the browser display it in its usual manner. In this case, we can replace the typical setContentType() and getWriter() calls with something like this:

response.sendError(HttpServletResponse.SC_NOT_FOUND);

If you want to specify your own error message (in addition to the web server's default message for a particular error code), you can call sendError() with an extra String parameter:

16.14.2 A File Serving Servlet

Example below demonstrates both of these error-handling techniques, along with another method for reading data from the server. *FileServlet* reads a pathname from a form parameter and returns the associated file. Note that this servlet is designed only to return HTML files. If the file can't be found, the servlet sends the browser a 404 error. If the servlet lacks sufficient access privileges to load the file, it sends an *UnavailableException* instead. Keep in mind that this servlet exists as a teaching exercise: you should not deploy it on your web server. (For one thing, any security exception renders the servlet permanently unavailable, and for another, it can serve files from the root of your hard drive.)

Example: *Serving Files*

```
import javax.servlet.*;
import javax.servlet.http.*;
import java.io.*;
public class FileServlet extends HttpServlet {
public void doGet(HttpServletRequest req, HttpServletResponse resp)
throws ServletException, IOException {
File r;
FileReader fr;
BufferedReader br;
try {
r = new File(req.getParameter("filename"));
fr = new FileReader(r);
br = new BufferedReader(fr);
if(!r.isFile()) { // Must be a directory or something else
resp.sendError(resp.SC_NOT_FOUND);
return;
}
}
catch (FileNotFoundException e) {
resp.sendError(resp.SC_NOT_FOUND);
return;
}
catch (SecurityException se) { // Be unavailable permanently
throw(new UnavailableException(this,
"Servlet lacks appropriate privileges."));
```

```
}
resp.setContentType("text/html");
PrintWriter out = resp.getWriter();
String text;
while( (text = br.readLine()) != null)
out.println(text);
br.close();
}
}
```

16.15 SECURITY

Servlets don't have to handle their own security arrangements. Instead, they can rely on the capabilities of the web server to limit access where required. The security capabilities of most web servers are limited to basic on-or-off access to specific resources, controlled by username and password (or digital certificate), with possible encryption-in-transmission using SSL. Most servers are limited to basic authentication, which transmits passwords more or less in the clear, while some support the more advanced digest authentication protocol, which works by transmitting a hash of the user's password and a server-generated value, rather than the password itself. Both of these approaches look the same to the user; the familiar "Enter username and password" window pops up in the web browser.

Recent versions of the Servlet API take a much less hands-off approach to security. The *web.xml* file can be used to define which servlets and resources are protected, and which users have access. The user access model is the J2EE User Role model, in which users can be assigned one or more Roles. Users with a particular role are granted access to protected resources. A user named Admin might have both the Administrator role and the User role, while users Bob and Ted might only have the User role.

In addition to basic, digest and SSL authentication, the web application framework allows for HTML form-based logins. This approach allows the developer to specify an HTML or JSP page containing a form like the following:

```
<form method="POST" action="j_security_check">
<input type="text" name="j_username">
<input type=password" name="j_password">
<input type="submit" value="Log In">
</form>
```

Note that forms-based authentication is insecure, and will only work if the client session is being tracked via Cookies or SSL signatures. In Servlets 2.0, the HttpServletRequest interface included a pair of basic methods for retrieving standard HTTP user authentication information from the web server. If your web server is equipped to limit access, a servlet can retrieve the username with getRemoteUser() and the authentication method (basic, digest, or SSL) with getAuthType(). Version 2.2 of the Servlet API added the isUserInRole() and getUserPrincipal() methods to HttpServletRequest. isUserInRole() allows the program to query whether the current user is member of a particular role (useful for dynamic content decisions that can not be made at the container level). The getUserPrincipal() method returns a java.security.Principal object identifying the current user. The process used to authenticate users (by validating their usernames and passwords) is up the developer of the servlet container.

16.16 SERVLET CHAINS AND FILTERS

So far, we have looked at servlets that take requests directly from the server and return their results directly to the client. Servlets were designed as a generic server extension technology, however, rather than one devoted solely to performing CGI like functions. A servlet can just as easily take its input from another servlet, and a servlet really doesn't care very much about where its output goes. Most web servers that implement servlets have also implemented a feature called *servlet chaining*, where the server routes a request through an administrator defined chain of servlets. At the end of the sequence, the server sends the output to the client. Alternately, some servers can be configured to route certain MIME types through certain servlets. If a filtering servlet is configured to take all of the output with the MIME type "servlet/filterme," another servlet can produce data with that MIME type, and that data will be passed to the filtering servlet. The filtering servlet, after doing its work, can output HTML for the browser. MIME based filtering also allows servlets to filter objects that don't come from a servlet in the first place, such as HTML files served by the web server.

Example below demonstrates a basic servlet, derived from HttpServlet, that examines incoming text for a <DATE> tag and replaces the tag with the current date. This servlet is never called on its own, but instead after another servlet (such as an HTML generator) has produced the actual content.

The DateFilter servlet works by reading each line of input, scanning for the text <DATE>, and replacing it with the current date. This example introduces the getReader() method of HttpServletRequest, which returns a PrintReader that points to the original request body. When you call getReader() in an HttpServlet, you can read the original HTTP form variables, if any. When this method is used within a filtering servlet, it provides access to the output of the previous servlet in the chain.

Example: *Date Filtering Servlet*

```
import javax.servlet.*;
import javax.servlet.http.*;
import java.io.*;
import java.util.*;
public class DateFilter extends HttpServlet {
public void doGet(HttpServletRequest req, HttpServletResponse resp)
throws ServletException, IOException {
PrintWriter out = resp.getWriter();
String contentType = req.getContentType();
if (contentType == null)
return; // No incoming data
// Note that if we were using MIME filtering we would have to set this to
// something different to avoid an infinite loop
```

```
resp.setContentType(contentType);
BufferedReader br = new BufferedReader(req.getReader());
String line = null;
Date d = new Date();
while ((line = br.readLine()) != null) {
int index;
while ((index=line.indexOf("<DATE>")) >= 0)
line = line.substring(0, index) + d + line.substring(index + 6);
out.println(line);
}
br.close();
}
}
```

16.16.1 Filters

Version 2.3 of the Servlet API introduced a new method of handling requests, via the javax.servlet. Filter class. When filters are used, the servlet container creates a *filter chain*. This consists of zero or more Filter objects and a destination resource, which can be either a servlet or another resources available on the web server (such as an HTML or JSP file). Filters are installed in the server and associated with particular request paths (just like servlets). When a filtered resource is requested, the servlet constructs a filter chain and calls the doFilter() method of the first filter in the filter chain, passing a ServletRequest, a ServletResponse, and the FilterChain object. The filter can then perform processing on the request. The processing is sometimes noninterventionary (such as logging characteristics of the request or tracking a clickstream). However, the filter can also wrap the ServletRequest and ServletResponse classes with its own versions, overriding particular methods. For instance, one of the example filters included with the Tomcat server adds support for returning compressed output to browsers that support it.

After the filter has processed the response, it can call the doFilter() method of the FilterChain to invoke the next filter in the sequence. If there are no more filters, the request will be passed on to its ultimate destination. After calling doFilter(), the filter can perform additional processing on the response received from farther down the chain.

In the event of an error, the filter can stop processing, returning to the client whatever response has already been created, or forwarding the request on to a different resource. Example below duplicates the form-based authentication feature that already exists in the servlet API, but could be customized to provide additional functionality not available directly from the server (for instance, authenticating users against systems other than those supported by the servlet container). It works by intercepting each request and checking the HttpSession for an attribute called "enterprise.login." If that attribute contains a Boolean.TRUE, access is permitted. If not, the filter checks for request parameters named "login_name" and "login_pass," and searches for a match in a hashtable containing valid username/password pairs. If valid login credentials are found, processing the filter chain is allowed to continue. If not, the user is served a login page located at */login.jsp*, retrieved via a RequestDispatcher. Astute readers will note that we try to retrieve the users' hashtable from a servlet context attribute. We showed how to set this attribute at server startup in the section "Custom Servlet Initialization." In case you don't have that set up, the Filter's init() method will create its own if it can't find one in the context.

Example: *AuthenticationFilter*

```
import javax.servlet.*;
import javax.servlet.http.*;
import java.util.Hashtable;
public class AuthenticationFilter implements Filter {
private Hashtable users = null;
public void init(FilterConfig config)
throws javax.servlet.ServletException {
users = (Hashtable)config.getServletContext().getAttribute(
"enterprise.users");
if(users == null) {
users = new Hashtable(5);
users.put("test", "test");
}
}
public void doFilter(
ServletRequest req, ServletResponse res, FilterChain chain)
throws java.io.IOException, javax.servlet.ServletException {
HttpServletRequest request = (HttpServletRequest)req;
HttpSession sess = request.getSession(true);
if(sess != null) {
Boolean loggedIn = (Boolean)sess.getAttribute("enterprise.login");
if (loggedIn != Boolean.TRUE) {
String login_name = request.getParameter("login_name");
String login_pass = request.getParameter("login_pass");
if((login_name != null) && (login_pass != null))
if(users.get(login_name).toString().equals(login_pass)) {
loggedIn = Boolean.TRUE;
sess.setAttribute("enterprise.login", Boolean.TRUE);
sess.setAttribute("enterprise.loginname", login_name);
}
}
if (loggedIn == Boolean.TRUE) {
chain.doFilter(req, res);
} else {
request.setAttribute("originaluri", request.getRequestURI());
request.getRequestDispatcher("/login.jsp").forward(req, res);
}
```

```
}
}
public void destroy() {
// Code cleanup would be here
}
}
```

Here's the JSP page used to display the login form. The important thing to note is that the form submits back to the original URI. The filter uses the setAttribute() method of HttpServletRequest to specify the URI to post the form back to; the filter is then reapplied, and if the user has provided appropriate credentials access to the resource is granted.

```
<html><body bgcolor="white">
<% out.print ("<FORM METHOD=POST ACTION=\""+request.
getAttribute("originaluri").toString() +"\">"); %>
Login Name: <INPUT TYPE=TEXT NAME="login_name"><br>
Password: <INPUT TYPE=PASSWORD NAME="login_pass">
<INPUT TYPE=SUBMIT VALUE="Log In">
</FORM>
</body></html>
```

When configuring the filter, map it to the paths you wish to protect. Mapping it to /* will not work, as that would also protect the */login.jsp* file (which will be run through its own filter chain by the RequestDispatcher object). If you did want to protect your whole application, you could build the login form internally to the filter; but this is generally considered bad practice.

16.16.2 Thread Safety

In a typical scenario, only one copy of any particular servlet or filter is loaded at any given time. Each servlet might, however, be called upon to deal with multiple requests at the same time. This means that a servlet needs to be thread-safe. If a servlet doesn't use any class variables (that is, any variables with a scope broader than the service method itself), it is generally already thread-safe. If you are using any third-party libraries or extensions, make sure that those components are also thread-safe. However, a servlet that maintains persistent resources needs to make sure that nothing untoward happens to those resources. Imagine, for example, a servlet that maintains a bank balance using an int in memory.* If two servlets try to access the balance at the same time, you might get this sequence of events:

1. User 1 connects to the servlet to make a $100 withdrawal.
2. The servlet checks the balance for User 1, finding $120.
3. User 2 connects to the servlet to make a $50 withdrawal.
4. The servlet checks the balance for User 2, finding $120.
5. The servlet debits $100 for User 1, leaving $20.
6. The servlet debits $50 for User 2, leaving –$30.
7. The programmer is fired.

Obviously, this is incorrect behavior, particularly that last bit. We want the servlet to perform the necessary action for User 1, and then deal with User 2 (in this case, by giving him an insufficient funds message). We can do this by surrounding sections of code with synchronized blocks. While a particular synchronized block is executing, no other sections of code that are synchronized on the same object (usually the servlet or the resource being protected) can execute. For more information on thread safety and synchronization, Example below implements the ATM display for the First Bank of Java. The doGet() method displays the current account balance and provides a small ATM control panel for making deposits and withdrawals, The control panel uses a POST request to send the transaction back to the servlet, which performs the appropriate action and calls doGet() to redisplay the ATM screen with the updated balance.

Example: *An ATM Servlet*

```
import javax.servlet.*;
import javax.servlet.http.*;
import java.util.*;
import java.io.*;
public class AtmServlet extends HttpServlet {
Account act;
public void init(ServletConfig conf) throws ServletException {
super.init(conf);
act = new Account();
act.balance = 0;
}
public void doGet(HttpServletRequest req, HttpServletResponse resp)
throws ServletException, IOException {
resp.setContentType("text/html");
PrintWriter out = resp.getWriter();
out.println("<HTML><BODY>");
out.println("<H2>First Bank of Java ATM</H2>");
out.println("Current Balance: <B>" + act.balance + "</B><BR>");
out.println("<FORM METHOD=POST ACTION=/servlet/AtmServlet>");
out.println("Amount: <INPUT TYPE=TEXT NAME=AMOUNT SIZE=3><BR>");
out.println("<INPUT TYPE=SUBMIT NAME=DEPOSIT VALUE=\"Deposit\">");
out.println("<INPUT TYPE=SUBMIT NAME=WITHDRAW VALUE=\"Withdraw\">");
out.println("</FORM>");
out.println("</BODY></HTML>");
}
public void doPost(HttpServletRequest req, HttpServletResponse resp)
throws ServletException, IOException {
int amt=0;
try {
amt = Integer.parseInt(req.getParameter("AMOUNT"));
}
catch (NullPointerException e) {
```

```
// No Amount Parameter passed
}
catch (NumberFormatException e) {
// Amount Parameter was not a number
}
synchronized(act) {
if(req.getParameter("WITHDRAW") != null) && (amt < act.balance)
act.balance = act.balance - amt;
if(req.getParameter("DEPOSIT") != null) && (amt > 0)
act.balance = act.balance + amt;
} // end synchronized block
doGet(req, resp); // Show ATM screen
}
public void destroy() {
// This is where we would save the balance to a file
}
class Account {
public int balance;
}
}
```

The doPost() method alters the account balance contained within an Account object act (since Account is so simple, we've defined it as an inner class). In order to prevent multiple requests from accessing the same account at once, any code that alters act is synchronized on act. This ensures that no other code can alter act while a synchronized section is running. The destroy() method is defined in the AtmServlet, but it contains no actual code.

16.16.3 Cookies

Cookies spent a year or two as a little-known feature of Netscape Navigator before becoming the focus of a raging debate on electronic privacy. Ethical and moral considerations aside, cookies allow a web server to store small amounts of data on client systems. Cookies are generally used to store basic user identification or configuration information. Because a cookie's value can uniquely identify a client, cookies are often used for session tracking.

To create a cookie, the server (or, more precisely, a web application running on the server) includes a Cookie header with a specific value in an HTTP response. The browser then transmits a similar header with that value back to the server with subsequent requests, which are subject to certain rules. The web application can use the cookie value to keep track of a particular user, handle session tracking, etc. Because cookies use a single Cookie header, the syntax for a cookie allows for multiple name/value pairs in the overall cookie value.

The Servlet API includes a class, javax.servlet.http.Cookie, that abstracts cookie syntax and makes it easy to work with cookies. In addition, HttpServletResponse provides an addCookie() method and HttpServletRequest provides a getCookies() method to aid in writing cookies to and reading cookies from the HTTP headers, respectively. To find a particular cookie, a servlet needs to read the entire collection of values and look through it:

```
Cookie[] cookies;
cookies = req.getCookies();
String userid = null;
for (int i = 0; i < cookies.length; i++)
if (cookies[i].getName().equals("userid"))
userid = cookies[i].getValue();
```

A cookie can be read at any time, but can be created only before any content is sent to the client. This is because cookies are sent using HTTP headers. These headers can be sent to the client before the regular content. Once any data has been written to the client, the server can flush the output and send the headers at any time, so you can't create any new cookies safely. You must create new cookies before sending any output. Here's an example of creating a cookie:

```
String userid = createUserID(); // Create a unique ID
Cookie c = new Cookie("userid", userid);
resp.addCookie(c); // Add the cookie to the HTTP headers
```

Note that a web browser is only required to accept 20 cookies per site and 300 total per user, and the browser can limit each cookie's size to 4096 bytes. Cookies can be customized to return information only in specific circumstances. In particular, a cookie can specify a particular domain, a particular path, an age after which the cookie should be destroyed, and whether the cookie requires a secure (HTTPS) connection. A cookie is normally returned only to the host that specified it. For example, if a cookie is set by *server1.company.com,* it isn't returned to *server2.company.com*. You can get around this limitation by setting the domain to *.company.com* with the setDomain() method of Cookie. By the same token, a cookie is generally returned for pages only in the same directory as the servlet that created the cookie, or it's returned under that directory. We can get around this limitation using setPath(). Here's a cookie that is returned to all pages on all toplevel servers at *company.com*:

```
String userid = createUserID(); // Create a unique ID
Cookie c = new Cookie("userid", userid);
c.setDomain(".company.com"); // *.company.com, but not *.web.company.com
c.setPath("/"); // All pages
resp.addCookie(c); // Add the cookie to the HTTP headers
```

16.16.4 Session Tracking

Very few web applications are confined to a single page, so having a mechanism for tracking users through a site can often simplify application development. The Web, however, is an inherently stateless environment. A client makes a request, the server fulfills it, and both promptly forget about each other. In the past, applications that needed to deal with a user through multiple pages (for instance, a shopping cart) had to resort to complicated dodges to hold onto state information, such as hidden fields in forms, setting and reading cookies, or rewriting URLs to contain state information.

The Servlet API provides classes and methods specifically designed to handle session tracking. A servlet can use the session-tracking API to delegate most of the user-tracking functions to the server. The first time a user connects to a session enabled servlet, the servlet simply creates a javax.servlet.http.HttpSession object. The servlet can then bind data to this object, so subsequent requests can read the data. After a certain amount of inactive time, the session object is destroyed.

A servlet uses the getSession() method of HttpServletRequest to retrieve the current session object. This method takes a single boolean argument. If you pass true, and there is no current session object, the method creates and returns a new HttpSession object. If you pass false, the method returns null if there is no current session object. For example:

```
HttpSession thisUser = req.getSession(true);
```

When a new HttpSession is created, the server assigns a unique session ID that must somehow be associated with the client. Since clients differ in what they support, the server has a few options that vary slightly depending on the server implementation. In general, the server's first choice is to try to set a cookie on the client (which means that getSession() must be called before you write any other data back to the client). If cookie support is lacking, the API allows servlets to rewrite internal links to include the session ID, using the encodeURL() method of HttpServletResponse. This is optional, but recommended, particularly if your servlets share a system with other, unknown servlets that may rely on uninterrupted session tracking. However, this on-the-fly URL encoding can become a performance bottleneck because the server needs to perform additional parsing on each incoming request to determine the correct session key from the URL. (The performance hit is so significant that the Java Web Server disables URL encoding by default.)

To use URL encoding run all your internal links through encodeURL(). If you have a line of code like this:

```
out.println("<A HREF=\"/servlet/CheckoutServlet\">Check Out</A>");
```

you should replace it with:

```
out.print("<A HREF=\"");
out.print(resp.encodeURL("/servlet/CheckoutServlet");
out.println("\">Check Out</A>");
```

JWS, in this case, adds an identifier beginning with $ to the end of the URL. Other servers have their own methods. Thus, with JWS, the final output looks like this:

```
<A HREF="/servlet/CheckoutServlet$FASEDAW23798ASD978">Check Out</A>"
```

In addition to encoding your internal links, you need to use encodeRedirectURL() to handle redirects properly. This method works in the same manner as encodeURL(). You can access the unique session ID via the getID() method of HttpSession. This is enough for most applications, since a servlet can use some other storage mechanism (*i.e.*, a flat file, memory, or a database) to store the unique information (e.g., hit count or shopping cart contents) associated with each session.

However, the API makes it even easier to hold onto session-specific information by allowing servlets to bind objects to a session using the putValue() method of HttpSession. Once an object is bound to a session, you can use the getValue() method.†

Objects bound using putValue() are available to all servlets running on the server. The system works by assigning a user-defined name to each object (the String argument); this name is used to identify objects at retrieval time. In order to avoid conflicts, the general practice is to name bound objects with names of the form *applicationname.objectname*. For example:

```
session.putValue("myservlet.hitcount", new Integer(34));
```

Now that object can be retrieved with:

```
Integer hits = (Integer)session.getValue("myservlet.hitcount")
```

Example below demonstrates a basic session-tracking application that keeps track of the number of visits to the site by a particular user. It works by storing a counter value in an HttpSession object and incrementing it as necessary. When a new session is created (as indicated by isNew(), which returns true if the session ID has not yet passed through the client and back to the server), or the counter object is not found, a new counter object is created.

Example: *Counting Visits with Sessions*

```
import javax.servlet.*;
import javax.servlet.http.*;
import java.io.*;
public class VisitCounterServlet extends HttpServlet {
public void doGet(HttpServletRequest req, HttpServletResponse resp)
throws ServletException, IOException {
PrintWriter out = resp.getWriter();
resp.setContentType("text/html");
HttpSession thisUser = req.getSession(true);
Integer visits;
if(!thisUser.isNew()) { //Don't check newly created sessions
visits = (Integer)thisUser.getValue("visitcounter.visits");
if(visits == null)
visits = new Integer(1);
else
visits = new Integer(visits.intValue() + 1);
}
else
visits = new Integer(1);
// Put the new count in the session
thisUser.putValue("visitcounter.visits", visits);
// Finally, display the results and give them the session ID too
out.println("<HTML><HEAD><TITLE>Visit Counter</TITLE></HEAD>");
out.println("<BODY>You have visited this page " + visits + " time[s]");
out.println("since your last session expired.");
out.println("Your Session ID is " + thisUser.getId());
out.println("</BODY></HTML>");
}
}
```

16.16.5 HttpSessionBindingListener

Sometimes it is useful to know when an object is getting bound or unbound from a session object. For instance, in an application that binds a JDBC java.sql. Connection object to a session (something that, by the way, is ill-advised in all but very low traffic sites), it is important that the Connection be explicitly closed when the session is destroyed.

The javax.servlet.http.HttpSessionBindingListener interface handles this task. It includes two methods, valueBound() and valueUnbound(), that are called whenever the object that implements the interface is bound or unbound from a session, respectively. Each of these methods receives an HttpSessionBindingEvent object that provides the name of the object being bound or unbound and the session involved in the action. Here is an object that implements the HttpSessionBindingListener interface in order to make sure that a database connection is closed properly:

```
class ConnectionHolder implements HttpSessionBindingListener {
java.sql.Connection dbCon;
public ConnectionHolder(java.sql.Connection con) {
dbCon = con;
}
public void valueBound(HttpSessionBindingEvent event) {
// Do nothing
}
public void valueUnbound(HttpSessionBindingEvent event) {
dbCon.close();
}
}
```

16.16.6 Session Contexts

Version 2.0 of the Servlet API included the getContext() method of HttpSession, coupled with an interface named HttpSessionContext. Together, these allowed servlets to access other sessions running in the same context. Unfortunately, this functionality also allowed a servlet to accidentally expose all the session IDs in use on the server, meaning that an outsider with knowledge could spoof a session. To eliminate this minor security risk, the session-context functionality was deprecated in Version 2.1 of the Servlet API. Instead, web applications can use the getAttribute() and setAttribute() methods of ServletContext to share information across sessions.

16.17 DATABASES AND NON-HTML CONTENT

Most web applications need to communicate with a database, either to generate dynamic content or collect and store data from users, or both. With servlets, this communication is easily handled using the JDBC API .

Thanks to JDBC and the generally sensible design of the servlet lifecycle, servlets are an excellent intermediary between a database and web clients.Servlet developers should keep a few things in mind for optimal performance.

First, JDBC Connection objects can be created in the servlet's init() method. This allows the servlet to avoid reconnecting to the database (a la CGI) with each request, saving up to a second or more on every single page request. If you anticipate high volume, you may want to create several connections and rotate between them. An excellent freeware connection-pooling system is available at *http://www.javaexchange.com*. Or, if you're using JDBC 2.0, the javax.sql package provides a connection-pooling mechanism. Finally, if you plan on using JDBC's transaction support, you need to create individual connections for each request or obtain exclusive use of a pooled connection. So far, all our servlets have produced standard HTML content. Of course, this is all most servlets ever do, but it's not all that they can do. Say, for instance, that your company stores a large database of PDF documents within an Oracle database, where they can be easily accessed. Now say you want to distribute these documents on the Web. Luckily, servlets can dish out any form of content that can be defined with a MIME header. All you have to do is set the appropriate content type and use a ServletOuputStream if you need to transmit binary data. Example below shows how to pull an Adobe Acrobat document from an Oracle database.

Example: *A Servlet That Serves PDF Files from a Database*

```
import java.io.*;
import java.sql.*;
import javax.servlet.*;
import javax.servlet.http.*;
public class DBPDFReader extends HttpServlet {
Connection con;
public void init(ServletConfig config) throws ServletException {
super.init(config);
try {
Class.forName("oracle.jdbc.driver.OracleDriver");
con = DriverManager.getConnection("jdbc:oracle:oci8:@DBHOST",
"user", "passwd");
}
catch (ClassNotFoundException e) {
throw new UnavailableException(this, "Couldn't load OracleDriver");
}
catch (SQLException e) {
throw new UnavailableException(this, "Couldn't get db connection");
}
}
public void doGet(HttpServletRequest req, HttpServletResponse res)
throws ServletException, IOException {
try {
res.setContentType("application/pdf");
ServletOutputStream out = res.getOutputStream();
Statement stmt = con.createStatement();
ResultSet rs = stmt.executeQuery(
"SELECT PDF FROM PDF WHERE PDFID = " + req.getParameter("PDFID"));
if (rs.next()) {
BufferedInputStream pdfData =
```

```
new BufferedInputStream(rs.getBinaryStream("PDF"));
byte[] buf = new byte[4 * 1024]; // 4K buffer
int len;
while ((len = pdfData.read(buf, 0, buf.length)) != -1) {
out.write(buf, 0, len);
}
}
else {
res.sendError(res.SC.NOT_FOUND);
}
rs.close();
stmt.close ();
}
catch(SQLException e) {
// Report it
}
}
}
```

QUESTIONS WITH ANSWERS

1. *What is Servlet?*

Solution: A servlet is a Java technology-based Web component, managed by a container called servlet container or servlet engine, that generates dynamic content and interacts with web clients via a request\/response paradigm.

2. *Why is Servlet so popular?*

Solution: Because servlets are platform-independent Java classes that are compiled to platform-neutral byte code that can be loaded dynamically into and run by a Java technologyenabled Web server.

3. *What is servlet container?*

Solution: The servlet container is a part of a Web server or application server that provides the network services over which requests and responses are sent, decodes MIME-based requests, and formats MIME-based responses. A servlet container also contains and manages servlets through their lifecycle.

4. *When a client request is sent to the servlet container, how does the container choose which servlet to invoke?*

Solution: The servlet container determines which servlet to invoke based on the configuration of its servlets, and calls it with objects representing the request and response.

5. *If a servlet is not properly initialized, what exception may be thrown?*

Solution: During initialization or service of a request, the servlet instance can throw an UnavailableException or a ServletException.

6. *Given the request path below, which are context path, servlet path and path info?*

Solution: /bookstore/education/index.html

context path: /bookstore

servlet path: /education

path info: /index.html

7. *What is filter? Can filter be used as request or response?*

Solution: A filter is a reusable piece of code that can transform the content of HTTP requests,responses, and header information. Filters do not generally create a response or respond to a request as servlets do, rather they modify or adapt the requests for a resource, and modify or adapt responses from a resource.

8. *When using servlets to build the HTML, you build a DOCTYPE line, why do you do that?*

Solution: I know all major browsers ignore it even though the HTML 3.2 and 4.0 specifications require it. But building a DOCTYPE line tells HTML validators which version of HTML you are using so they know which specification to check your document against. These validators are valuable debugging services, helping you catch HTML syntax errors.

9. *What is new in ServletRequest interface ? (Servlet 2.4)*

Solution: The following methods have been added to ServletRequest 2.4 version:

public int getRemotePort()

public java.lang.String getLocalName()

public java.lang.String getLocalAddr()

public int getLocalPort()

10. *Request parameter How to find whether a parameter exists in the request object?*

Solution:

(*i*) boolean hasFoo = !(request.getParameter("foo") == null || request.getParameter("foo") .equals(""));

(*ii*) boolean hasParameter = request.getParameterMap().contains(theParameter); (which works in Servlet 2.3+)

11. *How can I send user authentication information while making URL Connection?*

Solution: You'll want to use HttpURLConnection.setRequestProperty and set all the appropriate headers to HTTP authorization.

12. *Can we use the constructor, instead of init(), to initialize servlet?*

Solution: Yes , of course you can use the constructor instead of init(). There's nothing to stop you. But you shouldn't. The original reason for init() was that ancient versions of Java couldn't dynamically invoke constructors with arguments, so there was no way to give the constructur a ServletConfig. That no longer applies, but servlet containers still will only call your no-arg constructor. So you won't have access to a ServletConfig or ServletContext.

13. *How can a servlet refresh automatically if some new data has entered the database?*

Solution: You can use a client-side Refresh or Server Push.

14. *The code in a finally clause will never fail to execute, right?*

Solution: Using System.exit(1); in try block will not allow finally code to execute.

15. *What mechanisms are used by a Servlet Container to maintain session information?*

Solution: Cookies, URL rewriting, and HTTPS protocol information are used to maintain session information

16. *Difference between GET and POST.*

Solution: In GET your entire form submission can be encapsulated in one URL, like a hyperlink. query length is limited to 260 characters, not secure, faster, quick and easy.

In POST Your name/value pairs inside the body of the HTTP request, which makes for a cleaner URL and imposes no size limitations on the form's output. It is used to send a chunk of data to the server to be processed, more versatile, most secure.

17. *What is session?*

Solution: The session is an object used by a servlet to track a user's interaction with a Web application across multiple HTTP requests.

18. *What is servlet mapping?*

Solution: The servlet mapping defines an association between a URL pattern and a servlet. The mapping is used to map requests to servlets.

19. *What is servlet context ?*

Solution: The servlet context is an object that contains a servlet's view of the Web application within which the servlet is running. Using the context, a servlet can log events, obtain URL references to resources, and set and store attributes that other servlets in the context can use. (Answer supplied by Sun's tutorial).

20. *Which interface must be implemented by all servlets?*

Solution: Servlet interface.

21. *Explain the life cycle of Servlet.*

Solution: Loaded(by the container for first request or on start up if config file suggests load-on-startup), initialized(using init()), service(service() or doGet() or doPost()..), destroy(destroy()) and unloaded.

EXERCISE

1. Explain the need for Servlets?
2. What do you mean by Servlets?
3. What are various characteristics of Servlets?
4. Differentiate between Applets and Servlets.
5. Explain the lifecycle of Servlets.
6. What do you mean by JSDK?
7. Explain the servlet API and Servlet Packages.
8. How will you Deploy Servlet?
9. Explain the HTTP package.

17

JAVA SERVER PAGES

17.0 INTRODUCTION

Java Server pages are a way of providing server side executable content in a web page. In other words, a way of providing a Web page, which is varied depending on conditions on the server, information, filled in to a form, etc. The original way of providing server side executable content was through the Common Gateway Interface (CGI) and a variety of programming languages such as C, C++ and (most prevalent) Perl. Indeed, Perl and CGI are still growing though not to the same extent as some other technologies. More recently, Java servlets have been introduced and they allow you to use a similar approach to writing server side executable content — a program which produces an HTML page as its output. Java servlets are more efficient in operation than CGI programs, and for heavily used servers they provide an excellent solution.

Many web servers can support "Server Side Includes" — where a page is parsed by the web server on its way from the document directory to the browser, and substitutions of certain variable are made. Using SSI, operating system commands can even be run and their outputs written in to the page sent to the browser — such a web page looks different if you examine the source on the server's discs and if you ask your browser to "view source".

Active Server Pages (ASP) from Microsoft takes a similar approach to SSI. You write Web pages which include chunks of one or more of VBScript, PerlScript and JavaScript, and the page is parsed and the script run as the server feeds the page through to the browser. The facilities provided are much more extensive that SSI, but with the "interpret every time" approach efficient of operation is not a strong point of this scheme — even the Microsoft documentation warns you of the fact! The SSI/ASP approach is a good one, but there's a requirement for something that works along the same lines as part as the provider is concerned: "A page of HTML that changes is not a program" but doesn't have the same run time resource inefficiencies. Of course, to make it portable a language like Java would be nice, especially if your programmers already know Java. The OO abilities and large class libraries will minimize what's needed in each individual web page ... and so came about Java Server pages, or JSP. JSP is much more recent than ASP (SSI has been around for a very long time); much of the documentation, etc, being dated early 2000 and as I write this material, anyone who's already using it is an "early adoptor" whereas ASP, servlets, etc., are already well established. Time will tell us if the design promise of JSP gets translated into a heavily used product.

The JSP specification was written by Sun, and they provide a test reference server. However, you'll probably find that Apache "Tomcat" will become the big kid on the block as a JSP Server; it's open source, freely available, and we see no reason why it shouldn't be just as robust as the rest of Apache's Web server!

17.1 A SIMPLE WORKED EXAMPLE

Let's do a very simple worked example. Write a JSP page locally on our workstation, upload it to a server and view it there:

1. Create a file with HTML and extra JSP tags on your local machine. Call it *[yourname].jsp*

```
<html>
<head><title>Example for first JSP Practical</title></head>
<body><h1>JSP is like a Jumbo Jet Driver</h1>
Because the smallest of operators can do a mighty lot<hr>
The total age of the kids is
<%
int fred = 14;
int doris = 13;
int totalage = fred + doris;
out.print(totalage);
%><br>
Copyright ....
</body>
</html>
```

2. ftp 192.168.200.190 log in as trainee, password of abc123
3. cd /usr/local/tomcat/webapps (to root of the web tree)
4. cd octj (and check via an ls)
5. put [yourname.jsp]
6. quit
7. View *http://192.168.200.190:8080/octj/gje2.jsp*

17.2 THE STRUCTURE OF A JSP PAGE

A JSP page, then, looks like an extended HTML page. Java server pages files have a dot jsp extension.

Within your HTML, JSP directives are written within a tag

```
<%@ ...... %>
```

Examples of directives:

```
<%@ include file="morestuff.html" %>
```

JSP directives, and most of the parameters associated with them are case sensitive. In any case, with XML standards becoming more relevant, we'll encourage you to use lower case tags in your HTML these days, and to match all your open tags with a matching close tag.

17.3 ENTERING DATA INTO A FORM

One of the most common parts of an electronic commerce application is an HTML form in which a user enters some information. The information might be a customer's name and address, a word or phrase entered for a search engine, or a set of preferences gathered as market research data.

The information the user enters in the form is stored in the request object, which is sent from the client to the JSP engine.

The JSP engine sends the request object to whatever server-side component (Java— Beans component, servlet, or enterprise bean) the JSP file specifies. The component handles the request, possibly retrieving data from a database or other data store, and passes a response object back to the JSP engine. The JSP engine passes the response object to the JSP page, where its data is formatted according the page's HTML design. The JSP engine and Web server then send the revised JSP page back to the client, where the user can view the results in the Web browser. The communications protocol used between the client and server can be HTTP, or it can be some other protocol.

Example - form, data validation, initial page and response in single script

```
<%
String elder = request.getParameter("age1");
String younger = request.getParameter("age2");
boolean first = false;
int totalage = 0;
String message = "";
if (elder == null) {
first = true;
message = "Your results will appear here";
} else {
try {
int fred = Integer.parseInt(elder);
int doris = Integer.parseInt(younger);
totalage = fred + doris;
} catch (Exception e) {
message = "You must enter two Integers";
first = true;
}
}
//------------------------------
%>
```

```
<html>
<head><title>Example for first JSP Practical</title></head>
<body><h1>JSP is like a Jumbo Jet Driver</h1>
Because the smallest of operators can do a mighty lot<hr>
<% if (! first) { %>
Inputs were <%= elder %> and <%= younger %><br>
The total age of the kids is <%= totalage %>
<% } else { %>
<%= message %>
<% } %>
<hr>
<form>Please enter age 1 <input name=age1> and
age 2 <input name=age2> and <input type=submit></form>
Copyright ....
</body>
</html>
```

How to Create a Form

You typically define an HTML form in a JSP source file using JSP tags to pass data between the form and some type of server-side object (usually a Bean). In general, you do the following things in your JSP application:

1. Start writing a JSP source file, creating an HTML form and giving each form element a name.
2. Write the Bean in a *java* file, defining properties, get, and set methods that correspond to the form element names (unless you want to set one property value at a time explicitly).
3. Return to the JSP source file. Add a **<jsp:useBean>** tag to create or locate an instance of the Bean.
4. Add a **<jsp:setProperty>** tag to set properties in the Bean from the HTML form (the Bean needs a matching set method).
5. Add a **<jsp:getProperty>** tag to retrieve the data from the Bean (the Bean needs a matching get method).
6. If you need to do even more processing on the user data, use the **request** object from within a scriptlet.

The *Hello, User* example will make these steps more clear.

A Simple Hello Application

The JSP application is very simple. It continues the illustrious computer science tradition known as *Hello, World,* but with a twist.

Example code:

The Duke Banner (*dukebanner.html*)

```
<table border="0" width="400" cellspacing="0"
```

```
cellpadding="0">
<tr>
<td height="150" width="150">   </td>
<td width="250">   </td>
</tr>
<tr>
<td width="150">   </td>
<td align="right" width="250">
<img src="duke.waving.gif"> </td>
</tr>
</table>
<br>
```

The Main JSP File (*hellouser.jsp*)

```
<%@ page import="hello.NameHandler" %>
<jsp:useBean id="mybean" scope="page"
class="hello.NameHandler" />
<jsp:setProperty name="mybean" property="*" />
<html>
<head><title>Hello, User</title></head>
<body bgcolor="#ffffff" background="background.gif">
<%@ include file="dukebanner.html" %>
<table border="0" width="700">
<tr>
<td width="150">   </td>
<td width="550">
<h1>My name is Duke. What's yours?</h1>
</td>
</tr>
<tr>
<td width="150"   </td>
<td width="550">
<form method="get">
<input type="text" name="username" size="25">
<br>
<input type="submit" value="Submit">
<input type="reset" value="Reset">
</td>
</tr>
</form>
</table>
```

```
<%
if ( request.getParameter("username") != null ) {
%>
<%@ include file="response.jsp" %>
<%
}
%>
</body>
</html>
```

The Response File (*response.jsp*)

```
<table border="0" width="700">
<tr>
<td width="150">   </td>
<td width="550">
<h1>Hello, <jsp:getProperty name="mybean"
property="username" />!
</h1>
</td>
</tr>
</table>
```

The Bean That Handles the Form Data (*namehandler.java*)

```
package hello;
public class NameHandler {
private String username;
public NameHandler() {
username = null;
}
public void setUsername( String name ) {
username = name;
}
public String getUsername() {
return username;
}
}
```

Constructing the HTML Form

An HTML form has three main parts: the opening and closing **<form>** tags, the input elements, and the Submit button that sends the data to the server. In an ordinary HTML page, the opening **<form>** tag usually looks something like this:

```
<form method=get action=someURL>
```

In other Web applications, the action attribute specifies a CGI script or other program that will process the form data. In a JSP file, you can omit the action attribute if you want the data sent to the Bean specified in the <jsp:useBean> tag or specify another JSP file. The rest of the form is constructed just like a standard HTML form, with input elements, a Submit button, and perhaps a Reset button. Be sure to give each input element a name, like this:

<input type="text" name="username">

Using the GET and POST Methods

The HTTP **GET** and **POST** methods send data to the server. In a JSP application, **GET** and **POST** send data to the Bean, servlet, or other server-side component that is handling the form data.

In theory, **GET** is for getting data from the server and **POST** is for sending data there. However, **GET** appends the form data (called a query string) to an URL, in the form of key/value pairs from the HTML form, for example, **name=John**. In the query string, key/value pairs are separated by **&** characters, spaces are converted to **+** characters, and special characters are converted to their hexadecimal equivalents. Because the query string is in the URL, the page can be book marked or sent as email with its query string. The query string is usually limited to a relatively small number of characters.

The **POST** method, however, passes data of unlimited length as an HTTP request body to the server. The user working in the client Web browser cannot see the data that is being sent, so POST requests are ideal for sending confidential data (such as a credit card number) or large amounts of data to the server.

Writing the Bean

If your JSP application uses a Bean, you can write the Bean according to the design patterns outlined in the JavaBeans API Specification, remembering these general points:

- If you use a **<jsp:getProperty>** tag in your JSP source file, you need a corresponding get method in the Bean.
- If you use a **<jsp:setProperty>** tag in your JSP source file, you need one or more corresponding set methods in the Bean.

Setting properties in and getting properties from a Bean is explained a bit more in the next section.

Getting Data From the Form to the Bean

Setting properties in a Bean from an HTML form is two-parts:

- Creating or locating the Bean instance with **<jsp:useBean>**
- Setting property values in the Bean with **<jsp:setProperty>**

The first step is to instantiate or locate a Bean with a **<jsp:useBean>** tag before you set property values in the Bean. In a JSP source file, the **<jsp:useBean>** tag must appear above the **<jsp:setProperty>** tag. The **<jsp:useBean>** tag first looks for a Bean instance with the name you specify, but if it doesn't find the Bean, it instantiates one. This allows you to create a Bean in one JSP file and use it in another, as long as the Bean has a large enough scope. The second step is to set property values in the Bean with a **<jsp:setProperty>** tag. The easiest way to use **<jsp:setProperty>** is to define properties in the Bean with names that match the names of the form elements. You would also define corresponding set methods for each property. For example, if the form element is named username, you would define a property username property and methods getUsername and setUsername in the Bean. If you use different names for the form element and the Bean property, you can still set the property value with **<jsp:setProperty>**, but you can only set one value at a time. For more information on the syntax variations of **<jsp:setProperty>**, see the JavaServer Pages Syntax Card.

Checking the Request Object

The data user enters is stored in the request object, which usually implements **javax.servlet. HttpServletRequest** (or if your implementation uses a different protocol, another interface that is subclassed from **javax.servlet.ServletRequest**).

You can access the request object directly within a scriptlet, or a fragment of code written in a scripting language and placed within <% and %> characters. In JSP 1.0, you must use the Java programming language as your scripting language.

Getting data from the Bean to the JSP Page

Once the user's data has been sent to the Bean, you may want to retrieve the data and display it in the JSP page. To do this, use the **<jsp:getProperty>** tag, giving it the Bean name and property name:

<h1>Hello, <jsp:getProperty name="mybean" property="username"/>!

The Bean names you use on the **<jsp:useBean>**, **<jsp:setProperty>**, and **<jsp:getProperty>** tags must match, for example:

hellouser.jsp:
<jsp:useBean id="mybean" scope="session" class="hello.NameHandler" / >
<jsp:setProperty name="mybean" property="*" />
response.jsp:
<h1>Hello, <jsp:getProperty name="mybean" property="username"/>!

In this example, the tags are in two files, but the Bean names still must match. If they don't, the Sun JSP reference implementation throws an error, possibly a fatal one. The response the JSP engine returns to the client is encapsulated in the implicit response object, which the JSP engine creates.

How to Run the Example

The instructions given here use a UNIX-style pathname. If you are working on Windows, use the same pathname with the proper separator.

1. Create the directory (or folder) *../jswdk-1.0/examples/jsp/tutorial/hellouser* Place the following files in the *../tutorial/hellouser* directory:
2. *background.gif, duke.waving.gif, dukebanner.html, hellouser.jsp,* and *response.jsp* Create the directory (or folder)
3. *../jswdk-1.0/examples/WEB-INF/jsp/beans/hello* Note that this directory is named *hello*, not *hellouser*.
4. Place the files *NameHandler.java* and *NameHandler.class* in the *../beans/hello* directory Start the Sun JSP reference implementation
5. *cd ../jswdk-1.0* **startserver**
6. Open a Web browser and go to *http://yourMachineName:8080/examples/jsp/tutorial/hellouser/hellouser.jsp.*

17.4 USING SCRIPTING ELEMENTS

At some point, you will probably want to add some good, old-fashioned programming to your JSP files. The JSP tags are powerful and encapsulate tasks that would be difficult or time-consuming to program. But even so, you will probably still want to use scripting language fragments to supplement the JSP tags.

The scripting languages that are available to you depend on the JSP engine you are using. With Sun's JSP reference implementation, you must use the Java programming language for scripting, but other vendors' JSP engines may include support for other scripting languages).

How to Add Scripting

First, you'll need to know a few general rules about adding scripting elements to a JSP source file:

1. Use a page directive to define the scripting language used in the JSP page (unless you are using the Java language, which is a default value).
2. The declaration syntax <%! .. %> declares variables or methods.
3. The expression syntax <%= .. %> defines a scripting language expression and casts the result as a String.
4. The scriptlet syntax <% .. %> can handle declarations, expressions, or any other type of code fragment valid in the page scripting language.
5. When you write a scriptlet, end the scriptlet with %> before you switch to HTML, text, or another JSP tag.

The difference between <%, <%=, and <%!

Declarations, expressions, and scriptlets have similar syntax and usage, but also some important differences. Let's explore the similarities and differences here, with some examples.

Declarations (between <%! and %> tags) contain one or more variable or method declarations that end or are separated by semicolons:

```
<%! int i = 0; %>
<%! int a, b; double c; %>
<%! Circle a = new Circle(2.0); %>
```

You must declare a variable or method in a JSP page before you use it in the page. The scope of a declaration is usually a JSP file, but if the JSP file includes other files with the include directive, the scope expands to cover the included files as well.

Expressions (between <%= and %> tags) can contain any language expression that is valid in the page scripting language, but without a semicolon:

```
<%= Math.sqrt(2) %>
<%= items[i] %>
<%= a + b + c %>
<%= new java.util.Date() %>
```

The definition of a valid expression is up to the scripting language. When you use the Java language for scripting, what's between the expression tags can be any expression defined in the Java Language Specification. The parts of the expression are evaluated in left-to-right order. One key difference between expressions and scriptlets (which are described next and appear between **<%** and **%>** tags) is that a semicolon is not allowed within expression tags, even if the same expression requires a semicolon when you use it within scriptlet tags.

Scriptlets (between **<%** and **%>** tags) allow you to write any number of valid scripting language statements, like this:

```
<%
String name = null;
if (request.getParameter("name") == null) {
%>
```

Remember that in a scriptlet you must end a language statement with a semicolon if the language requires it.

When you write a scriptlet, you can use any of the JSP implicit objects or classes imported by the page directive, declared in a declaration, or named in a **<jsp:useBean>** tag.

The Number Guess Game

The Number Guess game is fun and makes good use of scriptlets and expressions, as well as using the knowledge of HTML forms you gained in the last example.

About to Guess a Number

Example Code

Displaying the Number Guess Screen (*numguess.jsp*)

```
<!-- -->
<%@ page import = "num.NumberGuessBean" %>
<jsp:useBean id="numguess" class="num. NumberGuessBean" scope="session" />
<jsp:setProperty name="numguess" property="*" />
<html>
<head><title>Number Guess</title></head>
<body bgcolor="white">
<font size=4>
<% if (numguess.getSuccess() ) { %>
Congratulations! You got it.
And after just <%= numguess.getNumGuesses() %>
tries.<p>
<% numguess.reset(); %>
Care to <a href="numguess.jsp">try again</a>?
<% } else if (numguess.getNumGuesses() == 0) { %>
Welcome to the Number Guess game.<p>
I'm thinking of a number between 1 and 100.<p>
<form method=get>
What's your guess? <input type=text name=guess>
<input type=submit value="Submit">
```

```
</form>
<% } else { %>
Good guess, but nope. Try <b><%= numguess.
getHint() %></b>.
You have made <%= numguess.getNumGuesses() %>
guesses.<p>
I'm thinking of a number between 1 and 100.<p>
<form method=get>
What's your guess? <input type=text name=guess>
<input type=submit value="Submit">
</form>
<% } %>
</font>
</body>
</html>
```

Handling the Guess (NumberGuessBean.java)

```
package num;
import java.util.*;
public class NumberGuessBean {
int answer;
boolean success;
String hint;
int numGuesses;
public NumberGuessBean() {
reset();
}
public void setGuess(String guess) {
numGuesses++;
int g;
try {
g = Integer.parseInt(guess);
}
catch (NumberFormatException e) {
g = -1;
}
if (g == answer) {
success = true;
}
else if (g == -1) {
hint = "a number next time";
}
```

```
else if (g < answer) {
hint = "higher";
}
else if (g > answer) {
hint = "lower";
}
}
public boolean getSuccess() {
return success;
}
public String getHint() {
return "" + hint;
}
public int getNumGuesses() {
return numGuesses;
}
public void reset() {
answer = Math.abs(new Random().nextInt() % 100)
+ 1;
success = false;
numGuesses = 0;
}
}
```

Using Scripting Elements in a JSP File

The file *numguess.jsp* is an interesting example of the use of scripting elements because it is structured as you might structure a source file, with a large **if** ... **else** statement within scriptlet tags. The difference is that the body of each statement clause is written in HTML and JSP tags, rather than in a programming language. You are not required to write scriptlets mingled with HTML and JSP tags, as shown in *numguess.jsp*. Between the <% and %> tags, you can write as many lines of scripting language code as you want. In general, doing less processing in scriptlets and more in components like servlets or Beans makes your application code more reusable and portable. Nonetheless, how you write your JSP application is your choice, and Sun's JSP 1.0 reference implementation specifies no limit on the length of a scriptlet.

Mingling Scripting Elements with Tags

When you mingle scripting elements with HTML and JSP tags, you must always end a scripting element before you start using tags and then reopen the scripting element afterwards, like this:

```
<% } else { %> <!-- closing the scriptlet before the tags start -->
... tags follow ...
<% } %> <!-- reopening the scriptlet to close the language block -->
```

At first, this may look a bit strange, but it ensures that the scripting elements are transformed correctly when the JSP source file is compiled.

How to Run the Example

The instructions given here use a UNIX-style pathname. If you are working on Windows, use the same pathname with the proper separator.

1. The Number Guess example is already installed in the JSP reference implementation.
2. The *.jsp* and *.html* files are in the directory *../jswdk-1.0/examples/jsp/num*
3. The *.java* and *.class* files are in the directory *../jswdk-1.0/examples/WEB-INF/jsp/beans/num*
4. Open a Web browser and go to *http://yourMachineName/examples/jsp/num/numguess.jsp*

17.5 A JSP THAT MAINTAINS STATE

Example showing use of JSP in a rudimentary shopping cart application. The file *products.txt* (in the */data* directory on the server) contains a file of products (one per line); within each line is the product description, unit price, and the size of a unit (e.g. kilos).

The first time a visitor comes to this JSP, the data file is read into a vector, the user is welcomed and presented with a form into which he or she can complete the number of each item wanted. On subsequent visits, the session data is remembered and the JSP gives a total of the number of units ordered. By parsing the data held in the "Store6" class, prices and an invoice could also be produced.

```
###########################################################################
/home/html/shop6.jsp
Remember - within a JSP
<%@ is a directive
<%! is a variable declaration
<%= is an expression to output (so no ; chactacter)
<% is a piece of Java - also known as a scriptlet
###########################################################################
<%@ page session="true"%>
<html>
<head>
<title>Shopping in Java</title>
</head>
<body bgcolor=white>
<%! Store6 Christmas; %>
<% if (session.isNew()) { %>
<h1>Welcome to the Christmas Dinner Store</h1>
<% Christmas = new Store6("/data/products.txt");
} else {
int nitems = Christmas.remember(session,request);
%>
```

```
<h1>So far you have selected ...</h1>
<%= nitems %> items so far
<% } %>
<HR>
<%=
Christmas.offer(session)
%>
</body> </html>
#####################################################################
/home/html/WEB-INF/classes/Store6.java
#####################################################################
import java.io.*;
import java.util.*;
import javax.servlet.*;
import javax.servlet.http.*;
public class Store6 {
Vector instore;
public Store6 (String filename) {
instore = new Vector();
try {
BufferedReader fred = new BufferedReader(
new FileReader(filename));
String inline;
while ((inline = fred.readLine())!= null) {
instore.addElement(inline);
}
} catch (Exception e) {
instore = null;
}
}
public int remember (HttpSession s,HttpServletRequest rq) {
int nprods = 0;
for (int i=0;i<instore.size();i++) {
String n = rq.getParameter(""+i);
if (n != null) {
s.setAttribute(""+i,n);
nprods += Integer.parseInt(n);
}
}
return nprods;
}
```

```
public String offer (HttpSession s) {
StringBuffer makeup = new StringBuffer
("<form>");
for (int i=0;i<instore.size();i++) {
String v = (String)(s).getAttribute(""+i);
if (v == null) v = "0";
makeup.append("<input name="+i+" size=3 value="
+v+"> ");
makeup.append(instore.elementAt(i));
makeup.append("<BR>");
}
makeup.append("<input type=submit></form>");
return makeup.toString();
}
}
```

/data/products.txt

The sample data file ....

Frozen Turkey 9.50 each
Brussel Sprouts 0.80 kilo
Stuffing 2.20 kilo
Potatoes 0.60 kilo
White Bread 0.49 each
Carrots 0.35 kilo
Xmas Pudding 4.99 800 gramms
Brandy 12.99 700 ml
Beer 1.20 550 ml can
Crackers 5.99 box of 6

JSP INTERVIEW QUESTIONS AND ANSWERS

1. *What is a JSP and what is it used for?*

Solution: Java Server Pages (JSP) is a platform independent presentation layer technology that comes with SUN s J2EE platform. JSPs are normal HTML pages with Java code pieces embedded in them. JSP pages are saved to *.jsp files. A JSP compiler is used in the background to generate a Servlet from the JSP page.

2. *What is difference between custom JSP tags and beans?*

Solution: Custom JSP tag is a tag you defined. You define how a tag, its attributes and its body are interpreted, and then group your tags into collections called tag libraries that can be used in any number of JSP files. To use custom JSP tags, you need to define three separate components:

1. the tag handler class that defines the tag\'s behavior
2. the tag library descriptor file that maps the XML element names to the tag implementations
3. the JSP file that uses the tag library

When the first two components are done, you can use the tag by using taglib directive:

<%@ taglib uri="xxx.tld" prefix="..." %>

Then you are ready to use the tags you defined. Let's say the tag prefix is test:

MyJSPTag or

JavaBeans are Java utility classes you defined. Beans have a standard format for Java classes. You use tags to declare a bean and use to set value of the bean class and use to get value of the bean class.

<%=identifier.getclassField() %>

Custom tags and beans accomplish the same goals -- encapsulating complex behavior into simple and accessible forms. There are several differences:

Custom tags can manipulate JSP content; beans cannot.

Complex operations can be reduced to a significantly simpler form with custom tags than with beans. Custom tags require quite a bit more work to set up than do beans.

Custom tags usually define relatively self-contained behavior, whereas beans are often defined in one servlet and used in a different servlet or JSP page.

Custom tags are available only in JSP 1.1 and later, but beans can be used in all JSP 1.x versions.

3. *What are the two kinds of comments in JSP and what's the difference between them ?*

Solution: <%-- JSP Comment --%>

<!-- HTML Comment -->

4. *What is JSP technology?*

Solution: Java Server Page is a standard Java extension that is defined on top of the servlet Extensions. The goal of JSP is the simplified creation and management of dynamic Web pages. JSPs are secure, platform-independent, and best of all, make use of Java as a server-side scripting language.

5. *What is JSP page?*

Solution: A JSP page is a text-based document that contains two types of text: static template data, which can be expressed in any text-based format such as HTML, SVG, WML, and XML, and JSP elements, which construct dynamic content.

6. *What are the implicit objects?*

Solution: Implicit objects are objects that are created by the web container and contain information related to a particular request, page, or application. They are:

-- request

-- response

-- pageContext

-- ion

-- application

-- out

-- config

-- page
-- exception

7. *How many JSP scripting elements and what are they?*

Solution: There are three scripting language elements:

-- declarations
-- scriptlets
-- expressions

8. *Why are JSP pages the preferred API for creating a web-based client program?*

Solution: Because no plug-ins or security policy files are needed on the client systems(applet does). Also, JSP pages enable cleaner and more module application design because they provide a way to separate applications programming from web page design. This means personnel involved in web page design do not need to understand Java programming language syntax to do their jobs.

9. *Is JSP technology extensible?*

Solution: YES. JSP technology is extensible through the development of custom actions, or tags, which are encapsulated in tag libraries.

10. *Can we use the constructor, instead of init(), to initialize servlet?*

Solution: Yes , of course you can use the constructor instead of init(). There's nothing to stop you. But you shouldn't. The original reason for init() was that ancient versions of Java couldn't dynamically invoke constructors with arguments, so there was no way to give the constructur a ServletConfig. That no longer applies, but servlet containers still will only call your no-arg constructor. So you won't have access to a ServletConfig or ServletContext.

11. *How can a servlet refresh automatically if some new data has entered the database?*

Solution: You can use a client-side Refresh or Server Push.

12. *The code in a finally clause will never fail to execute, right?*

Solution: Using System.exit(1); in try block will not allow finally code to execute.

13. *How many messaging models do JMS provide for and what are they?*

Solution: JMS provide for two messaging models, publish-and-subscribe and point-to-point queuing.

14. *What information is needed to create a TCP Socket?*

Solution: The Local Systems IP Address and Port Number. And the Remote System's IPAddress and Port Number.

15. *What Class.forName will do while loading drivers?*

Solution: It is used to create an instance of a driver and register it with the DriverManager. When you have loaded a driver, it is available for making a connection with a DBMS.

16. *How to Retrieve Warnings?*

Solution: SQLWarning objects are a subclass of SQLException that deal with database access warnings. Warnings do not stop the execution of an application, as exceptions do; they simply alert the user that something did not happen as planned. A warning can be reported on a Connection object, a Statement object (including PreparedStatement and CallableStatement objects), or a ResultSet object. Each of these classes has a getWarnings method, which you must invoke in order to see the first warning reported on the calling object.

```
SQLWarning warning = stmt.getWarnings();
if (warning != null)
{
while (warning != null)
{
System.out.println(\"Message: \" + warning.getMessage());
System.out.println(\"SQLState: \" + warning.getSQLState());
System.out.print(\"Vendor error code: \");
System.out.println(warning.getErrorCode());
warning = warning.getNextWarning();
}
}
```

17. *How many JSP scripting elements are there and what are they?*

Solution: There are three scripting language elements: declarations, scriptlets, expressions.

18. *In the Servlet 2.4 specification SingleThreadModel has been deprecated, why?*

Solution: Because it is not practical to have such model. Whether you set isThreadSafe to true or false, you should take care of concurrent client requests to the JSP page by synchronizing access to any shared objects defined at the page level.

19. *What are stored procedures? How is it useful?*

Solution: A stored procedure is a set of statements/commands which reside in the database. The stored procedure is pre-compiled and saves the database the effort of parsing and compiling sql statements every time a query is run. Each database has its own stored procedure language, usually a variant of C with a SQL preproceesor. Newer versions of db's support writing stored procedures in Java and Perl too. Before the advent of 3-tier/n-tier architecture it was pretty common for stored procs to implement the business logic(A lot of systems still do it). The biggest advantage is of course speed. Also certain kind of data manipulations are not achieved in SQL. Stored procs provide a mechanism to do these manipulations. Stored procs are also useful when you want to do Batch updates/exports/houseKeeping kind of stuff on the db. The overhead of a JDBC Connection may be significant in these cases.

20. *How do I include static files within a JSP page?*

Solution: Static resources should always be included using the JSP include directive. This way, the inclusion is performed just once during the translation phase. Do note that you should always supply a relative URL for the file attribute. Although you can also include static resources using the action, this is not advisable as the inclusion is then performed for each and every request.

21. *Why does JComponent have add() and remove() methods but Component does not?*

Solution: Because JComponent is a subclass of Container, and can contain other components and jcomponents. How can I implement a thread-safe JSP page? - You can make your JSPs thread-safe by having them implement the SingleThreadModel interface. This is done by adding the directive <%@ page isThreadSafe="false" % > within your JSP page.

22. *How do I prevent the output of my JSP or Servlet pages from being cached by the browser?*

Solution: You will need to set the appropriate HTTP header attributes to prevent the dynamic content output by the JSP page from being cached by the browser. Just execute the following scriptlet at the beginning of your JSP pages to prevent them from being cached at the browser. You need both the statements to take care of some of the older browser versions.

23. *How do you restrict page errors display in the JSP page?*

Solution: You first set "Errorpage" attribute of PAGE directory to the name of the error page (*i.e* Errorpage="error.jsp")in your jsp page .Then in the error jsp page set "isErrorpage=TRUE". When an error occur in your jsp page it will automatically call the error page.

24. *How can I enable session tracking for JSP pages if the browser has disabled cookies?*

Solution: We know that session tracking uses cookies by default to associate a session identifier with a unique user. If the browser does not support cookies, or if cookies are disabled, you can still enable session tracking using URL rewriting. URL rewriting essentially includes the session ID within the link itself as a name/value pair.

However, for this to be effective, you need to append the session ID for each and every link that is part of your servlet response. Adding the session ID to a link is greatly simplified by means of a couple of methods: response.encodeURL() associates a session ID with a given URL, and if you are using redirection, response.encodeRedirectURL() can be used by giving the redirected URL as input.

Both encodeURL() and encodeRedirectedURL() first determine whether cookies are supported by the browser; if so, the input URL is returned unchanged since the session ID will be persisted as a cookie. Consider the following example, in which two JSP files, say hello1.jsp and hello2.jsp, interact with each other.

Basically, we create a new session within hello1.jsp and place an object within this session. The user can then traverse to hello2.jsp by clicking on the link present within the page.Within hello2.jsp, we simply extract the object that was earlier placed in the session and display its contents. Notice that we invoke the encodeURL() within hello1.jsp on the link used to invoke hello2.jsp; if cookies are disabled, the session ID is automatically appended to the URL, allowing hello2.jsp to still retrieve the session object. Try this example first with cookies enabled. Then disable cookie support, restart the brower, and try again. Each time you should see the maintenance of the session across pages.

Do note that to get this example to work with cookies disabled at the browser, your JSP engine has to support URL rewriting.

```
hello1.jsp
hello2.jsp
hello2.jsp
<%
Integer i= (Integer )session.getValue("num");
out.println("Num value in session is "+i.intValue());
```

25. *What JSP lifecycle methods can I override?*

Solution: You cannot override the _jspService() method within a JSP page. You can however, override the jspInit() and jspDestroy() methods within a JSP page. jspInit() can be useful for allocating resources like database connections, network connections, and so forth for the JSP page. It is good programming practice to free any allocated resources within jspDestroy().

The jspInit() and jspDestroy() methods are each executed just once during the lifecycle of a JSP page and are typically declared as JSP declarations:

26. *How do I perform browser redirection from a JSP page?*

Solution: You can use the response implicit object to redirect the browser to a different resource, as:

response.sendRedirect("http://www.exforsys.com/path/error.html");

You can also physically alter the Location HTTP header attribute, as shown below:

You can also use the:

Also note that you can only use this before any output has been sent to the client. I beleve this is the case with the response.sendRedirect() method as well. If you want to pass any paramateres then you can pass using >

27. *How does JSP handle run-time exceptions?*

Solution: You can use the errorPage attribute of the page directive to have uncaught runtime exceptions automatically forwarded to an error processing page.

For example:

redirects the browser to the JSP page error.jsp if an uncaught exception is encountered during request processing. Within error.jsp, if you indicate that it is an error-processing page, via the directive:

the Throwable object describing the exception may be accessed within the error page via the exception implicit object.

Note: You must always use a relative URL as the value for the errorPage attribute.

28. *How do I use comments within a JSP page?*

Solution: You can use "JSP-style" comments to selectively block out code while debugging or simply to comment your scriptlets. JSP comments are not visible at the client.

For example:

--%>

You can also use HTML-style comments anywhere within your JSP page. These comments are visible at the client. For example:

Of course, you can also use comments supported by your JSP scripting language within your scriptlets.

29. *Is it possible to share an HttpSession between a JSP and EJB? What happens when I change a value in the HttpSession from inside an EJB?*

Solution: You can pass the HttpSession as parameter to an EJB method, only if all objects in session are serializable. This has to be consider as "passed-by-value", that means that it's read-only in the EJB.

If anything is altered from inside the EJB, it won't be reflected back to the HttpSession of the Servlet Container.The "pass-byreference" can be used between EJBs Remote Interfaces, as they are remote references.

While it IS possible to pass an HttpSession as a parameter to an EJB object, it is considered to be "bad practice" in terms of object oriented design. This is because you are creating an unnecessary coupling between back-end objects (ejbs) and front-end objects (HttpSession). Create a higher-level of abstraction for your ejb's api. Rather than passing the whole, fat, HttpSession (which carries with it a bunch of http semantics), create a class that acts as a value object (or structure) that holds all the data you need to pass back and forth between front-end/back-end.

Consider the case where your ejb needs to support a non-http-based client. This higher level of abstraction will be flexible enough to support it.

30. *How can I implement a thread-safe JSP page?*

Solution: You can make your JSPs thread-safe by having them implement the SingleThreadModel interface. This is done by adding the directive <%@ page isThreadSafe="false" %> within your JSP page.

31. *How can I declare methods within my JSP page?*

Solution: You can declare methods for use within your JSP page as declarations. The methods can then be invoked within any other methods you declare, or within JSP scriptlets and expressions.

Do note that you do not have direct access to any of the JSP implicit objects like request, response, session and so forth from within JSP methods. However, you should be able to pass any of the implicit JSP variables as parameters to the methods you declare.

For example:

Another Example:

file1.jsp:

file2.jsp

<%test(out);% >

32. *Can I stop JSP execution while in the midst of processing a request?*

Solution: Yes. Preemptive termination of request processing on an error condition is a good way to maximize the throughput of a high-volume JSP engine. The trick (assuming Java is your scripting language) is to use the return statement when you want to terminate further processing.

33. *Can a JSP page process HTML FORM data?*

Solution: Yes. However, unlike Servlet, you are not required to implement HTTP-protocol specific methods like doGet() or doPost() within your JSP page. You can obtain the data for the FORM input elements via the request implicit object within a scriptlet or expression as.

34. *Is there a way to reference the "this" variable within a JSP page?*

Solution: Yes, there is. Under JSP 1.0, the page implicit object is equivalent to "this", and returns a reference to the Servlet generated by the JSP page.

35. *How do you pass control from one JSP page to another?*

Solution: Use the following ways to pass control of a request from one servlet to another or one jsp to another.

The RequestDispatcher object's forward method to pass the control.

The response.sendRedirect method.

36. *Is there a way I can set the inactivity lease period on a per-session basis?*

Solution: Typically, a default inactivity lease period for all sessions is set within your JSPengine admin screen or associated properties file. However, if your JSP engine supports the Servlet 2.1 API, you can manage the inactivity lease period on a per-session basis.

This is done by invoking the HttpSession.setMaxInactiveInterval() method, right after the session has been created.

37. *How does a servlet communicate with a JSP page?*

Solution: The following code snippet shows how a servlet instantiates a bean and initializes it with FORM data posted by a browser. The bean is then placed into the request, and the call is then forwarded to the JSP page, Bean1.jsp, by means of a request dispatcher for downstream processing.

```
public void doPost (HttpServletRequest request, HttpServletResponse response)
{
try {
govi.FormBean f = new govi.FormBean();
String id = request.getParameter("id");
f.setName(request.getParameter("name"));
f.setAddr(request.getParameter("addr"));
f.setAge(request.getParameter("age"));
//use the id to compute
//additional bean properties like info
//maybe perform a db query, etc.
//...
f.setPersonalizationInfo(info);
request.setAttribute("fBean",f);
getServletConfig().getServletContext().getRequestDispatcher
("/jsp/Bean1.jsp").forward(request, response);
} catch (Exception ex) {
...
}
}
```

The JSP page Bean1.jsp can then process fBean, after first extracting it from the default request scope via the useBean action.

jsp:useBean id="fBean" class="govi.FormBean" scope="request"/ jsp:getProperty name="fBean" property="name" / jsp:getProperty name="fBean" property="addr" / jsp:getProperty name="fBean" property="age" / jsp:getProperty name="fBean" property="personalizationInfo" /

38. *Can you make use of a ServletOutputStream object from within a JSP page?*

Solution: No. You are supposed to make use of only a JSPWriter object (given to you in the form of the implicit object out) for replying to clients.

A JSPWriter can be viewed as a buffered version of the stream object returned by response.getWriter(), although from an implementational perspective, it is not.

A page author can always disable the default buffering for any page using a page directive as.

39. *How do I include static files within a JSP page?*

Solution: Static resources should always be included using the JSP include directive. This way, the inclusion is performed just once during the translation phase.

The following example shows the syntax:

```
< % @ include file="copyright.html" % >
```

Do note that you should always supply a relative URL for the file attribute. Although you can also include static resources using the action, this is not advisable as the inclusion is then performed for each and every request.

How do I have the JSP-generated servlet subclass my own custom servlet class, instead of the default? One should be very careful when having JSP pages extend custom servlet classes as opposed to the default one generated by the JSP engine. In doing so, you may lose out on any advanced optimization that may be provided by the JSPengine.

In any case, your new super class has to fulfill the contract with the JSP engine by: Implementing the HttpJspPage interface, if the protocol used is HTTP, or implementing JspPage otherwise Ensuring that all the methods in the Servlet interface are declared final.

Additionally, your servlet super class also needs to do the following:

The service() method has to invoke the _jspService() method

The init() method has to invoke the jspInit() method

The destroy() method has to invoke jspDestroy()

If any of the above conditions are not satisfied, the JSP engine may throw a translation error. Once the super class has been developed, you can have your JSP extend it as follows:

40. *Can a JSP page instantiate a serialized bean?*

Solution: No problem! The use Bean action specifies the beanName attribute, which can be used for indicating a serialized bean.

For example:

A couple of important points to note. Although you would have to name your serialized file "filename.ser", you only indicate "filename" as the value for the beanName attribute. Also, you will have to place your serialized file within the WEB-INFjspbeans directory for it to be located by the JSP engine.

41. *What is JSP?*

Solution: Let's consider the answer to that from two different perspectives: that of an HTML designer and that of a Java programmer.

If you are an HTML designer, you can look at JSP technology as extending HTML to provide you with the ability to seamlessly embed snippets of Java code within your HTML pages. These bits of Java code generate dynamic content, which is embedded within the other HTML/XML content you author. Even better, JSP technology provides the means by which programmers can create new HTML/XML tags and JavaBeans components, which provide new features for HTML designers without those designers needing to learn how to program.

Note: A common misconception is that Java code embedded in a JSP page is transmitted with the HTML and executed by the user agent (such as a browser). This is not the case. A JSP page is translated into a Java servlet and executed on the server. JSP statements embedded in the JSP page become part of the servlet generated from the JSP page. The resulting servlet is executed on the server. It is never visible to the user agent.

If you are a Java programmer, you can look at JSP technology as a new, higher-level means to writing servlets. Instead of directly writing servlet classes and then emitting HTML from your servlets, you write HTML pages with Java code embedded in them. The JSP environment takes your page and dynamically compiles it. Whenever a user agent requests that page from the Web server, the servlet that was generated from your JSP code is executed, and the results are returned to the user.

42. *How do I mix JSP and SSI #include?*

Solution: If you're just including raw HTML, use the #include directive as usual inside your .jsp file.

<!--#include file="data.inc"-->

But it's a little trickier if you want the server to evaluate any JSP code that's inside the included file. Ronel Sumibcay (ronel@LIVESOFTWARE.COM) says: If your data.inc file contains jsp code you will have to use

<%@ vinclude="data.inc" %>

The <!--#include file="data.inc"--> is used for including non-JSP files.

43. *How do I mix JSP and SSI #include? What is the difference between include directive & jsp:include action?*

Solution: Difference between include directive and jsp: include action

(*i*) provides the benefits of automatic recompliation,smaller class size ,since the code corresponding to the included page is not present in the servlet for every included jsp page and option of specifying the additional request parameter.

(*ii*) The also supports the use of request time attributes values for dynamically specifying included page which directive does not.

(*iii*) the include directive can only incorporate contents from a static document.

(*iv*) can be used to include dynamically generated output e.g., from servlets.

(*v*) include directive offers the option of sharing local variables, better run time efficiency.

(*vi*) Because the include directive is processed during translation and compilation, it does not impose any restrictions on output buffering.

44. *How do you prevent the Creation of a Session in a JSP Page and why? What is the difference between include directive & jsp:include action?*

Solution: By default, a JSP page will automatically create a session for the request if one does not exist.

However, sessions consume resources and if it is not necessary to maintain a session, one should not be created. For example, a marketing campaign may suggest the reader visit a web page for more information. If it is anticipated that a lot of traffic will hit that page, you may want to optimize the load on the machine by not creating useless sessions.

45. *How do I use a scriptlet to initialize a newly instantiated bean?*

Solution: A jsp:useBean action may optionally have a body. If the body is specified, its contents will be automatically invoked when the specified bean is instantiated. Typically, the body will contain scriptlets or jsp:setProperty tags to initialize the newly instantiated bean, although you are not restricted to using those alone.

The following example shows the "today" property of the Foo bean initialized to the current date when it is instantiated. Note that here, we make use of a JSP expression within the jsp:setProperty action.

value=""/>

46. *How can I set a cookie and delete a cookie from within a JSP page?*

Solution: A cookie, mycookie, can be deleted using the following scriptlet.

47. *How do you connect to the database from JSP?*

Solution: A Connection to a database can be established from a jsp page by writing the code to establish a connection using a jsp scriptlets.

Further then you can use the resultset object "res" to read data in the following way.

48. *What is the page directive used to prevent a JSP page from automatically creating a session?*

Solution: <%@ page session="false">

49. *How do you delete a Cookie within a JSP?*

Solution: Cookie mycook = new Cookie("name","value");

response.addCookie(mycook);

Cookie killmycook = new Cookie("mycook","value");

killmycook.setMaxAge(0);

killmycook.setPath("/");

killmycook.addCookie(killmycook);

50. *What is the difference between ServletContext and PageContext?*

Solution: ServletContext: Gives the information about the container

PageContext: Gives the information about the Request.

51. *What is the difference in using request.getRequestDispatcher() and context.getRequest Dispatcher()?*

Solution: request.getRequestDispatcher(path): In order to create it we need to give the relative path of the resource context.getRequestDispatcher(path): In order to create it we need to give the absolute path of the resource.

52. *How to pass information from JSP to included JSP?*

Solution: Using <%jsp:param> tag.

53. *How is JSP include directive different from JSP include action?*

Solution: When a JSP include directive is used, the included file's code is added into the added JSP page at page translation time, this happens before the JSP page is translated into a servlet. While if any page is included using action tag, the page's output is returned back to the added page. This happens at runtime.

54. *Can we override the jspInit(), _jspService() and jspDestroy() methods?*

Solution: We can override jspinit() and jspDestroy() methods but not _jspService().

55. *Why is _jspService() method starting with an '_' while other life cycle methods do not?*

Solution: _jspService() method will be written by the container hence any methods which are not to be overridden by the end user are typically written starting with an '_'. This is the reason why we don't override _jspService() method in any JSP page.

56. *What happens when a page is statically included in another JSP page?*

Solution: An include directive tells the JSP engine to include the contents of another file (HTML, JSP, etc.) in the current page. This process of including a file is also called as static include.

57. *A JSP page, include.jsp, has a instance variable "int a", now this page is statically included in another JSP page, index.jsp, which has a instance variable "int a" declared. What happens when the index.jsp page is requested by the client?*

Solution: Compilation error, as two variables with same name can't be declared. This happens because, when a page is included statically, entire code of included page becomes part of the new page. At this time there are two declarations of variable 'a'. Hence compilation error.

58. *Can you override jspInit() method? If yes, In which cases?*

Solution: Yes, we can. We do it usually when we need to initialize any members which are to be available for a servlet/JSP throughout its lifetime.

59. *What is the difference between directive include and jsp include?*

Solution: <%@ include> : Used to include static resources during translation time. : Used to include dynamic content or static content during runtime.

60. *What is the difference between RequestDispatcher and sendRedirect?*

Solution: RequestDispatcher: server-side redirect with request and response objects. sendRedirect: Client-side redirect with new request and response objects.

61. *How does JSP handle runtime exceptions?*

Solution: Using errorPage attribute of page directive and also we need to specify isErrorPage= true if the current page is intended to URL redirecting of a JSP.

62. *How can my application get to know when a HttpSession is removed?*

Solution: Define a Class HttpSessionNotifier which implements HttpSessionBindingListener and implement the functionality what you need in valueUnbound() method.

Create an instance of that class and put that instance in HttpSession.

63. *What Class.forName will do while loading drivers?*

Solution: It is used to create an instance of a driver and register it with the DriverManager. When you have loaded a driver, it is available for making a connection with a DBMS.

64. *How to Retrieve Warnings?*

Solution: SQLWarning objects are a subclass of SQLException that deal with database access warnings. Warnings do not stop the execution of an application, as exceptions do; they simply alert the user that something did not happen as planned. A warning can be reported on a Connection object, a Statement object (including PreparedStatement and CallableStatement objects), or a ResultSet object. Each of these classes has a getWarnings method, which you must invoke in order to see the first warning reported on the calling object

```
SQLWarning warning = stmt.getWarnings();
if (warning != null)
{
while (warning != null)
{
System.out.println(\"Message: \" + warning.getMessage());
System.out.println(\"SQLState: \" + warning.getSQLState());
System.out.print(\"Vendor error code: \");
System.out.println(warning.getErrorCode());
warning = warning.getNextWarning();
}
}
```

65. *How many JSP scripting elements are there and what are they?*

Solution: There are three scripting language elements: declarations, scriptlets, expressions.

66. *In the Servlet 2.4 specification SingleThreadModel has been deprecated, why?*

Solution: Because it is not practical to have such model. Whether you set isThreadSafe to true or false, you should take care of concurrent client requests to the JSP page by synchronizing access to any shared objects defined at the page level.

67. *Is JSP technology extensible?*

Solution: Yes, JSP technology is extensible through the development of custom actions, or tags, which are encapsulated in tag libraries.

68. *Can we use the constructor, instead of init(), to initialize servlet?*

Solution: Yes, of course you can use the constructor instead of init(). There's nothing to stop you. But you shouldn't. The original reason for init() was that ancient versions of Java couldn't dynamically invoke constructors with arguments, so there was no way to give the constructur a ServletConfig. That no longer applies, but servlet containers still will only call your no-arg constructor. So you won't have access to a ServletConfig or ServletContext.

69. *How can a servlet refresh automatically if some new data has entered the database?*

Solution: You can use a client-side Refresh or Server Push.

70. *The code in a finally clause will never fail to execute, right?*

Solution: Using System.exit(1); in try block will not allow finally code to execute.

71. *How many messaging models do JMS provide for and what are they?*

Solution: JMS provide for two messaging models, publish-and-subscribe and point-to-point queuing.

MULTIPLE CHOICE QUESTIONS

1. Choose the statement that best describes the relationship between JSP and servlets:
   (*a*) Servlets are built on JSP semantics and all servlets are compiled to JSP pages for runtime usage.
   (*b*) JSP and servlets are unrelated technologies.
   (*c*) Servlets and JSP are competing technologies for handling web requests. Servlets are being superseded by JSP, which is preferred. The two technologies are not useful in combination.
   (*d*) JSPs are built on servlet semantics and all JSPs are compiled to servlets for runtime usage.
2. What is a benefit of using JavaBeans to separate business logic from presentation markup within the JSP environment?
   (*a*) It allows the JSP to access middleware.
   (*b*) It creates a cleaner role separation between the web-production team and the software development team, so that the web-production team can focus on presentation markup, while the software team can focus on building reusable software components for helping to generate dynamic displays.
   (*c*) It provides a dynamic markup environment, such that JavaBeans are integrated seamlessly with the template presentation content, in order to create the dynamic display for the client.
   (*d*) It provides the developer with full access to the Java 2 Platform Enterprise Edition (J2EE), which is unavailable from outside the JavaBean environment.
3. Why use `RequestDispatcher` to forward a request to another resource, instead of using a `sendRedirect`?
   (*a*) Redirects are no longer supported in the current servlet API.
   (*b*) Redirects are not a cross-platform portable mechanism.
   (*c*) The `RequestDispatcher` does not use the reflection API.
   (*d*) The `RequestDispatcher` does not require a round trip to the client, and thus is more efficient and allows the server to maintain request state.

4. What alternatives exist to embedding Java code directly within the HTML markup of your JSP page?
   (*a*) Moving the code into your session manager.
   (*b*) Moving the code into scriptlets.
   (*c*) Moving the code into JavaBeans and servlets.
   (*d*) Moving the code into a transaction manager.
5. What type of scriptlet code is better-suited to being *factored forward* into a servlet?
   (*a*) Code that deals with logic that is common across requests.
   (*b*) Code that deals with logic that is vendor specific.
   (*c*) Code that deals with logic that relates to database access.
   (*d*) Code that deals with logic that relates to client scope.
6. Choose the statement that best describes how to connect JSP pages and Enterprise JavaBeans (EJBs):
   (*a*) Lookup the EJBs from within a JSP, but use the EJBs from within a basic JavaBean.
   (*b*) Lookup and use the EJBs from a separate business delegate. The JavaBeans that work with JSP pages are clients to these business delegates and know nothing about EJB specifics.
   (*c*) Lookup and use the EJBs from within a JSP page, but only as remote references.
   (*d*) Lookup the EJBs from within a servlet, delegating usage to specific JSP pages.
7. Are custom tags available in JSP 1.0? If not, how else might you implement iteration from within a JSP?
   (*a*) Yes, but the only tags available relate to database access.
   (*b*) No. To iterate over a collection of values, one must use scriptlet code.
   (*c*) No, but there is a standard <iterate> tag that may be used.
   (*d*) Yes, but custom tags will not help developers create tags for use in iterating over a collection.
8. What is the initial contact point for handling a web request in a *Page-Centric* architecture?
   (*a*) A JSP page. (*b*) A JavaBean. (*c*) A servlet. (*d*) A session manager.
9. What is the difference between doing an *include* or a *forward* with a RequestDispatcher?
   (*a*) The forward method transfers control to the designated resource, while the include method invokes the designated resource, substitutes its output dynamically in the display, and returns control to the calling page.
   (*b*) The two methods provide the same functionality, but with different levels of persistence.
   (*c*) The forward method is deprecated as of JSP 1.1 and the include method should be used in order to substitute portions of a dynamic display at runtime.
   (*d*) The include method transfers control to a dynamic resource, while the forward method allows for dynamic substitution of another JPS pages output, returning control to the calling resource.
10. What line of code below might be combined in the same JSP page with a validation guard (for example, `<% bean.validationGuard(); %>`), in order to create an alternate flow of control for scenarios in which exceptions arise. The validationGaurd method might throw an exception, which should cause the flow of control to continue in another user-defined page (assume JSP 1.0).
   (*a*) `<jsp:error page="errorPage.jsp" guard="true" />`
   (*b*) `<%@ page language="java" buffer="8k" %>`
   (*c*) `<jsp:useBean id="bean" class="examples.Bean" scope="request" />`
   (*d*) `<%@ page language="java" errorPage="errorPage.jsp" buffer="8k" %>`

Answers of Multiple Choice Questions

1. (*d*),	**2.** (*b*),	**3.** (*d*),	**4.** (*c*),	**5.** (*a*),
6. (*b*),	**7.** (*b*),	**8.** (*a*),	**9.** (*a*),	**10.** (*d*),

EXERCISE

1. What do you mean by page directive and include directive and also explain the purpose of these directives.
2. Write a program for error handling and debugging in JSP.
3. Describe the attributes of Taglib directive.
4. What are JSP actions?
5. Compare JSP and Java Beans.
6. What is the procedure to initialize the Java Beans?
7. Write a program in JSP using Java Beans.
8. Describe request, response and session objects.

18

DATABASE CONNECTIVITY

18.0 INTRODUCTION

Java's JDBC API gives us a shared language through which our applications can talk to database engines. Following in the tradition of its other multi-platform APIs such as the AWT, JDBC provides us with a set of interfaces that create a common point at which database applications and database engines can meet.

18.1 WHAT IS JDBC?

Working with leaders in the database field, JavaSoft developed a single API for database access--JDBC. As part of this process, they kept three main goals in mind:

- JDBC should be an SQL-level API.
- JDBC should capitalize on the experience of existing database APIs.
- JDBC should be simple.

An SQL-level API means that JDBC allows us to construct SQL statements and embed them inside Java API calls. In short, you are basically using SQL. But JDBC lets you smoothly translate between the world of the database and the world of the Java application. Your results from the database, for instance, are returned as Java variables, and access problems get thrown as exceptions. Because of the confusion caused by the proliferation of proprietary database access APIs, the idea of a universal database access API to solve this problem is not a new one. In fact, JavaSoft drew upon the successful aspects of one such API, Open DataBase Connectivity (ODBC). ODBC was developed to create a single standard for database access in the Windows environment. Although the industry has accepted ODBC as the primary means of talking to databases in Windows, it does not translate well into the Java world. First of all, ODBC is a C API that requires intermediate APIs for other languages. But even for C developers, ODBC has suffered from an overly complex design that has made its transition outside of the controlled Windows environment a failure. ODBC's complexity arises from the fact that complex, uncommon tasks are wrapped up in the API with its simpler and more common functionality. In other words, in order for you to understand a little of ODBC, you have to understand a lot.

In addition to ODBC, JDBC is heavily influenced by existing database programming APIs such as X/OPEN SQL Call Level Interface. JavaSoft wanted to re-use the key abstractions from these

APIs, which would ease acceptance by database vendors and capitalize on the existing knowledge capital of ODBC and SQL CLI developers. In addition, JavaSoft also realized that deriving an API from existing ones can provide quick development of solutions for database engines that support the old protocols. Specifically, JavaSoft worked in parallel with Intersolv to create an ODBC bridge that maps JDBC calls to ODBC calls, thus giving Java applications access to any database management system (DBMS) that supports ODBC.

18.2 THE STRUCTURE OF JDBC

JDBC accomplishes its goals through a set of Java interfaces, each implemented differently by individual vendors. The set of classes that implement the JDBC interfaces for a particular database engine is called a JDBC driver. In building a database application, you do not have to think about the implementation of these underlying classes at all; the whole point of JDBC is to hide the specifics of each database and let you worry about just your application. Figure below shows the JDBC classes and interfaces.

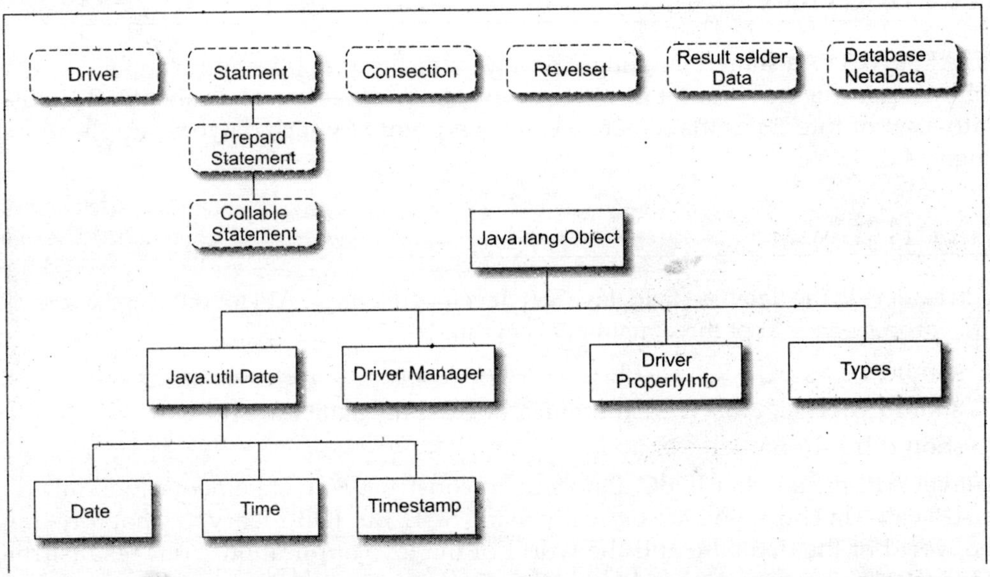

Fig. 18.1 *The classes and interfaces of java.sql, the JDBC API package*

Example : A Simple SELECT Application from the Imaginary JDBC Implementation for mSQL

```
import java.sql.*;

public class SelectApp {
 public static void main(String args[]) {
  String url = "jdbc:msql://athens.imaginary.com:4333/db_web";

  try {
   Class.forName("imaginary.sql.iMsqlDriver");
  }
  catch( Exception e ) {
   System.out.println("Failed to load mSQL driver.");
   return;
  }
```

```
    try {
      Connection con = DriverManager.getConnection(url, "borg", "");
      Statement select = con.createStatement();
      ResultSet result = select.executeQuery
                       ("SELECT key, val FROM t_test");
      System.out.println("Got results:");
      while(result.next()) { // process results one row at a time
        int key = result.getInt(1);
        String val = result.getString(2);
        System.out.println("key = " + key);
        System.out.println("val = " + val);
      }
      select.close();
      con.close();
    }
    catch( Exception e ) {
      e.printStackTrace();
    }
  }
}
```

If you already have Java experience, then you should be able to understand the flow of the code in Example 18.1 without knowing any JDBC. There are no references to specific database engine classes. Instead, the code simply uses JDBC interfaces to provide a facade for the DBMS-specific implementation. The JDBC implementation, in turn, performs the actual database access somewhere behind the scenes.

In this simple application, the SelectApp class asks the JDBC DriverManager to hand it the proper database implementation based on a database URL. The database URL looks similar to other Internet URLs. The actual content of the URL is loosely specified as *jdbc:subprotocol:subname*. The subprotocol identifies which driver to use, and the subname provides the driver with any required connection information. For the Imaginary JDBC Implementation for mSQL that I used in testing the above example, the URL is *jdbc:msql://athens.imaginary.com:4333/db_web*. In other words, this URL says to use the mSQL JDBC driver to connect to the database db_web on the server running at port 4333 on *athens.imaginary.com*. Each URL, however, is specific to the JDBC implementation being sought, and so I can't say anything more explicit about it. Whatever its format, the primary function of a database URL is to uniquely identify the implementation needed by the application and pass that implementation any information it needs in order to connect to the proper database.

18.3 DATABASES AND DRIVERS

Once your database engine is installed and your database is all set up, you will need a JDBC driver for that database engine. You can find an mSQL JDBC driver at http://www.imaginary.com/Java. The more commercial database engines like Oracle have commercial JDBC drivers. Most of them, however, allow you to have a free trial period for experimenting with the driver. Follow the install instructions for the driver you choose, and remember that some JDBC drivers require to you install native code on client machines. To help you understand what different drivers require, JavaSoft has defined the following driver categorization system:

Type 1

These drivers use a bridging technology to access a database. The JDBC-ODBC bridge that comes with the JDK 1.1 is a good example of this kind of driver. It provides a gateway to the ODBC API. Implementations of that API in turn do the actual database access. Bridge solutions generally require software to be installed on client systems, meaning that they are not good solutions for applications that do not allow you to install software on the client.

Type 2

The type 2 drivers are native API drivers. This means that the driver contains Java code that calls native C or C++ methods provided by the individual database vendors that perform the database access. Again, this solution requires software on the client system.

Type 3

Type 3 drivers provide a client with a generic network API that is then translated into database specific access at the server level. In other words, the JDBC driver on the client uses sockets to call a middleware application on the server that translates the client requests into an API specific to the desired driver. As it turns out, this kind of driver is extremely flexible since it requires no code installed on the client and a single driver can actually provide access to multiple databases.

Type 4

Using network protocols built into the database engine, type 4 drivers talk directly to the database using Java sockets. This is the most direct pure Java solution. In nearly every case, this type of driver will come only from the database vendor.

18.4 ALTERNATIVES TO JDBC

Without JDBC, only disparate, proprietary database access solutions exist. These proprietary solutions force the developer to build a layer of abstraction on top of them in order to create database independent code. Only after that abstraction layer is complete can the developer move to actually writing the application. In addition, the experience you have with that abstraction layer does not translate immediately to other projects or other employers who are almost certainly using their own abstraction layers to provide access to a variety of database engines.

Of course, the ODBC specification exists to provide this universal abstraction layer for languages like C and C++ as well as popular development tools such as Delphi, PowerBuilder, and VisualBasic. Unfortunately, ODBC does not enjoy the platform independence of Java. Using the JDBC interface design, however, your server application can pick the database at runtime based on which client is connecting. The ATM front-end of the banking application, for example, could have some legacy data stored in an Oracle system that is not yet converted to the Informix system against which the rest of the application is running. You write the application without writing special access code for the legacy data. The ATM client just passes the Oracle URL when requesting the connect. Once its data has been converted to Informix, all you have to do to switch the application to the new database is tell the ATM machine about the new database URL. No new code needs to be written for the migration.

18.5 CONNECTING TO THE DATABASE

Now I am going to dive into the details about JDBC calls and how to use them. Any JDBC application we write needs to be able to run from start to finish without ever referencing a specific JDBC implementation. Figure below shows how an application uses JDBC to talk to one or more databases without knowing any of the details concerning the driver implementation for that database. An application uses JDBC as an interface through which it passes all of its databases requests.

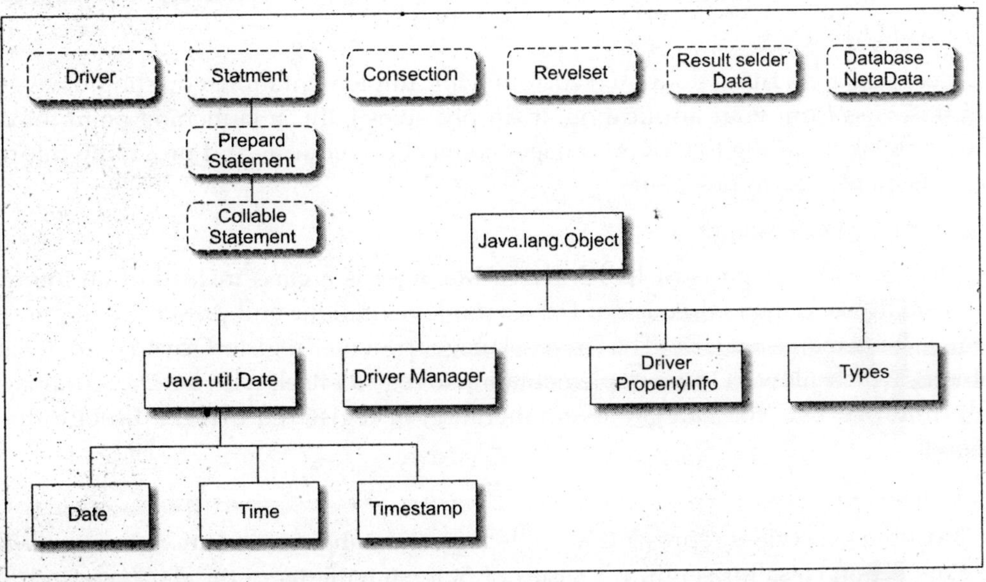

Fig. 18.2 *JDBC shields an application from the specifics of individual database implementations*

When you write a Java database applet or application, the only driver-specific information JDBC requires from you is the database URL. You can even build your application so that it derives the URL at runtime--based on user input or applet parameters.

Using the database URL, a user name, and password, your application will first requests a java.sql.Connection implementation from the DriverManager. The DriverManager in turn will search through all of the known java.sql.Driver implementations for one that will connect with the URL you provided. If it exhausts all of the implementations without finding a match, it throws an exception back to your application.

Once a Driver recognizes your URL, it creates a database connection using the user name and password you specified. It then provides the DriverManager with a java.sql.Connection implementation representing that database connection. The DriverManager then passes that Connection object back to the application. In your code, the entire database connection process is handled by this one-liner:

```
Connection con = DriverManager.getConnection(url, uid, password);
```

Of course, you are probably wondering just how the JDBC DriverManager learns about a new driver implementation. The DriverManager actually keeps a list of classes that implement the java.sql.Driver interface. Somehow, somewhere, your application needs to load the Driver implementations for any potential database drivers it might require. JDBC requires a Driver class to register itself with the DriverManager when it gets loaded. The very act of loading a Driver class thus enters it in the DriverManager's list. Your only task is thus to determine the somehow and somewhere of loading those Driver implementations.

18.6 THE JDBC CLASSES FOR CREATING A CONNECTION

As you can see from the process flow above, JDBC uses one class (java.sql.DriverManager) and two interfaces (java.sql.Driver and java.sql.Connection) for connecting to a database.

java.sql.Driver

Unless you are writing your own custom JDBC implementation, you should never have to deal with this class from your application. It simply gives JDBC a launching point for database connectivity by responding to DriverManager connection requests and providing information about the implementation in question.

java.sql.DriverManager

Unlike most other parts of JDBC, DriverManager is a class instead of an interface. Its main responsibility is to maintain a list of Driver implementations and present an application with one that matches a requested URL. The DriverManager provides registerDriver() and deregisterDriver() methods, which allow a Driver implementation to register itself with the DriverManager or remove itself from that list. You can get an enumeration of registered drivers through the getDrivers() method.

java.sql.Connection

The Connection class represents a single logical database transaction. In other words, you use the Connection class for sending a series of SQL statements to the database and managing the committing or aborting of those statements.

Example 18.2 puts the process of connecting to the database into a more concrete format.

Example 18.2: ***A Simple Database Connection***

```
package example.sql;

import java.sql.Connection;
import java.sql.DriverManager;
import java.sql.SQLException;

/**
 * The SimpleConnection class is a command line application that accepts
 * the following command line:
 * java SimpleConnection DRIVER URL UID PASSWORD
 * If the URL fits the specified driver, it will then load the driver and
 * get a connection.
 */
public class SimpleConnection {
  static public void main(String args[]) {
    Connection connection = null;
```

```
// Process the command line
if( args.length != 4 ) {
  System.out.println("Syntax: java SimpleConnection " +
                    "DRIVER URL UID PASSWORD");
  return;
}
try { // load the driver
  Class.forName(args[0]);
}
catch( Exception e ) { // problem loading driver, class not exist?
  e.printStackTrace();
  return;
}
try {
  connection = DriverManager.getConnection(args[1], args[2], args[3]);
  System.out.println("Connection successful!");
  // Do whatever queries or updates you want here!!!
}
catch( SQLException e ) {
  e.printStackTrace();
}
finally {
  try {
    connection.close();
  }
  catch( SQLException e ) {
    e.printStackTrace();
  }
}
}
```

In connecting to the database, this example catches an SQLException. This is a sort of catch-all exception for database errors. Just about any time something goes wrong between JDBC and the database, JDBC throws an SQLException. In addition to the information you commonly find in Java exceptions, SQLException also provides database specific error information, such as the SQLState value and vendor error code. JDBC SQLExceptions may be chained together so that you can find out everything that went wrong with a catastrophic database call.

18.7 BASIC DATABASE ACCESS

Now that you are connected to the database, you can begin making updates and queries. The most basic kind of database access involves writing JDBC code where you know ahead of time whether the statements you are sending are updates (INSERT, UPDATE, or DELETE) or queries (SELECT). In the next chapter, we will discuss more complex database access that allows you to execute statements of unknown types.

When this object first gets created, it is simply a direct link to the database. You use a Connection object to generate implementations of java.sql.Statement tied to the same database transaction. After you have used one or more Statement objects generated by your Connection, you can use it to commit or rollback the Statement objects associated with that Connection.

A Statement is very much what its name implies--an SQL statement. Once you get a Statement object from a Connection, you have what amounts to a blank check that you can write against the transaction represented by that Connection. You do not actually assign SQL to the Statement until you are ready to send the SQL to the database.

18.8 THE JDBC SUPPORT CLASSES

JDBC provides a handful of other classes and interfaces that support JDBC's core functionality. Many of them are more SQL-friendly extensions of java.util classes like java.sql.Date and java.sql.Numeric. Others are exception classes that get thrown by JDBC calls.

java.sql.Types

The Types class provides constants that identify SQL data types. Each constant that represents an SQL data type that is mapped to an integer is defined by the XOPEN SQL specification. You will see this class used extensively in the next chapter.

java.sql.SQLException

The SQLException class extends the general java.lang.Exception class that provides extra information about a database error. The information provided by a SQLException includes:

- The SQLState string describing the error according to the XOPEN SQLState conventions. The different values of this string are defined in the XOPEN SQL specification.
- The database-specific vendor error code. This code is usually some number that you have to look up in the obscure reference section of your database's documentation. Fortunately, the error should be sufficiently described through the Java Exception class's getMessage() method.
- A chain of exceptions leading up to this one. This is one of the niftier features of this class. Specifically, if you get several errors during the execution of a transaction, you can chain them all together in this class. This is frequently useful when you have exceptions that you want to let the user to know about, but you do not want to stop processing.

  try { Connection connection = DriverManager.getConnection(url, uid, pass); } catch(SQLException e) { e.printStackTrace(); while((e = e.getNextException()) != null) { // while more exceptions e.printStackTrace(); } }

java.sql.SQLWarning and java.sql.DataTruncation

Depending on the driver you are using, non-fatal errors might occur that should not halt application processing. JDBC provides an extension to the SQLException class called SQLWarning. When a JDBC object--like a ResultSet--encounters a warning situation internally, it creates an SQLWarning object and adds it to a list of warnings that it keeps. At any point, you can get the warnings for any JDBC object by repeatedly calling the getWarnings() method until it returns null.

The DataTruncation class is a special kind of warning that a JDBC implementation throws when JDBC unexpectedly truncates a data value. A DataTruncation object is chained as a warning on a read operation and thrown as an exception on a write.

java.sql.Date, java.sql.Time, and java.sql.Timestamp

Portable date handling among database engines can be very complex--each relational database management system (RDBMS) seems to have its own unique way of representing date information. These three classes all extend the functionality of other Java objects to provide a portable representation of their SQL counterparts. The Date and Time classes represent different levels of granularity as well as different means of expressing information already found in the java.util.Date class. The java.sql.Date class, for example, provides methods to express just the date, month, and year, while the Time class works in terms of hours, minutes, and seconds. And finally the Timestamp class takes the java.util.Date class down to nanosecond granularity.

java.sql.DriverPropertyInfo

I can almost guarantee that you will never use this class. It is designed for Rapid Application Development (RAD) tools like Symantec VisualCafe and Borland JBuilder. In order to provide a graphical user interface for rapid prototyping, these tools need to know what properties are required by a given JDBC implementation in order to connect to the database. Most drivers, for example, need to know the user name and password of the user connecting to the database. That and anything else the driver needs in order to connect to the database will be returned as an array of DriverPropertyInfo objects from the java.sql. Driver getPropertyInfo() method. Development tools can call this method to find out what information they should prompt the user for before connecting to the database.

QUESTIONS WITH ANSWERS

1. *I have the choice of manipulating database data using a byte[] or a java.sql.Blob. Which has best performance?*

Solution: java.sql.Blob, since it does not extract any data from the database until you explicitly ask it to. The Java platform 2 type Blob wraps a database locator (which is essentially a pointer to byte). That pointer is a rather large number (between 32 and 256 bits in size) - but the effort to extract it from the database is insignificant next to extracting the full blob content. For insertion into the database, you should use a byte[] since data has not been uploaded to the database yet. Thus, use the Blob class only for extraction.

Conclusion: use the java.sql.Blob class for extraction whenever you can.

2. *I have the choice of manipulating database data using a String or a java.sql.Clob. Which has best performance?*

Solution: java.sql.Clob, since it does not extract any data from the database until you explicitly ask it to. The Java platform 2 type Clob wraps a database locator (which is essentially a pointer to char). That pointer is a rather large number (between 32 and 256 bits in size) - but the effort to extract it from the database is insignificant next to extracting the full Clob content. For insertion into the database, you should use a String since data need not been downloaded from the database. Thus, use the Clob class only for extraction.

Conclusion: Unless you always intend to extract the full textual data stored in the particular table cell, use the java.sql.Clob class for extraction whenever you can.

3. *Do I need to commit after an INSERT call in JDBC or does JDBC do it automatically in the DB?*

Solution: If your autoCommit flag (managed by the Connection.setAutoCommit method) is false, you are required to call the commit() method - and vice versa.

4. *How can I retrieve only the first n rows, second n rows of a database using a particular WHERE clause ? For example, if a SELECT typically returns a 1000 rows, how do first retrieve the 100 rows, then go back and retrieve the next 100 rows and so on ?*

Solution: Use the Statement.setFetchSize method to indicate the size of each database fetch. Note that this method is only available in the Java 2 platform. For Jdk 1.1.X and Jdk 1.0.X, no standardized way of setting the fetch size exists. Please consult the Db driver manual.

5. *What does ResultSet actually contain? Is it the actual data of the result or some links to databases? If it is the actual data then why can't we access it after connection is closed?*

Solution: A ResultSet is an interface. Its implementation depends on the driver and hence, what it "contains" depends partially on the driver and what the query returns.

For example with the Odbc bridge what the underlying implementation layer contains is an ODBC result set. A Type 4 driver executing a stored procedure that returns a cursor - on an oracle database it actually returns a cursor in the database. The oracle cursor can however be processed like a ResultSet would be from the client.

Closing a connection closes all interaction with the database and releases any locks that might have been obtained in the process.

6. *What are SQL3 data types?*

Solution: The next version of the ANSI/ISO SQL standard defines some new datatypes, commonly referred to as the SQL3 types. The primary SQL3 types are:

STRUCT: This is the default mapping for any SQL structured type, and is manifest by the java.sql.Struct type.

REF: Serves as a reference to SQL data within the database. Can be passed as a parameter to a SQL statement. Mapped to the java.sql.Ref type.

BLOB: Holds binary large objects. Mapped to the java.sql.Blob type.

CLOB: Contains character large objects. Mapped to the java.sql.Clob type.

ARRAY: Can store values of a specified type. Mapped to the java.sql.Array type.

You can retrieve, store and update SQL3 types using the corresponding getXXX(), setXXX(), and updateXXX() methods defined in ResultSet interface.

7. *How can I manage special characters (for example: " _ ' %) when I execute an INSERT query? If I don't filter the quoting marks or the apostrophe, for example, the SQL string will cause an error,*

Solution: The characters "%" and "_" have special meaning in SQL LIKE clauses (to match zero or more characters, or exactly one character, respectively). In order to interpret them literally, they can be preceded with a special escape character in strings, e.g. "\". In order to specify the escape character used to quote these characters, include the following syntax on the end of the query:

{escape '*escape-character*'}

For example, the query

Select Name from Identifiers Where ID Like '_%' {escape '\'}

finds identifier names that begin with an underbar.

8. *What is SQLJ and why would I want to use it instead of JDBC?*

Solution: SQL/J is a technology, originally developed by Oracle Corporation, that enables you to embed SQL statements in Java. The purpose of the SQLJ API is to simplify the development requirements of the JDBC API while doing the same thing. Some major databases (Oracle, Sybase) support SQLJ, but others do not. Currently, SQLJ has not been accepted as a standard, so if you have to learn one of the two technologies, I recommend JDBC.

9. *How do I insert an image file (or other raw data) into a database?*

Solution: All raw data types (including binary documents or images) should be read and uploaded to the database as an array of bytes, byte[]. Originating from a binary file,

(*i*) Read all data from the file using a FileInputStream.

(*ii*) Create a byte array from the read data.

(*iii*) Use method setBytes(int index, byte[] data); of java.sql.PreparedStatement to upload the data.

10. *How can I pool my database connections so I don't have to keep reconnecting to the database?*

Solution:

- you gets a reference to the pool
- you gets a free connection from the pool
- you performs your different tasks
- you frees the connection to the pool

Since your application retrieves a pooled connection, you don't consume your time to connect/ disconnect from your data source.

11. *Will a call to PreparedStatement.executeQuery() always close the ResultSet from the previous executeQuery()?*

Solution: A ResultSet is automatically closed by the Statement that generated it when that Statement is closed, re-executed, or is used to retrieve the next result from a sequence of multiple results.

12. *How do I upload SQL3 BLOB & CLOB data to a database?*

Solution: Although one may simply extract BLOB & CLOB data from the database using the methods of the java.sql.CLOB and java.sql.BLOB, one must upload the data as normal java datatypes. The example below inserts a BLOB in the form of a byte[] and a CLOB in the form of a String into the database.

Inserting SQL3 type data [BLOB & CLOB]

```
private void runInsert() {
```

```
try {
  // Log
this.log("Inserting values ... ");
  // Open a new Statement
PreparedStatement stmnt = conn.prepareStatement(
            "insert Lobtest (image, name) values (?, ?)");
  // Create a timestamp to measure the insert time
  Date before = new java.util.Date();
    for(int i = 0; i < 500; i++) {
  // Set parameters
  stmnt.setBytes(1, blobData);
  stmnt.setString(2, "i: " + i + ";" + clobData);
  // Perform insert
  int rowsAffected = stmnt.executeUpdate();
    }

    // Get another timestamp to complete the time measurement
    Date after = new java.util.Date();
    this.log(" ... Done!");
    log("Total run time: " + (
          after.getTime() - before.getTime()));
    // Close database resources
    stmnt.close();
    } catch(SQLException ex) {
  this.log("Hmm... " + ex);
    }
}
```

13. *What is the difference between client and server database cursors?*

Solution: What you see on the client side is the current row of the cursor which called a Result (ODBC) or ResultSet (JDBC). The cursor is a server-side entity only and remains on the server side.

14. *Are prepared statements faster because they are compiled? if so, where and when are they compiled?*

Solution: Prepared Statements aren't actually compiled, but they are bound by the JDBC driver. Depending on the driver, Prepared Statements can be a lot faster - if you re-use them. Some drivers bind the columns you request in the SQL statement. When you execute Connection. prepareStatement(), all the columns bindings take place, so the binding overhead does not occur each time you run the Prepared Statement. For additional information on Prepared Statement performance and binding.

15. *Is it possible to connect to multiple databases simultaneously? Can one extract/update data from multiple databases with a single statement?*

Solution: In general, subject, as usual, to the capabilities of the specific driver implementation, one can connect to multiple databases at the same time. At least one driver (and probably others) will also handle commits across multiple connections. Obviously one should check the driver documentation rather than assuming these capabilities.

As to the second part of the question, one needs special middleware to deal with multiple databases in a single statement or to effectively treat them as one database. DRDA (Distributed Relational Database Architecture — I, at least, make it rhyme with "Gerta") is probably most commonly used to accomplish this.

Oracle has a product called Oracle Transparent Gateway for IBM DRDA and IBM has a product called DataJoiner that make multiple databases appear as one to your application. No doubt there are other products available. XOpen also has papers available regarding DRDA.

16. *Why do I get an UnsupportedOperationException?*

Solution: JDBC 2.0, introduced with the 1.2 version of Java, added several capabilities to JDBC. Instead of completely invalidating all the older JDBC 1.x drivers, when you try to perform a 2.0 task with a 1.x driver, an UnsupportedOperationException will be thrown. You need to update your driver if you wish to use the new capabilities.

17. *What advantage is there to using prepared statements if I am using connection pooling or closing the connection frequently to avoid resource/connection/cursor limitations?*

Solution: The ability to choose the 'best' efficiency (or evaluate tradeoffs, if you prefer,) is, at times, the most important piece of a mature developer's skillset. This is YAA (Yet Another Area,) where that maxim applies. Apparently there is an effort to allow prepared statements to work 'better' with connection pools in JDBC 3.0, but for now, one loses most of the original benefit of prepared statements when the connection is closed. A prepared statement obviously fits best when a statement differing only in variable criteria is executed over and over without closing the statement.

However, depending on the DB engine, the SQL may be cached and reused even for a different prepared statement and most of the work is done by the DB engine rather than the driver. In addition, prepared statements deal with data conversions that can be error prone in straight ahead, built on the fly SQL; handling quotes and dates in a manner transparent to the developer, for example.

18. *What is JDBC, anyhow?*

Solution: JDBC is Java's means of dynamically accessing tabular data, and primarily data in relational databases, in a generic manner, normally using standard SQL statements.

19. *Can I reuse a Statement or must I create a new one for each query?*

Solution: When using a JDBC compliant driver, you can use the same Statement for any number of queries. However, some older drivers did not always "respect the spec." Also note that a Statement SHOULD automatically close the current ResultSet before executing a new query, so be sure you are done with it before re-querying using the same Statement.

20. *What is a three-tier architecture?*

Solution: A three-tier architecture is any system which enforces a general separation between the following three parts:

(*i*) **Client Tier** or user interface

(*ii*) **Middle Tier** or business logic

(*iii*) **Data Storage Tier**

Applied to web applications and distributed programming, the three logical tiers usually correspond to the physical separation between three types of devices or hosts:

21. *What separates one tier from another in the context of n-tiered architecture?*

Solution: It depends on the application.

In a web application, for example, where tier 1 is a web-server, it may communicate with a tier 2 Application Server using RMI over IIOP, and subsequently tier 2 may communicate with tier 3 (data storage) using JDBC, etc.

Each of these tiers may be on separate physical machines or they may share the same box.

The important thing is the functionality at each tier.

- Tier 1 - Presentation - should be concerned mainly with display of user interfaces and/ or data to the client browser or client system.
- Tier 2 - Application - should be concerned with business logic
- Tier 3+ - Storage/Enterprise Systems - should be focused on data persistence and/or communication with other Enterprise Systems.

22. *What areas should I focus on for the best performance in a JDBC application?*

Solution: These are few points to consider:

- Use a connection pool mechanism whenever possible.
- Use prepared statements. These can be beneficial, for example with DB specific escaping, even when used only once.
- Use stored procedures when they can be created in a standard manner. Do watch out for DB specific SP definitions that can cause migration headaches.
- Even though the jdbc promotes portability, true portability comes from NOT depending on any database specific data types, functions and so on.
- Select only required columns rather than using select * from Tablexyz.
- Always close Statement and ResultSet objects as soon as possible.
- Write modular classes to handle database interaction specifics.
- Work with DatabaseMetaData to get information about database functionality.
- Softcode database specific parameters with, for example, properties files.
- Always catch AND handle database warnings and exceptions. Be sure to check for additional pending exceptions.
- Test your code with debug statements to determine the time it takes to execute your query and so on to help in tuning your code. Also use query plan functionality if available.
- Use proper (and a single standard if possible) formats, especially for dates.
- Use proper data types for specific kind of data. For example, store birthdate as a date type rather than, say, varchar.

23. *How can I insert multiple rows into a database in a single transaction?*

Solution:

```
//turn off the implicit commit
Connection.setAutoCommit(false);
//..your insert/update/delete goes here
```

Connection.Commit();

a new transaction is implicitly started.

24. *How do I convert a java.sql.Timestamp to a java.util.Date?*

Solution: While Timesteamp extends Date, it stores the fractional part of the time within itself instead of within the Date superclass. If you need the partial seconds, you have to add them back in.

Date date = new Date(ts.getTime() + (ts.getNanos() / 1000000));

25. *What is SQL?*

Solution: SQL is a standardized language used to create, manipulate, examine, and manage relational databases.

26. *Is Class.forName(Drivername) the only way to load a driver? Can I instantiate the Driver and use the object of the driver?*

Solution: Yes, you can use the driver directly. Create an instance of the driver and use the connect method from the Driver interface. Note that there may actually be two instances created, due to the expected standard behavior of drivers when the class is loaded.

27. *What's new in JDBC 3.0?*

Solution: Probably the new features of most interest are:

- Savepoint support
- Reuse of prepared statements by connection pools
- Retrieval of auto-generated keys
- Ability to have multiple open ResultSet objects
- Ability to make internal updates to the data in Blob and Clob objects
- Ability to Update columns containing BLOB, CLOB, ARRAY and REF types
- Both java.sql and javax.sql (JDBC 2.0 Optional Package) are expected to be included with J2SE 1.4.

28. *Why do I get the message "No Suitable Driver"?*

Solution: Often the answer is given that the correct driver is not loaded. This may be the case, but more typically, the JDBC database URL passed is not properly constructed. When a Connection request is issued, the DriverManager asks each loaded driver if it understands the URL sent. If no driver responds that it understands the URL, then the "No Suitable Driver" message is returned.

29. *When I create multiple Statements on my Connection, only the current Statement appears to be executed. What's the problem?*

Solution: All JDBC objects are required to be threadsafe. Some drivers, unfortunately, implement this requirement by processing Statements serially. This means that additional Statements are not executed until the preceding Statement is completed.

30. *Can a single thread open up mutliple connections simultaneously for the same database and for same table?*

Solution: The general answer to this is yes. If that were not true, connection pools, for example, would not be possible. As always, however, this is completely dependent on the JDBC driver.

You can find out the theoretical maximum number of active Connections that your driver can obtain via the DatabaseMetaData.getMaxConnections method.

31. *Can I ensure that my app has the latest data?*

Solution: Typically an application retrieves multiple rows of data, providing a snapshot at an instant of time. Before a particular row is operated upon, the actual data may have been modified by another program. When it is essential that the most recent data is provided, a JDBC 2.0 driver provides the ResultSet.refreshRow method.

32. *What does normalization mean for java.sql.Date and java.sql.Time?*

Solution: These classes are thin wrappers extending java.util.Date, which has both date and time components. java.sql.Date should carry only date information and a normalized instance has the time information set to zeros. java.sql.Time should carry only time information and a normalized instance has the date set to the Java epoch (January 1, 1970) and the milliseconds portion set to zero.

33. *What's the best way, in terms of performance, to do multiple insert/update statements, a PreparedStatement or Batch Updates?*

Solution: Because PreparedStatement objects are precompiled, their execution can be faster than that of Statement objects. Consequently, an SQL statement that is executed many times is often created as a PreparedStatement object to increase efficiency.

A CallableStatement object provides a way to call stored procedures in a standard manner for all DBMSes. Their execution can be faster than that of PreparedStatement object.

Batch updates are used when you want to execute multiple statements together. Actually, there is no conflict here. While it depends on the driver/DBMS engine as to whether or not you will get an actual performance benefit from batch updates, Statement, PreparedStatement, and CallableStatement can all execute the addBatch() method.

34. *What is JDO?*

Solution: JDO provides for the transparent persistence of data in a data store agnostic manner, supporting object, hierarchical, as well as relational stores.

35. *What is the difference between setMaxRows(int) and SetFetchSize(int)? Can either reduce processing time?*

Solution: setFetchSize(int) defines the number of rows that will be read from the database when the ResultSet needs more rows. The method in the java.sql.Statement interface will set the 'default' value for all the ResultSet derived from that Statement; the method in the java.sql.ResultSet interface will override that value for a specific ResultSet. Since database fetches can be expensive in a networked environment, fetch size has an impact on performance.

setMaxRows(int) sets the limit of the maximum nuber of rows in a ResultSet object. If this limit is exceeded, the excess rows are "silently dropped". That's all the API says, so the setMaxRows method may not help performance at all other than to decrease memory usage. A value of 0 (default) means no limit.

36. *What is DML?*

Solution: DML is an abbreviation for Data Manipulation Language. This portion of the SQL standard is concerned with manipulating the data in a database as opposed to the structure of a database. The core verbs for DML are SELECT, INSERT, DELETE, UPDATE, COMMIT and ROLLBACK.

37. *What is DDL?*

Solution: DDL is an abbreviation for Data Definition Language. This portion of the SQL standard is concerned with the creation, deletion and modification of database objects like tables, indexes and views. The core verbs for DDL are CREATE, ALTER and DROP. While most DBMS engines allow DDL to be used dynamically (and available to JDBC), it is often not supported in transactions.

38. *How can I get information about foreign keys used in a table?*

Solution: DatabaseMetaData.getImportedKeys() returns a ResultSet with data about foreign key columns, tables, sequence and update and delete rules.

39. *How do I disallow NULL values in a table?*

Null capability is a column integrity constraint, normally aplied at table creation time. Note that some databases won't allow the constraint to be applied after table creation. Most databases allow a default value for the column as well. The following SQL statement displays the NOT NULL constraint:

```
CREATE TABLE CoffeeTable (
Type VARCHAR(25) NOT NULL,
Pounds INTEGER NOT NULL,
Price NUMERIC(5, 2) NOT NULL
)
```

40. *What isolation level is used by the DBMS when inserting, updating and selecting rows from a database?*

Solution: The answer depends on both your code and the DBMS. If the program does not explicitly set the isolation level, the DBMS default is used. You can determine the default using DatabaseMetaData.getDefaultTransactionIsolation() and the level for the current Connection with Connection.getTransactionIsolation(). If the default is not appropriate for your transaction, change it with Connection.setTransactionIsolation(int level).

EXERCISE

1. What are the features of JDBC API?
2. What are different types of JDBC Drivers? Write type of Driver is the best for use?
3. Write the steps to connect the application to the database.
4. How will you create DSN?
5. What is Struts Framework?
6. What are the features of Struts?
7. Explain the MVC architecture in brief?
8. Describe the working of Servlets.

19

Introduction to Web Services Management

19.0 INTRODUCTION

With the boom in distributed computing, the Internet world is heading towards Services Oriented Technologies. Web Services have become the buzzword of today. Web Services offer easy and standardized communication for loosely coupled and dynamically discovered software components over the Internet. Enterprises have started experimenting with Web Services at their corporate intranets before actually going live to their customers over the Web.

Being distributed and dynamic in nature, Web Services need to be managed with care.

Web Services Management is what we are going to talk about now. This article analyses the requirements of Web Services Management (referred to as WSM in this article) Platform. To address the functionalities required in WSM, we'll introduce the basic components of WSM. This article, then, aims to develop a basic understanding of the core components of the Web Services Management Platform.

In the forthcoming articles, we will discuss each one of the components of WSM in detail and propose implementation architectures for them.

19.1 WHAT ARE WEB SERVICES?

Even if the technologies such as CORBA and COM introduced the services-oriented distributed concepts, they could never become the universal choice of enterprises and developers. In search of standardization and simplicity, e-business technologists and customers looked forward for a loosely coupled and dynamically discovered services technology, which is known as Web Services. These services are software components developed by their vendors to solve some business problems. These services can reside on different systems and can be implemented by vastly different technologies, but they are packaged and transported using standard Web protocols, such as XML and HTTP, thus making them easily accessible by any user on the Web. Web Services Technology has become a key to the Service Oriented Internet World in a very short time period because it promises the interaction of unknown and unrelated applications on the Internet in a more standardized and simpler way than any other approach ever claimed.

19.2 WHY MANAGE WEB SERVICES?

After understanding the nature of Web Services, we can see their deployment scenarios where the following four players have vital roles to play:

1. Web Services Provider (WSP)-This is the entity (for example, a business organization) that designs and develops Web Services.
2. Web Services Infrastructure Provider (WSIP)-This entity provides the infrastructure services to deploy Web Services at its premises.
3. Web Services Broker (WSB)-Broker has the information of Web Services hosted by WSIP or WSP in the Web Services registries.
4. Web Services Client (WSC)-Clients are actual consumers (or, end-users or applications) of Web Services.

Web Services can be deployed in various fashions and on different platforms. This strongly urges a need to manage them in a centralized sphere of control depicted by Fig. 1:

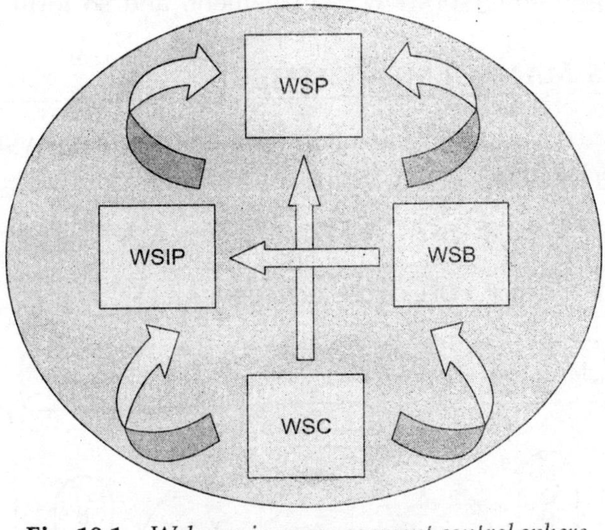

Fig. 19.1 *Web services management control sphere*

Note: The direction of the arrows shown in Fig. 1 is the direction of the flow of requests initiated by Web Service Clients. Consider an example of this flow: WSC requests WSB to provide the information of a registered Web Service. After getting the response, WSC invokes the Web Service provided by WSP and hosted by WSIP. This flow depends on the design and deployment of Web Services in a business scenario.

The previously-discussed four players (shown in Figure 1) may or may not play a role in the control sphere. Their participation depends upon the Web Services deployment configuration/ fashion. This control sphere is also referred as the heart of the Web Services Management Platform (referred to as WSMP hereafter).

Digging into the complexity of business in the present world, there are many development and deployment scenarios possible for Web Services. These scenarios, when needed to interoperate, create more complicated systems. If these systems are not operated carefully, they may hinder the advantages of Web Services. To have control over the above-mentioned complexity of the heart of WSMP, we must have a wrapper of management services over it. This wrapper is responsible for managing Web Services and the four players, which are operating in the heart of WSMP.

The primary goal of enterprises that are currently using Web Services is to derive a business sense out of this technology and drive their strategies based on that. This can only be done when they have proper control over Web Services offered to their customers. This control can be visualized by some infrastructure services in the above-mentioned Control Sphere. There are many core requirements for Web Services to work in a commercialized world where they can help enterprises get returns for their investments.

When we translate the above-discussed needs into the components of the wrapper over the heart of WSMP, we see these core modules:

- Access Mechanism (Authentication and Authorization)
- Web Services Provisioning (Subscription, SLA, and License (Contract) Management, Monitoring, Metering, and Billing)
- Secure Communications
- Service Virtualization and Workflow Management, and so forth

19.3 WEB SERVICES MANAGEMENT SPHERE

Having discussed the need of various infrastructure components of the WSM Sphere, we will now see that our Sphere looks like this:

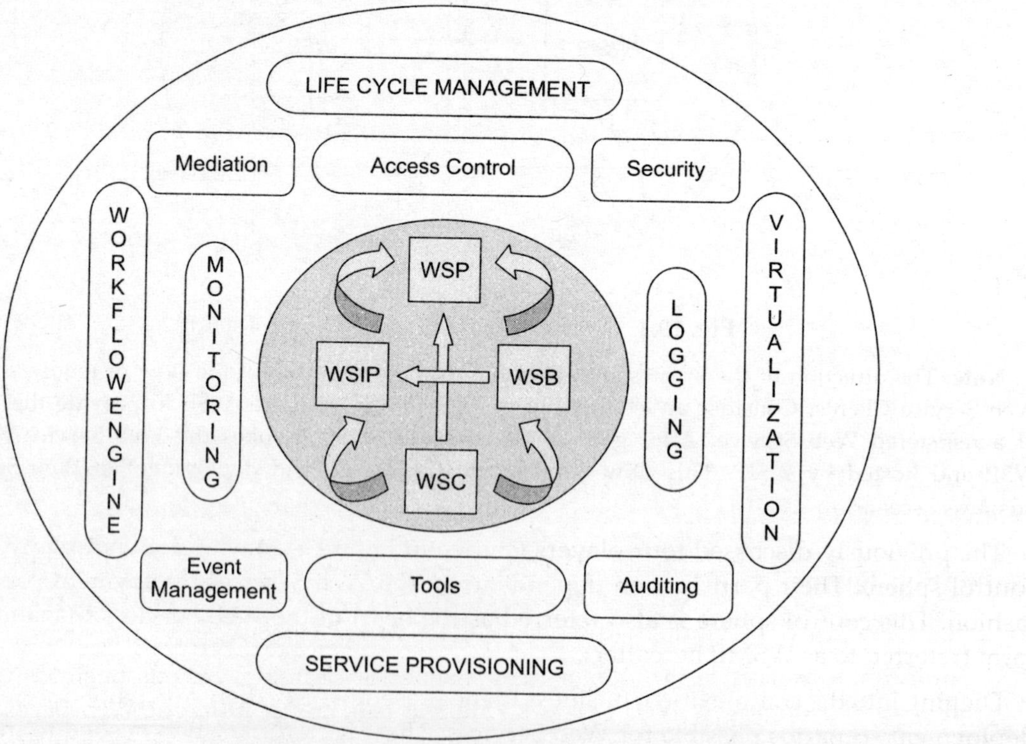

Fig. 19.2 *Web services management sphere-core infrastructure components*

Note: The components shown in the WSM sphere are the core functionality modules identified. Different vendors of the WSM platform may identify more advanced pieces in their WSM sphere.

Now, let us briefly discuss each one of the infrastructure components.

Tools

These tools aim to assist:

1. Web Services Providers develop their Web Services.
2. Web Services Infrastructure Providers deploy the Web Services.
3. Web Services Brokers provide Web Services information.
4. Web Services Clients invoke Web Services.

Access Control

The WSM infrastructure should be able to authenticate and authorize Web Services Clients. When a client logs in, a session is created and maintained until he/she logs out of the system. Sessions are used in various other components of WSM as well.

Logging

Web Services requests, responses, client session-related information, various events, and so forth should be logged. These logs are used for various vital operations, such as Services Provisioning, Monitoring, Performance Evaluations, Business Trend Analysis, and so on.

Monitoring

Web Services monitoring is essential as a part of management functionalities. Web Services Administrators should be able to monitor various events of all the deployed Web Services. This helps the administrators analyze business trends and manage Web Services.

Service Provisioning

Web Services Provisioning is responsible for defining the system behavior in terms of its technical and business functionalities.

For example, Web Services Clients should subscribe to Web Services. Clients are authenticated and authorized based on their subscription account before they access Web Services. Then, they are billed based on their usage of the system.

Here are the building blocks of the Web Service Provisioning System:

Subscription Engine

We can look into the subscription engine from these two perspectives:

- **Administrator:** This is the person responsible for defining various business terms and rules for the deployed Web Services. He/She can group different Web Services under Catalogs and set rules for the same. This way, all the Web Services having similar kinds of business functionalities can have the same sets of rules. The administrator should be able to manage various users (administrators and Web Services clients) and the subscription policies for Web Services.

- **Web Services Clients:** These are also called the business users of Web Services. Clients should be able to enroll themselves and then browse the directory of Web Services whose access has been given by the administrator. Clients, then, can apply for the subscription of listed Web Services.

Contract Management

Contracts are defined for linking the Web Services Clients to the terms of service (these terms include billing and rating packages). This contract is associated with each subscription of Web Services Clients. When the clients invoke the Web Services, authentication, authorization, and identity systems match the associated contract. Web Services Clients will not have access to invoked Web Services in case of an invalid contract.

In this process, Service Level Agreement (SLA) and Quality of Service (QoS) management applications play their role.

Metering and Billing

Clients will access Web Services based on the contract they have agreed upon when they subscribed to Web Services. To bill the clients, the system should be aware of the statistics of the contract, SLA, and QoS promised to the clients. A metering application gathers this usage and session statistics and the Billing application is responsible for co-relating the above-mentioned two statistics and produces a bill to the clients. Therefore, the Contract Management and Metering application should be treated as inputs to the Billing application.

Life Cycle Management

As the name of this WSM component suggests, it manages various stages of the Web Services life cycle. These stages are development, deployment, registering, and testing. The Life Cycle Manger keeps the information of each one of these stages and presents it to WSM administrator(s). It works in synchronization with WSM Tools, which control and manage various stages of Web Services (discussed under the "Tools" section, above).

Auditing

This WSM component is built on monitoring and logging components. The basic functionality it offers is to produce audit trails enabling the reconstruction and examination of a sequence of events in Web Services context. The Auditor fulfills this function by reliably and securely keeping records of security-related events. Various security event data can be obtained from the logging application. Security events could include authentication events, policy, enforcement decisions, and so forth. The resulting audit trails may be used to detect attacks, confirm compliances with policy, deter abuse, or other purposes.

Mediation

Mediation functionality enables the automated composition or federation of Web Services developed by various Web Services Providers (WSP) via a registry service. This component takes care of runtime dynamic discovery, subsequent binding, and execution of Web Services, from both a technical and business perspective.

Event Management

There are various events defined in the Web Services life cycle; these events can be grouped together in technical as well as business contexts. Event Manager is responsible for keeping stock of these events per Web Services basis. Various rules can also be configured using Event Manager; for example, sending alerts if any event occurs, setting thresholds for events, and so on. All event information should be able to be presented to administrator(s) for further analysis or feeding to other WSM components.

Security

Security Manager offers and guarantees authentication, authorization, privacy, trust, integrity, confidentiality, secure communication channels, federation, delegation, and auditing across a wide variety of Web Services.

The security mechanism enables us to achieve the following goals by a process in which:

1. A Web Service can mandate an incoming message proving a set of claims (name, key, permission, capability, and so forth). If a message arrives without having the required claims, the service may ignore or reject the message. We refer to the set of required claims and related information as policy.
2. A requester can send messages with proof of the required claims by associating security tokens with the messages. Thus, messages both demand a specific action and prove that their sender has the claim to demand the action.
3. When a requester does not have the required claims, the requester or someone on its behalf can try to obtain the necessary claims by contacting other Web Services. These other Web Services, which we refer to as security token services, may in turn require their own set of claims. Security token services broker trust between different trust domains by issuing security tokens.

   This mechanism can be developed implemented by using the WS-Security specifications.

Workflow Engine

Workflow is a very prevalent concept in today's business world and it applies to Web Services as well. As we know, Web Services are software components developed to solve some particular business problem. It makes a lot more sense to design business functionalities by visualizing a flow of more than one Web Service. This flow finally solves a bigger business problem than solved by its constituting Web Services when operated in an isolated manner.

Workflow Manger fulfills the above-mentioned need. It creates, tests, and manages the logical flows of Web Services. Dynamic discovery from registries, Security, and Transactional aspects of workflow are also covered in the engine.

Virtualization

A Virtualization application creates and manages 'virtual' endpoints for Web Services. The virtual endpoints can be dynamically associated with 'real' endpoints to manage fail-over, provide load balancing, and concurrently manage multiple versions of Web Services.

Note: As the readers must have noticed, some functionalities are covered in more than one WSM component. Actually, this is because some of the WSM components (Security, Life Cycle Manager, and so forth) have vast scope and their requirements overlap the need of relatively small WSM components (Auditor, Monitor, Logger, and so on).

Web Services Management Platform vendors should carefully design the WSM components and they may logically combine WSM functionalities into various WSM components.

EXERCISE

1. What are Web Services?
2. Why Manage Web Services?
3. Describe Web Services Management Sphere.
4. What do you mean by Virtualization application?

APPENDIX I

J2EE INTERVIEW QUESTIONS AND ANSWERS

1. *What is J2EE?*

Solution: J2EE is an environment for developing and deploying enterprise applications. The J2EE platform consists of a set of services, application programming interfaces (APIs), and protocols that provide the functionality for developing multitier, web-based applications.

2. *What is the J2EE module?*

Solution: A J2EE module consists of one or more J2EE components for the same container type and one component deployment descriptor of that type.

3. *What are the components of J2EE application?*

Solution: A J2EE component is a self-contained functional software unit that is assembled into a J2EE application with its related classes and files and communicates with other components. The J2EE specification defines the following J2EE components:

Application clients and applets are client components.

Java Servlet and JavaServer PagesTM (JSPTM) technology components are web components.

Enterprise JavaBeansTM (EJBTM) components (enterprise beans) are business components.

Resource adapter components provided by EIS and tool vendors.

4. *What are the four types of J2EE modules?*

Solution: 1. Application client module

2. Web module

3. Enterprise JavaBeans module

4. Resource adapter module

5. *What does application client module contain?*

Solution: The application client module contains:

—class files,

—an application client deployment descriptor.

Application client modules are packaged as JAR files with a .jar extension.

6. *What does web module contain?*

Solution: The web module contains:

— JSP files,
— class files for servlets,
— GIF and HTML files, and
— a Web deployment descriptor.

Web modules are packaged as JAR files with a .war (Web ARchive) extension.

7. *What are the differences between Ear, Jar and War files? Under what circumstances should we use each one?*

Solution: There are no structural differences between the files; they are all archived using zip-jar compression. However, they are intended for different purposes.

— Jar files (files with a .jar extension) are intended to hold generic libraries of Java classes, resources, auxiliary files, etc.
— War files (files with a .war extension) are intended to contain complete Web applications. In this context, a Web application is defined as a single group of files, classes, resources, .jar files that can be packaged and accessed as one servlet context.
— Ear files (files with a .ear extension) are intended to contain complete enterprise applications. In this context, an enterprise application is defined as a collection of .jar files, resources, classes, and multiple Web applications.

Each type of file (.jar, .war, .ear) is processed uniquely by application servers, servlet containers, EJB containers, etc.

8. *What is the difference between Session bean and Entity bean?*

Solution: The Session bean and Entity bean are two main parts of EJB container.

Session Bean

— represents a workflow on behalf of a client
— one-to-one logical mapping to a client.
— created and destroyed by a client
— not permanent objects
— lives its EJB container(generally) does not survive system shut down
— two types: stateless and stateful beans

Entity Bean

— represents persistent data and behavior of this data
— can be shared among multiple clients
— persists across multiple invocations
— findable permanent objects
— outlives its EJB container, survives system shutdown
— two types: container managed persistence(CMP) and bean managed persistence(BMP)

9. *What is "applet" ?*

Solution: A J2EE component that typically executes in a Web browser but can execute in a variety of other applications or devices that support the applet programming model.

10. *What is "applet container" ?*

Solution: A container that includes support for the applet programming model.

11. *What is "application assembler" ?*

Solution: A person who combines J2EE components and modules into deployable application units.

12. *What is "application client" ?*

Solution: A first-tier J2EE client component that executes in its own Java virtual machine. Application clients have access to some J2EE platform APIs.

13. *What is "application client container" ?*

Solution: A container that supports application client components.

14. *What is "application client module" ?*

Solution: A software unit that consists of one or more classes and an application client deployment descriptor.

15. *What is "application component provider" ?*

Solution: A vendor that provides the Java classes that implement components' methods, JSP page definitions, and any required deployment descriptors.

16. *What is "application configuration resource file" ?*

Solution: An XML file used to configure resources for a Java Server Faces application, to define navigation rules for the application, and to register converters, Validator, listeners, renders, and components with the application.

17. *What is "archiving" ?*

Solution: The process of saving the state of an object and restoring it.

18. *What is "asant" ?*

Solution: A Java-based build tool that can be extended using Java classes. The configuration files are XML-based, calling out a target tree where various tasks get executed.

19. *What is "attribute"?*

Solution: A qualifier on an XML tag that provides additional information.

20. *What is authentication ?*

Solution: The process that verifies the identity of a user, device, or other entity in a computer system, usually as a prerequisite to allowing access to resources in a system. The Java servlet specification requires three types of authentication-basic, form-based, and mutual-and supports digest authentication.

21. *What is authorization ?*

Solution: The process by which access to a method or resource is determined. Authorization depends on the determination of whether the principal associated with a request through authentication is in a given security role. A security role is a logical grouping of users defined by the person who assembles the application. A deployer maps security roles to security identities. Security identities may be principals or groups in the operational environment.

22. *What is authorization constraint ?*

Solution: An authorization rule that determines who is permitted to access a Web resource collection.

23. *What is backing bean ?*

Solution: A JavaBeans component that corresponds to a JSP page that includes JavaServer Faces components. The backing bean defines properties for the components on the page and methods that perform processing for the component. This processing includes event handling, validation, and processing associated with navigation.

24. *What is basic authentication ?*

Solution: An authentication mechanism in which a Web server authenticates an entity via a user name and password obtained using the Web application's built-in authentication mechanism.

25. *What is bean-managed persistence ?*

Solution: The mechanism whereby data transfer between an entity bean's variables and a resource manager is managed by the entity bean.

26. *What is bean-managed transaction ?*

Solution: A transaction whose boundaries are defined by an enterprise bean.

27. *What is binding (XML) ?*

Solution: Generating the code needed to process a well-defined portion of XML data.

28. *What is binding (JavaServer Faces technology) ?*

Solution: Wiring UI components to back-end data sources such as backing bean properties.

29. *What is build file ?*

Solution: The XML file that contains one or more asant targets. A target is a set of tasks you want to be executed. When starting asant, you can select which targets you want to have executed. When no target is given, the project's default target is executed.

30. *What is business logic ?*

Solution: The code that implements the functionality of an application. In the Enterprise JavaBeans architecture, this logic is implemented by the methods of an enterprise bean.

31. *What is business method ?*

Solution: A method of an enterprise bean that implements the business logic or rules of an application.

32. *What is callback methods ?*

Solution: Component methods called by the container to notify the component of important events in its life cycle.

33. *What is caller principal ?*

Solution: The principal that identifies the invoker of the enterprise bean method.

34. *What is cascade delete ?*

Solution: A deletion that triggers another deletion. A cascade delete can be specified for an entity bean that has container-managed persistence.

35. *What is CDATA ?*

Solution: A predefined XML tag for character data that means "don't interpret these characters," as opposed to parsed character data (PCDATA), in which the normal rules of XML syntax apply. CDATA sections are typically used to show examples of XML syntax.

36. *What is certificate authority ?*

Solution: A trusted organization that issues public key certificates and provides identification to the bearer.

37. *What is client-certificate authentication ?*

Solution: An authentication mechanism that uses HTTP over SSL, in which the server and, optionally, the client authenticate each other with a public key certificate that conforms to a standard that is defined by X.509 Public Key Infrastructure.

38. *What is comment ?*

Solution: In an XML document, text that is ignored unless the parser is specifically told to recognize it.

39. *What is commit ?*

Solution: The point in a transaction when all updates to any resources involved in the transaction are made permanent.

40. *What is component contract ?*

Solution: The contract between a J2EE component and its container. The contract includes life-cycle management of the component, a context interface that the instance uses to obtain various information and services from its container, and a list of services that every container must provide for its components.

41. *What is component-managed sign-on ?*

Solution: A mechanism whereby security information needed for signing on to a resource is provided by an application component.

42. *What is connector ?*

Solution: A standard extension mechanism for containers that provides connectivity to enterprise information systems. A connector is specific to an enterprise information system and consists of a resource adapter and application development tools for enterprise information system connectivity. The resource adapter is plugged in to a container through its support for system-level contracts defined in the Connector architecture.

43. *What is container-managed persistence ?*

Solution: The mechanism whereby data transfer between an entity bean's variables and a resource manager is managed by the entity bean's container.

44. *What is container-managed sign-on ?*

Solution: The mechanism whereby security information needed for signing on to a resource is supplied by the container.

45. *What is container-managed transaction ?*

Solution: A transaction whose boundaries are defined by an EJB container. An entity bean must use container-managed transactions.

46. *What is content ?*

Solution: In an XML document, the part that occurs after the prolog, including the root element and everything it contains.

47. *What is context attribute ?*

Solution: An object bound into the context associated with a servlet.

48. *What is context root ?*

Solution: A name that gets mapped to the document root of a Web application.

49. *What is conversational state ?*

Solution: The field values of a session bean plus the transitive closure of the objects reachable from the bean's fields. The transitive closure of a bean is defined in terms of the serialization protocol for the Java programming language, that is, the fields that would be stored by serializing the bean instance.

50. *What is CORBA ?*

Solution: Common Object Request Broker Architecture. A language-independent distributed object model specified by the OMG.

51. *What is create method ?*

Solution: A method defined in the Interview Questions — Home interface and invoked by a client to create an enterprise bean.

52. *What is credentials ?*

Solution: The information describing the security attributes of a principal.

53. *What is CSS ?*

Solution: Cascading style sheet. A stylesheet used with HTML and XML documents to add a style to all elements marked with a particular tag, for the direction of browsers or other presentation mechanisms.

54. *What is CTS ?*

Solution: Compatibility test suite. A suite of compatibility tests for verifying that a J2EE product complies with the J2EE platform specification.

55. *What is data ?*

Solution: The contents of an element in an XML stream, generally used when the element does not contain any subelements. When it does, the term content is generally used. When the only text in an XML structure is contained in simple elements and when elements that have subelements have little or no data mixed in, then that structure is often thought of as XML data, as opposed to an XML document.

56. *What is DDP ?*

Solution: Document-driven programming. The use of XML to define applications.

57. *What is declaration ?*

Solution: The very first thing in an XML document, which declares it as XML. The minimal declaration is. The declaration is part of the document prolog.

58. *What is declarative security ?*

Solution: Mechanisms used in an application that are expressed in a declarative syntax in a deployment descriptor.

59. *What is delegation ?*

Solution: An act whereby one principal authorizes another principal to use its identity or privileges with some restrictions.

60. *What is deployer ?*

Solution:A person who installs J2EE modules and applications into an operational environment.

61. *What is deployment ?*

Solution: The process whereby software is installed into an operational environment.

62. *What is deployment descriptor ?*

Solution: An XML file provided with each module and J2EE application that describes how they should be deployed. The deployment descriptor directs a deployment tool to deploy a module or application with specific container options and describes specific configuration requirements that a deployer must resolve.

63. *What is destination ?*

Solution: A JMS administered object that encapsulates the identity of a JMS queue or topic. See point-to-point messaging system, publish/subscribe messaging system.

64. *What is digest authentication ?*

Solution: An authentication mechanism in which a Web application authenticates itself to a Web server by sending the server a message digest along with its HTTP request message. The digest is computed by employing a one-way hash algorithm to a concatenation of the HTTP request message and the client's password. The digest is typically much smaller than the HTTP request and doesn't contain the password.

65. *What is distributed application ?*

Solution: An application made up of distinct components running in separate runtime environments, usually on different platforms connected via a network. Typical distributed applications are two-tier (client-server), three-tier (client-middleware-server), and multitier (client-multiple middleware-multiple servers).

66. *What is document ?*

Solution: In general, an XML structure in which one or more elements contains text intermixed with subelements.

67. *What is Document Object Model ?*

Solution: An API for accessing and manipulating XML documents as tree structures. DOM provides platform-neutral, language-neutral interfaces that enables programs and scripts to dynamically access and modify content and structure in XML documents.

68. *What is document root ?*

Solution: The top-level directory of a WAR. The document root is where JSP pages, client-side classes and archives, and static Web resources are stored.

69. *What is DTD ?*

Solution: Document type definition. An optional part of the XML document prolog, as specified by the XML standard. The DTD specifies constraints on the valid tags and tag sequences that can be in the document. The DTD has a number of shortcomings, however, and this has led to various schema proposals. For example, the DTD entry says that the XML element called username contains parsed character data-that is, text alone, with no other structural elements under it. The DTD includes both the local subset, defined in the current file, and the external subset, which consists of the definitions contained in external DTD files that are referenced in the local subset using a parameter entity.

70. *What is durable subscription ?*

Solution: In a JMS publish/subscribe messaging system, a subscription that continues to exist whether or not there is a current active subscriber object. If there is no active subscriber, the JMS provider retains the subscription's messages until they are received by the subscription or until they expire.

71. *What is EAR file ?*

Solution: Enterprise Archive file. A JAR archive that contains a J2EE application.

72. *What is ebXML ?*

Solution: Electronic Business XML. A group of specifications designed to enable enterprises to conduct business through the exchange of XML-based messages. It is sponsored by OASIS and the United Nations Centre for the Facilitation of Procedures and Practices in Administration, Commerce and Transport (U.N./CEFACT).

73. *What is EJB container ?*

Solution: A container that implements the EJB component contract of the J2EE architecture. This contract specifies a runtime environment for enterprise beans that includes security, concurrency, life-cycle management, transactions, deployment, naming, and other services. An EJB container is provided by an EJB or J2EE server.

74. *What is EJB container provider ?*

Solution: A vendor that supplies an EJB container.

75. *What is EJB context ?*

Solution: A vendor that supplies an EJB container. An object that allows an enterprise bean to invoke services provided by the container and to obtain the information about the caller of a client-invoked method.

76. *What is EJB Home object ?*

Solution: An object that provides the life-cycle operations (create, remove, find) for an enterprise bean. The class for the EJB Home object is generated by the container's deployment tools. The EJB Home object implements the enterprise bean's Home interface. The client references an EJB Home object to perform life-cycle operations on an EJB object. The client uses JNDI to locate an EJB Home object.

77. *What is EJB JAR file ?*

Solution: A JAR archive that contains an EJB module.

78. *What is EJB module ?*

Solution: A deployable unit that consists of one or more enterprise beans and an EJB deployment descriptor.

79. *What is EJB object ?*

Solution: An object whose class implements the enterprise bean's remote interface. A client never references an enterprise bean instance directly; a client always references an EJB object. The class of an EJB object is generated by a container's deployment tools.

80. *What is EJB server ?*

Solution: Software that provides services to an EJB container. For example, an EJB container typically relies on a transaction manager that is part of the EJB server to perform the two-phase commit across all the participating resource managers. The J2EE architecture assumes that an EJB container is hosted by an EJB server from the same vendor, so it does not specify the contract between these two entities. An EJB server can host one or more EJB containers.

81. *What is element ?*

Solution: A unit of XML data, delimited by tags. An XML element can enclose other elements.

82. *What is empty tag ?*

Solution: A tag that does not enclose any content.

83. *What is enterprise bean ?*

Solution: A J2EE component that implements a business task or business entity and is hosted by an EJB container; either an entity bean, a session bean, or a message-driven bean.

84. *What is enterprise bean provider ?*

Solution: An application developer who produces enterprise bean classes, remote and Interview Questions — Home interfaces, and deployment descriptor files, and packages them in an EJB JAR file.

85. *What is enterprise information system ?*

Solution: The applications that constitute an enterprise's existing system for handling companywide information. These applications provide an information infrastructure for an enterprise. An enterprise information system offers a well-defined set of services to its clients. These services are exposed to clients as local or remote interfaces or both. Examples of enterprise information systems include enterprise resource planning systems, mainframe transaction processing systems, and legacy database systems.

86. *What is enterprise information system resource ?*

Solution: An entity that provides enterprise information system-specific functionality to its clients. Examples are a record or set of records in a database system, a business object in an enterprise resource planning system, and a transaction program in a transaction processing system.

87. *What is Enterprise JavaBeans (EJB) ?*

Solution: A component architecture for the development and deployment of object-oriented, distributed, enterprise-level applications. Applications written using the Enterprise JavaBeans architecture are scalable, transactional, and secure.

88. *What is Enterprise JavaBeans Query Language (EJB QL) ?*

Solution: Defines the queries for the finder and select methods of an entity bean having container-managed persistence. A subset of SQL92, EJB QL has extensions that allow navigation over the relationships defined in an entity bean's abstract schema.

89. *What is an entity ?*

Solution: A distinct, individual item that can be included in an XML document by referencing it. Such an entity reference can name an entity as small as a character (for example, <, which references the less-than symbol or left angle bracket, <). An entity reference can also reference an entire document, an external entity, or a collection of DTD definitions.

90. *What is entity bean ?*

Solution: An enterprise bean that represents persistent data maintained in a database. An entity bean can manage its own persistence or can delegate this function to its container. An entity bean is identified by a primary key. If the container in which an entity bean is hosted crashes, the entity bean, its primary key, and any remote references survive the crash.

91. *What is entity reference ?*

Solution: A reference to an entity that is substituted for the reference when the XML document is parsed. It can reference a predefined entity such as < or reference one that is defined in the DTD. In the XML data, the reference could be to an entity that is defined in the local subset of the DTD or to an external XML file (an external entity). The DTD can also carve out a segment of DTD specifications and give it a name so that it can be reused (included) at multiple points in the DTD by defining a parameter entity.

92. *What is error ?*

Solution: A SAX parsing error is generally a validation error; in other words, it occurs when an XML document is not valid, although it can also occur if the declaration specifies an XML version that the parser cannot handle. See also fatal error, warning.

93. *What is external entity ?*

Solution: An entity that exists as an external XML file, which is included in the XML document using an entity reference.

94. *What is external subset ?*

Solution: That part of a DTD that is defined by references to external DTD files.

95. *What is fatal error ?*

Solution: A fatal error occurs in the SAX parser when a document is not well formed or otherwise cannot be processed. See also error, warning.

96. *What is filter ?*

Solution: An object that can transform the header or content (or both) of a request or response. Filters differ from Web components in that they usually do not themselves create responses but rather modify or adapt the requests for a resource, and modify or adapt responses from a resource. A filter should not have any dependencies on a Web resource for which it is acting as a filter so that it can be composable with more than one type of Web resource.

97. *What is filter chain ?*

Solution: A concatenation of XSLT transformations in which the output of one transformation becomes the input of the next.

98. *What is finder method ?*

Solution: A method defined in the Interview Questions - Home interface and invoked by a client to locate an entity bean.

99. *What is form-based authentication ?*

Solution: An authentication mechanism in which a Web container provides an application-specific form for logging in. This form of authentication uses Base64 encoding and can expose user names and passwords.

100. *What is general entity ?*

Solution: An entity that is referenced as part of an XML document's content, as distinct from a parameter entity, which is referenced in the DTD. A general entity can be a parsed entity or an unparsed entity.

101. *What is group ?*

Solution: An authenticated set of users classified by common traits such as job title or customer profile. Groups are also associated with a set of roles, and every user that is a member of a group inherits all the roles assigned to that group.

102. *What is handle ?*

Solution: An object that identifies an enterprise bean. A client can serialize the handle and then later deserialize it to obtain a reference to the enterprise bean.

103. *What is Interview Questions - Home handle ?*

Solution: An object that can be used to obtain a reference to the Interview Questions - Home interface. A Interview Questions - Home handle can be serialized and written to stable storage and de-serialized to obtain the reference.

104. *What is Interview Questions - Home interface ?*

Solution: One of two interfaces for an enterprise bean. The Interview Questions - Home interface defines zero or more methods for managing an enterprise bean. The Interview Questions - Home interface of a session bean defines create and remove methods, whereas the Interview Questions - Home interface of an entity bean defines create, finder, and remove methods.

105. *What is HTML ?*

Solution: Hypertext Markup Language. A markup language for hypertext documents on the Internet. HTML enables the embedding of images, sounds, video streams, form fields, references to other objects with URLs, and basic text formatting.

106. *What is HTTP ?*

Solution: Hypertext Transfer Protocol. The Internet protocol used to retrieve hypertext objects from remote hosts. HTTP messages consist of requests from client to server and responses from server to client.

107. *What is HTTPS ?*

Solution: HTTP layered over the SSL protocol.

108. *What is IDL ?*

Solution: Interface Definition Language. A language used to define interfaces to remote CORBA objects. The interfaces are independent of operating systems and programming languages.

109. *What is IIOP ?*

Solution: Internet Inter-ORB Protocol. A protocol used for communication between CORBA object request brokers.

110. *What is impersonation ?*

Solution: An act whereby one entity assumes the identity and privileges of another entity without restrictions and without any indication visible to the recipients of the impersonator's calls that delegation has taken place. Impersonation is a case of simple delegation.

111. *What is initialization parameter ?*

Solution: A parameter that initializes the context associated with a servlet.

112. *What is ISO 3166 ?*

Solution: The international standard for country codes maintained by the International Organization for Standardization (ISO).

113. *What is ISV ?*

Solution: It stands for Independent software vendor.

114. *What is J2EE application ?*

Solution: Any deployable unit of J2EE functionality. This can be a single J2EE module or a group of modules packaged into an EAR file along with a J2EE application deployment descriptor. J2EE applications are typically engineered to be distributed across multiple computing tiers.

115. *What is J2EE component ?*

Solution: A self-contained functional software unit supported by a container and configurable at deployment time. The J2EE specification defines the following J2EE components: Application clients and applets are components that run on the client. Java servlet and JavaServer Pages (JSP) technology components are Web components that run on the server. Enterprise JavaBeans (EJB) components (enterprise beans) are business components that run on the server. J2EE components are written in the Java programming language and are compiled in the same way as any program in the language. The difference between J2EE components and "standard" Java classes is that J2EE components are assembled into a J2EE application, verified to be well formed and in compliance with the J2EE specification, and deployed to production, where they are run and managed by the J2EE server or client container.

116. *What is J2EE module ?*

Solution: A software unit that consists of one or more J2EE components of the same container type and one deployment descriptor of that type. There are four types of modules: EJB, Web, application client, and resource adapter. Modules can be deployed as stand-alone units or can be assembled into a J2EE application.

117. *What is J2EE product ?*

Solution: An implementation that conforms to the J2EE platform specification.

118. *What is J2EE product provider ?*

Solution: A vendor that supplies a J2EE product.

119. *What is J2EE server ?*

Solution: The runtime portion of a J2EE product. A J2EE server provides EJB or Web containers or both.

120. *What is JAR ?*

Solution: Java archive. A platform-independent file format that permits many files to be aggregated into one file.

121. *What is Java 2 Platform, Enterprise Edition (J2EE) ?*

Solution: An environment for developing and deploying enterprise applications. The J2EE platform consists of a set of services, application programming interfaces (APIs), and protocols that provide the functionality for developing multitiered, Web-based applications.

122. *What is Java 2 Platform, Micro Edition (J2ME) ?*

Solution: A highly optimized Java runtime environment targeting a wide range of consumer products, including pagers, cellular phones, screen phones, digital set-top boxes, and car navigation systems.

123. *What is Java API for XML Processing (JAXP) ?*

Solution: An API for processing XML documents. JAXP leverages the parser standards SAX and DOM so that you can choose to parse your data as a stream of events or to build a tree-structured representation of it. JAXP supports the XSLT standard, giving you control over the presentation of the data and enabling you to convert the data to other XML documents or to other formats, such as HTML. JAXP provides namespace support, allowing you to work with schema that might otherwise have naming conflicts.

124. *What is Java API for XML Registries (JAXR) ?*

Solution: An API for accessing various kinds of XML registries.

125. *What is Java API for XML-based RPC (JAX-RPC) ?*

Solution: An API for building Web services and clients that use remote procedure calls and XML.

126. *What is Java IDL ?*

Solution: A technology that provides CORBA interoperability and connectivity capabilities for the J2EE platform. These capabilities enable J2EE applications to invoke operations on remote network services using the Object Management Group IDL and IIOP.

127. *What is Java Message Service (JMS) ?*

Solution: An API for invoking operations on enterprise messaging systems.

128. *What is Java Naming and Directory Interface (JNDI) ?*

Solution: An API that provides naming and directory functionality.

129. *What is Java Secure Socket Extension (JSSE) ?*

Solution: A set of packages that enable secure Internet communications.

130. *What is Java Transaction API (JTA) ?*

Solution: An API that allows applications and J2EE servers to access transactions.

131. *What is Java Transaction Service (JTS) ?*

Solution: Specifies the implementation of a transaction manager that supports JTA and implements the Java mapping of the Object Management Group Object Transaction Service 1.1 specification at the level below the API.

132. *What is JavaBeans component ?*

Solution: A Java class that can be manipulated by tools and composed into applications. A JavaBeans component must adhere to certain property and event interface conventions.

133. *What is JavaMail ?*

Solution: It is An API for sending and receiving email.

134. *What is JavaServer Faces Technology ?*

Solution: A framework for building server-side user interfaces for Web applications written in the Java programming language.

135. *What is JavaServer Faces conversion model ?*

Solution: A mechanism for converting between string-based markup generated by JavaServer Faces UI components and server-side Java objects.

136. *What is JavaServer Faces event and listener model ?*

Solution: A mechanism for determining how events emitted by JavaServer Faces UI components are handled. This model is based on the JavaBeans component event and listener model.

137. *What is JavaServer Faces expression language ?*

Solution: A simple expression language used by a JavaServer Faces UI component tag attributes to bind the associated component to a bean property or to bind the associated component's value to a method or an external data source, such as a bean property. Unlike JSP EL expressions, JavaServer Faces EL expressions are evaluated by the JavaServer Faces implementation rather than by the Web container.

138. *What is JavaServer Faces navigation model ?*

Solution: A mechanism for defining the sequence in which pages in a JavaServer Faces application are displayed.

139. *What is JavaServer Faces UI component ?*

Solution: A user interface control that outputs data to a client or allows a user to input data to a JavaServer Faces application.

140. *What is JavaServer Faces UI component class ?*

Solution: A JavaServer Faces class that defines the behavior and properties of a JavaServer Faces UI component.

141. *What is JavaServer Faces validation model ?*

Solution: A mechanism for validating the data a user inputs to a JavaServer Faces UI component.

142. *What is JavaServer Pages (JSP) ?*

Solution: An extensible Web technology that uses static data, JSP elements, and server-side Java objects to generate dynamic content for a client. Typically the static data is HTML or XML elements, and in many cases the client is a Web browser.

143. *What is JavaServer Pages Standard Tag Library (JSTL) ?*

Solution: A tag library that encapsulates core functionality common to many JSP applications. JSTL has support for common, structural tasks such as iteration and conditionals, tags for manipulating XML documents, internationalization and locale-specific formatting tags, SQL tags, and functions.

144. *What is JAXR client ?*

Solution: A client program that uses the JAXR API to access a business registry via a JAXR provider.

145. *What is JAXR provider ?*

Solution: An implementation of the JAXR API that provides access to a specific registry provider or to a class of registry providers that are based on a common specification.

146. *What is JDBC ?*

Solution: An JDBC for database-independent connectivity between the J2EE platform and a wide range of data sources.

147. *What is JMS ?*

Solution: JMS stands for Java Message Service.

148. *What is JMS administered object ?*

Solution: A preconfigured JMS object (a resource manager connection factory or a destination) created by an administrator for the use of JMS clients and placed in a JNDI namespace.

149. *What is JMS application ?*

Solution: One or more JMS clients that exchange messages.

150. *What is JMS client ?*

Solution: A Java language program that sends or receives messages.

151. *What is JMS provider ?*

Solution: A messaging system that implements the Java Message Service as well as other administrative and control functionality needed in a full-featured messaging product.

152. *What is JMS session ?*

Solution: A single-threaded context for sending and receiving JMS messages. A JMS session can be nontransacted, locally transacted, or participating in a distributed transaction.

153. *What is JNDI ?*

Solution: Abbreviate of Java Naming and Directory Interface.

154. *What is JSP action ?*

Solution: A JSP element that can act on implicit objects and other server-side objects or can define new scripting variables. Actions follow the XML syntax for elements, with a start tag, a body, and an end tag; if the body is empty it can also use the empty tag syntax. The tag must use a prefix. There are standard and custom actions.

155. *What is JSP container ?*

Solution: A container that provides the same services as a servlet container and an engine that interprets and processes JSP pages into a servlet.

156. *What is JSP container, distributed ?*

Solution: A JSP container that can run a Web application that is tagged as distributable and is spread across multiple Java virtual machines that might be running on different hosts.

157. *What is JSP custom action ?*

Solution: A user-defined action described in a portable manner by a tag library descriptor and imported into a JSP page by a taglib directive. Custom actions are used to encapsulate recurring tasks in writing JSP pages.

158. *What is JSP custom tag ?*

Solution: A tag that references a JSP custom action.

159. *What is JSP declaration ?*

Solution: A JSP scripting element that declares methods, variables, or both in a JSP page.

160. *What is JSP directive ?*

Solution: A JSP element that gives an instruction to the JSP container and is interpreted at translation time.

161. *What is JSP document ?*

Solution: A JSP page written in XML syntax and subject to the constraints of XML documents.

162. *What is JSP element ?*

Solution: A portion of a JSP page that is recognized by a JSP translator. An element can be a directive, an action, or a scripting element.

163. *What is JSP expression ?*

Solution: A scripting element that contains a valid scripting language expression that is evaluated, converted to a String, and placed into the implicit out object.

164. *What is JSP expression language ?*

Solution: A language used to write expressions that access the properties of JavaBeans components. EL expressions can be used in static text and in any standard or custom tag attribute that can accept an expression.

165. *What is JSP page ?*

Solution: A text-based document containing static text and JSP elements that describes how to process a request to create a response. A JSP page is translated into and handles requests as a servlet.

166. *What is JSP scripting element ?*

Solution: A JSP declaration, scriptlet, or expression whose syntax is defined by the JSP specification and whose content is written according to the scripting language used in the JSP page. The JSP specification describes the syntax and semantics for the case where the language page attribute is "java".

167. *What is JSP scriptlet ?*

Solution: A JSP scripting element containing any code fragment that is valid in the scripting language used in the JSP page. The JSP specification describes what is a valid scriptlet for the case where the language page attribute is "java".

168. *What is JSP standard action ?*

Solution: An action that is defined in the JSP specification and is always available to a JSP page.

169. *What is JSP tag file ?*

Solution: A source file containing a reusable fragment of JSP code that is translated into a tag handler when a JSP page is translated into a servlet.

170. *What is JSP tag handler ?*

Solution: A Java programming language object that implements the behavior of a custom tag.

171. *What is JSP tag library ?*

Solution: A collection of custom tags described via a tag library descriptor and Java classes.

172. *What is JSTL ?*

Solution: Abbreviate of JavaServer Pages Standard Tag Library.

173. *What is JTA ?*

Solution: Abbreviate of Java Transaction API.

174. *What is JTS ?*

Solution: Abbreviate of Java Transaction Service.

175. *What is keystore ?*

Solution: A file containing the keys and certificates used for authentication

176. *What is life cycle (J2EE component) ?*

Solution: The framework events of a J2EE component's existence. Each type of component has defining events that mark its transition into states in which it has varying availability for use. For example, a servlet is created and has its init method called by its container before invocation of its service method by clients or other servlets that require its functionality. After the call of its init method, it has the data and readiness for its intended use. The servlet's destroy method is called by its container before the ending of its existence so that processing associated with winding up can be done and resources can be released. The init and destroy methods in this example are callback methods. Similar considerations apply to the life cycle of all J2EE component types: enterprise beans, Web components (servlets or JSP pages), applets, and application clients.

177. *What is life cycle (JavaServer Faces) ?*

Solution: A set of phases during which a request for a page is received, a UI component tree representing the page is processed, and a response is produced. During the phases of the life cycle: The local data of the components is updated with the values contained in the request parameters. Events generated by the components are processed. Validators and converters registered on the components are processed. The components' local data is updated to back-end objects. The response is rendered to the client while the component state of the response is saved on the server for future requests.

178. *What is local subset ?*

Solution: That part of the DTD that is defined within the current XML file.

179. *What is managed bean creation facility ?*

Solution: A mechanism for defining the characteristics of JavaBeans components used in a JavaServer Faces application.

180. *What is message ?*

Solution: In the Java Message Service, an asynchronous request, report, or event that is created, sent, and consumed by an enterprise application and not by a human. It contains vital information needed to coordinate enterprise applications, in the form of precisely formatted data that describes specific business actions.

181. *What is message consumer ?*

Solution: An object created by a JMS session that is used for receiving messages sent to a destination.

182. *What is message-driven bean ?*

Solution: An enterprise bean that is an asynchronous message consumer. A message-driven bean has no state for a specific client, but its instance variables can contain state across the handling of client messages, including an open database connection and an object reference to an EJB object. A client accesses a message-driven bean by sending messages to the destination for which the bean is a message listener.

183. *What is message producer ?*

Solution: An object created by a JMS session that is used for sending messages to a destination.

184. *What is mixed-content model ?*

Solution: A DTD specification that defines an element as containing a mixture of text and one more other elements. The specification must start with #PCDATA, followed by diverse elements, and must end with the "zero-or-more" asterisk symbol (*).

185. *What is method-binding expression ?*

Solution: A Java Server Faces EL expression that refers to a method of a backing bean. This method performs either event handling, validation, or navigation processing for the UI component whose tag uses the method-binding expression.

186. *What is method permission ?*

Solution: An authorization rule that determines who is permitted to execute one or more enterprise bean methods.

187. *What is mutual authentication ?*

Solution: An authentication mechanism employed by two parties for the purpose of proving each other's identity to one another.

188. *What is namespace ?*

Solution: A standard that lets you specify a unique label for the set of element names defined by a DTD. A document using that DTD can be included in any other document without having a conflict between element names. The elements defined in your DTD are then uniquely identified so that, for example, the parser can tell when an element should be interpreted according to your DTD rather than using the definition for an element in a different DTD.

189. *What is naming context ?*

Solution: A set of associations between unique, atomic, people-friendly identifiers and objects.

190. *What is naming environment ?*

Solution: A mechanism that allows a component to be customized without the need to access or change the component's source code. A container implements the component's naming environment and provides it to the component as a JNDI naming context. Each component names and accesses its environment entries using the java:comp/env JNDI context. The environment entries are declaratively specified in the component's deployment descriptor.

191. *What is normalization ?*

Solution: The process of removing redundancy by modularizing, as with subroutines, and of removing superfluous differences by reducing them to a common denominator. For example, line endings from different systems are normalized by reducing them to a single new line, and multiple whitespace characters are normalized to one space.

192. *What is North American Industry Classification System (NAICS) ?*

Solution: A system for classifying business establishments based on the processes they use to produce goods or services.

193. *What is notation ?*

Solution: A mechanism for defining a data format for a non-XML document referenced as an unparsed entity. This is a holdover from SGML. A newer standard is to use MIME data types and namespaces to prevent naming conflicts.

194. *What is OASIS ?*

Solution: Organization for the Advancement of Structured Information Standards. A consortium that drives the development, convergence, and adoption of e-business standards.

195. *What is OMG ?*

Solution: Object Management Group. A consortium that produces and maintains computer industry specifications for interoperable enterprise applications.

196. *What is one-way messaging ?*

Solution: A method of transmitting messages without having to block until a response is received.

197. *What is ORB ?*

Solution: Object request broker. A library that enables CORBA objects to locate and communicate with one another.

198. *What is OS principal ?*

Solution: A principal native to the operating system on which the J2EE platform is executing.

199. *What is OTS ?*

Solution: Object Transaction Service. A definition of the interfaces that permit CORBA objects to participate in transactions.

200. *What is parameter entity ?*

Solution: An entity that consists of DTD specifications, as distinct from a general entity. A parameter entity defined in the DTD can then be referenced at other points, thereby eliminating the need to recode the definition at each location it is used.

201. *What is parsed entity ?*

Solution: A general entity that contains XML and therefore is parsed when inserted into the XML document, as opposed to an unparsed entity.

202. *What is parser ?*

Solution: A module that reads in XML data from an input source and breaks it into chunks so that your program knows when it is working with a tag, an attribute, or element data. A nonvalidating parser ensures that the XML data is well formed but does not verify that it is valid. See also validating parser.

203. *What is passivation ?*

Solution: The process of transferring an enterprise bean from memory to secondary storage. See activation.

204. *What is persistence ?*

Solution: The protocol for transferring the state of an entity bean between its instance variables and an underlying database.

205. *What is persistent field ?*

Solution: A virtual field of an entity bean that has container-managed persistence; it is stored in a database.

206. *What is POA ?*

Solution: Portable Object Adapter. A CORBA standard for building server-side applications that are portable across heterogeneous ORBs.

207. *What is point-to-point messaging system ?*

Solution: A messaging system built on the concept of message queues. Each message is addressed to a specific queue; clients extract messages from the queues established to hold their messages.

208. *What is primary key ?*

Solution: An object that uniquely identifies an entity bean within a home.

209. *What is principal ?*

Solution: The identity assigned to a user as a result of authentication.

210. *What is privilege ?*

Solution: A security attribute that does not have the property of uniqueness and that can be shared by many principals.

211. *What is processing instruction ?*

Solution: Information contained in an XML structure that is intended to be interpreted by a specific application.

212. *What is programmatic security ?*

Solution: Security decisions that are made by security-aware applications. Programmatic security is useful when declarative security alone is not sufficient to express the security model of an application.

213. *What is prolog ?*

Solution: The part of an XML document that precedes the XML data. The prolog includes the declaration and an optional DTD.

214. *What is public key certificate ?*

Solution: Used in client-certificate authentication to enable the server, and optionally the client, to authenticate each other. The public key certificate is the digital equivalent of a passport. It is issued by a trusted organization, called a certificate authority, and provides identification for the bearer.

215. *What is publish/subscribe messaging system ?*

Solution: A messaging system in which clients address messages to a specific node in a content hierarchy, called a topic. Publishers and subscribers are generally anonymous and can dynamically publish or subscribe to the content hierarchy. The system takes care of distributing the messages arriving from a node's multiple publishers to its multiple subscribers.

216. *What is query string ?*

Solution: A component of an HTTP request URL that contains a set of parameters and values that affect the handling of the request.

217. *What is queue ?*

Solution: A messaging system built on the concept of message queues. Each message is addressed to a specific queue; clients extract messages from the queues established to hold their messages.

218. *What is RAR ?*

Solution: Resource Adapter Archive. A JAR archive that contains a resource adapter module.

219. *What is RDF ?*

Solution: Resource Description Framework. A standard for defining the kind of data that an XML file contains. Such information can help ensure semantic integrity-for example-by helping to make sure that a date is treated as a date rather than simply as text.

220. *What is RDF schema ?*

Solution: A standard for specifying consistency rules that apply to the specifications contained in an RDF.

221. *What is realm ?*

Solution: See security policy domain. Also, a string, passed as part of an HTTP request during basic authentication, that defines a protection space. The protected resources on a server can be partitioned into a set of protection spaces, each with its own authentication scheme or authorization database or both. In the J2EE server authentication service, a realm is a complete database of roles, users, and groups that identify valid users of a Web application or a set of Web applications.

222. *What is reentrant entity bean ?*

Solution: An entity bean that can handle multiple simultaneous, interleaved, or nested invocations that will not interfere with each other.

223. *What is reference ?*

Solution: A reference to an entity that is substituted for the reference when the XML document is parsed. It can reference a predefined entity such as < or reference one that is defined in the DTD. In the XML data, the reference could be to an entity that is defined in the local subset of the DTD or to an external XML file (an external entity). The DTD can also carve out a segment of DTD specifications and give it a name so that it can be reused (included) at multiple points in the DTD by defining a parameter entity.

224. *What is registry ?*

Solution: An infrastructure that enables the building, deployment, and discovery of Web services. It is a neutral third party that facilitates dynamic and loosely coupled business-to-business (B2B) interactions.

225. *What is registry provider ?*

Solution: An implementation of a business registry that conforms to a specification for XML registries (for example, ebXML or UDDI).

226. *What is relationship field ?*

Solution: A virtual field of an entity bean having container-managed persistence; it identifies a related entity bean.

227. *What is remote interface ?*

Solution: One of two interfaces for an enterprise bean. The remote interface defines the business methods callable by a client.

228. *What is remove method ?*

Solution: Method defined in the Home interface and invoked by a client to destroy an enterprise bean.

229. *What is render kit ?*

Solution: A set of renderers that render output to a particular client. The JavaServer Faces implementation provides a standard HTML render kit, which is composed of renderers that can render HMTL markup.

230. *What is renderer ?*

Solution: A Java class that can render the output for a set of JavaServer Faces UI components.

231. *What is resource adapter ?*

Solution: A system-level software driver that is used by an EJB container or an application client to connect to an enterprise information system. A resource adapter typically is specific to an enterprise information system. It is available as a library and is used within the address space of the server or client using it. A resource adapter plugs in to a container. The application components deployed on the container then use the client API (exposed by the adapter) or tool-generated high-level abstractions to access the underlying enterprise information system. The resource adapter and EJB container collaborate to provide the underlying mechanisms-transactions, security, and connection pooling-for connectivity to the enterprise information system.

232. *What is resource adapter module ?*

Solution: A deployable unit that contains all Java interfaces, classes, and native libraries, implementing a resource adapter along with the resource adapter deployment descriptor.

233. *What is resource manager ?*

Solution: Provides access to a set of shared resources. A resource manager participates in transactions that are externally controlled and coordinated by a transaction manager. A resource manager typically is in a different address space or on a different machine from the clients that access it. Note: An enterprise information system is referred to as a resource manager when it is mentioned in the context of resource and transaction management.

234. *What is resource manager connection ?*

Solution: An object that represents a session with a resource manager.

235. *What is resource manager connection factory ?*

Solution: An object used for creating a resource manager connection.

236. *What is RMI ?*

Solution: Remote Method Invocation. A technology that allows an object running in one Java virtual machine to invoke methods on an object running in a different Java virtual machine.

237. *What is RMI-IIOP ?*

Solution: A version of RMI implemented to use the CORBA IIOP protocol. RMI over IIOP provides interoperability with CORBA objects implemented in any language if all the remote interfaces are originally defined as RMI interfaces.

238. *What is role (development) ?*

Solution: The function performed by a party in the development and deployment phases of an application developed using J2EE technology. The roles are application component provider, application assembler, deployer, J2EE product provider, EJB container provider, EJB server provider, Web container provider, Web server provider, tool provider, and system administrator.

239. *What is role mapping ?*

Solution: The process of associating the groups or principals (or both), recognized by the container with security roles specified in the deployment descriptor. Security roles must be mapped by the deployer before a component is installed in the server.

240. *What is role (security) ?*

Solution: An abstract logical grouping of users that is defined by the application assembler. When an application is deployed, the roles are mapped to security identities, such as principals or groups, in the operational environment. In the J2EE server authentication service, a role is an abstract name for permission to access a particular set of resources. A role can be compared to a key that can open a lock. Many people might have a copy of the key; the lock doesn't care who you are, only that you have the right key.

241. *What is rollback ?*

Solution: The point in a transaction when all updates to any resources involved in the transaction are reversed.

242. *What is root ?*

Solution: The outermost element in an XML document. The element that contains all other elements.

243. *What is SAX ?*

Solution: Abbreviation of Simple API for XML.

244. *What is Simple API for XML ?*

Solution: An event-driven interface in which the parser invokes one of several methods supplied by the caller when a parsing event occurs. Events include recognizing an XML tag, finding an error, encountering a reference to an external entity, or processing a DTD specification.

245. *What is schema ?*

Solution: A database-inspired method for specifying constraints on XML documents using an XML-based language. Schemas address deficiencies in DTDs, such as the inability to put constraints on the kinds of data that can occur in a particular field. Because schemas are founded on XML, they are hierarchical. Thus it is easier to create an unambiguous specification, and it is possible to determine the scope over which a comment is meant to apply.

246. *What is Secure Socket Layer (SSL) ?*

Solution: A technology that allows Web browsers and Web servers to communicate over a secured connection.

247. *What is security attributes ?*

Solution: A set of properties associated with a principal. Security attributes can be associated with a principal by an authentication protocol or by a J2EE product provider or both.

248. *What is security constraint ?*

Solution: A declarative way to annotate the intended protection of Web content. A security constraint consists of a Web resource collection, an authorization constraint, and a user data constraint.

249. *What is security context ?*

Solution: An object that encapsulates the shared state information regarding security between two entities.

250. *What is security permission ?*

Solution: A mechanism defined by J2SE, and used by the J2EE platform to express the programming restrictions imposed on application component developers.

251. *What is security permission set ?*

Solution: The minimum set of security permissions that a J2EE product provider must provide for the execution of each component type.

252. *What is security policy domain ?*

Solution: A scope over which security policies are defined and enforced by a security administrator. A security policy domain has a collection of users (or principals), uses a well-defined authentication protocol or protocols for authenticating users (or principals), and may have groups to simplify setting of security policies.

253. *What is security role ?*

Solution: An abstract logical grouping of users that is defined by the application assembler. When an application is deployed, the roles are mapped to security identities, such as principals or groups, in the operational environment. In the J2EE server authentication service, a role is an abstract name for permission to access a particular set of resources. A role can be compared to a key that can open a lock. Many people might have a copy of the key; the lock doesn't care who you are, only that you have the right key.

254. *What is security technology domain ?*

Solution: A scope over which the same security mechanism is used to enforce a security policy. Multiple security policy domains can exist within a single technology domain.

255. *What is security view ?*

Solution: The set of security roles defined by the application assembler.

256. *What is server certificate ?*

Solution: Used with the HTTPS protocol to authenticate Web applications. The certificate can be self-signed or approved by a certificate authority (CA). The HTTPS service of the Sun Java System Application Server Platform Edition 8 will not run unless a server certificate has been installed.

257. *What is server principal ?*

Solution: The OS principal that the server is executing as.

258. *What is service element ?*

Solution: A representation of the combination of one or more Connector components that share a single engine component for processing incoming requests.

259. *What is service endpoint interface ?*

Solution: A Java interface that declares the methods that a client can invoke on a Web service.

260. *What is servlet ?*

Solution: A Java program that extends the functionality of a Web server, generating dynamic content and interacting with Web applications using a request-response paradigm.

261. *What is servlet container ?*

Solution: A container that provides the network services over which requests and responses are sent, decodes requests, and formats responses. All servlet containers must support HTTP as a protocol for requests and responses but can also support additional request-response protocols, such as HTTPS.

262. *What is servlet container, distributed ?*

Solution: A servlet container that can run a Web application that is tagged as distributable and that executes across multiple Java virtual machines running on the same host or on different hosts.

263. *What is servlet context ?*

Solution: An object that contains a servlet's view of the Web application within which the servlet is running. Using the context, a servlet can log events, obtain URL references to resources, and set and store attributes that other servlets in the context can use.

264. *What is servlet mapping ?*

Solution: Defines an association between a URL pattern and a servlet. The mapping is used to map requests to servlets.

265. *What is session ?*

Solution: An object used by a servlet to track a user's interaction with a Web application across multiple HTTP requests.

266. *What is session bean ?*

Solution: An enterprise bean that is created by a client and that usually exists only for the duration of a single client-server session. A session bean performs operations, such as calculations or database access, for the client. Although a session bean can be transactional, it is not recoverable should a system crash occur. Session bean objects either can be stateless or can maintain conversational state across methods and transactions. If a session bean maintains state, then the EJB container manages this state if the object must be removed from memory. However, the session bean object itself must manage its own persistent data.

267. *What is SGML ?*

Solution: Standard Generalized Markup Language. The parent of both HTML and XML. Although HTML shares SGML's propensity for embedding presentation information in the markup, XML is a standard that allows information content to be totally separated from the mechanisms for rendering that content.

268. *What is SOAP ?*

Solution: Simple Object Access Protocol. A lightweight protocol intended for exchanging structured information in a decentralized, distributed environment. It defines, using XML technologies, an extensible messaging framework containing a message construct that can be exchanged over a variety of underlying protocols.

269. *What is SOAP with Attachments API for Java (SAAJ) ?*

Solution: The basic package for SOAP messaging, SAAJ contains the API for creating and populating a SOAP message.

270. *What is SQL ?*

Solution: Structured Query Language. The standardized relational database language for defining database objects and manipulating data.

271. *What is SQL/J ?*

Solution: A set of standards that includes specifications for embedding SQL statements in methods in the Java programming language and specifications for calling Java static methods as SQL stored procedures and user-defined functions. An SQL checker can detect errors in static SQL statements at program development time, rather than at execution time as with a JDBC driver.

272. *What is SSL ?*

Solution: Secure Socket Layer. A security protocol that provides privacy over the Internet. The protocol allows client-server applications to communicate in a way that cannot be eavesdropped upon or tampered with. Servers are always authenticated, and clients are optionally authenticated.

273. *What is stateful session bean ?*

Solution: A session bean with a conversational state.

274. *What is stateless session bean ?*

Solution: A session bean with no conversational state. All instances of a stateless session bean are identical.

275. *What is system administrator ?*

Solution: The person responsible for configuring and administering the enterprise's computers, networks, and software systems.

276. *What is tag ?*

Solution: In XML documents, a piece of text that describes a unit of data or an element. The tag is distinguishable as markup, as opposed to data, because it is surrounded by angle brackets (< and >). To treat such markup syntax as data, you use an entity reference or a CDATA section.

277. *What is template ?*

Solution: A set of formatting instructions that apply to the nodes selected by an XPath expression.

278. *What is tool provider ?*

Solution: An organization or software vendor that provides tools used for the development, packaging, and deployment of J2EE applications.

279. *What is transaction attribute ?*

Solution: A value specified in an enterprise bean's deployment descriptor that is used by the EJB container to control the transaction scope when the enterprise bean's methods are invoked. A transaction attribute can have the following values: Required, RequiresNew, Supports, NotSupported, Mandatory, or Never.

280. *What is transaction ?*

Solution: An atomic unit of work that modifies data. A transaction encloses one or more program statements, all of which either complete or roll back. Transactions enable multiple users to access the same data concurrently.

281. *What is transaction isolation level ?*

Solution: What is transaction isolation level The degree to which the intermediate state of the data being modified by a transaction is visible to other concurrent transactions and data being modified by other transactions is visible to it.

282. *What is transaction manager ?*

Solution: Provides the services and management functions required to support transaction demarcation, transactional resource management, synchronization, and transaction context propagation.

283. *What is Unicode ?*

Solution: A standard defined by the Unicode Consortium that uses a 16-bit code page that maps digits to characters in languages around the world. Because 16 bits covers 32,768 codes, Unicode is large enough to include all the world's languages, with the exception of ideographic languages that have a different character for every concept, such as Chinese.

284. *What is Universal Description, Discovery and Integration (UDDI) project ?*

Solution: An industry initiative to create a platform-independent, open framework for describing services, discovering businesses, and integrating business services using the Internet, as well as a registry. It is being developed by a vendor consortium.

285. *What is Universal Standard Products and Services Classification (UNSPSC) ?*

Solution: A schema that classifies and identifies commodities. It is used in sell-side and buy-side catalogs and as a standardized account code in analyzing expenditure.

286. *What is unparsed entity ?*

Solution: A general entity that contains something other than XML. By its nature, an unparsed entity contains binary data.

287. *What is URI ?*

Solution: Uniform resource identifier. A globally unique identifier for an abstract or physical resource. A URL is a kind of URI that specifies the retrieval protocol (http or https for Web applications) and physical location of a resource (host name and host-relative path). A URN is another type of URI.

288. *What is URL ?*

Solution: Uniform resource locator. A standard for writing a textual reference to an arbitrary piece of data in the World Wide Web. A URL looks like this: protocol://host/local info where protocol specifies a protocol for fetching the object (such as http or ftp), host specifies the Internet name of the targeted host, and local info is a string (often a file name) passed to the protocol handler on the remote host.

289. *What is URL path ?*

Solution: The part of a URL passed by an HTTP request to invoke a servlet. A URL path consists of the context path + servlet path + path info, where Context path is the path prefix associated with a servlet context of which the servlet is a part. If this context is the default context rooted at the base of the Web server's URL namespace, the path prefix will be an empty string. Otherwise, the path prefix starts with a / character but does not end with a / character. Servlet path is the path section that directly corresponds to the mapping that activated this request. This path starts with a / character. Path info is the part of the request path that is not part of the context path or the servlet path

290. *What is URN ?*

Solution: Uniform resource name. A unique identifier that identifies an entity but doesn't tell where it is located. A system can use a URN to look up an entity locally before trying to find it on the Web. It also allows the Web location to change, while still allowing the entity to be found.

291. *What is user data constraint ?*

Solution: Indicates how data between a client and a Web container should be protected. The protection can be the prevention of tampering with the data or prevention of eavesdropping on the data.

292. *What is user (security) ?*

Solution: An individual (or application program) identity that has been authenticated. A user can have a set of roles associated with that identity, which entitles the user to access all resources protected by those roles.

293. *What is validating parser ?*

Solution: A parser that ensures that an XML document is valid in addition to being well formed. See also parser.

294. *What is value-binding expression ?*

Solution: A JavaServer Faces EL expression that refers to a property of a backing bean. A component tag uses this expression to bind the associated component's value or the component instance to the bean property. If the component tag refers to the property via its value attribute, then the component's value is bound to the property. If the component tag refers to the property via its binding attribute then the component itself is bound to the property.

295. *What is virtual host ?*

Solution: Multiple hosts plus domain names mapped to a single IP address.

296. *What is W3C ?*

Solution: World Wide Web Consortium. The international body that governs Internet standards. Its Web site is http://www.w3.org/.

297. *What is WAR file ?*

Solution: Web application archive file. A JAR archive that contains a Web module.

298. *What is warning ?*

Solution: A SAX parser warning is generated when the document's DTD contains duplicate definitions and in similar situations that are not necessarily an error but which the document author might like to know about, because they could be. See also fatal error, error.

299. *What is Web application ?*

Solution: An application written for the Internet, including those built with Java technologies such as JavaServer Pages and servlets, as well as those built with non-Java technologies such as CGI and Perl.

300. *What is Web application, distributable ?*

Solution: A Web application that uses J2EE technology written so that it can be deployed in a Web container distributed across multiple Java virtual machines running on the same host or different hosts. The deployment descriptor for such an application uses the distributable element.

301. *What is Web component ?*

Solution: A component that provides services in response to requests; either a servlet or a JSP page.

302. *What is Web container ?*

Solution: A container that implements the Web component contract of the J2EE architecture. This contract specifies a runtime environment for Web components that includes security, concurrency, life-cycle management, transaction, deployment, and other services. A Web container provides the same services as a JSP container as well as a federated view of the J2EE platform APIs. A Web container is provided by a Web or J2EE server.

303. *What is Web container, distributed ?*

Solution: A Web container that can run a Web application that is tagged as distributable and that executes across multiple Java virtual machines running on the same host or on different hosts.

304. *What is Web module ?*

Solution: A deployable unit that consists of one or more Web components, other resources, and a Web application deployment descriptor contained in a hierarchy of directories and files in a standard Web application format.

305. *What is Web resource ?*

Solution: A static or dynamic object contained in a Web application that can be referenced by a URL.

306. *What is Web resource collection ?*

Solution: A list of URL patterns and HTTP methods that describe a set of Web resources to be protected.

307. *What is Web server ?*

Solution: Software that provides services to access the Internet, an intranet, or an extranet. A Web server hosts Web sites, provides support for HTTP and other protocols, and executes server-side programs (such as CGI scripts or servlets) that perform certain functions. In the J2EE architecture, a Web server provides services to a Web container. For example, a Web container typically relies on a Web server to provide HTTP message handling. The J2EE architecture assumes that a Web container is hosted by a Web server from the same vendor, so it does not specify the contract between these two entities. A Web server can host one or more Web containers.

308. *What is Web service ?*

Solution: An application that exists in a distributed environment, such as the Internet. A Web service accepts a request, performs its function based on the request, and returns a response. The request and the response can be part of the same operation, or they can occur separately, in which case the consumer does not need to wait for a response. Both the request and the response usually take the form of XML, a portable data-interchange format, and are delivered over a wire protocol, such as HTTP.

309. *What is well-formed ?*

Solution: An XML document that is syntactically correct. It does not have any angle brackets that are not part of tags, all tags have an ending tag or are themselves self-ending, and all tags are fully nested. Knowing that a document is well formed makes it possible to process it. However, a well-formed document may not be valid. To determine that, you need a validating parser and a DTD.

310. *What is XHTML ?*

Solution: An XML look-alike for HTML defined by one of several XHTML DTDs. To use XHTML for everything would of course defeat the purpose of XML, because the idea of XML is to identify information content, and not just to tell how to display it. You can reference it in a DTD, which allows you to say, for example, that the text in an element can contain <em> and <b> tags rather than being limited to plain text.

311. *What is XLink ?*

Solution: The part of the XLL specification that is concerned with specifying links between documents.

312. *What is XLL ?*

Solution: The XML Link Language specification, consisting of XLink and XPointer.

313. *What is XML ?*

Solution: Extensible Markup Language. A markup language that allows you to define the tags (markup) needed to identify the content, data, and text in XML documents. It differs from HTML, the markup language most often used to present information on the Internet. HTML has fixed tags that deal mainly with style or presentation. An XML document must undergo a transformation into a language with style tags under the control of a style sheet before it can be presented by a browser or other presentation mechanism. Two types of style sheets used with XML are CSS and XSL. Typically, XML is transformed into HTML for presentation. Although tags can be defined as needed in the generation of an XML document, a document type definition (DTD) can be used to define the elements allowed in a particular type of document. A document can be compared by using the rules in the DTD to determine its validity and to locate particular elements in the document. A Web services application's J2EE deployment descriptors are expressed in XML with schemas defining allowed elements. Programs for processing XML documents use SAX or DOM APIs.

314. *What is XML registry ?*

Solution: An infrastructure that enables the building, deployment, and discovery of Web services. It is a neutral third party that facilitates dynamic and loosely coupled business-to-business (B2B) interactions.

315. *What is XML Schema ?*

Solution: The W3C specification for defining the structure, content, and semantics of XML documents.

316. *What is XPath ?*

Solution: An addressing mechanism for identifying the parts of an XML document.

317. *What is XPointer ?*

Solution: The part of the XLL specification that is concerned with identifying sections of documents so that they can be referenced in links or included in other documents.

318. *What is XSL-FO ?*

Solution: A subcomponent of XSL used for describing font sizes, page layouts, and how information flows from one page to another.

319. *What is component (JavaServer Faces technology) ?*

Solution: A user interface control that outputs data to a client or allows a user to input data to a JavaServer Faces application.

Appendix II

Glossary on Web Technologies

Agent A program that can travel over the Internet and access remote resources, on behalf of a user. A proper agent should be able to run on remote machines and travel freely from machine to machine. The Java language shows promise for permitting safe agents, since the Java interpreter does not let Java applets harm the computers they contact.

Anchor The location of a hypertext link in a document. An anchor can be either the start of a hypertext link or the destination of a hypertext link.

Anonymous FTP Computers can run an anonymous FTP server, which lets anyone log into the computer under the username anonymous, and access public resources. In general, when you log in as user anonymous, you (or your browser) use your e-mail address for the password string.

Applet A program or mini-application that can be downloaded over a network and activated on the user's computer. To do this safely, you must have a secure way of running applets. The Java language is designed to support safe applets.

Archie A system that automatically generates and maintains a database for anonymous FTP servers' contents. An archie server accesses information from FTP servers and archives the directory listings. An archie client can access these databases and search for programs or files matching a particular name.

Archive file A single file that contains a collection of different files and/or directories. Archive files are often used to transport collections of files across the Internet, since you can transport a large collection in a single archive file. UNIX archives have the extension .tar (for Tape ARchive). PKZIP is often used to create archives on DOS computers (suffix .zip), while Stuffit is often used to create Macintosh archives (suffixes .sea or .sit). PKZIP and Stuffit archives are also compressed.

ASCII American Standard Code for Information Interchange. This is a 7-bit character code capable of representing 128 characters. Several of these characters are special control characters used in communications control, and are not printable.

ibute A quantity that defines a special property of an HTML element. Attributes are specified within an element start tag. For example, <IMG SRC="image.gif"> means that the element IMG has an attribute SRC, which is assigned the indicated value.

Browser Any program used to view material prepared for the World Wide Web. Mosaic, Netscape, and lynx are some examples. Browsers are able to interpret URLs and HTML markup and also understand Internet protocols such as HTTP, FTP, and Gopher.

CERN Centre Européen pour la Récherche Nucleaire; a large particle-accelerator laboratory located near Geneva, on the French-Swiss border. The World Wide Web originated here, largely due to the efforts of Tim Berners-Lee.

CGI Common Gateway Interface, the specification for how an HTTP server should communicate with server gateway programs. Most servers support the CGI specification.

Character reference A way, within an SGML language such as HTML, of referencing a character using a simple string of numbers reflecting the position of the character in the current character set. For example, the character reference é is the reference for e with an acute accent (é) within the ISO Latin-1 character set. Note, however, that character reference will produce a different character if a different character set is involved. For a character-set independent representation, see entity reference.

Chinese/Japanese/Korean, often used in the discussion of character sets and of the issues important to these language/character set groups.

Client Any program used to extract information from a server. For example, a browser such as Mosaic is a client that can access data from HTTP (and other) servers. All browsers are Web clients.

Compressed Many files on the Internet are compressed—this reduces the space taken up by a file and makes transmission over the Internet faster. The client must then have software able to decompress the file.

Cookie A small quantity of data exchanged between (and then stored on) a client and a server, and usually hidden from the user. An example is the Netscape cookie mechanism, discussed in Chapters 7 and 8.

CRLF The combination of carriage-return (CR) and linefeed (LF) characters. This combination is used by several Internet protocols, including HTTP, to denote the end of a line.

CSO Computing Services Office, a system that lets users search for student and/or faculty names at a school or university. It is one approach at creating "white pages" for Internet e-mail addresses.

CWIS Campus Wide Information Systems, electronic systems for distributing campus information, which first became common with university-based Gopher servers.

Dial-up connection The action of using a telephone and modem to connect to a remote computer. Dial-up connections are slow compared with direct connections, or ISDN.

Domain name A symbolic name for a computer, that can be translated by a nameserver into a computers formal numeric Internet address (IP address). Domain names let users reference Internet sites without having to know the numerical address.

Download Transfer of a file from a remote computer to a local computer.

DTD Document Type Definition. An SGML document type definition is a specific description of a markup language. This description is written as a plain text file, often with the filename extension .dtd. The HyperText Markup Language (HTML) has its own Document Type Definition file, often called html.dtd.

E-mail Electronic mail.

Element (HTML) The basic unit of an HTML document. HTML documents use start and stop tags to define structural elements in the document. These elements are arranged hierarchically, to define the overall document structure. The name of the element is given by the tag, and indicates the meaning associated with the block. Some elements are empty, since they don't affect a block of text. Elements that have content are also often called containers.

End tag A markup tag that denotes the end of an element.

Entity reference A way, within an SGML language such as HTML, of referencing a character using a simple string of ASCII characters. For example, the entity reference é is the reference for e with an acute accent (é). See also character reference.

FAQ Frequently Asked Questions, on the Internet, a FAQ is a document that answers the most frequently asked questions on a particular topic. Most newsgroups have FAQs that are frequently posted to the newsgroup.

Firewall A firewall is used to separate a local network from the outside world. In general a local network is connected to the outside world by a "gateway" computer. This gateway machine can be converted into a firewall by installing special software that does not let unauthorized TCP/IP packets pass from inside to outside and vice versa. You can give users on the local network, and "inside" the firewall, access to the outside world using the SOCKS package or by installing the a proxy server on the firewall machine.

Fragment identifier A text string included using a NAME attribute in an A element, that labels the anchored location in a document—thus the word fragment, since it references a document fragment.

FTP File Transfer Protocol, an Internet client-server protocol for transferring files between computers.

GIF Graphics Interchange Format, a format for storing image files. It is the most common format for inline images in HTML documents. The other common format is JPEG.

Gopher A protocol for information delivery used in distributed information systems. Gopher clients give you access to this information. Gopher is a menu-based delivery system and does not have hypertext capabilities. Gopher has been largely supplanted by HTTP.

Header The leading part of a data message. HTTP messages are sent with an HTTP header preceding the actual communicated data.

Helper A program launched or used by a browser (such as Netscape Navigator) to process files that the browser cannot handle internally. Most users have helper applications to play sound or movie files, to uncompress compressed files or to unstuff archives.

Hits In database searches, the number of documents that resulted from the search; for servers, the number of document requests received by a server.

Home page The introductory page for a World Wide Web site. A home page usually provides an introduction to the site, along with hypertext links to local resources.

HTML HyperText Markup Language, a markup language defined by an SGML Document Type Definition (DTD). To a document writer, HTML is simply a collection of tags used to mark blocks of text and assign them special meanings.

Hypertext Any document that contains hypertext links to other documents. HTML documents are almost always hypertext documents.

Hypertext link A hypertext relationship between two anchors, leading from the head anchor to the tail anchor. On the Web, this is usually a link from one hypertext document to another. Lining points are associated with anchors.

Inline image An image that is merged with the displayed text. Placing images in this manner is often described as "inlining" the images.

I18N See internationalization.

IANA Internet Assigned Naming Authority, the agency which registers name for common use on the Internet. General information is found at: ftp://ftp.isi.edu/in-notes/iana/

IETF Internet Engineering Task Force, a collection of task forces at work on developing standards for Internet protocols and architectures. There

Internet You mean you don't know? The Internet is the world wide network of computers communicating via the TCP/IP protocols.

Internationalization Software development aimed at providing software that can serve a multilingual, internationalized audience. Often abbreviated as I18N (Internationalization).

Internet provider A company from whom users purchase Internet connectivity. This could either be a dedicated connection (for example, a telephone connection that stays open twenty-four hours a day) or a dial-up connection. Usually users run software such as PPP or SLIP to allow Internet connectivity across the line.

Internet resources The collection of data, documents, and databases available on the Internet.

Intranet An Intranet is a collection of services that use an Internet as the underlying communications technology, designed to support business operations and applications. Basically just another buzzword, like enterprise computing, and mission-critical applications.

IP Address The numerical Internet protocol address of a computer on the Internet. Every computer on the Internet has a unique numerical address.

ISO International Standards Organization, an international organization responsible for setting international standards, such as the ISO Latin-1 character set.

ISO 10646 A multi-byte character set proposed by the ISO as a universal character set for the characters and symbols used by all the world's languages. The most important 2-byte subset of this language, know as the basic multilingual plane, is equivalent to the Unicode character set.

ISO Latin-1 An 8-bit character code developed by the International Standards Organization. An 8-bit code contains 256 different characters. In the ISO Latin-1 code, the first 128 characters are the equivalent to the 128 characters of the US-ASCII character set (also called the ISO 646 character set). The remaining 128 characters consist of control characters and a large collection of accented and other characters commonly used in European languages.

Java A programming language, developed by Sun Microsystems, designed specifically for use in applet and agent applications. Java programs can only run under a Java interpreter, which is designed to eliminate the risk of a rogue Java applet damaging the local computer.

JavaScript A scripting language developed by Netscape Inc. Javascript program listings can be included within an HTML document, and are then executed by the Web browser when the document is loaded. A similar scripting language, known as VBScript, has been developed by Microsoft.

JPEG Joint Photographic Experts Group, an image format. In general JPEG allows for higher quality images than GIF. Browsers cannot display JPEG images inline, and instead must display them using helper programs.

Kerberos A network authentication system, based on the key distribution model. It allows machines communicating over networks to prove their identity to each other through a trusted third party. It also prevents eavesdropping or replay attacks (recording and retrying encryption information "snooped" off the network), through support for a variety of data encryption schemes.

LAN Local Area Network.

Link See hypertext link.

Linux A freeware clone of UNIX for 386-based PC computers. Linux consists of the linux kernel (core operating system), originally written by Linus Torvalds, along with utility programs developed by the Free Software Foundation and by others. Since PC hardware is inexpensive and linux is essentially free the combination of the two is a practical way of developing inexpensive and reliable HTTP service.

Listserv An automated electronic mailing list, managed by a listserv program. Listservs are commonly used by discussion groups.

Lynx A popular character-mode (text-only). World Wide Web browser.

MIME Multipurpose Internet Mail Extensions, a scheme that lets electronic mail messages contain mixed media (sound, video, image, and text). The World Wide Web uses MIME content-types to specify the type of data contained in a file or being sent from an HTTP server to a client.

Mosaic A graphical browser for the World Wide Web, developed at NCSA. There are several commercial browsers based on Mosaic.

MPEG Motion Picture Experts Group, a common video file compression method.

multimedia A mixture of media—text, audio, and video, under the control of a computer. The World Wide Web is a form of multimedia.

name token In SGML, this is a character string composed of the ASCII letters a-z or A-Z, the numerals, 0-9, a dash (-) or a period (.), and that must begin with a letter. Name tokens are usually case-insensitive. Many attribute values are defined as name tokens.

Name server A computer (and a program on the computer) that translates domain names into the proper numeric IP address (or vice versa).

NCSA National Center for Supercomputing Applications. The NCSA is situated at the Urbana-Champaign campus of the University of Illinois. The NCSA software development team developed the Mosaic and NCSA HTTPD server programs.

NNTP Network News Transfer Protocol, used for communicating USENET articles across the Internet.

packet A small package of data. TCP/IP breaks messages up into packets, and sends each packet independently to the message destination. The protocol ensures that there is no error in transmission and that the entire message arrives.

Partial URL A location scheme containing only partial information about the resource location. To access the resource, the client must construct a full URL, based on the partial URL. It does so by assuming that all the information not found in the partial URL is the same as that used when the client accessed the document containing the partial URL reference. A partial URL is often called a relative URL, since the location of the linked resource is determined relative to the location of the document containing the partial URL.

PEM Privacy Enhanced Mail, a special mail protocol that provides encryption of mail message content.

perl Practical Extraction and Reporting Language, a scripting language created by Larry Wall. Because powerful data and text manipulation programs can be written quickly and easily using perl, it has become a popular language for writing CGI applications.

PGP Pretty Good Privacy, a publicly available encryption scheme that uses the "public key" approach—messages are encrypted using a "public" key, but can only be decrypted by a "private" key, retained by the intended recipient of the message.

Plug-in A program module that adds inline functionality to a Web browser (or, in general, any other program). On the Web, plugins let Web browsers display data such as VRML scenes, real-time video, or multimedia data inline with the HTML document. Plugins, when available, are accessed through HTML EMBED or OBJECT elements.

Port number Any Internet application communicates at a particular port number specific to the application. For example FTP, HTTP, Gopher and telnet are all assigned unique port numbers so that the computer knows what to do when contacted at a particular port. There are accepted standard numbers for these ports so that computers know which port to connect to for a particular service. For example, Gopher servers generally "talk" at port 70, while HTTP servers generally "talk" at port 80. These default values can be overridden in a URL.

PPP Point to Point Protocol, a communications protocol that turns a dial-up telephone connection into a point-to-point Internet connection. This is commonly used to run WWW browsers over a phone line.

Provider See Internet provider.

Protocol In computer networks, a protocol is simply an agreed convention for inter-computer communication. Thus the TCP/IP protocol defines how messages are passed on the Internet, while the FTP protocol, which is built using the TCP/IP protocol, defines how FTP messages should be sent and received.

Proxy server A server that acts as an intermediary between a user's computer and the computer they want to access. If a user makes a request for a resource from computer "A," this request is directed to the proxy server, which makes the request, gets the response from computer "A," and then forwards the response to the client. Proxy servers are useful for accessing World Wide Web resources from inside a firewall.

RFC Request For Comments, is a document, written by groups or individuals involved in Internet development, that describes agreed-upon standards or proposes new standards for Internet protocols. For example, the rules for electronic mail message composition are specified in the document RFC 822.

Robots On the World Wide Web, a program that autonomously searches through trees of hypertext documents, retrieving files for indexing (or other purposes). Also called a worm.

Router A computer that determines, on a local basis, which route packets will take en route to their destination.

RSA A common, commercial public-key encryption technology, owned by RSA Data Security Inc. RSA Inc. also holds several patents on public-key encryption in general, so that popular publicly available encryption tools, such as PGP and PEM, infringe on RSA patents. PGP and PEM therefore cannot be used in commercial products without licensing approval of RSA Inc.

Server A program, running on a networked computer, that responds to requests from client programs running on other networked computers. The server and client communicate using a client-server protocol.

SGML Standard Generalized Markup Language, is a standard for describing markup languages. HTML is defined as an instance of SGML.

Shell The UNIX shell is the program that interprets the commands typed at the terminal. A shell can also be used to run simple script programs called shell scripts. There are several different shells, with slightly different commands and syntax. The most common are the Bourne shell (sh), the C shell (csh), and the Korn dhell (ksh). The DOS command-line interpreter can be thought of as a shell.

SLIP Serial Line Internet Protocol, a communications protocol that that can turn a dial-up telephone connection into an Internet connection. SLIP can be used to run Web browsers over a phone line, but is less stable than a PPP connection.

SMTP Simple Mail Transfer Protocol, the standard by which electronic mail messages are communicated over the Internet.

SOCKS A software package that allows hosts inside a firewall to communicate with the outside world. To allow access to the outside world a secure network can run a SOCKS server on its gateway/firewall machine; all networking software inside the network must be configured to talk to the SOCKS server. SOCKS is a proxy server without the special caching capabilities of a caching HTTP proxy server.

SSL Secure Sockets Layer, is a technology developed by Netscape Communications Inc. for encrypting data sent between clients and servers. SSL is the basis for Netscape's secure communication technologies.

start tag (HTML) A markup tag that denotes the start of an element.

Tag (HTML) HTML marks documents using tags. A tag is simply typed text surrounded by the less than and greater than signs, for example: . An end tag has a slash in front of the tag name; for example .

Tar Tape archiver, a program (and file format) commonly used on UNIX systems for archiving and transporting large collections of files and/or directories.

TCP/IP Transmission Control Protocol/Internet Protocol, the basic communication protocol that is the foundation of the Internet. All the other protocols, such as HTTP, FTP, and Gopher, are built on top of TCP/IP.

Telnet A terminal emulation protocol that allows you to make a terminal connection to other computers on the Internet. This requires that you run a telnet client on your computer and connect to a telnet server on the other machine.

TIA The Internet Adapter, a program run under a dial-in UNIX account that supports SLIP-like connection between a dial-up computer and the dial-in site. TIA is useful if you have a UNIX account with a company that does not provide PPP or SLIP service.

TIFF Tag Image File Format, a graphic file format developed by Aldus Corporation. TIFF is the standard format of many graphics and desktop publishing programs.

tn3270 A variant of telnet that emulates the behavior of IBM model 3270 display terminals.

Unicode A 2-byte character set, developed as a universal character set for international use. The current 2 version of Unicode is equivalent to the basic multilingual plane subset of the ISO 10646 character set. Internationalized HTML uses Unicode as its base character set.

UNIX An operating system, commonly used on the backbone machines on the Internet. Most Web servers are run under the UNIX operating system.

URC Uniform Resource Characteristics, is an as-yet unspecified format for representing aggregate information about a resource or collection of resources.

URI Uniform Resource Identifier, the generic term for a coded string that identifies a (typically Internet) resource. There are currently two practical examples of URI's, namely Uniform Resource Locators (URLs) and partial URLs.

URL Uniform Resource Locator, the scheme used to address Internet resources on the World Wide Web. A URL specifies the protocol, domain name/IP address, port number, path, and resource details needed to access a resource from a particular machine. Partial URLs are an associated scheme that specify a location relative to the location of a document or resource containing the URL reference.

URN Uniform Resource Names, are as yet defined, but are the holy grail of addressing, as any file would retain the same URN, regardless of which computer the file resided on. URNs would be universal identifiers for Internet resources, regardless of the resource origins.

USENET The Internet's world wide bulletin board system, consisting of over 6,000 topical discussion groups, called newsgroups. The newsgroups related to the World Wide Web were mentioned at the end of Chapter 1. USENET postings are distributed around the world using the NNTP protocol.

VBScript A document scripting language developed by Microsoft, also known as Visual Basic Script. See Javascript for a description of document scripting languages.

Viewer A program launched by a browser to view files that the browser cannot handle internally and that are accessed by standard hypertext anchors. Thus you have viewers for JPEG images, sound files, and MPEG movies. Viewers are also often called helpers or helper applications. Viewers are distinct from plugins, since they work separately from the browser.

Visit When you access a World Wide Web document you are said to be visiting the site.

W3C `World Wide Web Consortium, an academic and industrial consortium devoted to the development of Web standards and technologies.

White space Any combination of space or tab characters that separate two characters or two character strings.

WAIS Wide Area Information Servers, a system and protocol for Internet accessible databases. The WAIS protocol is based on the Z39.50 protocol.

WAN Wide Area Network.

worms A computer program that can make copies of itself. Alternatively, on the Web, a worm is synonymous with a robot.

WWW The World Wide Web. Also called the Web or W3.

Z39.50 A protocol for communicating search information and search results, allowing remote searching of databases. Many library systems support the Z39.50 protocol.

APPENDIX III

INTRODUCTION TO XHTML

WHAT IS XHTML?

- XHTML stands for EXtensible HyperText Markup Language
- XHTML is aimed to replace HTML
- XHTML is almost identical to HTML 4.01
- XHTML is a stricter and cleaner version of HTML
- XHTML is HTML defined as an XML application
- XHTML is a W3C Recommendation

  XHTML 1.0 became a W3C Recommendation January 26, 2000. W3C defines XHTML as the latest version of HTML. XHTML will gradually replace HTML.
- XHTML is a combination of HTML and XML (EXtensible Markup Language).
- XHTML consists of all the elements in HTML 4.01 combined with the syntax of XML.

WHY XHTML?

We have reached a point where many pages on the WWW contain "bad" HTML.

The following HTML code will work fine if you view it in a browser, even if it does not follow the HTML rules:

```
<html>
<head>
<title>This is bad HTML</title>
<body>
<h1>Bad HTML
</body>
```

XML is a markup language where everything has to be marked up correctly, which results in "well-formed" documents.

XML was designed to describe data and HTML was designed to display data.

Today's market consists of different browser technologies, some browsers run Internet on computers, and some browsers run Internet on mobile phones and hand helds. The last-mentioned do not have the resources or power to interpret a "bad" markup language.

Therefore - by combining HTML and XML, and their strengths, we got a markup language that is useful now and in the future - XHTML.

XHTML pages can be read by all XML enabled devices AND while waiting for the rest of the world to upgrade to XML supported browsers, XHTML gives you the opportunity to write "well-formed" documents now, that work in all browsers and that are backward browser compatible !!!

XHTML IS NOT VERY DIFFERENT FROM THE HTML

In addition, you should start NOW to write your HTML code in lowercase letters, and NEVER skip ending tags (like </p>).

The Most Important Differences:

- XHTML elements must be properly nested
- XHTML elements must always be closed
- XHTML elements must be in lowercase
- XHTML documents must have one root element
- Attribute names must be in **lower case**
- Attribute values must be **quoted**
- Attribute minimization is **forbidden**
- The id attribute **replaces** the name attribute
- The XHTML DTD defines **mandatory** elements

XHTML ELEMENTS MUST ALWAYS BE CLOSED

Non-empty elements must have an end tag.

```
<p>This is a paragraph</p>
<p>This is another paragraph</p>
```

EMPTY ELEMENTS MUST ALSO BE CLOSED

Empty elements must either have an end tag or the start tag must end with />.

```
Abreak: <br />
A horizontal rule: <hr />
An image: <img src="happy.gif" alt="Happy face" />
```

XHTML ELEMENTS MUST BE IN LOWER CASE

The XHTML specification defines that the tag names and attributes need to be lower case.

```
<body>
<p>This is a paragraph</p>
</body>
```

XHTML DOCUMENTS MUST HAVE ONE ROOT ELEMENT

All XHTML elements must be nested within the <html> root element. All other elements can have sub (children) elements. Sub elements must be in pairs and correctly nested within their parent element. The basic document structure is:

```
<html>
<head> ... </head>
<body> ... </body>
</html>
```

Attribute Names must be in Lower Case

```
<table width="100%">
```

Attribute Values must be Quoted

```
<table width="100%">
```

Attribute Minimization is Forbidden

```
<input checked="checked" />
<input readonly="readonly" />
<input disabled="disabled" />
<option selected="selected" />
<frame noresize="noresize" />
```

Here is a list of the minimized attributes in HTML and how they should be written in XHTML:

HTML	XHTML
compact	compact="compact"
checked	checked="checked"
declare	declare="declare"
readonly	readonly="readonly"
disabled	disabled="disabled"
selected	selected="selected"
defer	defer="defer"
ismap	ismap="ismap"
nohref	nohref="nohref"
noshade	noshade="noshade"
nowrap	nowrap="nowrap"
multiple	multiple="multiple"
noresize	noresize="noresize"

THE ID ATTRIBUTE REPLACES THE NAME ATTRIBUTE

HTML 4.01 defines a name attribute for the elements a, applet, frame, iframe, img, and map. In XHTML the name attribute is deprecated. Use id instead.

```
<img src="picture.gif" id="picture1" />
```

Note: To interoperate with older browsers for a while, you should use both name and id, with identical attribute values, like this:

```
<img src="picture.gif" id="picture1" name="picture1" />
```

Important Compatibility Note:

To make your XHTML compatible with today's browsers, you should add an extra space before the "/" symbol.

The Lang Attribute

The lang attribute applies to almost every XHTML element. It specifies the language of the content within an element.

If you use the lang attribute in an element, you must add the xml:lang attribute, like this:

```
<div lang="no" xml:lang="no">Heia Norge!</div>
```

MANDATORY XHTML ELEMENTS

<!DOCTYPE> Is Mandatory

An XHTML document consists of three main parts:

- the DOCTYPE
- the Head
- the Body

The basic document structure is:

```
<!DOCTYPE ...>
<html>
<head>
<title>... </title>
</head>
<body> ... </body>
</html>
```

The DOCTYPE declaration should always be the first line in an XHTML document.

An XHTML Example

This is a simple (minimal) XHTML document:

```
<!DOCTYPE html
PUBLIC "-//W3C//DTD XHTML 1.0 Strict//EN"
"http://www.w3.org/TR/xhtml1/DTD/xhtml1-strict.dtd">
<html>
<head>
<title>simple document</title>
```

```
</head>
<body>
<p>a simple paragraph</p>
</body>
</html>
The DOCTYPE declaration defines the document type:
<!DOCTYPE html
PUBLIC "-//W3C//DTD XHTML 1.0 Strict//EN"
"http://www.w3.org/TR/xhtml1/DTD/xhtml1-strict.dtd">
The rest of the document looks like HTML:
<html>
<head>
<title>simple document</title>
</head>
<body>
<p>a simple paragraph</p>
</body>
</html>
```

The 3 Document Type Definitions

- DTD specifies the syntax of a web page in SGML.
- DTD is used by SGML applications, such as HTML, to specify rules that apply to the markup of documents of a particular type, including a set of element and entity declarations.
- XHTML is specified in an SGML document type definition or 'DTD'.
- An XHTML DTD describes in precise, computer-readable language, the allowed syntax and grammar of XHTML markup.

There are currently 3 XHTML document types:

- STRICT
- TRANSITIONAL
- FRAMESET

XHTML 1.0 specifies three XML document types that correspond to three DTDs: Strict, Transitional, and Frameset.

XHTML 1.0 Strict

```
<!DOCTYPE html
PUBLIC "-//W3C//DTD XHTML 1.0 Strict//EN"
"http://www.w3.org/TR/xhtml1/DTD/xhtml1-strict.dtd">
```

Use this when you want really clean markup, free of presentational clutter. Use this together with Cascading Style Sheets.

XHTML 1.0 Transitional

```
<!DOCTYPE html
PUBLIC "-//W3C//DTD XHTML 1.0 Transitional//EN"
"http://www.w3.org/TR/xhtml1/DTD/xhtml1-transitional.dtd">
```

Use this when you need to take advantage of HTML's presentational features and when you want to support browsers that don't understand Cascading Style Sheets.

XHTML 1.0 Frameset

```
<!DOCTYPE html
PUBLIC "-//W3C//DTD XHTML 1.0 Frameset//EN"
"http://www.w3.org/TR/xhtml1/DTD/xhtml1-frameset.dtd">
```

Use this when you want to use HTML Frames to partition the browser window into two or more frames.

INDEX

L

M

N

O

P

Q

R